ELDERCARE
911

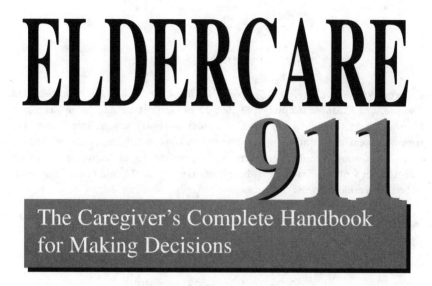

ELDERCARE 911

The Caregiver's Complete Handbook for Making Decisions

REVISED, UPDATED, AND EXPANDED

SUSAN BEERMAN, MS, MSW
JUDITH RAPPAPORT-MUSSON, CSA

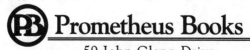
Prometheus Books

59 John Glenn Drive
Amherst, New York 14228-2119

Published 2008 by Prometheus Books

Inquiries should be addressed to
Prometheus Books
59 John Glenn Drive
Amherst, New York 14228–2119
VOICE: 716–691–0133, ext. 210
FAX: 716–691–0137
WWW.PROMETHEUSBOOKS.COM

12 11 10 09 08   5 4 3 2 1

Library of Congress Cataloging-in-Publication Data

Beerman, Susan, 1950–
    Eldercare 911 : the caregiver's complete handbook for making decisions —
revised, updated, and expanded ed. / Susan Beerman and Judith Rappaport-Musson.
        p. cm.
    Includes index.
    ISBN 978–1–59102–616–7 (pbk.)
    1. Aging parents—Care—Miscellanea. 2. Caregivers—Family relationships—
Miscellanea. 3. Older people—Care—Miscellanea. I. Rappaport-Musson, Judith,
1942– II. Title.

HQ1063.6 .B447 2008
646.7'9—dc22
                                                                                  2008007862

Printed in the United States of America on acid-free paper

To John, my loving husband whom I treasure more every day, and to my family, Kim, Tom, Nicholas, Jack, Harriet, and Allen, who fill my life with joy. JRM

To my loving husband, Alen, and children, Hal, Audra, and Michael, who always stand by me and support all of my dreams. I love you. SB

Special thanks to John Musson and Meyer Lurie for their immeasurable help with research and documentation.

CONTENTS

CONTENTS

10. HANDLING BURNOUT 245

11. HOW TO HIRE A HOMECARE WORKER 267

CONTENTS 15

20. EVALUATING THE MOVE TO A NURSING HOME

DISCLAIMER

The information provided in *Eldercare 911* is offered with the understanding that the authors are not engaged in rendering financial, legal, or medical advice. Readers who require such advice should not use this book as a replacement for professional counsel, but instead should seek the services of licensed financial, legal, and medical professionals.

PREFACE

A. YOU ARE NOT ALONE

"Dad desperately wanted to leave the nursing home. Every time I called him, I'd say 'Dad, I'm going to get you home by Christmas.' I got him home on 12/23 and I considered that one of my greatest accomplishments. When I found out Mom couldn't get him into bed without help, I laid awake the whole night wondering what the hell I had just done."

Carol, New York

"Mom had Parkinson's and couldn't manage her own care. I knew we had a finite amount of money and I was trying to balance that money for as long as possible so she could have help. I wasn't able to make it last—I don't know what would have happened if she'd lived several more years."

Fred, Pennsylvania

"The challenge is to appreciate when and how to offer these contributions in a healthy fashion, out of love rather than guilt.

Carrying a load of guilt served as a limitation on my fullest participation in life."

Dana, Oregon

Y ou are not alone. You weren't when we first wrote this book in
2002 and today, in 2008, you have more company than ever before
in the history of humankind. You are literally surrounded by people with
the same thoughts, feelings, and problems. If you feel overwhelmed and
burdened by an all-consuming caregiving situation that competes for
attention with your family, friends, and career, or you are one of the lucky
minority who feels blessed by a rewarding and loving caregiving relationship, *you are not alone.*

Twenty-first-century reality is that family caregivers like you, and
like the caregivers who generously shared their experiences with us for
this book, comprise one of the largest groups in the United States. In fact,
there are so many family caregivers that, if you asked them, you'd find
that a surprisingly large number of your neighbors, friends, coworkers,
and strangers sitting next to you at sporting events or standing in line with
you at the grocery store might be feeling just what you're feeling, or have
the same thoughts as Carol, Fred, and Dana.

In 2002, *Eldercare 911* was primarily for and about women. In 2008,
we recognize that men are increasingly more involved in caring for
elderly parents, so we are broadening our outreach to provide support and
guidance to help improve the lives of all caregivers, men and women
alike. We hope *Eldercare 911* will provide valuable insights and useful
advice as you continue to care for your parents.

We are honored to continue sharing your deepest feelings and your
unique relationships with your loved ones and friends. Your commitment
may be limited to calling your parent twice a week to be certain "everything is all right"; you may have taken on more responsibility such as
accompanying your parents to their physicians, or shopping for their groceries; or you may be totally engaged and sharing your home with your
parents. Whether you are minimally immersed or totally submerged, you
are still considered a family "elder-caregiver."

The good news is that experts in every walk of life, including the government, business, and clergy, are increasingly aware of the needs of family caregivers and trying to devise systems to ease their burdens. The bad news is that progress appears to be slow and inadequate, often placing even greater burdens on family caregivers.

Our caregiving dilemma owes many of its frustrations and heartaches to our parents' and society's centuries-old expectations that caregiving is "the children's job." This timeless status quo includes the inherent assumption that even though you have no medical or gerontological training, you will know when, how, and how much to intervene; how to manage insurance benefits; how to evaluate a nursing home; how to cope with Alzheimer's disease; and how to resolve a host of other new and life-altering caregiving dilemmas. The assumption also holds that you will find time to continue nurturing your children, being a good partner, working on your career, and maintaining your own personal time and space.

This unwritten caregivers' code equates resigned acceptance with loyalty and love. Nothing could be further from the truth. Acceptance of these rules often prevents adult children from seeking the assistance that would enable them to become more effective advocates and caregivers on behalf of their parents. It also lessens their ability to ensure a better financial, physical, and emotional quality of life for their parents, their families, and themselves. Efforts to share or shift responsibilities frequently result in family arguments and accusations of lack of love, ungratefulness, and selfishness.

The world is a very different place than it was when your parents cared for their parents. They were likely to live geographically closer together; the majority of caregivers were women who did not work outside the home; their doctors spent hours with patients; and medical science usually presented our grandparents with only one option: to sit down, age quietly, then pass away. Today, families may be disbursed over different continents; many of you have spent years creating families or building your careers; and the number of options for a functional, expanded life expectancy are so numerous they can only be understood by dedicated geriatric professionals.

Even so, the arguments and accusations usually have the desired effect. In many families, guilt wins out, so we continue the status quo. Most adult children accept the jobs of caregivers and give of themselves from love or from a sense of obligation or both. Some caregivers are their parents' only resource, some feel rewarded, and others use their parents' needs as a means to personal martyrdom. Still many others experience frustrations brought on by circumstances beyond their control. In the words of one Virginia caregiver, sarcastically describing recurrent conversations with her mother who is suffering from Alzheimer's, "It looks like her ability to lay a guilt trip on me will be the last skill to go."

You are the first generation, ever, in the entire history of the world, to face the difficulties of living in a time where you may spend more years caring for your elderly parents than you spent caring for your children.[1] We hope *Eldercare 911* will help you find your inner strength and create your own pathways to deal with the hundreds of real-world, everyday dilemmas caregivers face. Our recommendations come from personal experience with our own loved ones and from professional careers that have enabled us to talk with and help thousands of caregivers in every phase of eldercare.

The innermost thoughts of other family caregivers presented in *Eldercare 911* will comfort and surprise you. We hope you'll recognize many feelings and experiences that mirror your own or those of your friends. Our stories are a compilation of interviews and interactions with family caregivers. Their names and locations have been changed to protect their privacy. We and our contributing caregivers hope that together we will help you maintain a better quality of life by learning from our trials, tribulations, and victories.

Most of all, we hope you'll find more peace of mind knowing that you are not alone.

B. HOW TO USE THIS BOOK

Eldercare 911 understands and respects the many facets of a caregiver's busy life. Our goal is to deliver tested, practical problem-solving information that saves time and money.

For quick answers to specific issues, use the "read it as you need it" method to pinpoint just the information you need. Look up your problem in the index or table of contents, open *Eldercare 911* to the appropriate page, and you'll find a concise, practical explanation and recommendation that takes only a few minutes to read.

For preventive strategies, or when the situation dictates a broader review, you have the option of reading multiple associated topics or the entire book. It's your choice: read one subject, five subjects, or read them all. Whichever you choose, *Eldercare 911* will deliver the information you need to help you make informed decisions on most eldercare situations.

Eldercare 911 is a realistic guide for dealing with today's caregiving situations. It provides a frank look at many rarely discussed, sensitive issues that affect family communication and relationships. In addition, chapter 24 offers an extensive list of caregiver organizations and resources. To save you time, we've also listed each organization's address, telephone number, and e-mail address. You'll also find a comprehensive glossary of eldercare terms. The more informed you are, the more empowered you are to become a more effective caregiver.

Best wishes,

Judie Rappaport-Musson and Sue Beerman

1

THE PROS AND CONS
OF BEING A CAREGIVER

A. DO YOU WANT THIS RESPONSIBILITY?

"Before I became a caregiver I didn't realize how difficult it is to help a parent. I thought that if my mom needs my help, she'll listen to me. Wrong! This is an uphill battle that takes time and patience. And guess what? I don't have either. I want to do what is right for my mother, but I have a job and a family. This is a job and a half because sometimes she needs me in the morning and sometimes in the middle of the night. Maybe this job is just not for me. I need help."

Joyce, Connecticut

W hen you think about taking care of your aging parent, you probably put the emphasis on caring, loving, and fulfilling your responsibilities. You probably aren't thinking about it as a job, but that's exactly what it is. If you weren't doing the work—taking her to the doctor, handling finances, listening to her fears and frustrations, figuring out how to make her home safe, grocery shopping, doing laundry, cooking meals, and helping to buy clothes—someone else would have to do it. It may be a part-time or full-time job. Your parent may need you a few hours a day, a few days a week, or twenty-four hours a day, seven days a week. You may be living with your parent, or you may live nearby or even quite a distance away. You may talk once a week, or every day. You may get calls from your confused or disoriented parent several times a day, or even in the middle of the night. The problems and day-to-day dilemmas have endless possibilities. Sometimes you think you have heard it all, done it all, and felt every level of emotion. Then something else happens and you are thrust into yet another crisis.

Regardless of the scope or time commitment of the situation, taking care of your elderly parent is a job you must consider carefully. You may think that you have no choice, that you must do your duty. But the wiser course of action is to realize that you have the right to choose to take this job or not. You have the insight and power to decide whether this job is for you. Because the truth is that if you take on eldercare without considering the responsibilities and the needs that this job requires, you may not only feel unhappy or inadequate down the line, but your parent may suffer as well.

Being a caregiver to your parent may seem awkward and unnatural. After all, it may make you feel as if you're the parent to your parent. At times, it can be difficult and heartbreaking, and you just want to scream. Yet at other times the experience can be pleasant and fulfilling. Under any circumstances, it takes time, commitment, patience, and understanding. It also takes the courage to admit that at times you cannot do it alone. As an adult daughter of an aging parent, your parent may need you in a way no one, not even your child, spouse, or best friend, has needed you before. As an adult son, your sense of responsibility to your parent may not be clear or simple because of a poor past relationship or a less-than-loving present one. It's not a simple job, and it's not an easy one, but it's an important one. So make sure you're ready for it. How can you do that?

B. MAKING THE ELDERCARE DECISION

Begin by looking at your parents, seeing them as they really are today. This is one of the most difficult things an adult child has to do, but it is the first step, and it is essential for you and your parent's well-being to try. Once you start the process and open your eyes, you can begin to help your parent and yourself. Forget about what your parents did twenty years ago; forget that your father was a doctor and your mother was a bank executive or that your mother raised five children as a single parent and held two jobs to make ends meet. This may not be the parent you are looking at today. The parent you see today may not remember how to balance a checkbook, tie a shoe, cook an egg, drive a car, or walk to the bathroom. If this is the parent you see, begin making the eldercare decision by talking to him or her, providing he or she has the capacity to understand you and can contribute to the conversation. Most likely he will deny the need for help because he may feel embarrassed or fearful of losing his independence if you try to help him. Your conversation may leave you feeling frustrated, angry, and alone. Don't panic. You are not alone. Move on to step two and learn about your parent's needs and wants. Talk to your siblings, your parent's physician, clergy, therapist, and next-door neighbors. Get as much information as you can to make an informed decision for your parent and yourself. Ask questions about your parent's health, day-to-day activities, and other things that you may not know or see, because you are not with him all the time. If you do live with your parent, it is imperative that you get the input of others to help clarify your questions and get an objective picture of who your parent is today. In step three, think about what you have learned. If the information is overwhelming and you believe you are not the right person for the job of caregiver, it's okay because you have successfully completed the three most important steps to deciding if eldercare is for you. You opened your eyes to the problem, your ears to the answers, and your heart to the fact that no matter how you feel about your parent, you may or may not be the right person for this job. (See the next chapter for more information on understanding when your parent needs your help and when she doesn't.)

If Eldercare Is Not for You

If you decide caregiving is not for you and you want to refuse the responsibility, you will want to talk to your other family members as well as appropriate professionals and community resource specialists, so that you know what options are available and how your parent can be cared for.

This is not the time to be hard on yourself. Making this decision does not come easy and you are not a failure or a bad child. You are simply being realistic by understanding your strengths and limitations. Your next steps would be:

1. Call a family meeting to discuss how you feel and to determine if anyone is interested in assuming the responsibility. If the caregiver is not you, it may be your brother or sister or both. Everyone needs to be aware of who is taking charge and who will be responsible for the day-to-day problems. If no one agrees to accept the responsibility, the next step is to look for professional help. If paid care is involved, the family needs to be clear on who will pay for it. Sometimes care is provided by social service agencies at no cost or on a sliding scale based on your parent's income.

2. Contact your community associations; county, city, state, or federal government offices on aging; homecare agencies; and church or synagogue, for information regarding local and state services for the elderly, the cost of homecare in your community, support, and self-help groups. Explain your particular problem and ask for an appropriate referral to a geriatric professional such as a social worker, a registered nurse, a private geriatric care manager, a therapist, or a physician. Geriatric care managers often take over when the family is unable to handle the situation. They offer comprehensive assessments, make recommendations, coordinate and manage such essentials as homecare, living arrangements, healthcare, and daily activities. They may also supply referrals to physicians, dentists, therapists, and day care programs, as well as arrange appointments, and even provide transportation. An assessment by a geriatric professional may not only include medical data, but family, social, emotional, financial, and nutritional information. Once the assessment is completed, the geriatric professional can present concrete information regarding immediate solutions for most eldercare problems including options for care and support for you and your parent.

3. The geriatric professional may recommend an assessment or a combination of assessments. The dual assessment process provides a more complete picture and helps to determine your parent's needs.

For example, an assessment by a geriatric physician will equip you with medical and medication information to help the care manager provide the best possible care for your parent.

If You Decide to Care for Your Parent

If you decide this job is for you, you will need ongoing support to help you get through the daily problems and challenges of caregiving. You will make your life easier if you seek out guidance from professionals who will teach you, offer you choices, and provide you with encouragement and support. Asking for help is a wonderful sign of self-awareness and strength.

> "I got the help of a geriatric care manager. She gives me my only peace of mind. She is my eyes and ears. She is quickly able to get whatever is needed...home health aides, consults with specialists, and she facilitates interactions with facilities and agencies."
>
> *Carol, New Jersey*

> "Knowing that I wasn't alone helped me so much. I spend my life wanting to do the right thing and I really didn't know if asking for help was for me. But I did ask my friend who is a social worker for her guidance and for a hug. I got both and I am much stronger with her support."
>
> *Ellen, Rhode Island*

Once you have decided to care for your parent, you may begin to think about such necessities as reorganizing your work schedule if it is practical for you and your employer. Talk to your supervisor; maybe an earlier work schedule will accommodate your employer's needs as well as yours. Unfortunately, working nine to five does not leave much time in the day for doctors' appointments or contacting insurance companies for your parent. Think about your day, the time you need to work and relax, and then begin to consider how you can consolidate some of the things you have to do. If changing your parent's bank account to the same bank as yours will save you time and stress, try it. But make sure you alert your siblings to that fact if they are involved in your parent's financial business. If taking your mother to your beauty shop saves you time, try that. Don't be afraid to make a change that is difficult to explain to your parent in the beginning, but in the end saves you hours of time and stress.

Think about the effect of your caregiver responsibilities on your family and friends. Don't leave them out of the caregiver equation. Let them know that you are doing what you want to do, but that their support and love helps you through each day.

> "My sister lives in another state, and she really doesn't understand what is going on with Dad. I finally decided that I couldn't handle all of the problems, and I asked her to come out for a visit. We spent three very long and difficult days with Dad. Now she really understands what I am dealing with every day. Before I could even ask, she offered to do whatever she can to help me. We made a list of things that she could handle for Dad by telephone, such as following up with doctors, making appointments, and taking care of some of his financial questions and paperwork. What a difference for me, knowing that she supports my efforts and she can help."
>
> *Blossom, Maine*

No matter how well you plan your day, reality often strikes, and you may find yourself in the middle of a crisis. How can you be prepared to handle that first disaster? Use the skills you have developed over time as an adult. You have learned so much over the years that gives you the power and insight to make the best decisions for you and your parent.

C. HANDLING THAT FIRST CRISIS

To prepare for the first calamity, organize and list vital information such as the names of physicians, hospitals, homecare agencies, and pharmacies in a log, on a computer printout, or on the worksheets provided in this book. Keep a copy of the list in your purse or briefcase. If a caregiving situation thrusts you into a crisis or medical emergency, do not panic.

- Call immediately for emergency medical assistance.
- Once your parent is in the hospital emergency room, contact your parent's physician. The physician will alert the emergency room staff to your parent's special needs and condition.
- In any crisis situation, talk to anyone who has had recent contact with your parent, such as a family member, a neighbor, a physician, a pharmacist, or a social worker. The information they provide may contribute to understanding why the crisis occurred, how it can be resolved, and what to do to avoid a similar emergency.
- Help yourself, and you help your parent. Reach out to family, friends, and community services to help you through the crisis. At times, the comfort of a family member or a friend eases the pressure and stress during a crisis. Community services provide elder-care professionals who can guide and support you through an emergency. When the crisis has stabilized, reevaluate your role, your options, and your feelings about being a caregiver and then decide if you really want to continue with this job.

Believing in yourself, what you know, and what you can do is not easy. Every day our belief systems are challenged by our parents, our family, our friends, professionals, and even ourselves. We know professionals who find caregiving for their own parents challenging. A caregiver who is a geriatric social worker said, *"I think I was under a misconception that my parents would appreciate logic and respect my opinion consistently; after all, wasn't I the geriatric care manager for others who paid me to help them? They continued to treat me as if I was still a little girl. They nodded their heads as if they agreed with my suggestions, and then two minutes later they turned around and did exactly what they wanted. When something didn't work out the way they hoped, they called and asked me what they should do. We're in this terrible cycle, and I can't seem to stop it."*

Begin to think back to other times in your life when you had problems to solve and decisions to make. Draw on the strength of the past to get you through the present. It may help you to try to visualize an experience you had earlier in your life. Try to recall the problem and the steps you took to find a solution. By giving yourself a concrete example to ponder you may find answers to your current situation. You have the insight and power to make decisions. You've proven it dozens of times before. You also have the right to choose if this job is for you.

D. THE FIXER

Are you someone who fixes everything from a leaky faucet to a skinned knee? Are you the one person who makes everything better? We feel you smiling. You know who you are and you also know how difficult it is to always be known by your family and friends as "the fixer."

As a caregiver from New Jersey said, "*It's exhausting always trying to be the one who makes things better for my family and friends, but it seems to come naturally to me. I wonder if I was born this way.*"

Some people seem to have a knack and a need to take care of everyone and everything around them. If you have these character traits you may have an overwhelming sense of responsibility as a caregiver for your aging parent. Jenny from Washington, DC, said, "*I am a healthcare professional and I have always had an overwhelming sense of responsibility to people. Now that my father is eighty-three years old I feel it is my responsibility to make life as good as possible for him. Where does that leave me? I struggle every day trying to stop myself from doing too much for him and asking too much of myself.*"

As a "fixer," you often ask too much of yourself emotionally and intellectually because you do not know any other way of coping with problems, parents, and pressures. Unfortunately, you work hard and long to right wrongs and you often spend sleepless nights and restless days trying to figure out how you will fix any and all problems.

It is time for you to stop and take the time to realize that no matter what you do, no one can fix everything, and no one should feel that they have to try.

Can you change the recording in your mind that says you must be "the fixer"? You can do it, if you want to take a few steps toward change. Change is not easy because, at times, the things we do for our parents and others provide us with a secondary gain. This is not bad; it is simply a fact. Good deeds make us feel good. For example, if you help your parent every day with household chores, and someone says, "Your mom's house looks beautiful," you feel good because you took part in accomplishing that. Or if you are in charge of your parents' medical care and your parents are doing well, you feel good because you are instrumental in their care. But you still need to understand your limitations, so you won't feel overly burdened by your sense of responsibility.

Here are five tips to help you record a new mental message. In time you will learn that you can fix some things, you can't fix everything, but you can still embrace all of your wonderful qualities to be the most effective caregiver you can be.

1. Make a list of the tasks you do for your parent. Make a list of things you do for other family members and friends. Try to calculate the time you spend on all of the things you try to fix. Add the hours up and then take a realistic look at what you are doing. Now that it is in writing, do you see how much actual time you spend "fixing" everyone else's lives? It is time to say to yourself: "I do not have to do all of this for my parent or friend. I can delegate some of these responsibilities to my sister or brother or home health aide. I can be helpful, but I do not have to make everything right for everyone."

2. Learn the importance of saying "NO." As a "fixer" you do not seem to have that small, but powerful word in your vocabulary. At times everyone has to say NO to someone. Ask yourself, What are the most important things you do to help your parent? Keep your thoughts focused and then try and put the rest of the tasks on a mental shelf. If you have extra time and energy, you may remove one task at a time from your mental shelf or you have the ability to refuse to take on any further responsibilities. The choice is yours.

3. Forgive yourself. "Fixers" have a very difficult time forgiving themselves when they can't do everything they think they should accomplish. A "fixer" is self-critical and often self-deprecating. Change the recording in your mind to applaud all the things you do achieve and try not to concentrate on the things that you did not tackle or complete.

4. Peaceful thoughts are contagious. Once you think about what you accomplish and give yourself credit for your contributions you will find that your mind will begin to rest. The more you allow your mind to rest, the more peaceful you will become. People who

enjoy peace of mind, enjoy peace of body and spirit and actually become better caregivers.

5. Think of yourself as someone who is resourceful, successful, and focused. Take pride in your accomplishments. In time the recording in your mind will sound sweet and you will no longer have the need to fix everything and everyone. You will be a caregiver who is helpful, loving, and kind to your parent as well as yourself.

E. THE EFFECTS ON YOUR FAMILY, TIME, AND HEALTH

Caring for your parent is a job that affects the entire family, whether you take on this responsibility for a week, a month, or several years. As your involvement with your parent deepens and your commitment intensifies, you may find yourself exhausted, overwhelmed, and torn. On a daily basis, you may face many dilemmas that arouse feelings of anger, frustration, and guilt, especially when everything happens at once and everyone needs you at the same time. For example, you promised your eighteen-year-old daughter that you would shop with her for a prom dress. As you are about to leave the house, your husband telephones to tell you that out-of-town guests will be arriving for dinner. As you get into the car, your cell phone rings. Your father fell and is on the way to the hospital.

Or perhaps you took the day off from work to take your confused and disoriented mother to the geriatric specialist. As you leave the house, your supervisor telephones to tell you that you must make an unscheduled business trip tomorrow. Your head begins to pound, you appear anxious, and your mother reacts to your fear with increased anxiety and agitation. A sense of responsibility and a question of loyalty overwhelm you. How can you possibly be a responsible caregiver, a career woman, and a mother, and still maintain a sense of sanity and self? How can you reduce the negative effects of caregiving on your family and still focus on the things you want and need to do?

The first and one of the most crucial steps you can take to provide yourself and your family with a sense of priority and of control is to set realistic goals. Prioritize your concerns and realize that at times someone or something will not receive immediate care and attention. Making the decision to take care of one person over another is often heart wrenching and emotional. You will make the best decision once you are aware of the facts of the situation. For instance, if your father is rushed to the local hospital, he must be the focus of your attention. Some questions that must be answered immediately include:

- Is he in the emergency room, or is he immediately admitted to the hospital? When you call the hospital, you will be given the patient's location in the hospital and his general condition. For specific information, you will have to contact your parent's physician or the admitting doctor.
- If he is being admitted to the hospital, who is the admitting doctor, and what diagnosis has been made so far? If he is not being admitted, why not, and who will transport him home?
- Does he need homecare, and do you know if it is covered by insurance?
- Does your father need private-duty nursing in the hospital?
- Does the hospital provide the extra care, or do you have to call an agency?
- Is the hospital staff aware of your father's medication and know who his primary care physician is? (If possible, you should plan to bring the medications to the hospital in their original containers to provide the greatest amount of accuracy.)
- Ask the hospital staff to notify your father's primary care physician.
- Don't be afraid to ask questions, and if you find that you are not being provided with answers, ask to speak to a social worker or a patient advocate.
- Notify the rest of your family.

A productive and comforting way to keep your family informed and updated about your role as a caregiver is to have family meetings. In such meetings, you can talk about your feelings, your sense of responsibility, and the guilt you may feel because you are not always available. Family meetings are helpful in communicating other issues affecting the family, too, such as a job promotion and more job responsibility or the purchase of a car for the purpose of driving your parent. In time, your family will begin to understand what you are going through and how essential their cooperation is in the process. If your family is geographically scattered, modern technology can bring them home. E-mail, fax machines, speakerphones, and regular telephones can keep families informed and well connected.

"*As a working caregiver my e-mail is my quick link to my family. My sister and I e-mail once a day. I must admit I try to do it during my break or lunch hour, but that doesn't happen all the time. No matter what, it is fast and because we are not talking on the phone or in person we get right to the point. It helps both of us keep tabs on mom, dad, and each other, and to maintain our jobs.*"

At times, your own family at home will miss you and resent the intrusion on their lives. They may express their anger openly or in subtle ways such as not helping with household chores. At other times they will not realize or appreciate the impact of the hours you spend on the phone or away from home to set up appointments and help your parent. They will be preoccupied with their own problems.

School, work, vacation plans, and the ups and downs of personal relationships will also influence how your family responds to your job as a caregiver. Unfortunately, at times, you will feel alone, and your family will not or cannot be supportive. During those times reach out for a helping hand and caring heart from a spouse or friend, and go to the movies, or out to dinner, or contact your local Area Agency on Aging for help to find a support group or other eldercare services.

As you learn to establish realistic goals, communicate with your family, and prioritize your concerns, you will then be better able to balance the conflicting needs of your family, work, and parents.

F. WHAT IF YOU FAIL?

Ask a group of caregivers, "Are you successful at this job?" Most caregivers would probably shrug their shoulders and not agree about a definition of success. The idea of success or failure as caregivers is as individual as the problems they face. A woman once told us that the day her mother had a stroke, she felt like a failure. She said repeatedly, "*If I had only taken her to the doctor more often; if I only paid more attention to the medication she was taking.*" Fortunately, her mother recovered, and a few weeks later, she went home. I asked the woman, "Do you still feel like a failure now that your mother is well?" She looked at me and said,

"I'm okay now; until the next time." Another woman's goal was to keep her mother alive to see her hundredth birthday. Her mother died at the age of ninety-nine. How did she feel about her mother's death? She sadly whispered, *"She was only ninety-nine, you know."*

We all see success and failure in different ways. We often define our successes and failures by who we are, how we live, our individual goals, and sometimes by the measure of others, such as our family, friends, and co-workers. If you decide this job is for you, it is important to recognize that at times you may feel "successful" because your parent is doing well. But at other times your parent will not do as well, and you may end up blaming yourself for the problem. However, even you may not be your harshest critic. There will be times when your family, physicians, and even your parent may challenge your performance as a caregiver. When you feel challenged, you may try to protect yourself by saying things like, "If you don't like how I'm taking care of Mother, do it yourself," or "Mom, do your own shopping, laundry, and banking." In your heart, you know that no one else is volunteering for the job, and your mother cannot possibly take care of herself. If you decide this job is not for you and that someone else, such as a paid companion or nurse, should be the caregiver, you may find your family and friends second-guessing your decision. They may not fully understand the complexity of the situation or your personal reasons for making your decision. You may begin to doubt and question yourself, feeling inadequate, guilty, and alone.

"We've been married for twenty years and I have always been the 'good daughter-in-law.' I am always the one who prepares holiday parties, and I am the one who buys the presents and sends the birthday cards. My husband just signs the cards. When my father-in-law had a stroke, I visited him in the hospital, and my husband offered our house as his private rehabilitation center. I know I should have said no, but it is very hard for me to do that. I agreed for him to stay until he was stronger. I worked, cooked, cleaned, supervised his aides, and took him to the doctor. You know what I got, criticism from my brother-in-law and my husband. There is nothing worse or more hurtful then being criticized for doing something kind."

Samantha, Illinois

"I love Mom, but I know in my heart that I cannot take care of her. I am just not comfortable giving her a bath or feeding her. I sometimes feel guilty about the way I feel. I hired a wonderful lady to provide her with very good care. It's better for Mom. My mother's sister thinks I am wrong, and she lets me know how she feels every chance she gets. I can only do what I can."

Lena, New York

How do you accept the fact that no matter what decision you make, there will always be feelings of success and failure? The solution is not easy, but the following suggestions may help you come to terms with your decision and give you some peace of mind. The most difficult step is to come to terms with whatever decision you make. Listen carefully to your thoughts. Recognize and understand that you carefully weighed your decision, considered all of the options, and you know that it is the right decision for you and your parent. Open your heart to accept the fact that caring for an elderly parent has many ups and downs and no guarantees. If you do accept your decision and all of its uncertainties, you will never again have to ask yourself the question, what if I fail?

G. MY JOURNAL

Use this page as a safe place to express your feelings, thoughts, and concerns. Putting thoughts and feelings on paper helps us to see them more clearly. Do I really want this job? What is the best way for me to help my parents? How do I feel about taking on this difficult responsibility? For example:

"My father is so difficult and we never really got along. What makes me think I can do this . . . ?"

"I feel so angry and stuck. My sister doesn't help me and I feel so alone. . . ."

_____

_____

_____

H. TIP SHEET

- Ask yourself: Do I want this job or is eldercare not for me?
- Open your eyes to see who your parents are today and if they really need your help at this time. And how much time do they need?
- Get the help you need from family, friends, and professionals when you need it.
- Don't try to fix everything. You are not responsible for everyone and everything.
- Take care of yourself as well as you take care of everyone else.

2

KNOWING WHEN YOUR PARENTS NEED HELP

A. WHAT'S NORMAL?

"My eighty-six-year-old father lives alone and gets by pretty well. He and I have discussed that someday he may have to move out of his home. He says, 'I'll let you know when I can't handle this anymore.' I'm not sure he'll know when it's time and I don't know how I'm supposed to know whether he's in danger or just acting like a normal eighty-six-year-old."

Frank, Oregon

"My aunt's arthritis is so painful, she's stopped going out. She just stays home alone with her cats. I keep begging her to get another opinion, but she says her doctor told her that arthritis is a normal part of aging. I don't think that's right. I don't know what to do."

Sarah, Ohio

"Normal? You've got the wrong family! My biological father was old and sick at fifty-six and died at sixty. My eighty-seven-year-old mother has never been sick a day in her life. She's about to marry her fifth husband and we're all planning on dancing until dawn at her wedding—mostly because she won't let us go home until she's ready to leave! I think 'normal' is whatever works for you. Don't you?"

Jeff, Alabama

There is no *normal*. There never has been. The key to coping and understanding changes in your parent's changing needs is to learn to recognize actions and identify symptoms that fall outside of "expected and acceptable" changes. A good rule of thumb is this: as your parent ages, you may see changes in her physical activity, medication tolerance, memory, vision, and hearing. As long as these changes don't significantly interfere with her activities of daily living (ADLs), we usually categorize them as "expected and acceptable" changes. However, if these changes are severe enough that your mother can no longer safely evacuate her home in an emergency, self-manage her own dressing, walking, eating, bathing, toileting, or transferring from her bed to a chair, seek medical intervention.

We all change as we age. Just as your needs are different now than they were when you were a toddler or teenager, you can expect your parent's needs to be different at eighty-five years of age than they were at sixty-five. Since most of us haven't experienced the physical or emotional changes that come with older age, it's often difficult for us to know when a parent might need or appreciate our help, or when we're witnessing changes and needs that are attributable to normal aging.

Because we are all different from one another, we all age differently. A parent who has suffered from rheumatoid arthritis for decades will likely have more trouble with mobility than one who has not suffered from a similar disease. Similarly, if your mother has never been ill a day in her life and is still robust at seventy-four, you can reasonably expect her to walk with ease. If your father has never been compliant with physician's orders, has never taken medications properly, or has refused treatment regularly, we would not consider it unusual for his attitude to intensify with age; so we wouldn't be surprised if he became even more difficult with regard to medical issues. However, when a parent who has always enjoyed warm relationships with family and friends withdraws from activities that she previously enjoyed, that is unexpected and unacceptable. Or, when a kind, gentle, and loving parent undergoes a severe personality change and acts mean and aggressive, those unusual actions signify a change that is neither expected nor acceptable. Both usually signify a problem that warrants immediate medical attention.

If you see your parent regularly, it might be more difficult for you to recognize gradual changes in physical appearance, mental awareness, or emotional status. Many changes are subtle and inconsistent, and your parent may instinctively cope in a way that hides the change. When you see your parent once or twice a year, the changes may be more obvious because you witness the result of many months' changes all at once. In that situation you may be more apt to notice the bigger physical changes from visit to visit, but miss the smaller ones. Either way, identifying those changes doesn't always make it easy to know whether or not your parent needs your help. If your father is experiencing vision problems, you may find the furniture rearranged so that his chair is closer to the television, enabling him to see the picture better. As far as your father is concerned, the problem is solved. Does he need your help? Now, think back to the first time you had trouble reading without glasses. Did you make an appointment with an ophthalmologist? Most of us just thought our eyes were tired and resolved to get more sleep. Or, we just began to hold the paper an inch or two closer or farther from our eyes. Chances are, as far as we were concerned, the problem was solved—just like dad! Many changes are not life threatening and do not put your parent in danger. If your dad's vision keeps deteriorating, then his safety is unquestionably jeopardized and he may need help setting up an appointment with an ophthalmologist. One of the keys to knowing when your parent needs help is to learn to identify which changes affect your parent's health and safety.

B. LOSS OF LOVED ONES, TRUSTED FRIENDS, AND ADVISERS

> "My eighty-six-year-old mother-in-law has outlived her husband, both sisters, one grandchild, two ministers, all her doctors, and most of her lifelong friends. Except for church, she stays in the house. She eats alone, watches television alone, and reads alone. I live across the country from her, and she won't move to my area or come for an extended visit. She cries when I arrive for a visit and cries when I leave. I don't know how to help her."
>
> *Mary, Washington*

The older your parent becomes, the more likely she is to have experienced multiple emotional losses, such as the deaths of one or more partners, children, sisters, brothers, friends, and trusted advisers. Our role in society is often identified through the emotions we experience as a parent, spouse, sibling, and friend. The loss of any one of these identities can cause one to feel lonely and lost. Consider the added impact of multiple losses combined with a declining ability to walk, drive, prepare your own food, see clearly, hear well, read, watch television, remember the cards played during your weekly game, wear your favorite clothes and shoes, or wander about independently and free from pain. From your parent's point of view, the reward for having lived "this long" may feel, to some degree, more like a punishment. How hard it must be to carry the burden of losing so many of the things that made life warm, enjoyable, and interesting, while simultaneously facing your own inevitable decline. It's simple to see how trauma from emotional and physical losses can lead to withdrawal, serious injury, depression, self-neglect, and alcohol.

Loss of Self

How many times have you or someone you know looked in the mirror and groaned over a wrinkle, a few gray hairs, or a few pounds that will never disappear again? How many elderly people have you ever heard describe themselves or their friends as "beautiful"? What we usually hear is "Your mother was so beautiful when we met," or "Your father was the most

handsome man I had ever seen." In our society, the signs of age unfortunately are not always considered "beautiful." Your parent may talk about
physical changes with an implied negative comparison, such as "When I
was your age, I hit the ball so hard I broke the bat," or "When I was young,
I could have had three dates every Saturday night." How must that feel?
Imagine that the only compliments you received from others or could pay
yourself were in the past tense? Let yourself feel, just for a minute, what
life would be like with constant reminders that the best of life is behind
you. It's not difficult to understand why losing our physical self to changes
we'd rather not experience might lead to emotional decline.

The antidote to an emotional/physical decline is replacing our losses.
You can help your father by discussing in a frank manner his current
capabilities and working with him on ideas to live to his maximum level
of independence. People who have impaired mobility might find the intricacies and companionship of bridge or chess can help replace golf or
dancing. If your mother can no longer remember her cards well enough
to continue playing canasta or bridge, she may find mall walking or activities in groups at a community day care center just as stimulating and far
less frustrating. Don't be surprised if your parent rejects your suggestions,
saying, "I'm too old to make new friends," or, "I don't know anything
about bridge." Don't give up. Fear of the unknown is part of the loss of
self-esteem. After all, if your parent doubts his own self-worth, he most
likely doubts that others will find him worthwhile. Call the appropriate
community resources for ideas on how to help your parent become
involved in new activities. (You can review a list of organizations that
may be able to help you in chapter 24.) The best outcome is that your
parent will eventually thank you, and both your lives will be easier, happier, and more fulfilling. If your parent refuses your help, you will still
feel better for having tried.

Loss of Independence and Control

Loss of autonomy, control, and financial independence affect self-esteem,
an ingredient that is necessary for good mental health. If your mother can
no longer make consistently sound decisions and you step in to help, try
to involve her as much as possible so that she feels she is retaining some
control over her life. This is a good time to get help from professionals

who are experienced in your mother's illness (Alzheimer's, stroke, Parkinson's, and so on). They can help you with a list of activities that are appropriate to your mother's needs and capabilities, and help you create an approach to use when you talk to her. Your goal is to make your mother feel that her opinion still has value, and that she still has some control over her life.

A caregiver in New Jersey created this solution to the universal problem of helping a parent shop for groceries:

"I used to drive myself crazy when I took my mother shopping. She'd bring her coupons and I'd walk around the store with her, saying, 'Do you want the noodles? Do you need tissues? Are you getting low on tea? Sugar?' It took hours, and I'm sure she didn't like it, either. Now, I've given her back control over her own shopping and it's so much better for both of us. I tell her how much time I've got; I usually schedule about forty-five minutes or so. We go to the store, and she takes her own cart and does her shopping. Sometimes I just wait for her in the front of the store, and sometimes I do my own shopping while she's doing hers! At the end of the forty-five minutes, we get together, and I help her check to see if she missed anything that I know she needs. Then we go home. What a difference! She's got control, and neither one of us is as stressed out as we used to be."

A caregiver in New Hampshire offers this lesson learned from her father about control and independence:

"At lunch one afternoon, my dad casually mentioned that he went to the doctor for a hearing test and ended up with an MRI! When I asked why, he said, 'It's nothing. They found a little tumor.' With my heart in my throat, I asked, 'Where?' He answered, 'Pressing against the ear.' I blurted out, 'I want to talk to the doctor, Dad.' He looked at me and said, 'I'll write her a letter telling her it's okay to talk to you.' I started to tell him I wanted to call right away, that afternoon, not wait a week until she got the letter, when I suddenly realized he was gently but purposefully reminding me that he didn't intend to let me have total control. He wasn't adverse to my help, but I didn't have carte blanche to make decisions for him without involving him."

If you want your parent to agree to let you help him, learn to involve him in the decision-making process. It may take some time, but with a little practice, you'll find your parent will agree to your help with less trepidation, and you will accomplish more in less time and with fewer arguments. What if your mother believes she can still make her own decisions while you believe that allowing her to remain in control will put her in danger? How do you determine if your parent can make appropriate decisions? A word of caution: old age in and of itself does not always signify a need for help; neither does being disagreeable and unpleasant or making decisions that are harmless but different than those you would have made. Here are some guidelines that may help you identify problem areas that indicate a need for assistance:

- Consider your parent's physical safety. Has she fallen more than once? Each of us has the potential for a fall, but few healthy people fall or trip repeatedly. If your parent has cuts or bruises and you aren't satisfied with the reasons she gives for them, she needs your help.
- Can your parent hear and respond to fire or smoke alarms, telephone rings, or doorbells? If she has demonstrated increased difficulty with her hearing and refuses to wear a hearing aid that fits and works, this may be a good time to intervene.
- Is your parent able to follow directions for sequential tasks without getting confused? The phrase "Come in, take your coat off, and hang it in the closet" contains three sequential tasks, as does "Take the bus to 48th Street, walk over to Fifth, and I'll meet you in the restaurant." If she is having trouble with these or other day-to-day tasks, she needs your help.
- Consider your parent's ability to see clearly. Does he need brighter light or can he no longer read due to vision loss? If your parent's vision is deteriorating and he refuses to acknowledge or treat the problem, he needs your help.
- If you notice a change in your parent's speech pattern or you see involuntary body movements, your parent needs your immediate help to obtain a medical diagnosis and treatment.
- If your parent's judgment is impaired, he may be handling his financial affairs inappropriately. Look for a significant increase or decrease in the number and amount of bank withdrawals or checks written.
- If your parent has become incontinent, changed her personal

grooming habits, or lost interest in regular bathing, clean clothes, hair, and nails, she needs your help for a medical diagnosis and treatment.

- If your parent has become more confused or forgetful, is unreasonably anxious, cries frequently, or exhibits major irrational mood changes, intervene and help him obtain medical help.

You will find more information on assessing your parent's need, planning your intervention, and learning to be an advocate in chapters 3 and 4.

C. DECLINE IS A FACT OF LIFE

> "I'll never understand it. When I told my mother that the FDA approved a new treatment that would ease the arthritic problem in her knees and help her walk better, I expected her to be happy and impatient to get the treatment. Her response was, 'I never expected to live this long without pain.' She has no interest in the treatment, she's still in agony when she walks, and a year later, I still get angry and want to shake her every time I see her trying to walk without showing her pain."
>
> *Marjorie, Kansas*

Most of us don't really want to believe that our parents, who once seemed invulnerable, must face an inevitable decline. In our hearts and minds, when our parents' physical health and quality of life are compromised, it signifies the beginning of the end of the structure and support that shaped our lives. Witnessing the progressive deterioration that brings a parent's life to its inevitable conclusion is understandably often too hard for many of us to face or accept. To soften our pain, we may deny their illness or even become angry that they won't accept our help.

You can help yourself and your parent get through this difficult time by channeling your frustration and anger into positive actions such as trying to help your parent receive cutting-edge treatment and as much assistance as he needs.

- Get professional help from experts in your parent's illness. The heart, diabetes, stroke, Alzheimer's, and Parkinson's associations, and other groups can provide you with many resources, save you time and money, and help both you and your parent achieve a better quality of life. (See chapter 24 for contact information for these and other helpful resources.)
- Don't settle for a single diagnosis. Get a second opinion from an illness-specific specialist who doesn't know the original physician. Then return to the specialist at regular intervals to find out which medications or other treatments are newly available to help your parent.
- Do not settle for your parent's self-diagnosis: "My arthritis is so bad today I can hardly stand." If your parent can't stand, medical attention is needed to treat the severity of the problem. Without treatment, your parent may experience more pain and a faster decline than is necessary.
- Do your own research. Consult with a medical specialist, search the Internet, and contact the resources in chapter 24 to be certain your parent is receiving the latest and safest treatment techniques available. If you can afford it, retain the services of a geriatric care manager or another healthcare advocate to guide you through the intricacies of the healthcare system.

Regardless of the outcome of your efforts, these four steps will help you care for your parent. You will also achieve the peace of mind that comes with knowing that you have done everything you could possibly do.

D. WHY PARENTS REFUSE HELP

The best approach to a parent who refuses help is to back off and look at the situation from a different perspective. Take a moment to try to figure out why your mother might not want your help. Be sure you're thinking about the situation from her point of view, not yours. It's hard to do, but take a few minutes alone, in a quiet room, and imagine yourself in her shoes.

Begin with the premise that, like you, your mother treasures her independence and wants to make her own decisions. She realistically assumes that if she tells you something is wrong, you will want to help her and do something about the problem. If she is ill, she knows that in order for you to help her effectively, you must involve yourself in her private life, and that may jeopardize her independence. The result of your actions may mean the loss of her driving privileges or a move to an assisted living community or a nursing home. It may force her to admit she can no longer take care of herself and that she may have begun an irreversible slide into dependency. She senses that, from the moment you begin to help her, nothing in her life or your relationship will ever be the same. She is absolutely right. Do it anyway.

You will find ways to comfort your mother through the necessary changes, but for now, your assistance may be the only way to help ensure her health and safety. Your mother might not be sure which of her changing needs are natural with advancing age and which might signal a treatable problem. Rather than "pester" the doctor, she may decide to "wait," believing or hoping the problem will take care of itself or that there is nothing that can be done. "After all, dear, I am eighty-four."

Our parents rarely deceive us out of malice or harm, or to cause us more anxiety or pain. Most of our parents learned self-reliance as children and have practiced it their entire lives. Many come from a family tradition of not consulting doctors for seemingly ordinary occurrences like a cough, the flu, a pain, or even a broken toe. Their parents (your grandparents) had to be self-sufficient to survive. The nearest doctor may have been so far away, or so expensive, that treatment for less-than-life-threatening problems wasn't feasible.

Your mother could be responding to your questions and concerns with the same answers that her mother gave her. "*Worry about yourself; you look sicker than I do*," is a favorite, as are "*Stop worrying, this happens to everybody at my age*," and, "*I've been taking care of myself for years and I'm still here. I'll call you if I need help.*" For situations that involve memory loss, you may hear, "*At my age, I'm entitled to forget a few things.*" You may be tempted to accept your mother's explanation; after all, don't we all occasionally forget where we put our car keys, the name of an acquaintance, or even our own telephone numbers? Yes, we do forget those things, but our memory lapses are usually temporary: we eventually find our car keys, remember the person's name, and recall our own telephone number. Before you let your mother convince you she's fine, try to determine whether her lack of recall is sporadic and temporary, or recurring with growing confusion. If it's the latter, intervene quickly and see a board-certified geriatric physician.

To some of our parents, aging may be a metaphor for loss of independence, relinquishing the role as head of the family, and for becoming a burden to the family. For many, it can also mean a constant battle to maintain their privacy and control of their future. When we try to help, we have a tendency to "take over" and make immediate changes, regardless of the impact on our parents' lives. Although changes may be necessary for their health and safety, to our parents these changes may seem disheartening, disorienting, humiliating, and unnecessary. You can help prevent those feelings, or diminish them, by following these three steps:

1. Take time to think your ideas through and plan them out thoroughly. For example, if you know that your father can't drive safely and have removed his car, try to provide alternate transportation so your father can still run his errands, go to a movie, or to a restaurant for dinner. If you think your mother would be better off moving into an assisted living facility, work out the logistics with your mother and your family before making the final decision, rather than making her feel like a burden to you by arguing about them in front of her during and after her move.

2. Talk with your parent before you make any changes. If she is capable, develop a continuing strategy of working at trying to persuade her to do the right thing for her health and safety. It may take more than one meeting, but it's worth it. Don't expect an automatic or even a quick agreement to your recommendations. You may be asking your parent to change decades-old habits, a well-established routine, or even a total lifestyle. Unless we ask for help, very few of us want other family members meddling in our business and telling us what's best for us. Instead of forcing the issue, set a goal of trying to convince your mother to take care of her needs. When you talk to your mother about the benefits of following your suggestions, be sure to put yourself in her position. Forget about what you want. Try to figure out and stay focused on how your plan will help her achieve what she wants.

3. Present your parent with choices so that she can continue to main-

tain some control and autonomy. This approach is practical only if your parent is realistically able to make the decision. Don't attempt to make an agreement for a future date with a parent who exhibits midstage to advanced dementia symptoms. Your parent won't remember the discussion or the date, and constantly reminding her will only cause her more anxiety and confusion. For instance, if you are helping your mother move, identify several dates that work for you, and then give her the responsibility for choosing which date she wants to move. If you are hiring a home-care worker, interview several candidates and choose two or three that you feel are a match for your mother's healthcare needs and personality. Then let your mother interview your choices and choose the homecare worker she likes the best. You will still have the worker of your choice, and your mother will have had the final say in the decision. This approach will increase her control, which usually helps ensure more cooperation. You will receive fewer complaints from your mother and the worker, and you will have to replace fewer workers.

Difficult Parents

"My father has always been a tyrant. When he visits us, it's always a battle. He wants everything his way: dictating how my kids should behave, what time we should eat dinner, and what we should watch on TV. I've come to dread his visits. Now that he's sick, his attitude is worse. He's a living, breathing nightmare. I'm the only one who lives close enough to take care of him. I feel so guilty telling you this, God forgive me, but sometimes I actually have to stop myself from wishing he'd hurry up and die."

Serena, Virginia

Most of the time, difficult personalities intensify with age. If your father has always been difficult, you can reasonably expect him to stay difficult or become even more difficult as he ages. It isn't you, it isn't the noise your kids make, it isn't your cooking skills, and it isn't the amount of time you are spending or not spending with him. It's his personality, and it would be unusual for him to change and become the opposite of what he's been for years. However, if your father has had a personality change, from a flexible, gentle man to a difficult, demanding, and controlling parent, speak to your father's physician. If you think there is a possibility of recurring, untreated pain from an existing medical condition, a reaction from a medication change, a ministroke, depression, or another neurological problem, tell the physician. This caregiver's story demonstrates the need to talk to a parent's physician about safely trying to determine the cause of such problems before automatically adding another medication.

"When my father came for his semiannual visit, I was upset by the changes that seemed to have taken place since the last time I saw him. He seemed smaller, less energetic, and a little disoriented from time to time. I called his physician and spoke to him about it. The doctor's immediate response was, 'Thank you for telling me. I'll start him on Alzheimer's medication as soon as he gets back.' I was aghast! I never said anything about Alzheimer's! Just because he's seventy-four doesn't mean he has Alzheimer's! He could've had a stroke! What if he had developed a brain tumor or another neurological problem? It was all I could do to control myself."

Victoria, New York

Elderly people sometimes experience changing emotions, fear, denial, and depression. If no physiological reason is found for your father's personality change, ask the physician to refer you to a geriatric psychiatrist. Do you know anyone who actually welcomes growing older? Anyone who really believes that old age comes without some kind of an eventual decline? Anyone who wants to enter a nursing home? Or anyone who is eagerly waiting to become dependent? Society presents all of us with multiple reasons to fear and deny aging. We live in a youth-worshipping culture in which television programs, commercials, and magazine ads have conditioned us to believe that only young people are beautiful and important; employers surreptitiously value youth over experience; and the world openly wonders if people over the age of sixty-five will use up too many of its resources. The bias against age pervades society: store clerks often help younger customers first, and waiters often give spotty service to older people because they believe they will not leave a good tip. Even medical professionals may diagnose age or depression as the cause of a symptom without ever testing for other problems or diseases that might need treatment.

E. WHAT ARE THE WARNING SIGNS?

Memory Loss/Dementia

> "I didn't realize he needed help. I thought when he paid the rent bill twice it was an oversight. When the police called and said he drove the wrong way on the highway, I knew we were in trouble."
>
> *Johanna, Connecticut*

We all forget things. If your mother forgets today's date, or an acquaintance's last name, or to pick up the dry cleaning, that doesn't mean she has dementia. She may get frustrated for a short period of time, but eventually she should remember what she forgot and go on with her life. People with dementia can't remember what they forgot because they don't remember forgetting anything. They have lost the capacity to use clues and past memories to help themselves. Your mother, for example, may not be able to find the list she made to take to the grocery store. A person with dementia wouldn't look for the list because she wouldn't remember making the list or misplacing it. She would have lost all recall of the act.

One of the most important things for you to know about dementia is that it is not a disease. Dementia is the name given for a group of symptoms that occur in many diseases including adverse drug reactions (ADRs), Alzheimer's, AIDS, brain tumors, depression, drug and alcohol addictions, head injuries, hydrocephalus, nutritional deficiencies, Parkinson's, strokes, urinary tract infections (UTIs), and many others. It is also essential for you to recognize that the symptoms of Alzheimer's-type dementia usually progress gradually. If your mother was fine yesterday, but couldn't remember how to unlock her door today, that may signify a different medical problem. Whether your mother's symptoms progressed slowly or rapidly, she needs immediate medical attention by a board-certified geriatric physician or a neurologist who specializes in illnesses that manifest themselves in dementia symptoms. (You can read more about Alzheimer's-type dementia in chapter 16.)

Another critically important fact is that by the time you recognize the warning signs of dementia, the illness that caused the symptoms is usually already firmly established. Look for:

- A gradual or sudden loss of memory and language skills that may result in evasive answers to try and cover up the inability to remember words, places, and people
- A disinterest or decline in ability to perform routine tasks, particularly those with multiple parts and a sequential order, such as cooking from a recipe or participating in a hobby
- A decline in judgment such as forgetting to lock the door, opening the door to strangers, not remembering the meaning of a stop sign, leaving the water running, or forgetting to turn off the stove
- A change in social skills, such as a decline in ability to continue a conversation or eating with fingers instead of utensils
- Giving incorrect, almost correct, or evasive answers to questions (Q. Who is the current president of the United States? A. You mean you don't know?)
- A loss of attention and concentration skills, resulting in an inability to focus on a discussion, a television program, or a specific subject
- Becoming disoriented, frightened, or confused when faced with changing locations, such as traveling from one house to another, eating out in a restaurant, or visiting a doctor's office
- Becoming lost in familiar places (home, her doctor's office) or unable to recognize familiar landmarks or streets
- A loss of attention to hygiene, or behavior or gait changes, or other noticeable personality changes

Diminished Hearing

"I'd call my mother for hours, sometimes a couple of days before she answered the phone. I used to leave work and rush over to her house, wondering if she had fallen or had a heart attack. Every time I got there, she told me she'd just gotten back from the store, so I stopped rushing over. After months of terror, I finally figured out she couldn't hear the phone ring anymore."

Barbara, Iowa

"I thought my father was demented and not safe on his own. He never answered his phone. When I'd ask him a question, he'd answer with a question or statement that was totally unrelated to the subject I asked about. Finally, my sister and I hired a geriatric care manager to evaluate him and help us find a nursing home for him. Thank God for her. She recommended a geriatric physician who told us he wasn't demented, he was deaf! He had lost 80 percent of his hearing in one ear and 60 percent in the other ear."

Lorraine, Michigan

If these stories sound familiar, it will save you a lot of heartache, anxiety, and argumentative family gatherings if you can convince your parent to voluntarily visit an otologist or otolaryngologist. Examination and treatment might determine that the cause of your parent's hearing loss could be as simple as removing a wax buildup. Take this slowly, one step at a time. The fear many of us have of losing contact with the world and of exposing that loss publicly by wearing a hearing aid, plus simple vanity concerns, often results in anger and vehement denials of the problem.

The first step is not to convince your father to get a hearing aid. The first step is to secure his agreement for an exam by a board-certified specialist. That still leaves him free from acknowledging the seriousness of the problem or from making a commitment to wear a hearing aid. Talk to the doctor and ask him to present a variety of solutions that match the diagnosis and to work with your father to get a commitment for treatment. If your father needs a hearing aid, ask the doctor to take the time to talk with him about all the options, including size and visibility. You might also try researching the Internet for lists of famous people, or younger people, who wear hearing aids. This may provide your father with some comfort. By letting him know that others have taken the plunge to wear this assistive device, you will be reassuring him that the hearing aid won't reflect negatively on the image he has of himself.

Parents who are hearing-impaired often irritate other family members simply by trying to hear and understand what's being said so that they can remain involved in the family's activities. Helen Keller described deafness as worse than blindness because deafness severs contact with other people. Left untreated, deafness forces withdrawal, which often leads to isolation, depression, and further illness. A hearing impairment is a significant safety issue. If your parent cannot easily hear the telephone, a knock at the door, a siren or horn on a busy street, or a fire alarm, it is only a matter of time before an accident will happen. If your father refuses your first suggestion, try to enlist friends or other family members to help convince him.

If you can recognize these warning signs, your parent needs medical attention. Does your parent:

- Consistently raise the volume on the television or radio louder than is comfortable for others who are not impaired?
- Frequently ignore a direct question (because he hasn't heard it)?
- Continually say "What?" as a means of asking you to repeat what you said?
- Regularly repeat what you said back to you (as if to confirm hearing it correctly)?
- Often break into conversations or respond to questions with comments on completely different topics?
- Only understand you when your lips are visible and you speak clearly? (This signifies lip reading, which is a skill subconsciously acquired by many hearing-impaired people.)
- Generally have difficulty hearing and understanding high sounds?
- Have trouble distinguishing between certain sounds like *f*, *t*, and *z* so words like "zoo" and "food" might be heard as "too," resulting in often misunderstood requests?
- Nod and say "uh-huh" throughout your conversation? (With these actions, your parent is confirming, to you and to himself, that he is successfully following the conversation.)

Your persistence may annoy your father today, but may save his life tomorrow. Remember that even if your father continues to refuse your help, you will have helped yourself to more peace of mind by at least trying.

Diminished Sight

Vision loss is not a normal part of aging; it is a result of a medical problem.[1] Poor vision is a safety hazard. Your parent may not be able to tell the difference between red and green traffic lights, or may sign a financial or legal document without reading it. Untreated vision loss may also keep your parent from achieving an optimal quality of life. Your parent might not be able to recognize a friend across the room, read a menu in a restaurant, or enjoy watching television with the family. Not being able to see clearly often results in fear and anxiety that keeps your parent from taking part in outside-the-home activities.

Many of the symptoms of vision impairment are also symptoms of dementia. This often results in an "assumption" that your parent has Alzheimer's. This supposition may prevent him from seeking a complete examination for an accurate diagnosis. If you recognize these signs, your parent should visit a board-certified geriatric physician as soon as possible. This is not a typo: the reason we suggest seeing a *geriatric* physician instead of an eye doctor is because many of these signs can also indicate other medical problems. The geriatric physician will most likely perform a vision test; if he doesn't, then request one.

If you suspect a vision problem, look for these signs:

- Is your parent falling? Tripping? Bumping into things?
- Have you noticed a hesitancy in your parent's walk?
- Has your parent almost missed or actually missed a chair when trying to sit?
- Has your parent become "bored" with TV?
- Has your parent started wearing mismatched clothing or shoes?
- Has your parent gotten lost because he cannot read the street signs?
- Has your parent stopped reading, playing cards, or enjoying activities that require good eyesight?

Falls

If your parent has fallen or is at risk for falling, seek immediate medical attention from a board-certified geriatric physician. Look for these warning signs:

- Unexplained bruises
- Unexplained hospitalizations
- Explanations for cuts, bruises, or broken bones that don't have the ring of truth
- Hesitancy while walking
- Sudden, unexplained refusal to leave the familiarity of his own home

Falls are among the most dangerous occurrences for the elderly. Most experts agree that elders who fall once will fall again within the year unless they receive medical attention. A "fall" can take place in a dark or poorly lit room; exiting a shower, bath, or car; rising from bed or from a chair; bending to retrieve an object from the floor; walking up or down the stairs; and many other places. Your parent may be alone and not able to reach the telephone. If you see an unexplained bruise or broken bone, or your parent becomes timid and afraid to participate in activities that he used to enjoy, investigate further.

The best strategy is to avoid the causes of falls. If you recognize any of these physical problems or safety issues, work with your parents and their doctors or caregivers to eliminate the problem. It is very important to tell the physician how, when, and where the fall occurred. The time of day, the physical location, and what your parent was doing are all major clues to the cause. That type of information can suggest a neurological problem, a vision problem, or an emotional problem. Your intervention will help keep your parent safer.

Falls often result from:

- Poor physical health: osteoporosis, balance, eyesight, confusion, disorientation, adverse medication reactions, dizziness from low blood pressure, strokes, seizures, or lack of strength in arms or legs
- Poor safety habits: loose throw rugs; exposed wiring; slippery floors; poor lighting; lack of handrails in hallways, in bathrooms, and on stairs; and chairs that are difficult to get in and out of (too low or too high)
- Inappropriate clothing: non-supportive or ill-fitting shoes
- Not using needed assistive devices: cane, walker, wheelchair, eyeglasses, or hearing aid

Incontinence

> "My husband and I couldn't figure out why my father-in-law
> stopped coming over for dinner every week. After he missed a
> few weeks, Stuart and I got nervous and we went over to his
> apartment. The answer hit you as you walked in the door. He
> had become incontinent. We didn't mention it to him during
> that visit because we knew he'd be embarrassed. Frankly, so
> were we. We had no idea how to approach the subject with
> him. Stuart got some help from the human resources counselor
> at his office, but when he brought up the subject, my father-in-
> law became outraged. He said the whole idea that he was
> incontinent was 'nonsense' and asked Stuart to leave."
>
> *Polly, Arkansas*

Incontinence is one of the two most stressful situations for caregivers; the
other is dementia. Both contain elements of fear, anxiety, and embarrassment, because you never know when or where your parent will have an
episode of incontinence and embarrass himself or you.

Incontinence is an almost impossible subject to discuss with your
parent. This is a condition of the most personal and private nature. Your
parent will be humiliated by the episodes and try to keep them from you; he
may consider the subject too personal to even discuss with a physician. You
can begin by asking your parent's physician to call your parent and schedule
an appointment. Ask the physician to explain that incontinence is not a part
of old age; it is a physical condition that deserves a diagnosis to help determine its origin. When the physician knows the cause of the incontinence, he
can recommend guidelines for managing, treating, or even reversing your
parent's condition. Also ask the physician to take the time to clearly explain
the procedure he will use to diagnose the cause as well as the options for
treatment or cure. Follow up with the physician to be certain your father is
doing his part and is compliant with medications or other recommendations.

Look for these signs to identify incontinence:

- Clothing stains
- Odors emanating from furniture, clothing, or automobile seats
- Fear of leaving the house (due to embarrassment)

- Withdrawal from social activities to avoid embarrassment
- Daily or constant changing of bed linens or furniture covers

Self-Neglect

> "I've almost given up trying to figure out if my mother needs my help. She says that every one of her friends has arthritis and high blood pressure, and she doesn't know why I make 'such a big deal out of every little ache and pain.' I don't know what to think. Maybe she's right."
>
> *Debra, Vermont*

Your mother may assume that chronic pain is an unavoidable consequence of a medical condition and then neglect to speak with her doctor about pain-control treatment. A newly widowed parent may not eat properly, experience malnutrition, and suffer from one or more related illnesses, including depression and dementia symptoms. Your father may be accepting new prescriptions from new doctors without informing them of the medications he is currently taking, and adverse medication reactions may cause multiple illnesses. All of these situations and many others constitute self-neglect.

The warning signs of self-neglect may put your parent in physical, emotional, and practical danger. Take action and get help from a board-certified geriatrician. Ask questions. Get a second opinion. Remember that successful treatment begins with an accurate diagnosis. (For more information on getting an accurate diagnosis, see chapter 15.)

Warning signs of self-neglect include:

- Poor eating habits and inadequate nutrition
- Failure or inability to follow through on a physician's instructions
- Failure to observe standard safety guidelines such as traffic lights and locking doors
- Failure to obtain medical help when diagnosis and treatment are indicated
- Failure to continue good personal grooming habits such as bathing and washing soiled clothing
- Failure to dress appropriately for protection against cold, heat, or rain
- Putting oneself in harm's way without reason or sound thought

Drug or Alcohol Abuse

Drug and/or alcohol abuse is a very large, growing problem in our elder population. Your father may be continuing a lifelong habit of a "couple of drinks before dinner" or a sleeping pill at night. Your mother may be depressed and believe that a "little drink" will make her feel more positive about life, or an anti-anxiety medication will help her get through the day. What our parents rarely realize is that as they age, their tolerance for drugs and alcohol decreases, causing them to react differently to the same dosage. In addition, parents who are isolated and depressed, homebound or in pain, or newly widowed and without social interaction often increase their alcohol or drug intake and rely on the numbing effect for relief of loneliness, pain, or grief. It never works. It almost always leads to problems such as automobile accidents, broken bones, hospitalizations, entry into a nursing home, and even death from adverse interactions between alcohol and medications.

"When I got a call from my father's neighbor telling me the police had just brought him home with a gash on his head, in stained, filthy clothes, I didn't know what to think. He was always so fastidious. I took him to the doctor and, sometime later, after treatment for addiction, my father told me that when one drink made him feel a little better, he figured that two or three, or five or ten, would make him feel really good. He worked on the same premise for his pain medication. Then he combined them. He went to different doctors and complained of the same problem—each one gave him medication. He paid people to pick up his liquor and prescriptions, or called the stores for home delivery. He told me that it seemed so easy. Of course, it didn't work. He just slid into a haze. He crossed the street without looking, gave people hundreds of dollars to get the stuff for him when he was too stoned to walk, and ultimately nearly got himself killed."

Harold, Oklahoma

If your parent is addicted, he will go to unbelievable lengths to keep you from finding the evidence. If you suspect alcohol or drug abuse, talk to your parent's physician, the Area Agency on Aging, and Alcoholics

Anonymous to identify the options in your area for people your parent's age. You'll need a treatment program specifically designed for the elderly and administered and monitored by experienced geriatric practitioners.

Look for these signs:

- The first place your parent goes when entering a room is to the bar.
- Bottles of alcohol are found in the bedroom hidden under clothing or in drawers.
- Your parent goes out at approximately the same time every day to the same place (the "store," Aunt Martha's, and so on).
- There are multiple dents on your parent's car caused by driving under the influence of alcohol or drugs.
- Your parent generally drinks a clear liquid, often in a water or juice glass.
- You've noticed slurred speech or poor balance. (These symptoms could also represent strokes and a number of other serious problems; seek immediate medical attention.)
- You regularly find empty liquor bottles in the recycling bin or the garbage.
- If your parent refuses your help, try to understand that accepting your help may also mean an acknowledgment of "needing" help. Be patient, be gentle, and try to explain that the intervention is really for both of you; you are intervening because of love and concern, and also because of the pain you feel when witnessing his suffering. Your persistence may annoy your father today, but may save his life tomorrow. Remember that even if your father refuses your help, over time you will have the comfort of knowing you tried.

F. WORKSHEET: SAFETY QUIZ

Use this Safety Quiz for a realistic look at your parent's current capabilities. A better understanding of your parent's status and risk factors can help alleviate some of your confusion in assessing whether your parent needs your help or has just changed his attitude toward certain things.

Answer "yes" or "no":

1. My parent would be unable to call 911 or safely evacuate his home in an emergency without physical or verbal reminders. (Y or N)
2. My parent is often frightened because she perceives danger in living alone in her home. (Y or N)
3. My parent appears to be in significant pain. (Y or N)
4. My parent appears weaker every time I see him. (Y or N)
5. My parent has fallen more than once. (Y or N)
6. My parent's home has a strong urine or feces odor. (Y or N)
7. I often find spoiled food in my parent's refrigerator. (Y or N)
8. My parent sometimes has multiple bruises without a rational explanation for how she got them. (Y or N)
9. I'm concerned that my parent is being exploited by a family member or caregiver because they refuse to leave me alone with her unless I become very insistent. (Y or N)
10. My parent is often confused about simple things like whether she has eaten dinner or the names or relationships of many of her relatives. (Y or N)
11. My parent has forgotten to turn off the stove several times. (Y or N)
12. My parent frequently forgets to lock the door. (Y or N)
13. My parent has been spending money irrationally and writing multiple checks to cash or to people he doesn't remember. I think my parent is too confused to continue handling his own finances. (Y or N)
14. My parent has had multiple fender benders and my instincts tell me it's dangerous for him to continue driving. (Y or N)
15. My parent's vision is so bad he can't read signs. (Y or N)
16. I want to (have tried to) take my mother's car away but I don't know how. (Y or N)
17. My parent is very depressed and cries frequently. (Y or N)
18. My parent's hearing is so impaired that she frequently doesn't hear the phone or her doorbell. (Y or N)
19. My parent was not overweight, but has lost more than ten pounds in the last six months. (Y or N)
20. My parent has stopped bathing and wears soiled clothes. (Y or N)

Answering Yes to *any one* of these questions suggests your parent is at significant risk and should no longer live alone. For your next steps, refer back to the appropriate section in this chapter. For information on the different levels of intervention (Preventive, Partial, Total, Crisis, Legal, and Financial) and which option bests meets your parent's needs, see chapter 4.

G. MY JOURNAL

Expressing our thoughts on paper often helps us realize what our feelings are, which makes it easier to arrive at solutions to our problems. What bothers you? What changes do you want to make? What or who are you grateful for? When you read what you've written, you may see a new pathway to help resolve stressful issues. Use this page as a safe place to express your feelings. For example:

"I woke up in the middle of night again last night worrying about dad. I think he's ill but he won't talk to me about it. I would feel better if he'd at least tell me if he's seen a doctor or not. Should I argue with him and insist or should I find someone else to get the information from him? Whom does he trust who would help me out?"

"Mom knows she's losing her memory but won't let me help her. She's so afraid. It breaks my heart to sit back and do nothing but watch. I'm going to make some calls tomorrow and find out how I can help her."

_____

_____

_____

_____

_____

_____

_____

_____

_____

_____

_____

_____

_____

_____

_____

_____

_____

_____

H. TIP SHEET

- Evaluate whether changes and symptoms fall outside of expected and acceptable.
- Look at situations from your parent's perspective as well as yours.
- If you are unsure whether your parent is at risk, get a professional geriatric assessment.
- If you are sure your parent is at risk, seek an accurate diagnosis from a board-certified geriatric physician.
- If possible, involve your parent and family members in your decisions regarding your parent.

3

AGING IN PLACE

"My father always said, 'Stop wasting your breath. I'm not going anywhere. I've spent the last forty-five years in this house and when my time is up, I'm going to die in my own bed.' Unfortunately, that's as far as his planning went. He had enough money and plenty of room to reorganize and move his bedroom downstairs. He refused to consider that eventually he might not be able to climb the stairs safely, so he wouldn't discuss moving his bedroom downstairs. And that's exactly what happened. He fell once too often and eventually had to leave his home and die somewhere else. I can't remember a sadder day."

Fred, Oregon

"I've got to hand it to my parents. When they decided they wanted to retire in the same condominium they'd lived in for years, they started making changes right away. They started early enough to be able to take their time, so they didn't have to pay for it all at once. It took more than ten years, but when they were finished, everything in the house worked for their comfort.

Who knew there were gadgets designed to make life easier for old people? I'm still amazed at the stuff they found. Leave it to my mother, the decorating queen, to find grab bars in colors to match her bathrooms!"

Joan, New Jersey

A. WHAT IS *AGING IN PLACE*?

Staying home. If you are lucky enough to grow old without having to move out of your home, you are *Aging in Place.* It is no surprise that years of research continues to deliver the same answer: if given a choice, most older people opt for maintaining independence and continuing to live in their own homes. Almost no one is ever ready or ever wants to exchange the warmth and familiarity of his or her own home for a nursing home or even for an assisted living community. In other words, most people want to *Age in Place.* The good news is that most people fulfill that wish. However, while some live in safety and comfort, the bad news is that others remain at daily risk for accidents that can change their status in one heartrending moment.

Originally, Aging in Place meant your parent could grow older without leaving his home to move to another dwelling such as your home, an independent congregate community, an assisted living community, or a nursing home. Today the meaning has been changed to include Continuing Care Retirement Communities (CCRC), Naturally Occurring Retirement Communities (NORC), and other types of congregate housing that provide increased levels of services. (You can find in-depth information on the different types of care and services these alternative housing options provide in chapters 19 and 20.)

These options often present themselves as an opportunity to age in place based on the concept that your parent can stay in the same community when his healthcare needs increase. Although one of these communities may be the best choice for your parent, it's important to understand the complete picture. Your parent's move to a community with multiple levels of services may be only the first in a series of moves. The scenario looks like this: Your parent's first move is from her home to an independent apartment in a community that usually offers housekeeping, two meals each day, scheduled transportation, a wellness center, on-site social and educational activities, and other services that can enhance your parent's quality of life. This environment provides a safe place and peace of mind. As she needs more assistance, Mom will either have to hire a private home health aide or move into another building that houses people who need additional help: the assisted living building. When your parent needs even more support and services, she will be required to move again—this time to the wing or building that provides skilled nursing care. Although the buildings are in the same community, the reality is that each move means getting acquainted with a different home, a new staff, and leaving behind old acquaintances and friends.

These changes are often necessary, even beneficial, but are vastly different from the emotional and physical comfort associated with staying in our own homes, truly Aging in Place.

The Obstacles

> "My mother is determined to remain in her apartment. She's still pretty self-sufficient; the problem is the neighborhood is now a total dump. Drugs, gangs, I don't even like going to see her. She says, 'Where else should I grow old except my own house? Don't worry. They're just boys. I bake them cookies; they watch out for me. They call me "Grandma Millie."' She's so naive. But she's her own boss and I can't budge her on this. I don't know what to do. I can't stop going to see her. I feel as though the only option I have left is to buy a T-shirt that says, 'Don't hurt me. Grandma Millie is my mother.'"
>
> *Robert, Michigan*

The concept of Aging in Place (AIP) is far from new; in fact, it's just the opposite—literally as old as humankind. It was only a few decades ago that the possibility surfaced of living somewhere other than in our homes when we began needing assistance. The reasons are simple and complex at the same time:

- Today's fast-paced, ever-changing world often brings outside influences into the decision-making process. This is especially visible in the growing geographic separation among family; the dwindling availability of medical and other support services when the character of neighborhoods change; and the increased fear of crimes against seniors who live alone.
- Our continually expanding life expectancy adds a mixture of physical, emotional, and cognitive issues. Many parents receive treatment for multiple chronic diseases and are responsible for daily self-medicating with eight, ten, twelve, or more doses of powerful and potentially dangerous medications.
- Whether to remain at home or move is likely to be one of the most difficult decisions you and your parent will make. It's easy to feel inundated and overwhelmed. However, some conditions stand out as beyond your control and may force your hand in reaching a conclusion.
- These conditions put your parent at risk and make it unsafe for him to continue living in his home without assistance.
- Friends or family may no longer live close by and your parent may suffer from isolation and loneliness that can increase or initiate confusion and memory loss.
- The lack of nearby friends and neighbors can also put your parent at risk if he needs help.
- Changes in the neighborhood may mean decreased access (or no access) to physicians, transportation, grocery stores, banks, or other services your parent needs and used to easily walk or drive to.
- Your parent may no longer be able to afford home repairs for plumbing, painting, heat, air conditioning, and so on. Houses with poor exterior upkeep and visible structure decay are prime targets for break-ins and vandalism.
- Your parent's church, synagogue, or mosque may be closing due to the neighborhood's decreasing number of parishioners. This may deprive your parent of valued spiritual guidance and comfort.
- Your parent may no longer be able to safely navigate the steps to a porch, an upstairs bedroom, or the basement in a multistory home.
- Your parent is unsafe alone because of physical or cognitive impairments and the family cannot afford in-home assistance.

- Your parent refuses to recognize or acknowledge any risk factors that may lead to his having to involuntarily leave his home.

A resolute denial of his changing abilities, isolation from needed services, and lack of socialization leaves him without the support that he and all of us require every day to not only survive, but also to thrive and maintain a reasonable quality of life.

The Alternatives

"After my mother died, dad couldn't get out of their house fast enough. Mom ran the place and even though pop was a young seventy-nine, he said, 'At my age, why would I want to use up all my energy and the time I have left to fix pipes and worry about the roof? That would be nuts!' He moved to a gorgeous two-bedroom apartment in an Independent Community that has meals, trips, parties, housekeeping, laundry service—just about everything he wanted. Now, he's closer to me and his second bedroom means my kids and I can spend the day and night with him. It was one of the best things he ever did. He seems much happier. I think the companionship and activities have added years to his life."

Carla, New Jersey

It's often hard for adult children to emotionally accept that Aging in Place may not always be your parent's best option and that a parent may actually prefer the alternatives.

There are many life-enhancing reasons to move:

- Your parent may move to be closer to the family.
- Your parent's friends may have moved to the new area or specific community.
- Your parent may want the peace of mind that comes with knowing someone is always nearby in case of an emergency.
- Your parent may no longer want to expend the effort necessary to care for a large house.

- Your parent may no longer want the work and responsibility of yard care.
- Your parent may feel insecure driving and want the convenience of provided transportation.
- Your parent may be unable to afford needed in-home assistance or may not feel strong enough to manage an in-home caregiver.

Whether your parent moves by choice or because of circumstances beyond his control, it is in your parent's and your best interest to understand *the need and reason for the move* so that you can help your parent find an appropriate new home. Communities may have the same generic description, CCRC, NORC, Independent or Assisted Living, Nursing Home, but they do not always offer the same services or amenities.

Use the worksheet, *Making Decisions about Housing*, at the end of chapter 20 to help you choose a community that is appropriate for your parent. Since this will be your parent's new home, it's especially important to consider *his wants* alongside his *needs*. If he likes to walk, try to find a community with walking paths. If he has a pet he is still able to care for, look for a community that accepts pets. No matter how much you love "the look of the place," you'll need to protect yourself and your parent. Ask for the total monthly cost (in writing) of all the services your parent will use or charges he may incur from transportation to physical therapy to one-on-one assistance at meals to the barber/beauty shop *before you sign.* These ancillary costs can add 20, 40, or 50 percent or more to the base cost that is usually quoted. Read the contract thoroughly, particularly the portion regarding payment responsibility. If possible, ask an attorney to read it as well. Then determine whether your parent can afford this price on a continual basis.

Remember, all communities do not offer the same services. Choosing a community that will serve your parent's needs can be difficult.

- Taking an honest look at your parent's age and condition is one of the best tools to help determine which type of community will make him happiest and which will keep him as safe as possible.
- It's often difficult for children to see a true picture of their parents. If you can afford it, it's often beneficial to retain a geriatric care manager for an independent evaluation.

If your parent decides to move, he will need your help to make the move smoother and less traumatic. Moving a parent is a time-consuming, physically and emotionally demanding process that requires weeks or months of patient preparation and understanding. Chapter 19 is filled with time- and temper-saving tips that can help you and your parent plan the move. If this type of project doesn't sound like your forte, don't force it—get help from another family member, or a close friend (to whom you will owe a great favor). A geriatric care manager (www.caremanager.org) or a senior move specialist (www.nasmm.com) can assist you or take over the entire project. Regardless of who plans it, part of the move will entail deciding which possessions your parent can take and which he will be forced to leave behind as gifts to family members or friends, or to be donated.

If you hire a geriatric care manager or moving specialist, be sure to interview several before selecting one:

- Ask for a written cost estimate and how they arrived at that fee.
- Ask how many moves they've supervised and for examples of the types of services they provided.
- Ask how they handle sensitive issues, such as gently helping your parent choose which items to leave behind.
- Ask for references and check them thoroughly. Also check with other professionals such as elder law attorneys and geriatric physicians in your parent's community.
- If your parent complains, listen closely and investigate the complaint.

Without exception, you should expect the professional you hire to treat your parent and his belongings with profound respect and gentleness. Eldercare professionals are trained to expect problems with the elders whom they serve. They are skilled at diffusing or resolving issues. The professional's job is to help reduce your burden and help alleviate any uneasiness your parent may feel about the move. By hiring someone to handle the overall issues, you can spend your time emotionally and physically supporting your parent through a difficult time.

B. THE IMPORTANCE OF EARLY PLANNING

"My mother always wanted to talk about what would happen if she couldn't take care of herself without help. I usually panicked on two fronts: first, that she might have to go to a nursing home, and second, the most frightening thought of all, 'Oh God, what if she's waiting for me to say, "Don't worry mom, you can move in with us."' It took me years to get it. What she really wanted was for me to help her find a way to stay in her *own* home. She didn't want to live with me or anywhere else except the house she'd lived in for decades. Thank God I finally listened. Mom was ninety-three when she died in her own bed."

Jerry, Ohio

"My dad was a young, young seventy-eight. Everyone told him he looked sixty-eight and I guess he thought that meant he should try to act sixty-eight. But some things were just not as safe for him anymore. For instance, I begged him not get on a ladder when no one was home. 'I'm fine,' he'd say, and go on doing the same things he did when he was fifteen years younger. One day, he fell and broke his hip, elbow, and collarbone. His bones took a long time to heal and he was never the same. His health and strength deteriorated and he became confused. He ended up in a nursing home telling us, 'Please put me out of my misery. I want to die.' I still can't get over it—all of this misery came about because he didn't want anyone to think he was getting older. There must be more people like him. Are we all going to feel like that? Am I? The thought terrifies me."

Elaine, California

Will the future teach us that the primary obstacle to a good quality of life while growing older is that we were never taught or encouraged to prepare for aging? The heartbreaking reality is that many professionals believe more people may end up in nursing homes from the *failure to plan* for an illness rather than from the illness itself.

In truth, many of our parents won't consider or discuss the fact that they will someday need assistance—they are simply not emotionally prepared to age. This truth has two sides. The other side is that many children say they want to or feel they should talk with their parents about the future, but most don't. Whether you are uncomfortable with your parents' mortality, are afraid of your parents' reaction, or simply don't know where to start, it's important to try to face the obstacles that may prevent you from beginning the process that will help create a better quality of life for your parents and for you.

Before you begin to try and help your parent plan for the future, take some quiet time and look into your heart and mind for the honest answers to these two questions. Once you've answered them, you'll know where you both stand:

1. Is your parent emotionally prepared to accept the compromises he'll have to make to age safely?
2. Are you prepared to accept that your parent may not always show the strength you've always leaned on and, instead, she may need your help for many years?

How can you help your parent plan for a process that one or both of you refuse to acknowledge as real? If either or both of you remain in denial, the result will be that neither of you will have a working plan to minimize the risks your parent is almost certain to experience as she ages.

No one wants to become ill or dependent, but the reality is that most of us will need some assistance as we age. In the end, the deliberate avoidance of the "details" of your parent's future may force him to move from his home to assisted living or a nursing home. *There is no future in denying the possibilities.*

For example:

- If stiff, aging fingers prevent your parent from inserting a key or turning a heavy bolt in door locks, she may leave her door unlocked and put herself at risk for home break-ins.
- If your parent doesn't have the strength to carry her groceries, she may eventually buy fewer items and eat less—damaging her health and putting herself at risk for illnesses resulting from poor nutrition, including falls from dehydration, weakness, and dizziness.

- Without serious attention to potential future care needs, your parent is at risk for not receiving the care she needs. Now is the time to discuss whether your parent has made the appropriate arrangements and if she is able to afford the costs of those arrangements.

> "My mother was afraid she would slip and fall climbing in and out of her bathtub. She told dad and he told her that he was nervous about a few other things. That was all my take-charge dad needed. He spent weeks on the Internet researching Universal Design, then found a specialist for a consultation. They started with the biggest problem: the bathtub is now a walk-in shower. They're not wealthy and dad's talents stop at changing light bulbs, so they're spacing out the changes to keep the cost down, but what a difference the changes have made in their comfort level. Actually, I'm jealous. Who wouldn't want a keyless entry and faucets that go on without you touching them? I admired the way they faced reality. It really paid off."
>
> *Jack, Florida*

Science plans to continue extending our life expectancies with ways to prevent diseases that afflict the elderly and by changing deadly illnesses to chronic and treatable problems that allow elders to have a good quality of life. The only question left is how your parent will spend the gift of an extra ten or twenty years.

It's important to take steps today to make your parent's home (and your own!) safer and easier to live in tomorrow. Unless we exercise good judgment now, someone else will take over and make decisions for us in the future.

When and How to Talk to Your Parents

> "Me? Talk to my parents about them needing help? Please, please, oh, pulleeease, couldn't I dig up a sidewalk with my fingernails or have a tooth pulled instead? The last conversation turned into a screaming battle and we hardly spoke for a month. There has got to be a better way."
>
> *Ginger, Alabama*

"I was stumped. The odds of my father taking advice from me were less than zero. He'd do anything for my brother Sal, because Sal didn't rock the boat too much. He figured if Dad didn't want to take his medicine, no problem. It was Dad's decision. But when I explained the odds of Dad getting hurt, Sal jumped in and helped convince him. Now, the three of us are working on making Dad's home safer for him to live in. I knew he'd listen to Sal."

Jerome, Michigan

Talking to your parent may be difficult, but it is well worth the effort. Start as early as you can. The earlier you begin, the more likely you will finish before they need help. In fact, anyone who intends to Age in Place should begin adapting their homes the day they purchase them. From a practical position, home modifications take time and money. Many people find it more affordable to work on one room or one project at a time, instead of taking on the challenge and expense of upgrading the entire house at the same time.

While planning your approach to the conversation with your parent, remember that even if your father is open to the concept, he, like most people, may be resistant to change. Think through your strategy before you begin the conversation. Your parent may welcome your involvement, but you'll increase your chance for success if you play it safe and begin with three assumptions: (1) Your father doesn't believe he needs help. (2) It will not only be difficult, but also painful for him to imagine himself in a frail body in the future. (3) Your mother probably won't be thrilled if you tell her that you've got new and better ideas regarding how and where she should put her dishes and groceries—and that all she has to do is rearrange her perfectly ordered kitchen, or that you think her designer bathroom should include grab bars and other similar visible medical safety equipment; or that *because she's getting old* she has to remodel the lovely porch she added on to the house. In other words, the home she's spent forty years getting just the way she likes it needs to be changed to accommodate her advancing age.

Think back: how receptive has your parent been to previous recommendations you've made? If past discussions indicate that your mom won't accept *your* ideas, don't give up. Recognize the reality and look for a *different* spokesperson. Your goal is to succeed in helping her live more independently for a longer period of time. You may accomplish more by staying in the background and asking someone else to present your information. Think about your siblings: it's not unusual for parents to feel uncomfortable talking to one child and yet accept without question the exact same recommendations from another child. If this has been a thorn in your side for years, why not take this opportunity to pass this job to your sibling? Or someone outside the family who will work closely with you and whose guidance your parent may accept? The time and energy you invest in this effort will pay off for years to come.

If you are the spokesperson, these approaches will give you an idea of where and how to start. Wait for a time when you and your parent are enjoying a calm, stress-free afternoon or evening together. Broach the subject gently, and, if you feel it necessary, give Mom an example that relates to her situation.

- *"Mom, my friend at work told me her mother said she's tired of taking care of her house and is planning on moving to a place that's easier to keep up. Have you had any thoughts on whether you'd like to move or are you planning on staying here?"* If mom replies that she's staying, answer, *"If you want to stay, I think you should. I'd feel better if we could talk about some home improvements to make your life easier and the house a little safer for you."* Using the word "improvements" instead of "changes" removes the negative feeling of needing help and elevates the discussion to a positive future.

- *"Mom, I know your arthritis is giving you fits. Have you considered moving to a one-story home that's easier to get around in?"* If Mom rejects the concept, add, *"I thought you might feel that way. Would you consider talking about a few home improvements to make your life easier and the house a little safer for you?"* In many instances, the thought of packing up and moving might be overwhelming and may influence Mom's decision. If that's a possibility, add: *"If you're worried about the work involved in moving, I'll help you every step of the way."*

- *"Dad, I know you want to stay in this house forever and I support you on that. I wasn't sure whether you'd ever heard of all the great improvements they've come up with to make staying in your own home easier as you get a little older. Can I show you some of the ideas I found?"*

If your parent is receptive to your opening, this may be a good time to show Dad some of the improvements listed on the Minor Modification Worksheet at the end of this chapter. If your parent is not receptive to you or the surrogate spokesperson you've found, take a break and try again at a later date. You've given it your best for now and many would agree the only real failure is in not trying.

C. WHAT YOUR PARENT NEEDS TO AGE IN PLACE

Your parent doesn't have to be in perfect health to remain at home while she ages. The key is creating a support system within and outside of her home so that she can access services for help even when her health and care demands change. Your parent's support system should include:

- Neighbors, friends, and/or family nearby
- Home modifications for comfort and safety
- Medical, financial, and legal documents
- Lifestyle changes

Support from Family, Friends, and Neighbors

Few of us would survive without the help of others. We need our families and friends to share our happiness or to help us or to just listen with a loving heart during distressing times. Neighbors often become lifelong friends, sometimes closer than geographically distant family members. They add instant socialization and warmth to our homes and neighborhoods. Human touch and affection is necessary for us to thrive, beginning with the very moment we're born and increasing in emotional and practical value as we age.

It's a simple, yet hard to accept fact: if Mom is lucky enough to live to old age—perhaps eighty-eight, ninety-four, or one hundred years old—she may find it harder or even impossible to lift even a dinner plate to a high pantry shelf. Dad's decreasing strength and balance may dictate that he not climb a ladder to change a light bulb or his decreased vision may make it dangerous for him to drive home in the dark. He may no longer drive at all.

As you move through your daily routines, putting items back on a shelf, cooking, mowing a lawn, walking from one end of your homes to the other end, carrying groceries into your home, taking out a bag of garbage, putting laundry away, cleaning, and other chores or activities, ask yourself if your parent might need help with the same activity—and whether she can live comfortably or safely without that help.

The overall question is this: if your parent is going to Age in Place, what kind of help will she need and how will she or you provide it? A combination of these options usually does the job:

- Some adult children offer their time for personal errands, doctor's appointments, and social outings.
- Consider asking your teenagers to help with yard duty and miscellaneous household chores (perhaps work for their allowance).
- Look into professional homemakers/companions to help with housekeeping and meals, or to run errands one or two afternoons a week.
- Many parents are lucky enough to have friends or neighbors to look in on them and help with errands or home repairs.
- Check into whether your parent's grocery or pharmacy has a delivery service.
- Check with the Area Agency on Aging for community resources that can provide the services you need.
- Look for nearby high school or college organizations that have requirements for community service.
- Hire a geriatric care manager to create a lifestyle plan for your parent to safely Age in Place. (Be sure to ask for a cost estimate that includes a written report with the details of the plan.)

Always interview a potential professional helper *before* the person meets your parent. Request a current driver's license and keep a photocopy. Check references. Ask the person to tell you about himself or herself and then let the helper you are interviewing do most of the talking so you can assess whether he or she has the potential to create a relationship with your parent. Look for the helper's ability to speak clearly in a way your parent will be able to understand. Cleanliness, the helper's willingness to take on whatever job is needed, and a bright, open attitude are necessary to make this a success.

> "I'm over it. I give up. My mother can rot in that house for all I care now. I pay for a great homemaker/companion and she fires her. She says the woman was lazy and sat around all day. Yeah, right. That house never looked so good. She just doesn't want help."
>
> *Nick, Maryland*

There are many reasons you might not succeed in providing help for your parent on your initial try. Don't be dissuaded from trying again. Remember that even skilled professionals may have to try many times to fine-tune assistance for someone else. Trying to please your parent can make this slow process even more difficult. Celebrate small successes at every milestone. If your parent refuses to accept your assistance, acknowledge that some things are out of your control and take great comfort from your effort.

Medical, Financial, and Legal Documents

You can pretty much count on two things: (1) Your parent wants a voice in his future, and (2) He may be resistant to sharing personal healthcare and financial information with you.

To help ensure that his wishes are honored, your parent will need certain medical and financial documents and you or someone else will have to be given access to that information. In today's document-driven healthcare and legal systems, it's increasingly difficult, bordering on impossible, to have your healthcare wishes followed without an informed advocate at your side. Because these issues are often governed by the state your parent lives in, it is important to seek legal help in that state *regardless* of where you live. These laws change frequently. It is wise for your parent to update his wishes annually to comply with changes in the laws and changing circumstances within the family. If Aunt Ida is now eighty-seven and still has your parent's power of attorney, she may not be as appropriate for the job as she was ten years ago when Dad first appointed her as his agent. If Mom's brother lives two thousand miles away, he may not be as instantly accessible or may no longer want to be responsible for making emergency medical decisions—in fact, he may no longer have the capacity to make any decisions at all. If your parent hasn't updated his documents, both Aunt Ida and Mom's brother remain in charge of decisions that can affect your parent's care and even his or her life.

At a very *minimum* your parent should speak to a counselor about:

1. A Durable Power of Attorney for healthcare and Healthcare Surrogate that gives the appointed person the power to make healthcare and/or financial decisions for your parent if he can no longer make them for himself. That power may include consent, refusal of consent, or withdrawal of consent to any care, treatment, service, or procedure for healthcare, as well as any legal conditions your parent puts on those powers. The person named as "power of attorney" has a legal duty to implement and follow the wishes stated in that document. This person should be readily available for emergency decision making.

2. A Durable Power of Attorney for financial issues gives the appointed person the power to make financial decisions on behalf of your parent if your parent can no longer make those decisions for himself. The person appointed has the duty to follow your parent's previously documented or expressed instructions. This often has the added benefit of providing access to your parent's funds to pay for his care.

3. Advance Directives that instruct physicians, hospitals, emergency medical technicians, family, and powers of attorney as to your parent's wishes when your parent cannot express those wishes himself.

4. A legal document or will distributes his assets after he dies.

5. Elder law attorneys (www.naela.org) are specifically trained to discuss healthcare issues with your parent and help him complete documents that realistically express his wishes. Many of the laws involved are governed by the state your parent lives in, so it's always best to retain an attorney where your parent resides.

6. If your parent cannot afford legal counsel, many states provide free legal services to seniors. Call your local state attorney's office, Area Agency on Aging, or AARP chapter for information on where to find pro bono (no charge) help in your state. (See chapter 24 for resources.)

Flexibility and Lifestyle Changes

One of the most difficult aspects of helping a parent Age in Place is that you have virtually no control over how flexible your parent will be to any of the lifestyle changes discussed in this chapter. It's almost a certainty that some adjustments will have to be made if your parent wants to maintain her maximum independence and retain a good quality of life. It is far less certain that she will agree to do so.

If you feel angered or hurt by your parent's denial of his need, try not to add to your pain by deceiving yourself. Many loving, well-meaning children stubbornly hang on to unrealistic notions such as, "If I try harder, he'll change" or, "If only I had tried one more time, she wouldn't be sick today." You didn't fail; you didn't miss pushing the right buttons. This isn't your fault. You cannot control your parent's actions.

Your parent's unwillingness and emotional inability to accept the concept of aging shouldn't surprise anyone. Look around. Our country glorifies youth, while at best, it ignores aging. At worst, it portrays our elders as sexless, feeble-minded, frail-bodied people who can't think clearly or help themselves. We are constantly asked to ignore our future needs and spend thousands of dollars we may not have on one unproven method after another to avoid aging. Why shouldn't your parent try to avoid it as well?

If your parent does not have the capacity to make an appropriate decision, read chapter 4 to learn how and when to intervene for her safety. If your parent has capacity to make decisions, stand by and help as best you can. You may keep on trying because you love her or because your personality does not permit you to stop, but try to do so without destroying your own quality of life. Whether your parent accepts or refuses your help, know within your heart that you tried hard to protect her and make her future more secure. Now it's just as important to love yourself and your family enough to recognize what you've learned from this experience: if you intend to age in your current home, it's not too early to start making the personal and practical changes you'll need to give you and your children the peace of mind you all deserve.

Home Modification and Design

Unless your parent immediately agreed to a complete redesign with architectural changes when you broached the subject, it's best to begin with the small, minimally intrusive alterations you'll find on this Minor Home Modification checklist. Once your parent starts living with the practical benefits of the minor changes you've made, your chances will improve that he'll feel more comfortable permitting larger and more ambitious changes.

D. WORKSHEET: MINOR HOME MODIFICATIONS

If time or money is an issue for you, it's a good idea to spread the work over several months or even years. Go through this list and assign projects to others in your family, *including your parent:* your kids can plug in nightlights; your parents can sort through the items that need to be on lower shelves for easy access in everyday use. Most parents want control over the future. Involving them in the work is not only necessary to help secure their safety, it also gives them a voice in their future. Their participation also helps reinforce your primary message: *if you want to Age in Place, it's never to too early to start making the changes that will help you reach your goal.*

Don't be concerned about the length of this list. Just start somewhere and keep going at the pace that works best for you. You'll be surprised at how quickly you'll see changes and how more peace both you and your parent will feel with even the smallest change.

If your parent digs in and refuses any changes, don't argue. Wait and approach the subject again at a later date, but this time pick one simple change to make: lights? doorknobs? Find the one your parent will accept and when you're finished, give her a little while to enjoy it. Then pick your next project and keep going.

Bedroom

❑ If your parent's bedroom is on the second floor, discuss moving it to the first floor to eliminate negotiating the stairs every day. Close off upstairs rooms or use them as guest space and storage.

❑ Rearrange drawers and closets so that your parent doesn't have to stretch or stand on a stool to reach the items he most often uses.

❑ Install a light that goes on automatically whenever the closet door is opened.

❑ Install a light that turns on when you clap or by a heat sensor so that your parent does not have to navigate in a dark room.

Bathroom

❑ Purchase a nonslip shower seat and add a handheld shower that reaches the seat.

❑ Install a full set of grab bars inside and outside of the bath/shower and near the toilet.

❑ Install touchless faucets in the sink and shower.

❑ Set water temperature controls to 120°F to avoid scalds and burns.

❑ If your parent has poor balance; uses a cane, walker, or wheelchair; or has knee or back problems, install a raised toilet seat for safer, less painful lowering and standing up. If your parent is short, vary the height until his feet touch the floor.

❑ Move the toilet paper holder close enough so that your parent doesn't have to stretch to reach it.

❑ Install a light that goes on automatically when the bathroom door is opened. This is in addition to a night-light.

❑ Change the bathroom door so that it opens out instead of into the bathroom. Make sure there is a key to unlock the door from outside the bathroom.

❑ If possible, add a telephone extension to the master bath so your parent can call for help in an emergency.

❑ Replace space heaters with new ones that turn off automatically at preset temperatures. This helps prevent overheating and the danger of fire if your parent accidentally forgets to turn the heater off.

Every Room

- ❏ Remove on/off light switches and install rocker type switches thirty-six to forty inches above the floor for easier on/off and for the extra benefit of being able to use elbows to turn on lights when hands are holding parcels.
- ❏ Install lights that go on automatically when the door is opened in every closet and storage area.
- ❏ Install night-lights throughout the house. Pay particular attention to the bedrooms, hallways, stairs, bathrooms, garage, and kitchen. (Illuminating dark areas is even more important if your parent has a pet that can get underfoot and startle her in the dark.)
- ❏ Replace space heaters with new ones that turn off automatically at preset temperatures. This helps prevent overheating and the danger of fire if your parent accidentally forgets to turn the heater off.
- ❏ Upgrade bulbs or lighting in all areas, remembering older eyes need more light to see. Pay particular attention to stairways, hallways, garage, workshops, bathrooms, and areas where your parent likes to read, do crosswords, knit, write letters, and so on. Include outdoor areas in this project. Improved visibility will help reduce the risk of trips and falls, and of injuries from bumping into hard-to-see furniture.
- ❏ Make necessary repairs on loose steps and railings; install nonslip pads on inside stairs and the outside ramps or stairs.
- ❏ Change from round to levered door handles. Levers are much easier for arthritic fingers to grasp.
- ❏ Organize loose electrical cords to keep them out of pathways; replace frayed cords. Take the same action outside.
- ❏ Remove scatter or throw rugs from the floors throughout the house; they are notorious for causing trips and falls. The "why" remains elusive, but this issue often escalates into a deal breaker. If your parent threatens to derail all the other changes because of this, buy no-slip tape and secure the rugs to the floor as best you can for now. Retry removing them at a later date.
- ❏ Reorganize furniture groupings to help ensure sufficient space for your parent to walk around without bumping into the sharp corners of coffee tables or other furniture.

- [ ] Make sure the entry doors and all room-to-room doorways are free of clutter.
- [ ] If your parent uses a wheelchair or walker, make sure the entry and room-to-room doorways are wide enough for easy access. (This is a *major* modification that will be necessary for all doorways in the home.)
- [ ] Add lights that automatically go on when the front, back, or any other doors are opened.
- [ ] Remove doorway thresholds so that your parent can walk through on a level surface from one room to the other. This helps avoid bone-breaking trips and falls.

Kitchen

- [ ] Begin replacing irons, coffee pots, and other appliances with models that have automatic shut-off features. If your parent forgets to turn the appliance off, it will automatically shut itself off after a preset period of time.
- [ ] Install an antiscald device for the kitchen sink. (Hot water temp should not exceed 120°F.)
- [ ] Rearrange pantries and cupboards to provide plenty of easy-to-reach space for frequently used items.
- [ ] Look into adaptor kits that can fully automate kitchen or bathroom faucets. Touchless faucets are a boon for arthritic and reduced-strength fingers and hands.

Outside the Home

- [ ] Install censor lights outside the home to alert your parent when someone approaches the house and to help make the house less inviting to would-be intruders.
- [ ] Install an automatic garage door opener. This is helpful even if your parent doesn't drive.
- [ ] If there are steps from the garage into the home, install a strong railing and a nonslip surface on the steps.
- [ ] Consider installing a ramp with a gentle slope from the garage into the house. This will avoid the necessity to climb steps with packages.

❏ Install a light that goes on automatically when the door from the house is opened into the garage. Install the same light on the other side of the door inside the house.

❏ Make necessary repairs on loose porch steps and railings; install nonslip surfaces on all porches, ramps, and stairs.

Home modification to Age in Place is also known as Universal Design. You can find additional direction and ideas at www.naipc.org (National Aging in Place Council), www.aarp.org (American Association of Retired People, search words: Universal Design), and www.senior resource.com (Senior Resource, search words: Aging in Place).

If your parent thanks you for your help, congratulate yourself on a job well done. If Mom rejects your continuing intervention or asks you to stop after you replace the first doorknob, take it in stride. Applaud yourself (loudly!) for trying to help and don't give up—try again at the first opportunity. An added benefit is that you'll learn how *you* can Age in Place in the home of your dreams.

E. MY JOURNAL

Putting thoughts and feelings on paper can help us see them more clearly. What bothers you? What changes do you want to make? What or who are you grateful for? When you read what you've written, you may see a new pathway to help resolve stressful issues. Use this page as a safe place to express your feelings. For example:

"My mother will not even consider a few basic changes like lever doorknobs! What's wrong with her? How attached can she be to her damn doorknobs?"

"My wife wants me to stop remodeling my parent's home and take care of ours. She just doesn't understand. She's mad at me and I'm furious at her. Although now that I think about it, I may have done most of my explaining to Dad and forgotten to explain it to her. No wonder she's mad at me!"

_____
_____
_____
_____
_____
_____
_____
_____
_____
_____
_____
_____
_____
_____
_____
_____
_____
_____
_____
_____
_____

F. TIP SHEET

- Compare the obstacles to Aging in Place with your parent's current situation.
- Review this chapter to understand your parent's options.
- Get a professional assessment of your parent's capabilities to help you and your parent make decisions.
- Use this chapter's recommendations to begin your conversation with your parent.
- Use the Minor Home Modifications Worksheet to help you begin making safety adjustments in your parent's home.
- Involve your parent in as many decisions as he is capable of making.

4

INTERVENTION: WHEN? WHAT? HOW?

"I sometimes feel that if I had a crystal ball, I would know exactly when the right time is to intervene in my father's life. Day to day he seems OK and then he does or says something that makes my head whirl and my stomach sink. Is it time then? Should I wait until he does irrational things every day? Will it be too late? I'm getting a headache thinking about it. My friends tell me just do what you have to do, but they don't know my father. He was always tough; and now at eight-six years old, he's tougher and even more arrogant. I just wish I knew when."

Jim, Wisconsin

"She says, 'Beverly, I don't need your help and I don't want your help. Leave me alone.' I say, 'Ma you need my help, but you don't want it.' We have this fight week in and week out. She's stubborn and independent, but she's a mess. She used to be well groomed and beautifully dressed. Now she sits in a robe with her hair in curlers and doesn't even wash off her makeup. I'm not sure what to do or how to do it, but I know it's time for me to help my mom."

Pam, Delaware

A. TRUSTING YOUR INSTINCTS

How old are you? Forty? Fifty? Sixty? Seventy? You are a wife, mother, sister, friend, and daughter. You are a teacher, secretary, homemaker, truck driver, doctor, or lawyer. You manage an office for one hundred employees, stand before a judge and argue cases of law, organize a rally to benefit your children's school, fly an airplane, or drive a school bus. You are organized, methodical, and very talented. Everything you have done up to this point in your life enhances the tools that give you strength, wisdom, and courage. Life experience has taught you so much about people, their problems, and finding the best solutions. Year after year you use your experiences, knowledge, and instincts to find the answers to most problems. The decisions you make every day affect the lives of your family, friends, and coworkers. Use the strong skills you've developed over the years to do what you want and need to do for your parent. Talk to him about your concerns, but if he is capable of making appropriate decisions, try to respect his need and right to self-determination.

At times, fear and uncertainty take the place of courage and confidence when your parents have a problem and need you. You can be instantly transformed from a talented, bright, successful woman into an insecure girl. A long-distance caregiver revealed to us that when she visits her chronically ill mother in another state, she changes from the president of a thriving company to "a little five-year-old girl with a lollipop in her mouth." You have the answers inside you, so forget the lollipop; trust your instincts and search for the answers.

Trust yourself as others trust you. If you feel that you can handle some of the problems yourself, you probably can. Try to do what you can as long as you don't compromise your own health or well-being. Keep in mind that even strong, self-sufficient caregivers often need help. As you look inside yourself for the answers, remember that often the greatest inner strength comes from admitting you cannot do it alone. Physicians, nurses, and social workers, specializing in the care of the elderly, can evaluate your parent's needs and help you to understand what you have to do now and in the future. (For specific information on the assessment process, see section D in this chapter.)

B. PLANNING AHEAD

Caregivers often spend countless, exhausting, and unproductive hours worrying about their parents. Although we understand why you worry, we know that we cannot stop you from worrying. What we can do is to help you understand that there are things you can do to feel better, decrease the amount of time and energy you spend worrying, and at the same time help your parents. The idea that you can plan for every problem is unrealistic. But here are some steps to take today to plan for a less stressful, more peaceful tomorrow.

How do you think your parent may feel if you talk to him about planning for his future? Some parents may embrace the idea and feel that it is timely and appropriate; others may view this as a loss of control and independence or an invasion of privacy.

> "My parents were very receptive to my caring for them; it was formal care from outside resources that they did not like."
>
> *Margie, Massachusetts*

Still other parents may be fearful and anxious about what the future holds for their health, finances, or living arrangements.

> "My parents think that if you don't talk about a problem, it doesn't exist; and in fact it may even go away."
>
> *Sally, Vermont*

> "My mother couldn't have been clearer: 'You and your brother have no right to butt into my life. You two think you know everything. Butt out.' All my brother and I were trying to do was talk to her about planning for the future. We know that eventually we're going to be her caregivers. Wouldn't it be easier if we knew something about her health and finances before a crisis hits? What did we do wrong?"
>
> *Laverne, New Jersey*

When your parent creates a wall and stands firm, shutting you out, it is important for you to remember that if you are persistent, it is not because you are being intrusive or controlling. You are a practical, realistic, caring, and loving person because you are thinking about his future. These three steps will help you gather and organize the information you need to approach your parent and talk about the issues that are important to all of you.

1. Make a list of all the crucial information you know and don't know about your parent: medical diagnoses, medications, finances, insurance information, rent or mortgage, monthly expenses, support system, and social life. You will probably be surprised how little you know and how much your parent keeps to himself.

2. Observe your parent when you spend time together, such as going to a medical appointment, out to dinner, or to a family function. Don't be afraid to open your eyes and be honest with yourself. We know this process can be painful and frightening, but you can do it because you know how vital it is for all of you.

3. Think about how she managed six months ago, a year ago, five years ago. What has changed? If you do not see your parent on a regular basis, your observations will be different than someone who sees a parent several times a week or several times a month. Caregivers who see their parents weekly or more than once a week may not see physical or cognitive changes as clearly as those who see their parents less often. Changes in physical appearance or cognitive ability are often subtle and take weeks or even months to become obvious. All of your observations are valuable and important. The information you gather provides a strong foundation to facilitate communication with your parent and to begin thinking about and developing an appropriate, compassionate plan of care that can help you achieve peace of mind.

Once you have your list, it is time to try to talk to your parents. You may feel anxious, but don't panic. Make the attempt.

- Talk to your parent in an informal setting, such as while sitting at the dining room table or taking a walk.
- Ask questions that show you are interested, supportive, and caring. For instance, you might ask your parent how she spent the day or

what he prepared for last night's dinner. If your parent suffers from cognitive impairment or memory loss, provide a cue word or phrase, keep the sentence simple, ask one question at a time, and wait for an answer. For instance, "So Dad, I understand you went to the senior center today. What did you do during the morning exercise program? (Wait for an answer.) How was the lunch? (Wait for an answer.) What did you have to eat? (Wait for an answer.)"

- Listen to each answer, and you will learn new and significant information. Keep a mental note of your conversation. Later in the day, try to record some of the information in a notebook or log, on the appropriate worksheets in this book, or on a tape recording.

As you communicate more and more with your parents, you will begin to ask the harder questions about health issues, housing arrangements, and finances. Does it get easier as you go along? For some caregivers this process will grow easier because your parent may be more willing to participate in the process. For others the prospect of asking personal questions will always be very difficult. Often we see determined, well-meaning caregivers gather information, and communicate with their parent, only to hear, "No thanks, I don't want your help" or, "I don't need any help."

> "My father cries and cries but does not take my advice. He accepts help when he asks for it, but many times his requests are unreasonable. As for being compliant, don't make me laugh."
>
> Tom, New Jersey

If you are in this situation, try not to get discouraged. When your parents are ready to talk to you, listen carefully to their ideas, wants, and needs.

Even though this process can be difficult and frustrating, any information you obtain is valuable. Information empowers and enables you to see things more clearly in order to make the best decisions for you and your parent.

C. WHEN NOT TO INTERVENE

Before you intervene, take a long, hard look at your parents and ask yourself this question: Is there really a problem, or is this how my parents always functioned? If you stop to think about how your parents have interacted in the past—how they have shopped for groceries, managed money, and approached healthcare—you may be surprised to learn that they haven't changed. Your response to their lifestyle may be different because you are no longer a young child. As an adult you develop your own way of handling your life, and it may be in sharp contrast to your parents' way of doing things. This is not a right or wrong situation; it is just a case of different generations and different individuals dealing and coping with life in different ways.

> "My parents were really having a hard time handling all the chores around their house. Mom had bad arthritis, and Dad was becoming a little confused. So, my brother and I decided to look at several assisted living facilities. We hoped we could find one we liked and then talk to them about moving into it. One was more beautiful than another. Our parents lived a very simple and frugal lifestyle. My brother and I thought they would love the chance to live in luxury. We invited our parents to join us for a tour of both facilities. They couldn't get out of the buildings fast enough. My brother and I didn't get it. I called my friend who is a social worker, and she told us that our parents didn't see the facilities the way we did. They had never lived in that type of setting, and it probably made them very uncomfortable. She suggested another place that wouldn't have been our first choice, but that she thought would give our parents a sense of comfort and home. She was right."
>
> *Jennifer, Ohio*

> "Every time I went into my parents' home, I wanted to scream. It was always a mess. They always had stacks of books on the floor by their bed and by their chairs. They take way too many photos, and they never manage to get them in an album. When-

ever my mother asked me to get something for her out of a closet or drawer, I used to cringe. The closets and the drawers were so full I could barely get my hand in. She's seventy-two and still has kitchen bowls and tablecloths from before I was born. I was sure that no one would opt to live like that, so when they went to see my Aunt Rhoda for a week, I took two days off work and organized their whole house. I threw out things I'd never seen her use, got rid of old magazines, and gave away some of their really outdated clothes. I'm sure you know what happened. At first, they almost passed out from shock. At that point, I still thought I had done something wonderful. Then they got really angry. Then my mother began to cry and yell at the same time: 'How dare you! Who do you think you are? Who gave you permission to come into our home and arrange it the way you want us to live? Have you ever seen me move one item in your apartment? Where do you come off doing that to us?' She took back the key to their house and has still not returned it to me."

Beth Ann, Virginia

Intervention is only effective and necessary when something is different or wrong with your parents. They are entitled to live in the manner they have always lived, without intervention, as long as they are not in any kind of danger. Determining if something is different or wrong is not a difficult thing to do if you see your parents once a month, once every six months, or once a year. When you do not see someone for long periods of time, changes are generally more obvious. Caregivers who see their parents once a week, several times a week, or even every day will find that they may not be so aware of physical or cognitive changes because the changes are subtle and develop slowly over time. Make certain that you are seeing things clearly and accurately by following these steps.

- Speak to family members, neighbors, friends, and clergy. People who have known your parents for a long time and see them sporadically are probably better judges of any changes or problems than someone who is recently involved in their lives, and sees them only as they are today. Compare the way you view your parents with the way others see them. For instance, if your father always enjoyed gardening, ask his neighbor if he still spends time tending to his rose bushes. If he enjoyed weekly church services, ask his clergy if he continues to attend services on a regular basis. If your dad regularly met "the boys" for breakfast, ask his friends if he still joins them at the local diner. The answers to these and similar questions will provide you with a clearer picture and understanding of your parent today. Of course, do this in a tactful manner, so you don't appear as if you're checking on your parents.

- If you comfortably conclude that nothing has changed and nothing is different, there is no point in intervening right now. The observations you make over time are invaluable and will keep you alert, informed, and ready to intervene when it is necessary and appropriate.

> "My dad seemed a little forgetful, but I didn't think it was anything to worry about. He never used to ask me personal questions, but then he started asking and saying whatever was on his mind. When he asked my friend if she had gained weight, I figured it was time to find out what was happening to him. The human resources counselor at my office recommended a geriatric doctor. I asked my dad how he would feel about a checkup by this doctor. I was very surprised when he agreed. We went together, and after a very thorough examination and extensive laboratory testing, he said that Dad had mild dementia, but was actually doing quite well. This really helped me put things into perspective. It was very helpful to talk to someone who understands the situation."
>
> *Maxine, Washington*

D. GETTING A PROFESSIONAL ASSESSMENT

The purpose of a professional assessment is to provide you and your parents with the expertise of a specialist. She can often spot areas of concern that the family is not aware of. The benefit of an objective professional assessment is that it often validates what you are thinking, promotes problem solving, and encourages proactive behavior. A professional assessor views the patient and family with objectivity, and is thereby able to provide a sound, carefully thought-out plan of care that targets your parent's and family's needs.

The type of assessment your parent requires depends on her needs, finances, and the availability of services in her community. Her problems may include physical decline, cognitive impairment, as well as emotional and psychological issues. An objective assessment is essential because family relationships, emotions, and history play a large part on how we view our parents. Sometimes we just do not have the eyes to see the changes, the ears to hear the complaints, or the fortitude to make the first move.

Various community organizations, medical facilities, and social service agencies as well as private nurses and social workers provide assessments. The availability of these services varies with each community, and the cost for a professional assessment may range from no fee to more than one thousand dollars.

Before you take the steps to find the most appropriate type of assessment for your parent, keep in mind that your parent may not agree to participate in the process. Try not to pressure him into the situation, but provide gentle reminders that the purpose of this professional assessment is to take care of his needs so that he can maintain his independence as long as possible.

Private Assessments

A private assessment provides you with an objective opinion about your parent's overall condition. An increasing number of social workers with master degrees (MSWs) and registered nurses (RNs) are private consultants who give comprehensive assessments and geriatric care management. Geriatric care managers provide the assessment, a plan of care, and the ability to implement the plan of care if needed.

The cost for a private assessment can range from no fee to more than one thousand dollars. The fee may also reflect the experience level of the professional, or the going rate for this type of service that is considered acceptable within a community. Ask for a referral from your parent's physician, a disease-related organization, a local hospital, a geriatric clinic, or the National Association of Professional Geriatric Care Managers (see chapter 24 for more resources). Once you contact the geriatric care manager, you should expect to have an appointment within a few days. Ask for references and the person's training and experience level. To make you feel more comfortable, you might request an interview first alone with the assessor and see if she is someone who you can talk to and who can provide your parent with a level of comfort.

What you can expect from a comprehensive assessment is an overview of your parent's physical, cognitive, emotional, and social status. The report should include a thorough evaluation of his problems and a step-by-step plan of care to begin solving some of the issues. The assessor should ask you several preliminary questions before she meets with your parent. This provides her with accurate information and helps her determine if your parent has a good grasp of family, personal, and general history, or if he is having memory problems. For instance, the assessor may ask you how many siblings your parent has or how long he lived in his home. Once the assessor has this information, she will meet with your parent. Depending on the circumstances, the assessor will ask you to either be present during the assessment, request that you leave once the introductions are made, or not come at all. Once the assessment interview is complete, the written report should be available within a week or two. After you review the report, request an in-person meeting with the assessor or a phone conference to review the details. At that time you can determine if you wish to act on the suggestions. You may ask for help from the assessor or just retain the information for future use.

"When my dad was diagnosed with Parkinson's, I was frantic. He already had a heart condition. Now he was showing tremors and was unsteady on his feet, but he insisted on continuing as many activities as he could. Mother and I realized there must be some safety issues involved, but we had no idea what they were. I got the help of a geriatric care manager. It was absolutely beneficial. She helped coordinate homecare services and medical appointments. During an emergency hospitalization, she was able to meet my dad and his aide in the hospital. She gave the doctors his medical history so they could quickly treat him. My dad felt safer because he knew that he had an advocate. When the doctor told her that he was going to discharge my dad that same day, she advocated to keep him in the hospital overnight so that he could be monitored. It is a good thing she was there. He had a heart attack that night, but he was in the right place. I couldn't do this without her. She gives me my peace of mind."

Carly, Texas

"We made excellent connections with a freelance social worker during my mother's first illness, and with her help were able to put together a care plan and find a live-in attendant."

Aileen, California

The private-assessment process and the support of geriatric professionals can help you and your parents identify and face many challenging problems, and provide a plan of care that focuses on solutions to most situations that you and your family are facing.

Public Assessments

A public assessment furnishes you with a professional, comprehensive, and objective assessment of your parent. This type of assessment is generally provided by a social service agency, not-for-profit organization, local community center, hospital, or community-based clinic. Generally, a professional staff member conducts the assessment. There may be instances when a nonprofessional trained on the job or a trained volunteer will conduct the assessment. In these instances, a professional social worker or a nurse may supervise the worker. Ask for the credentials of the person assigned to your parent's case, the type of training she received, and how she is supervised. You are working hard to do all you can for your parent, and you are entitled to be informed, comfortable, and confident that the public system will supply the time and personnel to accommodate your parent's needs.

Fees vary according to location and the type of facility. There may not be any fee for the service or a small fee based on your income. This is called a sliding scale fee. Sometimes a donation to the specific organization or hospital is acceptable in lieu of a fee.

The assessment process may take place at your parent's home, or it may occur in the office of the social service agency, organization, or hospital. If your parent is homebound, ask about homebound programs or possible appropriate transportation to the assessment, such as an ambulette or van. An ambulette is a large vehicle that uses an electronic lift for wheelchair accessibility. Vans may have wheelchair accessibility as well. Transportation fees are typically flat fees or on a sliding scale based on your parent's ability to pay and are paid for out of pocket. Check with your parent's insurance company for possible coverage.

Because of the large numbers of cases and the availability of services in a given community, you may have to wait several weeks for an appointment if you choose the public-assessment route. If you are in a crisis situation, inquire about the availability of a crisis team, and how quickly it can respond. A crisis team is often composed of social workers and registered nurses who are available on an around-the-clock basis.

"My mom has severe dementia, and I am trying to keep her home. One night she became very agitated and refused her medication. Things escalated, and my neighbor called the local hospital. The hospital sent a crisis team. The team came to my house in their van. Their system gave them easy access to the police and other emergency personnel if we needed it. Fortunately, the nurse was able to give Mom her medication, and they waited until she was calm enough to go to sleep. They talked to me about how difficult this situation was for me and gave me referrals to counselors to help me make some decisions about my mom's care. They also told me to take Mom back to her doctor the next day for a reevaluation of her medications. I am so grateful for those people."

Lila, Kansas

For the availability of a crisis team in your parent's community, contact the Area Agency on Aging, local hospital, or geriatric medical clinic. But if you think the situation is unsafe or life threatening, do not wait for an appointment; immediately call 911 or contact your local hospital emergency department. If you are not in a crisis situation and you can wait for an appointment, you will likely receive a preliminary telephone call regarding the assessment, or in some instances you may be asked to fill out a questionnaire. The accurate information you provide is very helpful to the assessor when she evaluates your parent.

Your answers to the assessment questionnaire help the assessor learn as much as she can about your parent so she can recommend appropriate action. You're likely to be asked about the following:

1. Insurance information, advance directives, and medical contacts such as primary care physicians, specialists, dentists, psychiatrists, physical or occupational therapists.
2. Medical history, medication information, and your parent's perception of his needs, mood, and behavior if he is capable of participating in the assessment process.
3. Specific questions regarding activities of daily living, such as your parent's ability to dress, feed, or bathe himself.
4. An environmental and safety assessment of his home.
5. A summary of the assessor's findings for potential risks.
6. A detailed plan of care.

The information you receive from this type of assessment will aid you in helping your parent. Some of it will be helpful to you right now, and some of it you will save for another time. How you use the information is up to you. Depending on how busy the agency or facility is, you may receive the results of the assessment in a few days, or you may have to wait several weeks. You may receive a written report, a checklist with suggestions, or a specific date and time for a telephone conference with the assessor or her supervisor. If you receive a written report and wish to discuss it with the assessor or her supervisor, contact the facility immediately for an appointment. Make the most of your time by being prepared with your questions and concerns.

E. TALKING TO YOUR PARENT

You may feel that your parent doesn't understand you and you don't understand him or her. Some people refer to this as a "generation gap," but for many caregivers it is more like a bottomless cavern.

You may have visited your parent once a month and on holidays, and you talked on the telephone once or twice a week. Communicating with your parent was never easy, but now that he or she is declining, it has become increasingly difficult. How do you begin to communicate when communicating has never been a natural part of your relationship?

Begin in a social setting. Visit your parent at his home or invite him to your house for dinner. Ask him questions that are thoughtful and supportive about his friends, relatives, or how he spent his day. Talk about a happy childhood memory, a trip, a party, or an event such as an anniversary or a graduation. Bring a picture album to enhance the conversation. This approach is usually relaxing, invites conversation, and provides a level of comfort to discuss more difficult issues. Try not to begin your dialogue with a blunt statement, such as "Dad, you've been acting strange lately, and we think you need to see a psychiatrist." Although there may be some truth to the statement, the direct approach is insensitive and will almost certainly destroy any hope for future conversations.

You may find that you will need several of these informal, nonthreatening conversations before you can approach the more difficult topics, such as health, finances, living arrangements, and support systems. For some of you, the job will get easier because your parent is a willing participant, and you've always had good communication. For others, do not expect this to be easy, though you have opened a dialogue because you care. If you have a poor relationship with your parent, or are just returning from years away at school, in the armed services, or if you live in a different state, this may be a challenge. If you do not think you can do this, you may want to consider another family member, friend, clergy, or physician your parents like and trust to facilitate the conversation. One caregiver found that a doctor her father trusted and respected became her voice when dealing with such problems as medication management, driving a car, and moving to an adult home. Geriatric professionals such as social workers, nurses, or therapists may be able to pave the way and facilitate communication between you and your parent. Ask for help. You and your parents deserve the opportunity to listen and understand one another.

> "My dad had so many problems. He suffered from dementia, and we think that he had some psychiatric problems that no one ever diagnosed. Dad was a hunter his whole life, and he owned several

guns. He liked to look at the guns. We knew it was unsafe to leave him with a loaded weapon, so we disarmed the guns and threw out the bullets. One morning I got a frantic call from his home health aide. She said Dad went out hunting, and she saw the bullets. I started to panic, and I went to look for him. Then I realized I had to call the police and stop him before he hurt himself or someone else. The police found him in time, and they removed all of the guns. I searched the house and found more bullets and another gun. Calling the police was the best thing to do."

Margaret, Pennsylvania

A life-threatening situation may include a parent owning or using a gun or other dangerous weapon; a home that is on fire; a home that has no electricity, heat, or hot water in the winter, or no air conditioning or cooling system in the summer; or a medical emergency that requires immediate attention. If you believe the situation is life threatening, do not wait for the right time; take immediate action and contact your local emergency services.

F. TALKING TO YOUR FAMILY

As a caregiver, you have certain obligations and responsibilities that affect your husband, children, or significant other. When caregiver responsibilities increase, the time you spend with your immediate family may decrease, a situation that is not always fair or equal. It is your job to talk to your family about your role as a caregiver, what it means to you, how it has changed your life, what you expect from them, and what they can expect from you.

The most effective way to begin a discussion is to organize a family meeting. How do you do it when everyone in the family is on different schedules?

- Select a common meeting place. There are two places in the house frequented by all members of a family several times a day: the bathroom and the kitchen. The magical refrigerator door that opens and closes hundreds of times a day and the bathroom medicine cabinet that sees everyone's face at least once or twice a day make excellent places to display a notice. The notice should indicate that you are requesting a family meeting on such and such date at a time that does not interfere with school or work-related obligations. Request that any social engagements at that time be postponed. If you have a large family, you may want them to sign up for the meeting so that you are sure that everyone reads the notice. Once you confirm the day and time, begin to think about what you want to accomplish at the meeting.

- Write an agenda as if you are running a conference at your office or the school board. Use the skills you have acquired over the years. Include all of the points you wish to make to help your family understand your parents' problems. For instance, discuss some of the problems your parents are experiencing, how it affects them, and what you are trying to do to help them. Be clear, accurate, and do not give more details than your family can absorb. It doesn't matter if your parents live with you or somewhere else. The time you spend as a caregiver will impact everyone in your immediate family.

- Speak to your grade school–aged children in private and explain to them that although you have to spend more time with Grandma and Grandpa, you still love them. Take a few minutes a day to read a story or play a game with them. Check your local library and bookstore for children's books about the elderly, illness, death, and dying. Some of these books may help to demystify some of the things your children see, hear, and observe. (Chapter 9 provides you with details about a variety of support systems.)

- Talk to your family about the various caregiver duties you perform, such as preparing meals, doing laundry, or driving your parents to doctor appointments. Be specific, and let your family know how many hours a week you perform caregiver duties.

- Explain to your family how this affects your job and the time you spend with them. It is important for them to understand that this is how it is right now and that you need them to be flexible and understanding. Let them know that as the situation changes, the time you spend as a caregiver may increase or decrease, depending on the need.

- Explain what you want and expect from your family. Decide if you want to assign tasks or prepare a list of tasks and ask for volunteers. Keep in mind that caregivers who ask for volunteers are sometimes disappointed. Think about it, and use whichever method works for you and your family. If you decide to assign jobs, consider the age, amount of time the person has to complete the job, and the necessary skills and maturity level. A younger child can dry dishes and fold the towels and linens; a teenager can do the grocery shopping once a week for your home or possibly your parents' home. Your spouse or significant other can organize and drive the car pool a few days a week. Most likely everyone will comply if they do not feel overwhelmed or overburdened. If possible, alternate assignments twice a month or monthly to avoid boredom or monotony. If issues arise regarding specific assignments or if you find that some family members are not meeting their obligations, meet again and address these issues. You are not alone; you are now a member of a team, and you need all the players to support you and give you strength.

What if your family is not interested in talking, having a meeting, or helping you, for that matter? Sometimes you cannot do anything to change what they are willing to do and how they feel. Try to reach one member of the family by appealing to his sense of loyalty and love. If you win the support and help of just one member of the family, maybe the rest will follow.

"We are a family of five brothers and sisters. I am the only one who takes the time to help Mom with grocery shopping, cooking, and doing laundry. Everyone is always too busy. I decided to go to the senior center and ask for an appointment with one of the social workers. After we met a few times, she suggested a family meeting. I was surprised when everyone, even my two sisters-in-law, showed up. They all nodded their heads, and I actually thought we made some progress. I was disappointed. No one changed except my youngest brother. He offered to take Mom grocery shopping once a week. Then, a few weeks later, my sister-in-law said she would take Mom to the doctor. Not everyone came around, but a few of them did and it made all the difference to me."

Nina, Wisconsin

G. CHOOSING THE RIGHT INTERVENTION

Can we ever forget the haunting words of the *Apollo* 13 space crew: "Houston, we have a problem"? Within seconds of hearing those words, hundreds of skilled professionals intervened to find a solution. For some of you, eldercare is as daunting as the problems on *Apollo* 13, but the right intervention, at the right time, makes all the difference.

Once we recognize that there is a problem, selecting the right intervention is the first step in finding a solution. How do you know which intervention is appropriate when there may be so many possibilities?

Before you intervene, try to describe the problem. You can do this in several ways. Say it out loud, write it down, or talk to a friend or a professional. Once you say it, write it, and talk about it, the problem becomes real and much harder to deny. Here are examples of specific problems that may require some form of intervention.

- You feel that your mother has difficulty handling her money, but she does not ask to borrow any from you, and she seems to be managing. Even though you are a little suspect, you do not do anything about it. One day a friend of hers contacts you because she told him that she is uncharacteristically giving away large sums of money to some unknown charity. You know that you have a problem that requires immediate investigation and potential financial intervention to protect your parent from financial ruin.
- You speak to your father two times a week, visit every month, and describe him as a healthy, active, and social eighty-year-old. You look forward to seeing him. Suddenly, at two o'clock in the morning, you awake to the jolting ring of the telephone. The voice on the other end is your mother saying that your father had a stroke and is on his way to the hospital; please come right away. Your adrenaline skyrockets into high gear, and you face the fact that you are in the middle of a crisis and have to intervene immediately to advocate for your father in the hospital. (See chapter 17 for more information on advocating in hospitals.)

If you are concerned that your parents cannot take care of themselves any longer, think about some of the obvious and some of the less obvious changes in their lives. For example, your mother no longer bathes, washes her hair, or polishes her nails, and your father forgets to pay the telephone and light bills. The food in the house is sparse, old, and moldy. Your father blames your mother for his memory loss, and she blames him for everything else. They used to enjoy each other, but now they argue about the weather, politics, and how high to adjust the air-conditioner. As you review and examine all of these changes, you realize that they need help to sort out their lives. The impact of what this means to you and them is overwhelming, but you know that total intervention (twenty-four-hour supervision) is necessary for their safety and your peace of mind.

Preventive Intervention

You probably use preventive intervention every day for your own family and for yourself. If, for example, you have replaced a worn or torn electrical wire in your home because it represented a potential fire hazard, or if you taught your child to look both ways before crossing the street, or if you locked your door last night to avoid a break-in, you have taken preventive intervention. Applying the same thinking to your parent may mean you have to develop a knowledge of specific eldercare intervention techniques, but it's worth the time and effort. Intervening appropriately can literally change your future. Intervening as a preventive measure can help protect and preserve your parents' assets, improve their quality of life, maximize their independence, increase their safety, decrease hospitalizations, and decrease the need for future nursing home admissions.

The key to effective preventive intervention is to discuss with your parents their options and get your plans set before your parents show any sign of needing help; then, set your plan in motion when you first begin to see noticeable but not disabling changes in your parent's abilities to function easily in their surroundings. There are many steps you can take to help prevent relatively predictable accidents or curtail other serious problems before they mushroom into larger, more debilitating, or possibly life-threatening events. What you should not do if you want to create a successful plan is rush in, announce your intentions, and change everything you think needs changing. Your parent may consider your intervention as interference with his well-established lifestyle. Think it through, one issue at a time, and try to convince your parent to do what you believe to be in his own best interests.

Preventive intervention can mean almost anything, but often concerns itself with three main areas:

1. *Estate planning* is a tool to help you plan for your parent's financial future and healthcare needs. An attorney who specializes in trusts and estate or elder law planning will help you organize for future needs by creating documents that protect your parent's assets and make it mandatory that the appropriate steps are taken for your parent's healthcare. The documents outline what those steps are and establish that your parent's assets will be used for that purpose. The attorney will advise you on filing a durable power of attorney (DPOA), which is a legal document that allows a competent individual to appoint another individual to make decisions for her when she can no longer make her own decisions. This document remains in effect in the event the individual becomes incapacitated. The attorney will also advise you about a DPOA for healthcare decisions that allows a competent individual to make healthcare decisions for another individual when she can no longer make decisions for herself. This document remains effective in the event the individual becomes incapacitated. He may also advise you on a nondurable power of attorney that allows a competent individual to appoint another individual to make decisions for her. This document is generally used for a limited purpose such as providing an attorney with the legal power to represent an individual at a house closing or other business transaction. This document is no longer in effect if the individual becomes incapacitated.

   If your parent becomes incapacitated, everyone in the family may not agree on what type of healthcare to provide or how much money to spend on your parent's care. These documents will expedite, clarify, and validate your parent's wishes. Executing these documents now may help prevent disagreements among family members later.

2. *Healthcare planning* includes advance directives to ensure your

parent's wishes are known and followed if your parent cannot state them because of incapacity. These legal documents must be created in advance because when your parent needs them he may not be able to tell you what he wants or needs. These legal documents advise the family and medical caregivers as to what steps are to be taken, under what circumstances, to maintain life or to withhold lifesaving support. Another important part of healthcare planning is the appointment of a healthcare advocate who will take charge and obtain necessary care if your parent is unable to advocate for himself. This is often accomplished by appointing a durable power of attorney. The DPOA has the authority to make decisions on your father's behalf if he is unable to do so himself. Anyone over the age of eighteen who can cope with the stresses of carrying out his parent's wishes can assume this responsibility.

3. *Living arrangements* are difficult to change when your parent is ill and needs help but refuses to accept assistance. You may feel anxious about talking to your parent about alternative living arrangements while she is well, but you'll find it even more difficult when you need quick action. It's one of a caregiver's more frustrating "givens": When your parent needs help the most is when you can expect the strongest resistance to your intervention. Let your parent know that the reason you want to discuss this beforehand is so that you can do everything in your power to accommodate her wishes, but you cannot even attempt to do so unless you know what those wishes are. For example, if for instance you both feel it is safe and practical for your parent to remain in her own home, you may find a professional caregiver to help with personal needs or a homemaker/companion to help with transportation or shopping. You and your parent may want to tour assisted living facilities (ALFs) or skilled nursing facilities (SNFs) so that your parent can plan her own strategy for future needs. If you want to consider moving into your parent's home or bringing your parent into your home, you will need time to consider all the changes that will accompany this move, from how the furniture is arranged to bathroom alterations. (See chapters 19 and 20 for detailed information about ALFs and SNFs.)

Partial Intervention

As we age, it's not unusual to need help with one or two of our daily activities, and still remain functionally independent in most other areas of life. Transportation may be the most needed and most used form of partial intervention. Our parents often feel unsafe driving because of deteriorating vision or mobility problems, but often refuse to stop driving because they have no other means of maintaining their lifestyle. Those who live in areas with limited or unpredictable public transportation have no other options for obtaining food, socializing, attending religious services, or visiting a physician. Shopping is a necessity; we visit stores for almost everything we need to survive. In addition to basic driving, our parents may need assistance with shopping in extreme weather conditions such as heat, cold, or rain, and with carrying heavy packages. In areas where public transportation is readily available, it may be too far away or inappropriate for your parent's physical capabilities (that first step on a city bus can seem very high if you are eighty-six and you have arthritis).

Partial intervention often enables your parent to continue to live independently at home. Physical problems such as declining vision or arthritis may make it difficult for your parent to attend to household repairs, keep up with windows and floors that need cleaning, use a plunger for a sink or toilet, maintain the yard, or clear gutters. A home in obvious disrepair can be a signal to hoodlums that the resident is unable to defend against intruders; a poorly maintained rental apartment may cause problems with the property owner. Internal disrepair such as frayed carpets, wires in pathways, jagged edges on furniture, or burned-out bulbs in ceiling lights often result in accidents that might have been avoided through intervention.

Your mother may want to continue to live alone, but she has lost the motivation to "cook a whole meal for myself," or no longer feels safe going out for walks alone or showering without someone in the house. Paid companions, homecare workers, friends, or neighbors who work only a few hours each day can often help your parent remain independent. These helpers can also aid your mother to maintain or resume social activities to keep from becoming isolated and depressed.

Many elders have set up their own network of daily telephone calls to help keep each other safe. Mary might call Sarah, Sarah then calls Anne,

Anne then calls Martin, Martin then calls Harry, and so on. This form of partial intervention is a self-monitoring safeguard that allows Sarah, Anne, Martin, and Harry to remain independent, yet reassures them that a friend will call for help if they have an accident or fall ill and cannot answer the telephone. You and your family can set up your own monitoring system with a daily call schedule divided among you.

> "My mother and several of her friends who live in her apartment building have a reassurance and safety system fine-tuned to work with their lifestyles. Each member has two people to watch over. She has the key to their apartments and a list of emergency contacts' telephone numbers, such as my brother's and mine. Each member telephones those two people every morning at 8 AM. If a group member doesn't answer the phone, no one panics. The caller waits until about 3 or 4 PM and calls again. If there is still no answer, she calls someone on the emergency contact list. If no one has a rational explanation for why this person isn't answering the phone, she uses the key and checks inside the apartment. If my mother decides to stay with me for the weekend, she lets her contact know. It's a great system. They bring in each other's mail and newspapers, and even water the plants. They help each other feel safe."
>
> *Suzanne, Montana*

Another example of partial intervention is to help your parent with paperwork such as bill paying and/or insurance-claim filing as they age. Because of poor eyesight, memory loss, or physical problems such as arthritis in your parent's hand, he may not have the physical ability or the mental concentration to sort through the mail. Your newly widowed mother may be overwhelmed because your father handled all the financial transactions and she hasn't any idea where to start or how to balance a checkbook. If you notice stacks of mail, opened or unopened, sitting on a desk or counter, you're most likely looking at unpaid bills or insurance correspondence. Ask your parent if she would like help in handling her mail and paying her bills. Tell her that you understand how overwhelming these tasks can be and in order to avoid costly and annoying problems that may come from power shutoffs, telephone disconnections, and insurance cancellations, you hope she thinks about and accepts your offer.

> "It used to drive me crazy. My mother left piles of bills, magazines, and everything else all over the dining-room table. I'd ask her if I could help, and she would say, 'No, I can handle it.' One day I get a call from her doctor's office regarding her secondary insurance coverage. The billing person said the company canceled my mother's policy for lack of payment. I went over to the house, and at the bottom of the pile I found a bill for the insurance and two follow-up notices. Guess what? I got the job."
>
> *Janet, Illinois*

Total Intervention

If your parent cannot live safely without twenty-four-hour supervision or assistance with almost every aspect of daily life, it's time for total intervention. If you wake up every morning, wondering if your parent fell again last night, or forgot to lock the door again, or opened the door to a stranger again, total intervention is appropriate. Look for problems with food preparation or eating, toileting, personal grooming, and falling. Safety issues are major considerations. Is your parent a likely target for financial exploitation? Can your parent call 911 for help or dial your number in an emergency? Would your parent be able to evacuate in a fire? If your parent cannot self-manage physical needs and safety issues, then twenty-four-hour supervision is essential. You can provide twenty-four-hour assistance in your parent's home, your home, an assisted living facility (ALF), or in a nursing home (SNF). The final decision often depends on your parent's physical and mental status, finances, and your parent's wishes. Unless money is no object, take the time to find the cost of your options before entering into a discussion with your parent. Don't expect to get agreement after one conversation or meeting. In a lifetime of changes, this may be the most difficult change your parent will ever make. It signifies a permanent loss of control and independence, and the beginning of an irreversible decline. From your perspective, it may be the only way to help keep your parent safe.

Crisis Intervention

In a crisis, whether it's a medical emergency, accident, or crime, there is only one rule: Call 911 for professional assistance immediately. The rule remains the same for illness, violence, or accidents. Don't try to handle the situation alone; your best chance for recovery or effective treatment is to seek professional help as quickly as possible. If you're visiting your mother, for instance, and she has what appears to be a heart attack, your instinct might be to drive her to the nearest emergency room. However, experts advise that your mother has a better chance of survival and recovery if you call 911 immediately and follow their instructions. Think about it: If you take your mother to the hospital in your car and you are delayed with road or traffic problems, how would you prevent your mother from being further harmed by another attack or ancillary problems? In an ambulance, your mother will be assessed by trained personnel with lifesaving equipment that can help maintain her until she reaches the hospital. The scenario is exactly the same for any type of injury. Call 911 and follow instructions. The exception to this rule however is if you are in danger inside a building. For example, in case of fire, exit the building first, and then call 911.

Legal/Financial Intervention

As a rule, no matter how bad your father's dementia may have become, if he is not declared legally incapacitated, he still has the right to "not" take medicine, to "not" lock the door, and to give his home and all his other assets away to a man he met yesterday on the street because the law says he can do what he wants, when he wants. Work with an elder law or trust and estate attorney to guide you through the process of appointing a guardian or a durable power of attorney who can step in when your father is no longer able to make sound medical, financial, and safety decisions on his own behalf. An attorney will help you create the documents you need to give one or more of these surrogates the legal right to make decisions on your father's behalf and use his assets to care for him. The type of attorney you use is often determined by the size of your parent's estate. Because your options and the documents you need may be regulated by state laws, consult with an attorney who practices in the state your father lives.

H. TAKING THE CAR AWAY

There is nothing that strikes terror in the heart of an elderly driver more than the words, "It is time to stop driving." The impact of these words is even more powerful and devastating to some elderly people than a diagnosis of a debilitating illness. Some parents describe the loss of driving with the same emotion and regret as the loss of a friend or family member. An eighty-six-year-old gentleman said, *"After driving for almost seventy years, it feels like someone cut off my legs; my freedom is gone."*

The idea of taking the car away from a parent is difficult for two reasons. First, since the ability to drive a car is so closely related to a person's sense of independence, adult children feel that if they take the car away, they are to blame for their parent's loss of freedom. Second, if your parent can't drive himself, who is going to do the driving? Several years ago at a support group meeting, a caregiver related the story of her mother, Margaret. Margaret was eighty-two years old and in good physical health, but her memory was impaired. She insisted that driving is second nature and she would only drive in her neighborhood. On one of her excursions, Margaret took a wrong turn, and she found herself disoriented in an unfamiliar area of town. After work, Margaret's daughter stopped at her mother's house only to find no car or mother. She spoke to the neighbors, and no one had seen her mother all day. Just as she was about to call the police, her exhausted but unharmed mother arrived home. The daughter said that although it was a very stressful and frightening day, she still did not have the heart to take the car keys away.

Feelings often influence our decisions. It is not good or bad, it is just the way it is when we are involved in emotional family issues. As one caregiver said, *"It's so hard for me because my father refuses to give up driving. He gets lost all the time, and I feel like I have a three-year-old with a driver's license."*

When it is time for your parent to give up driving, emotions may run high, but it is important to base your discussion on concrete information. The following reality check should provide you with more leverage when you are approaching your parent on this issue.

To safely drive a car, you need to see and hear well, rely on quick physical reflexes, and have the ability to maintain clear and focused thinking. As parents age, they may suffer from hearing and vision impairment, memory loss, arthritis, or other physical or cognitive losses. For parents with any medical limitations, it is crucial that they receive medical clearance to drive. Depending on their overall condition, this clearance may be necessary several times a year. If your parent is cognitively impaired, getting lost, or upset and having accidents, he should not be driving. Sometimes asking someone else to help you stop your parent from driving is your only option. Try these suggestions to help you put the "red light" on unsafe driving.

- If your parent is cognitively impaired, getting lost, and having accidents, he should not be driving at all. State laws vary, and legal intervention may not be immediate. If you are waiting for the authorities to help you in this matter, don't wait any longer. Every day you wait, your father's life and the lives of other people are in danger. No matter how hard it is for you, your only option is to take the car away. If you feel this is something you can't do, speak to a geriatric specialist who can explain to you the implications of taking the car away or not taking the car away.

- Talk to a friend of your parent who recently gave up driving and is aware of the dangers of driving impaired. Ask this person to speak to your parent because the influence and understanding of peers is often very effective.

- Contact your parent's primary care physician. If your parent does not have a primary care physician, then contact any physician who sees your parent on a regular basis, such as a neurologist or a psychiatrist. Try this technique: ask the physician to write a prescription for your parent that states that because of her present condition, she is no longer able to drive a car. Sometimes your parent will accept this as a temporary situation. After a few months, the doctor may renew the prescription. This approach generally is more effective when the physician is one that your parent likes and respects.

- Make sure your parent's driver's license is current. If it is not, you can explain to him that it is illegal to drive without a valid license. If he insists on driving, he will require an eye test to renew the license. If he does not pass the eye test, he will not be able to legally drive a car.

There is no easy way to get your parent to stop driving; you either do it or you don't. If you are successful, we applaud you. But for those of you who are not, we know you tried, and sometimes nothing you do or say can change a situation. Accept the fact that you can take comfort in the trying, because sometimes that is all we have to give us peace of mind.

Providing Substitute Transportation

When driving a car is no longer an option for your parent, consider alternative means of transportation for visits to the doctor, for shopping, and for social events. As a caregiver, you may be tempted to offer to drive your parents to various appointments and functions, but if you are not available or you do not want that as a steady job, there are alternatives. Transportation options depend on four factors: your parent's physical and cognitive status, the geographic location, the availability of services in the community, and personal finances. If your parent lives in a large city, the options may include buses, subways, trains, taxi and car services, or private ambulette and van services. An ambulette transports people as they sit in wheelchairs. If your parents reside in the country or the suburbs, there may be some limitations on bus and train availability. Other means of transportation such as taxi and car services or ambulettes and vans may be more practical and accessible. Before privately paying for transportation, check with your parent's health insurance carrier to determine if she has transportation coverage.

The following information will help you determine what type of transportation is the safest, and the most comfortable and affordable, for your parent. If your parent is cognitively impaired and does not know his address, or is unable to give or understand directions, then public transportation is not an option, because it is unsafe unless he travels with a companion. Public transportation also may not be a safe option if your parent suffers from a physical problem such as difficulty walking or has the use of only one arm. In these situations, consider the need for transportation and the location he is going to and from. Inquire about van or ambulette service for visits to a hospital or physician's office. Some communities have volunteer services through a local hospital, community center, social service agency, church, or synagogue. Generally, the fee for the service is a small contribution, although some communities offer reduced rates on a sliding scale, determined by the person's income.

If your parent is financially able to afford a private taxi or car service, you can arrange for specific pickup times. This type of service is some- times expensive, but if your parent uses the service on a regular basis, there may be room to negotiate the price. Try to arrange for a charge account so that your parent does not have to pay the driver. Always pro- vide a contact name and telephone number in the event of an emergency. A caregiver reported that she made all of the taxi arrangements for her cognitively impaired mother, but instead of bringing her mother back to her home, the driver left her at a different location, lost, frightened, and alone. To avoid this type of situation, make sure that the car dispatcher communicates all of your directions to the driver, and if possible, request the same driver.

Transportation is sometimes available if your parent is a member of an adult day care program or other type of socialization program affiliated with a church, synagogue, or community center. Fees range according to the type of transportation, funding, and the location of the program.

Intervention may not be the easiest path, but when it's necessary, it may be the only way to keep your parent safe.

I. WORKSHEET: INTERVENTION: TRUSTING YOUR INSTINCTS

Knowing when to intervene and help your parents is as important as knowing when not to intervene. These eight important points will help you make this important determination.

INTERVENE IF:

- Your parent shows signs of cognitive impairment and memory loss.
- Your parent's physical condition is deteriorating, and she does not seem capable of taking care of herself.
- Your parent's doctor is concerned about his condition, and he believes your parent requires special care.

- Your parent is cognitively impaired or in poor physical health, and she still drives a car.
- You and other family members and friends notice changes in your parent's physical or cognitive status, and even if he denies that anything is wrong or different.

DO NOT INTERVENE IF:

- Your parent continues to function successfully at or about the same level as she did in the past.
- Your opinion or way of doing things is different from your parent's, and he simply does not agree with you.
- Your parent is high functioning, capable, and satisfied with her life.

Review this chapter for more information on the intervention that is best suited for your parent.

J. MY JOURNAL

Use this page as a safe place to express your thoughts and feelings. Putting your thoughts and feelings on paper helps you to see them more clearly. What bothers you? What changes do you want to make? How can you help yourself and your parent? When you read what you've written, you may see a new pathway to help you solve stressful issues. For example:

"I saw my mother today and she looked so old and frail. I need to help her now. . . ."

"When dad visited us last week he kept tripping and he even fell. He needs medical attention, but he rejects my help. I'm going to figure out a way to help him get what he needs to be safe and secure. . . ."

_____

_____

_____

_____

_____

_____
_____
_____
_____
_____
_____
_____
_____
_____
_____
_____
_____
_____
_____
_____
_____
_____
_____
_____

K. TIP SHEET

- Learn to trust your instincts. If you think that something is wrong, ask questions in order to problem-solve and find the solutions you need to help your parent.
- Ask for help from loved ones and professionals. Accept assistance to make decisions and carry out appropriate plans.
- Try to plan ahead in order to avoid crisis situations and emergencies.
- Do your best to take the car keys away from your cognitively impaired parent and try not to beat yourself up if you are not successful.
- Give yourself a well-deserved pat on the back when you intervene to help your parent remain safe, secure, and well cared for.

5

CAREGIVING REALITIES

A. DO YOU HAVE REALISTIC EXPECTATIONS?

"I wake up every morning and think about another day to worry about my dad. When my mom died I thought, 'OK, so I'll take care of dad because at ninety years old he needs me.' But you don't know how powerful and life altering those few words are to you until you live it. I weep for my life that has changed so much over the past year. I don't know how long dad will live, but I have to find a way to make this work for me and for him."

Jane, Ohio

Caring for a parent may be a temporary job for a few weeks or months, or it may be a job that lasts for years. No matter how long it lasts, caregivers need to establish realistic goals, understand their own individual limitations, and celebrate their accomplishments.

Unfortunately, guilt and responsibility often dictate a sense of duty, and often it is an adult child who takes on this role. Someone who lives three thousand miles away from her parent should not have the same expectations about caregiving as the woman who lives next door. Women who bathe their parents, prepare meals, and do laundry have very different obligations than those of long-distance caregivers who spend hours on the telephone coordinating and overseeing care. Your personal needs, individual circumstances, emotional connections, and history with your parents makes each situation unique. (See chapter 7 for more information on long-distance caregiving.)

Listen to the responses of these three adult children to the question "What motivates you?" Their answer to the question emphasizes the reality that each of you is a caregiver for different reasons.

> "I become guilty when I can't do more, guilty when I neglect my own needs, guilty when others need me and I can't be there for them. Guilty, guilty, guilty as charged!"
>
> *Margaret, Massachusetts*

> "A sense of responsibility. It's the right thing to do."
>
> *Peter, New York*

> "He's my father."
>
> *Sally, New Jersey*

Guilt, responsibility, and deep emotional connections are feelings shared and expressed by many caregivers. No matter how or why you became a caregiver, each one of you has the *power*, *right*, and *insight* to consider and take care of your own needs. You can successfully accomplish this if you are open to the possibility that just maybe you are doing too much, and trying too hard. Unfortunately, caregivers who are confused by their feelings or do not understand their feelings may become entrenched in their caregiver responsibilities. They may ignore many of the signs of their own physical and mental exhaustion, burnout, and emotional stress. Caregivers who have realistic expectations are often in tune with how they feel, and what they need. Try to consider how you feel, and what would make you feel better. The following suggestions should help you reach for and achieve your special comfort level.

- Ask yourself these questions: When was the last time I slept late? When was the last time I saw my doctor? When was the last time I went to the hair salon for a haircut? When did I last buy myself a new pair of shoes? If you have to think too hard about any of these questions, it's been much too long. You will probably be able to add another ten or twenty things you can do for yourself. Don't try to tackle everything—or even two things—at once. Choose one thing at a time, such as making an appointment, not setting your alarm clock one morning and sleeping a little longer, or going to the dentist. You'll see that even with the busiest schedule you can accomplish one thing at a time. As you do things for yourself you will be amazed and comforted that you can take care of yourself and still be a caring daughter, son, mother, father, and friend.

- Ask for help. If you are the caregiver who does the laundry, grocery shopping, bill paying, and cooking you are undoubtedly on overload. Once you become used to doing everything yourself, it is sometimes difficult to break your routine and let others help you. Let your spouse, significant other, son, daughter, neighbor, or friend know that you cannot do it alone, and that you need their help. Explain to them that helping you with just one thing, like the grocery shopping, cooking dinner, or folding the laundry, will make all the difference. Try to be specific with the assignment, and let them know that you appreciate their effort.

- Listen to your body, relax your mind, and nourish your spirit. Your body sends you signals when you are tired and hungry. If you listen to the signals, recognize your individual triggers such as feeling achy or lightheaded, and do what you need to do to feel better. It will renew your strength and stamina. Relax your mind. When you are overloaded and stressed, your thinking may be impeded and your ability to function may decrease. Take a walk, do a short relaxation exercise, watch the sunset, and experience what it feels like to rest and unwind. Comfort your spirit by reading a book, writing a poem, keeping a journal, visiting a friend, or speaking to your clergy. Revel in the tranquility and reward yourself as often as you can. No one deserves it more than you.

B. UNDERSTANDING YOUR RESPONSIBILITIES

You may have become a caregiver because of a parent's crisis or the diagnosis of a chronic illness. You may have noticed changes in your parent's ability to handle finances or take care of his needs. You may have experienced your life before caregiving as simple and uncomplicated. On a daily basis you went to work, enjoyed your children, grandchildren, and friends, and spent some time taking care of yourself. Amazingly, you found time to do it all. But in an instant everything changed and you found yourself in the middle of the most unusual role of your lifetime.

No one can diminish the difficulties and consequences of multiple generations' changing roles and alter some of the rules that dictate relationships between children and parents. Although you may have cared for your children, grandchildren, a brother, sister, significant other, or spouse, as a caregiver for your parents your sense of responsibility may feel and indeed be different. You may find it difficult to express yourself and how you feel because, after all, you are the child and your parents need you.

> "It is so hard for me to understand why I feel this way, but when I'm around my father I feel like I am three feet tall. He was always so powerful and controlling. I know he has dementia and he really can't make any decisions for himself, but it is so hard for me to take over. I am torn between what I have to do, what I can do, and what I want to do."
>
> Maggie, New Hampshire

This is an extraordinary situation that tests your emotional strength and physical stamina. *Nevertheless, it does not have to dominate your life.* The following exercise will help you find a workable balance to relieve some of the stress, so you can use your time efficiently. You will begin to understand that, no matter how hard you try, you cannot be in two places at the same time.

Think about how you spend an average day. Consider the fact that in a twenty-four-hour day, five to eight hours may be spent sleeping, which leaves you with sixteen to nineteen hours to take care of all the things you have to do. Suppose this is your schedule: You are up every morning at six AM, travel for one to hour, work from nine AM to five PM. From five thirty PM to six thirty PM you grocery shop for Mom; at seven PM you visit with Mom until eight thirty PM, pay some of her bills and go over the checking account. You arrive home at about nine PM, prepare a quick dinner, hem your daughter's skirt, hop into a shower, and go to bed. It is twelve thirty AM. Whom did you forget about in your busy schedule? Take a look in the mirror.

If you are ready for a change, you can do it by making some adjustments to your schedule. Speak to your boss or supervisor about a flextime or part-time schedule that allows you to adjust your hours. For instance, instead of working nine to five every day, your flextime schedule may be from eight to four. Or you may request a part-time schedule. Instead of working five days a week, you would work three days a week. When you do the grocery shopping for Mom, take a few extra minutes and do some of your own shopping and buy a cooked chicken for dinner. On the days that you go grocery shopping, shorten your visit at Mom's. If it's too much to shop and take care of finances on the same day, take the bills and bank statements home and deal with them when it is convenient for you. Keep in mind that a shorter visit with Mom does not preclude sharing a few stories and giving or receiving a few hugs. When you get home, serve the chicken and try to enjoy the time with your family. Explain to your daughter that you understand that her new skirt is important to her, but you've had a busy day, and the skirt can wait until the weekend. Take a shower, watch a television show, polish your nails, or chat on the telephone with a friend, because it is only nine PM.

If you accept the fact that every day will not be perfect, and sometimes you may be up until midnight or one AM, and other days you will have some free time to take care of yourself, you will be a more reasonable and responsible caregiver. You will not neglect yourself, and you will begin to appreciate that what you accomplish in one twenty-four-hour day is truly remarkable. (See chapter 10 for more timesaving tips.)

Learning to Be an Advocate

Some women seem to be born with the ability to march into most situations and take charge. Are you the one person friends or family members call on when they have a problem, need advice, or a shoulder to lean on?

Do you function at your best during a crisis or emergency? If you answered yes to one or both of these questions, it is probably one of the reasons that you are the caregiver for your parents. Others may not feel prepared to handle the responsibilities, demands, and the roller coaster of emotions that may result from being a caregiver. No matter how you feel, or what you know or don't know, everyone can benefit from learning new skills, approaches, and techniques. It is crucial to remember that you will gain strength from people who share their experiences, as well as gain knowledge from professionals in the field who offer information. But you have to ask the questions to get the answers. You have the power to be an effective advocate for your parent. If it is difficult for you, it is time to be proactive and take control. Try the process we call *C.O.P.E.*, a simple way to remember four steps to help you be a smart, effective, educated, and a prepared caregiver-advocate.

- Caregivers help caregivers and build amazing connections with those who share the same problems. Not only are they comforted but they also learn more in the process. Caregivers learn from one another through support groups, online chat rooms, social settings, and at work. The exchange of information, such as tips on saving time and money, and the warmth and understanding felt by the common bond of caregiving provides women and men with ongoing encouragement and support.

  > "I talk to everyone and anyone who will listen to me about my father. I go to support groups, individual therapy, and out to dinner with friends. I talk to them and they listen to me. I am very lucky, because I am always learning something new to help me with my dad."
  >
  > *Charles, Maine*

- Organizations such as the Alzheimer's Association, caregiver organizations, or other disease-related groups are there to inform, assist, and support the efforts of caregivers. Just one telephone call may provide you with the information you need. Information is sometimes available through newsletters, Web sites, telephone contact, and brochures. These groups are beneficial in keeping you informed about the latest medical research and breakthroughs, medications, and physicians who may be able to help your parent. Check with your local social service agency, Area Agency for Aging, and see our extensive list of Web sites and resources in chapter 24.

"I am a fairly intelligent person, but anytime I try to talk to my mom's doctor he makes me feel like I'm not too smart. When Mom was in the hospital I asked him how long he felt she would have to stay. He said, 'Until she is better.' I asked again for an educated guess. He said, 'When I say so.' I deserve better and so does my mom. When she felt better I told her the story and she said, 'Forget it, we're going to find someone else.'"

Lois, Ohio

"We feel so lucky with our father's doctor. We get nervous about everything and I guess we sometimes ask silly questions, but he always answers us. For instance, when Dad had pneumonia he had a funny sounding cough. I called the doctor and I described the cough by imitating it on the telephone. Instead of laughing at me or telling me it wasn't necessary, he thanked me for being so helpful. We feel like we have someone to talk to who really cares about all of us."

Michelle, Wisconsin

- Professionals in the field of geriatrics, such as social workers, registered nurses, and physicians, can help you understand your parent's diagnosis and medications, as well as the emotional and psychological problems you may face now and in the future. Sometimes caregivers may feel ill at ease when they approach a professional. You may feel as if you're asking stupid questions.
- As a consumer and an advocate for your parents you have the right to ask questions and receive appropriate and timely information and responses. Make the most of your appointment or telephone conversation by preparing a list of questions. If you are not satis-

fied with the answers, or you are still concerned and confused, don't give up the search for the information you need. You are entitled to ask to speak to a supervisor or get a second medical opinion. (See chapter 12 for information on speaking to doctors and other healthcare professionals.)

- Becoming educated empowers you with information, confidence, and the strength to be an effective advocate for your parent and yourself. As you learn from other advocates, professionals, and various organizations you are gaining and developing the tools you need now and will need in the future. Learn in your own way, and at your own pace. Allow yourself to feel empowered by what you know, and you will begin to tackle most situations feeling more comfortable and confident. If you feel frustrated or discouraged at first, give yourself credit for the things you have accomplished.

Hands-On Care

The actual physical care a person might require on a daily basis includes bathing, feeding, dressing, toileting, assistance with walking, and transferring (from a bed to a chair or from a wheelchair to a car), as well as medication management. Sometimes the care involves simply cueing your parent on how to put on her clothes, and sometimes you need to assist your parent with dressing. These are intimate and sometimes uncomfortable situations for parents and children. Even the adult child who enjoys a close, emotional, and loving relationship with his parent may find that some duties are too personal to share. For instance, during a support group meeting a caregiver said that although she took care of her mother for a few years, she could not continue when her mother became incontinent. She felt the intimate, personal care her mother needed was more than she could bear, and she made a conscious decision to get outside help. She said, *"That was my breaking point."* Fortunately, she recognized that her mother required a level of care that she could not provide physically or emotionally. Many of the other caregivers agreed with her and understood her feelings.

Your parent has the right to be taken care of with dignity and respect. Use common sense, and creativity, and try to learn to compromise to help you through the tough times.

- Providing your parent with personal care requires you to be honest with yourself from the first day through the last. Common sense dictates that you think about what you can and cannot do. There is no shame in admitting that at times some tasks may be too difficult. Caregivers often say that they do what they have to do, and they don't have a choice. At that moment you may not have a choice, but there are ways to make the job a little easier. If you are comfortable feeding and dressing your parent, but you find showering and toileting too difficult for both of you, then consider this idea. If your mother is physically frail but cognitively alert and oriented, talk to her about the best way to help. Allow her to enjoy as much independence as possible. You may be surprised that you are more uncomfortable than your parent, and talking about it relieves some of your tension and discomfort. For example, if you shower your parent, suggest that he wear a loose-fitting bathing suit to provide privacy and easy access. If your cognitively impaired parent always wears the same shirt and pants, buy two or three identical pieces of clothing and then switch the clean clothes for the soiled ones.
- Another caregiver described how she creatively outwitted her cognitively impaired father when he refused to change his underwear.

> "Every night my father dropped his clothes on the floor of the bedroom. Each morning before anyone else was awake he got up and put on the same clothes and underwear. One night I decided to sneak into the room while he was asleep and I replaced the dirty underwear with clean ones. After a while I did the same for his clothes. The floor became a very handy closet."
>
> *Linda, California*

- At times you may feel in conflict with what your parent wants and what he needs. As one caregiver said, "*I don't have time for what my father wants; I only have time for what he needs.*" This is understandable given the busy schedule, obligations, and responsibilities of most caregivers. However, it may raise some unnecessary conflicts and problems that you can avoid. Your mother, for example, used to enjoy a warm bath in the evening, but now she needs your assistance with bathing. The only time you have to help her with the bath is in the morning. She is very unhappy about this change in her schedule, but you are pressed for time. Consider a compromise. Set aside one or two nights each week for a luxurious bath, and then she can shower on the other days at your convenience. Suppose your father likes to take a walk around the pond near his home. Unfortunately, he is not steady on his feet so he cannot walk alone. Because of your job and your own family obligations you can join him only on Saturdays. Ask a friend, neighbor, or one of the grandchildren to take him for a walk once during the week. Explain to him that someone else will take him during the week and you will join him on the weekend. It may not be perfect, but making the time and effort to integrate your parent's wants and needs is often the key to a peaceful resolution.

Supervising Others

In most work-related settings the role of a supervisor is to delegate and oversee the work of other people. The same principle is applicable to the supervision of anyone who is helping you take care of your parent. The help may come from family, friends, or home health aides. You may call upon your family and friends to help you on a daily, weekly, or monthly basis, or just once in awhile. You may hire one home health aide or several over the course of time. No matter who helps you, they are all entitled to a job description, to understand what you expect of them, and to be made accountable for their work. Although this sounds very formal when you are talking about family and friends, it is important for everyone to understand that the type of care your parent needs and deserves. They can't do what you want if they don't know what it is. Open communication, cooperation, and consideration are critical for everyone involved. (See chapter 11 for a detailed description of how you select and screen professional caregivers.)

As the primary caregiver, you cannot make assumptions about what other people know or don't know about your parents, or know about the type of care your loved one needs. This is especially true if those who assist you never cared for your parent before, or they have not seen your parent in a long time. Family members may think they know your parent because you talk about him, but there is a significant difference between talking about a situation and actually being in it. Experienced homecare workers will tell you that each situation is different, and that families enjoy their own way of doing things. The following supervision guidelines will help you get organized, and encourage you to feel you have things well in hand. All of the suggestions apply to anyone who helps you take care of your parent.

- Provide the caregiver with the following information about your parent. List all of the information in a notebook, or attach a list to the refrigerator or medicine cabinet. The list should include all medical conditions; a list of medications, including the dosage and the time of day the medication is taken; any allergies to food or medications; dietary restrictions; the name and telephone number of the pharmacy; the primary care physician's name and telephone number, along with all the other healthcare specialists, such as a physical therapist, social worker, or nurse. Indicate the first, second, and third emergency contacts, with office, cell, and home telephone numbers, as well as e-mail addresses. Add the name of the homecare agency, its telephone number, and the agency contact's name to the list. This will ensure that everyone who takes care of your parent will have all the information they need.
- Instruct all caregivers that 911 is the only appropriate intervention for any emergency.
- Provide an envelope for petty cash. You determine the amount of petty cash by considering your parent's needs and expenses. For instance, your mother may require a visit to the beauty salon once a week, and the cost for her hair is, say, twenty-five dollars. If the caregiver and your mother have lunch in a restaurant once a week, consider adding a few extra dollars, and so on. Ask caregivers to keep all of the receipts and place them in the envelope. Make sure they keep a list of all of the expenses. This is to ensure the caregiver's accountability. A home health aide asked a family member if she needed the receipt for a cup of coffee and a doughnut. The daughter decided that anything the homecare worker bought for herself that was less than five dollars did not require a receipt. The system that you establish should provide you with an accurate

accounting of all financial transactions, a level of comfort, and over time a feeling of mutual trust.

- Instruct the caregiver about your parent's likes and dislikes. Talk to the caregiver about how your parent spends his day, which is his favorite chair, or which are his favorite television programs, or which television has a clearer picture. Informed caregivers are more in tune to your parent's needs. Your parent should be able to enjoy his special sweater or favorite food as long as it is not against the doctors' orders.

- Be specific about tasks you wish the caregiver to perform on a daily or weekly basis. If you do a complete grocery shopping once every two weeks, then explain to the caregiver that she may need to fill in with milk and bread during the alternating week. If her job is to do the laundry, explain to her how you would like it done and how often. If you are specific with your instructions, then it is more likely that the caregiver will complete the job in a timely and efficient manner.

- Communicate with the caregiver as often as you need to in order to establish a comfortable routine. Once you, the caregiver, and your parent have adjusted to one another, your communications may decrease. But if a telephone call in the middle of the day makes you feel better and less stressed, then make the call. It is perfectly normal to sometimes need reassurance from the caregiver that everything is all right. Eventually your motto should be, "*Assume wellness.*" Once you and the caregiver establish a level of trust, try to allow her to do her job. You'll know fast enough when something is wrong.

- Talk to the caregiver about the things she needs in order to be comfortable in your parent's home, and try to accommodate some of her needs. She may not enjoy watching television, but she might like a radio in her room. Or the caregiver may have certain dietary likes or restrictions that are different than your parent's.

- If you are dissatisfied with something she is doing, let her know as soon as possible, and give her the opportunity to change the situation. For example, if you like to see your mother dressed every day and the hired caregiver allows her to remain in nightclothes, talk to her about the problem. Tell her you will purchase items that are easy to put on and take off, such as a housecoat. If you observe the caregiver feeding your mother too quickly, talk to her about her pace. Ask her why and what is the hurry? Explain to her that your mother should comfortably enjoy her meal. If you continue to be dissatisfied, contact the homecare agency and request a replacement. If your friends or family members are not fulfilling their end of the bargain, talk about it and try to resolve the situation. When things are going well, say thank you as often as you can, because everyone appreciates a pat on the back for a job well done.

Financial Management

Some caregivers consider taking over financial control an integral part of their responsibilities. If your parent is physically ill or frail, she may appreciate your help in paying bills or taking care of banking tasks. (You can find timesaving tips for these chores in chapter 10.)

If your parent is cognitively impaired, it is very important that someone else take over the responsibility for his financial matters. If you let your parent remain in control, both you and he may be at a high risk for experiencing financial abuse or become the victim of a scam. Seniors are considered easy, lucrative targets by unscrupulous salespeople, because they have the time to read long letters and are often lonely or even eager to talk to strangers on the telephone. They are also concerned that they may outlive their assets and are easily interested in schemes that promise to increase their money. If your parent is confused and has trouble remembering appointments or when to take medications, it is unfair and unrealistic to expect him to pay his homeowner's, auto, or health insurance premiums on time, or to deal with many other similar issues that are a part of our lives.

The only way to safeguard against this is to make sure your parent cannot invest or spend money without the approval of a third party. A legal or financial professional can help you understand your options and take the appropriate steps to protect your parent's assets. Here's what you'll need to get started.

- Consider whether or not you have the time and skills to handle your parent's financial matters yourself. If you are a person who has trouble disciplining yourself to balance a checkbook or pay your own taxes on time, this may not be a job for you. Talk with other family members to see if someone else can help with this duty or speak to an elder-law attorney, trust officer at a bank, financial planner, or an accountant to help you with this situation.

- If your parent is legally incapacitated and you choose to handle his financial matters yourself or hire someone to take over for you, protect yourself. Talk to an attorney and obtain the legal authority to make financial decisions on your father's behalf. You'll need this if you want to sell investments or his house if you need the money from the sale of the house to pay for your father's healthcare. You'll also need authority to enter his safety deposit boxes and secure duplicate copies of items you cannot locate, such as birth certificates, life insurance policies, contracts, and so on.

- If you need someone just to pay bills, call your local Area Agency for Aging and ask for a referral to three people who pay bills for seniors. These professionals usually charge by the hour. Be sure to check references and obtain an estimate of the cost before you hire anyone. An experienced, qualified, and honest man or woman will be happy to give you both.

- Make an appointment with your parent's attorney and accountant to bring them up to date. Use this as a get-acquainted meeting to help you decide whether you want to continue the relationships. Depending on the size of your parent's estate, you may need either an elder law attorney or trust-and-estate attorney. You may also benefit from the services of a certified public accountant (CPA) or a certified financial planner (CFP). If you already work with one of these professionals, she can recommend others. Take the time to talk to more than one so that you're clear on the function they perform and what they charge for their services.

- Try to find the documents that affect your parent's assets. Look for a mortgage document and the homeowner's and auto insurance policies. There may be more than one life insurance policy; there may be several investment documents. You will also need your parent's health insurance policy or policies. Whoever handles the financial or legal matters may already have these documents or the documents may be in your parent's safety deposit box. When you find them, be certain you store them in a secure place, such as a safety deposit box.

- You'll also need to determine what other legal documents your parent has signed and obtain copies of all of them. Look for a passport; a will pertaining to asset distribution; a living will or other papers for healthcare matters, such as advance directives, burial plot papers, and notice of a designated healthcare surrogate; and state and federal income tax returns. Even if your mother has always been meticulous about filing and organizing, don't expect to finish this job in one afternoon. (Review the Honoring My Parent's Wishes worksheet in chapter 22 for a list of important documents and information.)

> "My mother always kept a file with what she called 'important papers.' She used to say, 'If anything happens to me, it's all in this box.' When I obtained power of attorney and took over the paperwork, I opened the box and guess what? She had opened the box—after the dementia set in. She hid the papers to protect them, but had no idea where she put them. It took me months of going through every drawer and every shoebox in her house to amass what I hope are all the documents. I even found one in the freezer and one in the flour canister. I won't know if I got them all until someone makes a demand for a document I don't have or a payment I don't know anything about."
>
> *Leah, Wisconsin*

- Talk to your legal and financial counselors about other documents you may need and about their distribution. For example, your attorney may want to keep a copy of the will, living will, and advance directives. Your accountant will want copies of the tax returns. This may be a difficult job in more ways than you think. Money combined with control issues or longtime sibling rivalries doesn't always bring out the best in families. You may be asked for loans or subjected to spiteful outbursts because you have assumed authority over the family's financial legacy. You may be asked to show proof of expenditures. Try to separate realistic requests from other issues. For example, keeping a record of expenditures so the family will know when and how much you spend on your father's behalf is a reasonable request. "You were always her favorite, and now you get all the money" is unreasonable, uncooperative, and disruptive. If you can remain secure and comfortable knowing that you are simply doing what you can to help, then you can ignore jealous rivalries. If these outbursts upset you, get help from your attorney, financial counselor, or a mental health counselor right away. They are experienced at helping families through the emotional and practical upheavals that arise from changes in financial control. (For more information on handling financial responsibilities, please read chapters 7 and 22.)

C. RECRUITING FRIENDS AND FAMILY

Women who spend the day "multitasking," or in our mother's jargon, "doing twenty things at once," often find it difficult to ask for help. Caregivers often describe a feeling of "spinning like a top," unable to stop, yet unable to move ahead. Unfortunately, the feeling does not go away by itself, but it is a warning. Just like a spinning top, eventually you will run out of the ability to spin. Don't wait until you topple over and fall. Ask for help, relief, and some needed time off before you spin out of control.

Asking for help is not a sign of weakness or frailty. It just means that you are tired, stressed, and need help from the people who love and need you. As one caregiver said, *"I was left feeling that I was taking care of everyone except myself."*

How do you ask for help when you never asked before? It is not as difficult as it seems, but it does take some planning so that you are clear on what you want, need, and expect from your family and friends. (See chapters 7, 9, and 10 for information on how to get the help you need.)

D. USING THE SKILLS YOU ALREADY HAVE

Several years ago a group of businesswomen met once a month for a support group meeting. The talent in the room extended from editors to accountants, executive secretaries to marketing consultants. These women represented the best and the brightest in their fields, and they all shared one thing in common: they cared for one or both parents. But when this amazing group of women sat around the table, they expressed feelings of anxiety, frustration, and an inability to focus on what they needed to do for their parents. Helping them to see their strengths was a challenge, but watching them find the solutions to their individual situations was inspirational.

No matter what each of us does or how we spend our time, we have skills that make us unique, special, and deserving of praise. Using the skills you already have when you care for your parent is something many women don't think about. No matter what type of work you do, it takes time management, organizational skills, and an ability to work with, and get along with, other people to accomplish many of your goals. As a caregiver you can use all of these skills to provide your parents with what they need and want: safety, and a sense of well-being. Hopefully, you will gain a feeling of satisfaction because you tried to do the right thing for all of you.

Figuring out what you know and how to use your skills is not that difficult. It starts with a long look in the mirror. No, not necessarily a glass mirror, but the mirror in your mind that makes you think about who you are, and what you can and cannot do. Your strength is in the skills you already have developed over the years. (See chapters 1, 4, and 7 for information to help you use your skills.)

E. WHERE TO GET THE TRAINING YOU NEED

You have many skills, but you may need some specific training to help you become a more effective caregiver. Education, information, training, and support enhance the skills you have, and help provide you with confidence and a feeling of control. Caregiver training empowers you by providing you with practical advice on a variety of eldercare issues. For example, if your loved one is diagnosed with Parkinson's disease, you may understand the long-term implications of the disease but need help on how to handle day-to-day physical, emotional, or cognitive changes and challenges. If your parent suffered a heart attack, you may want detailed information on diet, exercise, and medication management. Most of the time your parent's physician will provide you with some of the information you need. When you are dealing with a chronic or long-term problem you will need ongoing support, and practical information to help you through each day. Fees for caregiver training vary, and often there is no fee.

- Turn to disease-related organizations such as the Alzheimer's, Diabetes, and Heart associations (see chapter 24 for resources). Many organizations provide educational materials, support groups, and individual counseling. They often divide caregivers into beginning, middle, and end stage. This is important to help you cope with your current and ongoing changes, needs, and problems.
- Social service organizations in your community may have ongoing educational seminars, support groups, and individual and family counseling. Contact your local Area Agency for Aging to find out the availability of services and fee schedules from a variety of organizations that serve your community.
- Churches and synagogues sometimes help their congregants by providing educational seminars and support groups. Speaking to clergy brings a great deal of emotional consolation for many caregivers. Clergy are often knowledgeable about community resources and may be able to direct you to appropriate training services.
- If your employer is large enough to have a human resource director, speak to him or her. Many corporations have educational seminars on eldercare issues, called "lunch and learn," where they may invite a guest speaker or geriatric expert to talk to you. They may also provide counselors to advise you on community training and resources.

F. COPING WITH GUILT

"My sister and I take care of our mother and we work very well together. Mom is ninety-one years old and she has dementia. The doctors tell us that her dementia is caused by mini-strokes and there is no way to stop the strokes from occurring. Day to day we don't know what to expect from her. She lives in an assisted living facility and during one recent visit she and my sister had a terrible fight and they said awful things to one another. When we left my mother in the care of the staff, we both felt so sad that this happened and we both felt very guilty that we let it get out of hand. We get so frustrated trying to explain things to her that we sometimes just lose our cool. On the other hand, Mom's dementia is often very cruel."

Jamie, Minnesota

The voice of dementia is often uncensored, unfeeling, and uncontrollable. When we were children, our parent may have said, "Johnny, that's not a nice thing to say to Mary. You hurt her feelings." We learned from our mistakes and in many cases we became more conscious of other people's feelings. Hopefully, as we age we become more adept at censoring and filtering some of our thoughts and feelings in order not to hurt others. We may think something, we may even feel compelled to say it, but we just don't say it because we know that it is wrong or hurtful. However, individuals who suffer from dementia lose the filter and the ability to censor their thoughts; what is on the heart of the dementia patient is on her tongue. As hard as you may try to ignore your parent's hurtful words in a moment of anger or rage, the words sting and you react. It seems time and time again, you feel guilty about what you said or how you handled the situation. It is time to stop beating yourself up, because everyone loses their cool sometimes.

Women and men who never feel guilt or remorse are often considered seriously ill. Having feelings of guilt is natural and these feelings often give you the opportunity to think about specific problems in a new way. Have you ever heard someone say, "What do you have to be guilty about, you didn't do anything?" Or, "Guilt is a waste of time and I don't have the time to waste." Guilt has a place in all of our lives. The important thing is what you do with it and how you manage it in order for the guilty feelings not to overwhelm or over run your life and your emotional well-being.

As a caregiver you will continuously be confronted by new and difficult challenges. You will struggle making decisions and you will worry about what you finally decide regarding the care and management of your parent and loved ones. The pervasive, sometimes gripping feeling you will encounter will be guilt. Guilt with a small g is manageable because you recognize that it's just a feeling, and it does not have to overshadow every thought and decision you make. Guilt with a capital G feels overwhelming and painful and imposes itself on your every thought and action.

Accept the fact that nearly everyone feels guilty at one time or another. Keep in mind that at times you will feel overwhelmed by guilty thoughts and at other times you will be able to cope with your feelings and not allow the guilt to take over your thoughts.

1. Forgive yourself when you respond to a situation with anger. Everyone has feelings and sometimes we can control these feelings better than at other times. However, if you are afraid that you may physically or psychologically harm your loved one, step away from the situation immediately. Get the help you need from family, friends, and healthcare professionals such as a social worker, doctor, or clergy.

2. Do the best you can. When you feel as if you can always do better, you place unnecessary pressure on yourself. As often as you can, say to yourself, "I am doing the best I can for my parent and that is all I can do." If you say it often enough you will begin to believe in the fact that your best is good enough.

3. Allow other people to validate you. We all need to hear that we are doing a good job. You will begin to believe in yourself once you listen to the people around you who admire you for all of your efforts. Guilt ridden thoughts and feelings will begin to diminish as you learn to believe in yourself.

4. Give yourself a break. Allow yourself time away from caregiver problems. Time out will clear your head, and allow your body, mind, and spirit to heal from the emotional ups and downs. A few days away, a yoga class, or a drive to the country may be all you need to refresh and rejuvenate all of your senses. This renewed feeling will help you cope with any guilty feelings you have because you will be able to think clearer and begin to see guilt as a little g.

5. It is imperative for you to recognize that you will feel guilty at times about something that you have done or something that you have said. However, in time, and with some practice, you will be able to reduce the power that guilt has in your life.

G. WORKSHEET:
IMPORTANT TELEPHONE NUMBERS

Creating a list of telephone numbers for people who are crucial to your parent's well-being is a must for every caregiver. Having these numbers at your fingertips will add to your peace of mind.

In an emergency, always call 911 first.

1. Family members to contact in an emergency:

Name _____ Tel. _____

Name _____ Tel. _____

Name _____ Tel. _____

2. Physicians:

Name _____ Tel. _____

Name _____ Tel. _____

Name _____ Tel. _____

3. Pharmacy:

Name _____ Tel. _____

4. Neighbors:

Name _____ Tel. _____

Name _____ Tel. _____

5. Friends:

Name _____ Tel. _____

Name _____ Tel. _____

6. Other (geriatric care manager, elder-law attorney, financial adviser, bank, transportation service, homecare agency or worker, grocery store, plumber, home repair contractors, or others):

Title _____ Name _____ Tel. _____

Title _____ Name _____ Tel. _____

Title _____ Name _____ Tel. _____

Title _____ Name _____ Tel. _____

Title _____ Name _____ Tel. _____

Title _____ Name _____ Tel. _____

Title _____ Name _____ Tel. _____

Title _____ Name _____ Tel. _____

Title _____ Name _____ Tel. _____

Title _____ Name _____ Tel. _____

WORKSHEET: RECRUITING FRIENDS AND FAMILY

Asking for help is not always easy, but you have to decide what you need and want. First, get organized by answering questions 1–4. Second, take the time to make a list of some of the people who can help you.

1. What is the one thing I need or want most to do? _____

2. How much time do I need? _____

3. What day(s) of the week do I need? _____

4. What services do I need while I am out? _____

_____

5. When you call your friends and family, be very specific about what you want and need. For example: "Sally, I would like to take a course once a week on Wednesday nights six to eight PM. Could you stay with my mom once or twice a month?"

A. Name and Tel. _____

   Dates Available _____

B. Name and Tel. _____

   Dates Available _____

C. Name and Tel. _____

   Dates Available _____

D. Name and Tel. _____

   Dates Available _____

6. For more helpful information about recruiting friends and family, review this chapter.

H. MY JOURNAL

Use this space as a safe place to express your thoughts and feelings. Putting thoughts and feelings on paper helps you see them more clearly. What bothers you? What changes do you want to make? When you read what you've written, you may see a new pathway to help resolve stressful issues. For example:

"I want to help my dad, but I don't know if I'm the right one for this job. . . ."

"I feel trapped with nowhere to go. My world was turned upside down when Mom moved into my house. I think it's time I found an alternative to this situation. I need help. . . ."

I. TIP SHEET

- Ask yourself if you have realistic expectations about your role as a caregiver.
- Decide how much you can do and how much you want to do for your parent.
- Reach out for help and guidance from friends, family, and health-care professionals.
- Use the skills you already have to help you organize, plan, and cope with day-to-day problems.
- Recognize everything you do for your parent and give yourself credit for your strength and courage.

6

HOW TO PROTECT YOURSELF FROM TOXIC RELATIVES

A. WHY YOU NEED TO PROTECT YOURSELF

"My mother is the world's biggest bitch. She uses me for everything, and nothing I do is ever good enough for her. Last week she called, 'I need new sheets; these don't match my bed and I refuse to sleep one more night on them.' I brought exactly what she asked for and she refused them: 'No! No, no, no! Not those! Take them back right now!' Yesterday was the last straw for me. She called me at seven PM because she wanted 'her favorite snack to eat before she went to bed.' Like a fool, I got dressed and went to the store. When I got to her apartment, she greeted me with, 'I don't like these anymore. Bring me a different kind tomorrow.' My friends can't believe the crap I take from her. I stopped loving her years ago. I do this from obligation because it's hard to ignore that she was once my mother."

Brenda, South Carolina

"My sister expects me to put my life on hold every time she has a problem, which seems to be every day! She asks, 'do you have time to talk?' and if I say 'not right now,' she says, 'well this will only take a minute' and talks anyway. If I don't sit on the phone and listen for at least an hour, she says I'm not 'supportive.' I know she has problems with her husband and I don't think she means to burden me, but she's so uncaring when it comes to my time. I dread her calls."

Ellie, Louisiana

Whether you believe your relatives are acting deliberately or inadvertently in a toxic or damaging way, the result is the same: toxic people destroy your mental and physical health. In other words, they are "toxic" to you and others. It's true that many are too self-absorbed to even recognize their hurtful ways or speech; it's equally certain that others know exactly how much hurt they are causing and actually enjoy your discomfort and pain.

If you regularly dread a relative's visit, or feel that a sibling or parent is selfish, controlling, thoughtless, or devious, you've got a toxic relative. Communication is usually confined to the toxic person's needs with zero regard for yours, which makes sense when you understand that nothing she does has anything to do with you in any way; it's all about her.

Some "toxics" actually look forward to disrupting your life by invading your home and degrading your efforts to care for your parent, to cook, to landscape, to clean, or even to dress—any subject is fair game because to them, it is exactly that: a game. They cannot win unless they provoke you enough to see that you feel humiliated or angry. To continue generating that reaction, they will often increase the venom in their comments and make their remarks ever more hurtful so you don't become immune to them. Other "toxics" don't think about being malicious, but are so self-centered that your needs and your time are meaningless to them. Either way, you suffer.

If you are on the receiving end of abuse from toxic relatives, it's time to build your boundaries to reduce or eliminate your suffering. You can learn how to defend yourself, often without long-term damage to family relationships.

Picture yourself standing knee deep in the ocean when you see a chest-high wave coming right at you. If you continue facing the wave, its powerful wall of water may strike your body with enough force to knock you off your feet and injure you. At the very least, the wave may be strong enough to knock you off balance. Now picture the same wave coming at you, but since you know it's coming, you construct a defense to avoid the damage it can do: Instead of facing the wave, you turn *sideways* as it approaches. You'll diffuse the wave's power and avoid a great deal of the harmful impact because the wave has to divide and split in two to go around you. In effect, you've denied the wave its power over you. Read on to learn how to employ the same strategy to defend yourself and protect yourself from your toxic relatives.

It isn't always easy to say NO, but for most people it's critically important to try. If you continue to let your toxic relatives mistreat you, they consider your lack of resistance as giving them permission to continue their behavior. In essence, you are inadvertently helping them abuse you. You become their "enabler." Your continued silence and acceptance of their abuse gives them the green light to keep on angering, frustrating, embarrassing, and hurting you.

Learning to say NO from a position of strength and meaning it may not be as difficult as you believe. You already have the desire to stop their abuse—now all you need is a little practice. This chapter supplies strategies to deal with the Top 7 Toxic Relatives. Using these recommendations can help you create your own personal plan (and also give you a long-overdue laugh when you visualize your toxic person's shocked reaction). *Your own power will take you the rest of the way.*

If you need additional support to help you stand firm while you design your strategy, remember this overriding and life-saving rule: *Providing care to your loved one does not legally or morally require you to sign away your rights to your own happiness.*

Know-It-Alls

> "It was my decision to stay here and care for mom. I had a good job offer out of town, but my sister and brothers live out of state and I couldn't just leave Mom here alone. I accept the stress and loss of the career opportunity. What I don't accept is my know-it-all sisters and brothers who visit so sporadically that they have

no concept of what our lives are all about. Their major contribution is a lot of grief for me. Some of their observations are valuable, but mostly they don't realize the day-to-day stresses of caregiving. They never ask, 'How do you feel? Is there anything you need?' Instead I always feel like I'm under attack. 'Why isn't this done? Why haven't you done that? Look how awful this looks. When are you going to fix this?' They stay in a hotel for two or three days, 'educate us all' with their knowledge of how things 'should' be done and go back to their non-caregiving lives. If Mom didn't love their visits, I'd ask them to stop coming."

Mike, Wyoming

Know-It-Alls make life difficult in any situation, but they present special problems in caregiving. Some long-distance caregivers make things worse for hometown caregivers with every visit; others are downright dangerous. Unfortunately, there are enough of them to have created two stereotypes. The good news is we know enough about them to deal with their upsetting habits.

The *caring* Know-It-All suffers from guilt and anxiety. She may breeze in with a flurry of misguided activity and advice to show you and Mom, even the neighbors and other relatives, how much she really cares even though she is not involved in a "hands-on" way. She may feel badly that she isn't participating more. She may also be afraid that people will think ill of her or she may want to make certain that Mom will continue to love her as much as she used to, even though you are the central figure in Mom's life now. She performs a hurry-up show-and-tell, but she has little or no knowledge about what you actually do as a caregiver, so her advice is often unrealistic or even ridiculous. She is counting on Mom's not being able to discern the difference and hoping she can shine in Mom's eyes as well as yours. Unfortunately, Mom may be so happy for a visit from her absent children that she may not see their advice for the blustering show-off nonsense it is, or if she recognizes it, she may not care as long as they visit. Watching your mother praise your sibling while you are the one working hard to shoulder Mom's caregiving needs may leave you angry and frustrated.

If you are dealing with a sibling who feels guilt, try these approaches:

- *"You seem very interested in helping, Jan. I could use another brain and pair of hands. Mom's got some needs you can handle long-distance from your home. For example, I need to speak with her insurance company about some of the charges they denied. I'll write out the procedure for you. It would be so helpful to Mom and me if you could take this over."*

- If it's feasible for Mom, ask your sibling if she would like to have Mom visit for a few days. Tell her you'll send the necessary supplies along with written instructions with Mom so she'll know what to expect and that you'll drive her to your sibling's home (if you can).

- If neither of these is acceptable, ask her what she would like to contribute to the caregiving effort. Try to accommodate her choice if it makes sense and if you can do so without making your life more difficult. Remember, your goal is to help her feel good about her contributions so she will stop trying to run the entire show and perhaps take on additional duties.

- If your "don't fight me, join me" approach doesn't work, she is more likely to be the second type of Know-It-All, who is primarily interested in herself. This relative is so totally self-absorbed that she may neither notice nor care if she embarrasses or hurts others. In fact, this type of toxic relative may emotionally benefit from preying on others. In order to feel good about herself, she is compelled to advertise her (false) sense of superiority. She needs an audience to confirm that she is the dominant authority on every subject. Her cares and concerns begin and end with her own image.

If this sounds like your relative, try these two approaches:

1. Ask to speak with her privately. Be courteous but firm. Explain that you would value her help, but you don't appreciate her denigrating your efforts then disappearing without ever contributing anything concrete. Explain that if she continues acting in that manner, you will assume that she doesn't care about you or Mom, and that her only goal is showing off. Give her time to answer and if the answer is more BS, leave the room.

2. The next time she offers advice, respond by saying, *"You know so much about this and I know you want to help Mom, so I'm going to*

turn this over to you right now. I need a break and you and Mom could use some time together. I'll be back in a three or four hours." Leave the room, exit the house, and have a nice afternoon off!

Use these approaches every time your Know-It-All shows off with advice that makes no sense and she will get the message. Pat yourself on the back for resolving the issue with a diplomatic approach and reducing a previously traumatic situation to a minor annoyance. You're in control.

> "My brother Tom is a financial manager, and a physician and dietician. Or so he seems to think. Everything I do for Mom is wrong according to him. He has never spent even one day as caregiver and every time he reads an article or watches the news he wants to change Dad's diet, medication routine, or physical therapy. Sometimes I wonder if he could be right, but then I remember he gave me the exact opposite advice a couple of months ago, so I pass on his suggestions. The sad part is that even if some of his ideas would help Dad, I wouldn't believe he knew what he was talking about. If he's this stupid with his financial management, God help his clients. I just wish he'd shut the hell up."
>
> Rene, California

A Special Note about Know-It-Alls and Healthcare Issues

The axiom "a little knowledge can be dangerous" was never more important than when it applies to Know-It-Alls who try to manage a parent's healthcare. Their intent may be loving, but the results can be deadly.

Do not take advice or initiate your own changes in an ill parent's diet, treatment plan, or medications without consulting your parent's physician or another board-certified medical professional. Substituting your own plan may cause your parent to become ill, fall, break bones, have coronary problems, or suffer any number of other adverse reactions, many of which end with hospitalization, nursing home admittance, or even death.

If the Know-It-All in your life tries to make changes in your parent's diet, medicine, or treatment plan, it's in your parent's best interest for you to intervene. These guidelines will help you prepare:

- Set up a private meeting with the Know-It-All. Explain that you are very concerned about the advice he is giving your parent. State specific instances: "*I checked with the pharmacist and the supplement you brought Mom would have added so much more of the medication she already takes that her blood pressure might have skyrocketed to dangerous levels.*" Or, "*I looked up the treatment you suggested and it is not recommended for people who also have Mom's other conditions. I know your advice is well meant, but it can be very dangerous for Mom. Why don't we talk about these treatment ideas before you give them to Mom?*"
- Wait for a response. If your Know-It-All is angry or negative, simply repeat the reasons for your concerns and suggest that you and he or she visit a geriatric physician for a consultation.
- Alert the physician to the situation prior to your appointment and ask him to repeat the information he gave you to your Know-It-All.
- Hopefully he or she will begin to understand the potential for damage and continue to try to help Mom, but with some well-needed caution and in more beneficial ways.

Protecting Yourself from Know-It-Alls

At best, Know-It-Alls are annoying. At worst, they can aggravate and antagonize us until we dread their next contact or even inadvertently harm your parent. Suffering in silence invites them to continue ordering you around. It takes practice to put a stop to their orders and unsolicited suggestions, but it's worth the time.

- **I will be firm.** Every time my family member begins to give orders so she can show her false superiority, I will call her bluff.
- **I will be direct.** I will plan my dialogue and meet with my family member in private to clearly state my concerns with emphasis on those relating to my parent's healthcare.
- **I will be vigilant.** I will reinforce my feelings whenever necessary. I will not hesitate to repeat my responses to the specific issues over and over again.

Guilt Trippers

"My mother keeps saying, 'Just wait, your children will treat you like this someday.' If I'm as manipulative as she is, I'll deserve it. We almost never have a normal conversation. She always starts with, 'You probably don't have time for me, but when you needed me I always had time for you.' Another of her favorites is to pretend she cares about my time. She'll ask, 'Are you busy?' and if I say, 'Yes Mom, can I call you back later?' she responds, 'Oh, you're mad at me. What did I do?' or my all-time favorite, 'Take your time. I'll wait right here by the phone so I don't miss your call.' She's the queen of guilt. When she's through pushing my buttons, I end up apologizing to her and agreeing to whatever she wants. This conversation happens two or three times each week. She's got her act down pat. You'd think by now I could call her bluff. I'm not sure if I don't know how or don't want to hurt her. I should wear a sign around my neck, 'Hi, I'm Faye's personal doormat.'"

Bernice, Oregon

Many of us have Guilt Trippers in our families. Like your mother, they have mastered the art of manipulating us to make us feel guilty if we don't do whatever they ask. When they say, *"Never mind, I'll call your brother Frank. He's never too busy for me,"* they are actually threatening to punish you and cause you pain. When Mom threatens to take her request somewhere else, she is saying she will withhold her love from you and award it to the person who *"loves her enough"* to do what she wants. Or, she may be saying, *"It's obvious you don't love me, so I'll go where I'm loved."*

When Mom asks, *"Are you too busy for me"* and you respond *"Yes, I'm in the middle of a problem right now. Can I call you back in an hour?"* that should satisfy her unless it's an emergency. When she begins questioning your love much as a child might, it's important to recognize that she does it for the same reason a child does it: it's a battle for control and instant satisfaction. If you give in to her for convenience or you begin to believe her recriminations and try to do "more" so that you can be a "better" son or daughter, you've helped her formulate the process she needs to manipulate you.

The first step to saying NO from a position of strength is to accept the fact that for Guilt Trippers, doing "more" is not the solution; it is the worst possible response. You can never do enough "more" to satisfy a Guilt Tripper because each time you give in, your Guilt Tripper experiences the thrill of success. When we give in and let them rule our lives, we reinforce the concept that their bad habits work. With a model for successful manipulation in place, they will continue their lamentation and continue pushing our buttons no matter how much time, energy, or money we devote to them. "Practice makes perfect" and eventually Mom's practice will make her an expert at ruling your life.

Intellectually, you may have stepped back from your parent's manipulation. You may realize that you are a responsible son or daughter who has every right to control the time you spend with your parent in person or on the telephone. Now it's time to teach yourself how to control the emotional damage your parent inflicts.

You can save yourself a lot of heartache by developing your own approach; use these examples to help you create your own method of diluting your parent's ability to guilt-trip you. If you don't succeed the first time, try again. And try again. Keep trying until *you* control your buttons, not Mom. "Practice makes perfect" works for you, too!

Remember to check first to make certain that Mom isn't in danger. Absent a dangerous situation, try these responses when she begins her guilt trip:

- *"Mom, I'm happy to hear from you, but you have to accept that I can't always stop what I'm doing and spend time with you. I'm always happy to call you back later."* If Mom continues with more guilt dialogue, interrupt immediately and say, *"I'm sorry you feel that way, Mom. I'm doing the best I can. I'll call you back later. Bye Mom. I love you."*
- *"Mom, you'll have to wait until Monday. I can't do it right now."* When Mom begins to "punish" you emotionally, your response is the same: *"I'm sorry you feel that way Mom. I love you and I'm doing the best I can."* Then change the subject to something neutral or say good-bye.

- *"I'm sorry, Mom, Sal and I planned a day out with the kids tomorrow."* When Mom tries to push your buttons, your response is the same: *I'm sorry you feel that way, Mom. I love you and I'm doing the best I can."* Then change the subject to something neutral or say good-bye.

This is not a negotiation. Once you've said NO, don't argue and don't continue to discuss the subject. Turn to another topic or end the conversation. If you want your mother to believe you mean what you say, it's important for you to believe it as well.

You may never break your parent's habit of trying to manipulate you, but she will eventually learn that the subject is closed after you say NO and stick to it. Your quality of life will soar and you may also improve your relationship with your parent.

Protecting Yourself from Guilt Trippers

When we say NO to Guilt Trippers, then concede and give in, we confirm that if they continue guilt-tripping, we will eventually change our minds and say yes. It may seem difficult at first, but saying NO and meaning it is the only way to regain control of your life.

- **I recognize that "more" is not a solution.** I'm doing the best I can and no amount of "more" will ever be enough to satisfy my Guilt Tripper.
- **I won't let Guilt Trippers shake my confidence or alter my respect for myself.** Their version is not reality; it's part of their scam.
- **When I regain control, I will keep it.** I recognize that if I reward my Guilt Tripper's manipulation by reversing my decision, that gives them license to keep trying until their manipulation is successful.

Work Disrupters

"My mother doesn't think she is bothering me during the day because she doesn't call my work number...she calls my cell phone. I love cell phones, I hate cell phones. I actually have feelings about my cell phone. How crazy is that? It's really not the cell phone's fault; it's my mother. I have tried to tell her that the cell phone is strictly for emergency telephone calls when she can't reach me any other way. Well, yesterday in the middle of a staff meeting the phone rang...guess who? She actually called to tell me that she bought me a chicken for dinner so that I would not have to cook. Nice? No! She just doesn't get it. Emergency means blood, pain, or floods. Chicken can wait. I've had it."

Kim, Washington, DC

"I work from home. I love working from home, but my dad thinks that since I'm home he can visit any time of the day. Lunchtime is time to bond...no, it's time to catch up on my paperwork. I try to talk to him about it, but he doesn't want to listen. If he comes over I feel as if I have to entertain him. I have to put a stop to this interference now or else I will be out of business and I'll have all day for lunch."

Irving, New Jersey

Today's working caregiver balances multiple roles that include his family, friends, work, and caring for elderly relatives. It is no wonder that a caregiver from New Jersey said, "*Work is my escape. I lose myself in my computer, clients, and job-related dilemmas. The rest of my life is so complicated and overwhelming. I need my time at work to clear my head. Sure, there are problems at work, but it's different. I leave my feelings at home.*"

Dealing with Work Disrupters is not as difficult as you might imagine. Caregivers express feelings of guilt when they don't do something for a parent. Guilt is very burdensome and uses a great deal of emotional and psychological energy. Being at work provides you with somewhat of a "safety zone." The safety zone is your buffer against guilt. Think about it. When you are home watching television or enjoying dinner and your parent calls you, you may have an overwhelming sense of duty that you have to respond to the call. Why? The answer is simple: you are not working. However, when you are at work you can blame your inability to take the telephone call on your work. For instance, you may have a boss who doesn't like you to make personal calls, or a deadline on a project that is due that day. In your mind, you have a concrete reason for not being disrupted during the workday. Now take that one step fur-

HOW TO PROTECT YOURSELF FROM TOXIC RELATIVES

ther as you read some of the following reasons why you shouldn't be disrupted at work. As you read this list, think about your job and write your personal reasons why you should not be disturbed during your workday.

1. You are involved in a negotiation with a client and you will not be available until later in the day.
2. Your boss insists that you join her for lunch and you have to complete a report for the lunch meeting.
3. You are supervising your staff regarding new rules and regulations and they will be asked about these facts later in the day.
4. You are simply too busy catching up with your work after a vacation.
5. You were just promoted to manager of a store and you are trying to set an example for your employees by not taking or making personal telephone calls.

As you begin to understand that you do not have to take every telephone call, you will need to develop ways to assist your parent during your workday and decide which calls are emergencies and which can wait until later in the day or the next day. Try the following suggestions to help you set the boundaries that work the best for all of you.

- Consider the fact that emergency situations include medical problems that need immediate attention. If your parent is a chronic telephone caller, provide her with a list of reasons to call and a list of reasons that can wait until you arrive home in the evening. For example: an unexpected fall, injury, or medical emergency is a legitimate reason for being disrupted during the workday.
- Postpone a discussion about the garden, chicken dinner, or Sunday's card game until you are at home and relaxed.
- Set aside a chat time every day to talk to your parent. Some parents call because they are anxious or lonely. If your mother knows that she will have that special time with you, she may be less likely to bother you during the workday.
- Talk to your parent's home health aide or companion about reassuring your mother that you are well and busy at work. Sometimes telephone calls are simply your parent's way of checking up on you.
- Provide the home health aide or companion with a list of emer-

gency contacts, such as the primary care doctor, specialists, pharmacy, local hospital, and family members. You should be on the list, but you don't have to be the first contact. If you have siblings who don't work, or ones that do work and are actively involved in your mother's care, they may be willing to help out during a weekday emergency.

- Spend some of your chat time reassuring your mother that you care about her and understand her need to call you. Clearly let your mother know that she is important to you, but work is a part of your life that is also important.

Work disruptions are very annoying because we may lose our train of thought and concentration on our work. If we receive a disturbing telephone call it may interfere with our ability to go back to work productively. You can put an end to Work Disrupters by setting specific boundaries and providing your mother with the knowledge that you do care about her well-being and in the event of a real life emergency you are there to help.

Protecting Yourself from Work Disrupters

Help yourself be productive during your workday by reinforcing your needs and letting your family know that you *mean business.*

- **I will provide my family and friends with reminders.** I will provide a refresher course in the old-fashioned work ethic to help keep my parent off of the telephone.
- **I will provide my parent with options to keep her busy and involved.** I will discuss appropriate, stimulating daytime activities such as a membership to a senior center or a day care program to help fill my parent's day.
- **I will be available for emergencies only.** I will be clear to my parent and others involved in my parent's day-to-day life that I am available for emergencies only. I will clearly define an emergency such as an immediate medical problem. All nonemergency calls have to wait until after my office hours.

Parents in Denial

"My father believes that if you don't talk about it or think about it, whatever it is will not happen. We all know that my mother has dementia. She forgets everything—names, places, and events—and her judgment is so impaired. The other day she left the house at eight o'clock at night when my dad was dozing on the couch. When he woke up, she wasn't home. He panicked and called my son who lives two blocks away. The hunt for Grandma began and ended within fifteen minutes. We were so grateful that she was safe and sound. When we asked her why she left the house alone and at night she said, 'I wanted to visit my mother.' Her mother died in 1974. Another incident, proving that Dad needs help to take care of Mom. What does he say? 'She didn't mean what she said, she really went out for milk.' I can't take this anymore."

Penny, California

Some facts are undeniable—everyone has problems and everyone copes with problems in his own way. Penny's dad uses denial as a coping mechanism to keep him from seeing and accepting the fact that his wife has dementia. It protects him from the reality that he is losing someone he loves. The problem lies in the fact that because he is denying that there is a problem, Penny's mom is not safe.

Helping your parent accept the fact that he or his spouse needs help will take patience and planning. When your parent uses denial as a coping mechanism, he is employing a long-engrained method of dealing with problems. If you begin to look at how your parent coped in the past, you will find that denial was a means of getting through many family crises. For instance, if your brother had a drug or alcohol problem and he dropped out of school, your father may have used denial to deal with the problem and his own feelings. Your father may have said that your brother had better things to do than go to school or he was leaving town for a new job. He said whatever he had to in order to cope with the loss of control over a complicated and emotional situation. For some people, denying a problem makes it disappear into thin air. Magically the problem goes away only to reappear days, weeks, or months later. Unfortunately, a chronic denier's problems often escalate because they never deal with the source of the problem.

As the adult child of a denier you have the difficult job of helping your parent see the situation for what it is and then find appropriate solutions.

The following six steps will help you on this road to open the eyes and ears of the denier in your family:

1. Talk to your parent about past experiences where he denied a problem and the situation was clearly different. For example, you may say to your father, "Dad, do you remember when Tom left his job? You said it was because he had a better opportunity at another company, but he really had a serious alcohol problem. When you accepted the fact that Tom needed your help, you were the one who found him a rehabilitation facility. I remember how hard it was for you, but in the end you were such a great help to him." By pointing out how your father helped his son you are providing him with a historical reference. For better or worse, a history of denial can and does repeat itself, but can change if the person is willing to listen.

2. Provide your father with options. If your father is taking care of your mother, but he does not see the need for help, provide him with a list of two or three homecare agencies and a description of what they do. Leave the information for him to review in his own way and in his own time. Explain to your dad that you are not taking away his control of your mother's care, but you are simply trying to supplement what he does in order to make it easier for him.

3. Provide your father with ideas and options if he is taking care of himself. If your dad denies the need for help and you know that he can no longer take care of himself, once again draw from the past and give him examples of what he did and how he handled a particular situation. Try to use one specific example that occurred in the recent past. "Dad, I know you don't like to talk about your hearing problem, but do you remember a few months ago when the fire alarm sounded and you didn't hear the alarm go off? Luckily your neighbor was home and she helped you out of the apartment. Dad, after that incident you realized that you could no longer deny that you needed a hearing aid. Now you need to have

someone with you to help you with the chores and to drive you to the doctor or the park. I love you and I don't want to see you hurt. It's time to talk about hiring a home healthcare aide for a few hours a day to help you. Let's do this together."

4. Ask your family members to help you. Dad may be ready to hear some of what you have to say, but he may hear it more clearly from your older sister or brother. Engage the family member or members who communicate best with your dad. Some families feel that their dad relates better to the men in the family. Utilize whoever and whatever works best in your family.

5. Allow your parent the opportunity to express his feelings regarding the fact that he is facing new challenges. Remember, he is scared and denial has been a lifelong safety net. Providing your father with sound advice and concrete options may help to ease the situation.

6. Parents who deny the need for help can be very time consuming and frustrating. They cannot see the problem, because they deny that there are any problems. Therefore, they need you, a family member, or a geriatric professional such as a social worker, psychotherapist, or physician to say, "open your eyes; it's time to face the problem and find an appropriate solution." Once the parent who denies a need for help develops the eyes to see the problem, he may begin to recognize the need to find the answers.

Protecting Yourself from Parents in Denial

If you make the decision to step in and help your parent, it's important to judge how much assistance is necessary. If you are unsure, ask for a second opinion from a family member, friend, or a healthcare professional. Remember, you may meet with resistance, but you have the strength and courage to do what you need to do to help keep your parent safe.

- **I will gather the information I need to determine if my parent is really in danger.** I will engage the help of family, friends, and professional healthcare advocates to help assess and evaluate my parent's overall status.
- **I will act immediately if my parent is at risk.** I will not accept

NO for an answer. If I believe my parent is in danger. I will do what I need to do and act immediately, assess the danger, and provide my parent with a safe and appropriate solution.

- **I will accept my parent's capability and desire for independence.** I will take over only as much as I need to in order to ensure my parent's well-being. I will try not to take over any responsibilities that my parent wants to keep and can handle safely.

Disappointers

> "Promises, promises, promises. I will take Dad to the doctor. I will buy him new slacks. I will visit him this weekend. If my sister makes one more promise that she doesn't keep, I'm going to scream. You would think after years of looking after my dad I would know that my sister was useless. But I guess I'm the perpetual optimist, I think that maybe one day I can really count on her. NOT!"
>
> *Jim, Michigan*

> "My brother is a creep. He promises Dad everything from new clothes to a fishing trip. I tell him 'John, cut it out, you just keep disappointing Dad over and over.' He laughs it off. I've got to stop listening to him and just do what I can for our dad and let John take a hike, but it's so hard to do."
>
> *Madge, Iowa*

Every one of us wants to believe that we can count on someone in our life. It is comforting to think that there is one person to help us through difficult and stressful times, and holds us up when life gets us down. Consider yourself very fortunate if you have that person in your life. Many caregivers like Jim find that the one person they *thought* they could count on is the one person who continuously disappoints them, which hurts.

As you think about the Disappointers in your life, ask yourself the following questions. Do I want to remain friends with this person or do I want to close the door? Can I accept who she is and still have her as a part of my life? If you are inclined to close the door to the relationship, that is your choice, but think it through before you hear the door slam shut. It is often very difficult to reopen the door once it closes. If you feel that you would like to maintain the relationship but you are finding it difficult to do so after so many disappointments, try the following steps toward acceptance and understanding. Keep in mind that Disappointers are often family members, but they can also be your friends, or even colleagues.

- Write your Disappointer a letter. It is not necessarily a letter that you will mail, but it will contain your feelings and thoughts about the situation and how she makes you feel. Keep the letter for a few days, even weeks if you like, and then review it. As you read it, think about what things are really important for you to say and what things may just be spiteful or childish. You are entitled to have all of these feelings, but you may want to concentrate on the points that are most important to your relationship at this time in your life.
- Plan to meet in private with your sister, friend, or colleague. Some caregivers write notes for them to refer to during this meeting, because they feel that they will become too emotional and lose their train of thought. Others will review their letters and keep in mind some of the points they need to say.
- Try this conversation: "Jackie, I really care about you, but you have disappointed me so many times when it comes to helping me with Dad. I need help, I ask for help, and you promise to be there, but you're not. We are sisters and nothing will change that, but I need you to be there for me." Jackie may say that she will try or she may say that she is just not able to help you. If you decide to give her another chance you may want to say, "Jackie, can you take Dad to the doctor on Tuesday?" If she says yes after your heart-to-heart conversation, then you may be on your way. If she says "No, I don't want to," then you know where she stands and it is time for you to accept the fact that this Disappointer will always disappoint you.
- Learn to accept the fact that some people may be good and caring but they do not have the ability or the willingness to help anyone else. If you accept this fact then it may be easier for you to continue the relationship with your sister, friend, or colleague without feeling disappointed by his actions. A wonderful elderly lady once said, "People are like peaches; some are shiny and beautiful on the

outside and rotten on the inside. Some peaches don't look so nice, but they're very sweet. People are just the same, you have to take them as a whole."

- As a caregiver you are stressed and fatigued. At times your emotions are so frayed that it is difficult to express how you really feel. The Disappointers in your life are often people you love and expect so much more from. However, they are not capable of delivering and you are not able to understand their behavior. Take the time to talk to the person who disappoints you. Express your feelings and allow her to express how she feels. Together you may come to a better understanding of each other's needs and then you may not be so disappointed.

Protecting Yourself from Disappointers

There is nothing more disappointing as an unfulfilled promise, except for a promise that goes repeatedly unfulfilled. Protect yourself from Disappointers by following this two-step plan.

- **I will provide a test.** I will select a small task for my family member or friend to do. If he promises to complete the task and fulfills his promise, I will follow with other requests. If he does not fulfill his promise, I know exactly where I stand.
- **I will make every effort to protect myself.** I will protect myself from the people who disappoint me by trying to find alternatives to my dilemmas.

Sibling Battlers

"We couldn't even make it through one day in the emergency room while we waited to hear about how bad Mom's heart attack was. When we got there, it looked like my sisters and brothers and I were going to support each other, but it didn't take long for us to start fighting again and the nurses actually asked us to leave the surgical waiting area because we were disturbing other families. We've been bickering for years. Kathy has to have the last word, Neil knows everything about everything,

Bob makes so much money his answer is always 'hire someone' or 'no problem, buy it.' There are six of us and most of the time I wish I were an only child. Would it have killed them to shut up for a few hours, just this once, until we found out if Mom was going to live through surgery?"

Beth, Colorado

Most families have long histories filled with many or all of the emotions of life: love, sadness, worry, hate, anger, fear, frustration, and jealousy. For you and many others like you, the ideal family that comes together and stays together in times of illness or crisis may seem as elusive as a rainbow. It's the same for the majority of families. It may take five hours or five days, but eventually the feelings and issues that separated you in the past pop right back up to stress you again because *those feelings and issues haven't changed in any way.* They've simply been replaced by something newer and more urgent—something so powerful that it *temporarily* pushed your old feelings, the reasons for your past adversarial relationships with your siblings, to the back burner of your emotions. Your love, shock, fear, or concern for your parent has *temporarily* taken center stage. Once you adjust to the new emotions that are racking your psyche, the old feelings resurface. Sometimes stronger than before because of the fear associated with Mom's potential for survival.

- Call a family meeting to talk with your siblings. Express your feelings to them and ask them to share their emotions. At worst, they may refuse or walk out, leaving you with Mom's care. At best, you may open a dialogue with one or more of them for a long-term relationship filled with more open communication.

Whether or not your siblings cooperate, you will have tried your best and will know that you cannot change or even affect their toxic behavior. This knowledge will help you regain control of your own emotions and relieve you of some or all of the pain they cause by their antagonism. You will be able to emotionally move on and distance yourself from the negative influence they have on your life.

Protecting Yourself from Sibling Battlers

Sibling rivalries usually stem from long-term issues. Old habits are hard to break, but these suggestions can help with the immediate effects of arguments and ease the added stress they bring to your life. It's important to choose your battles and plan your responses to their provocations so that you can remain in control.

- **I will do my homework.** I will take the time to understand my parent's illness and capabilities as well as the treatment options. My knowledge will enable me to respond authoritatively when I disagree with my brother's or sister's recommendations.
- **I will not respond in anger.** I will do my best to step back and think about the reason for my anger. I will remember that a calm, measured response gives me more control, which can help me better influence them, or diffuse the confrontation or even ignore it.
- **I will choose my battles.** I will try to not follow years of habit and automatically respond to every taunt or comment because I recognize that many issues are not meaningful enough to argue about or worth my time to comment on.

Caregiver Self-Neglecters

> "I hurt all over, my back, my knees, my shoulder. I know I need surgery on my knees, but I just can't find the time to help myself. I sometimes wonder if I think by hurting all over I am really protecting myself from the real hurt . . . sick, old, demented parents. It's so hard to take the time I need to help myself when I spend so much physical and emotional time helping them get through one crisis after another. My friends tell me that I have to take care of myself because what would my family do without me. I'm tired and I just want all of the pain to stop."
>
> *Ellen, Connecticut*

> "There was an old song that said, 'I am woman hear me roar.' Well, I'm a man, 'watch me cry.' It is so difficult coping with my

mother and her problems. I moved away, as far away as I could. I hired a home health aide and I left. My business was going down the tubes, my social life was nonexistent. My best friend from college said, 'Joe, do something for yourself.' So I did; I left. I neglected my needs for too long. But I didn't leave Mom alone and my sister was willing to handle some of the problems. So here I am in California…and now I'm just feeling guilty. This caregiver stuff stinks."

Joe, California

As a caregiver you sacrifice so much for the people you love. Hours a day may be spent on caregiver issues that interfere with your work, family, and friends. Women and men express how disheartened they are because they have no time to enjoy their own lives. Giving up your life for the sake of a family member is not only self-destructive but also counterproductive to who you are and what your role is in the family. Think about the words "care" and "giver." By definition it is someone who provides care to another person, it doesn't mean at the expense of his own health and well-being. If you feel that you are a caregiver self-neglecter it is time to change the recording in your head that doesn't allow you to take care of yourself: the recording that says over and over again how much everyone needs you and how you have to be there for your parent, spouse, children, and friends. It is time for you to change that recording, move the dial to another station and take charge of your life. Draw upon the same gusto and strength that you use when you take care of the people you love and help every day. The first step is to stand firm and say out loud, *"This is the day I am going to face myself, decide what it is I need, and then do something about it."* Keep in mind that when you help yourself you are not a neglectful son or daughter or self-centered. It just means that you are wise enough to take care of yourself.

Here are several suggestions to get you started. Remember that changing old habits and the recording in your head takes time. Read on for a new beginning.

- Tune in to your thoughts and actions. If you have been listening to a mental recording that compels you to do too much for everyone, change the recording. Say to yourself, "I don't have to see Mom every day; I can try and see her every other day." Or, "I don't have to make dinner for my family every night; I can order a pizza and sit back and relax." Taking time for yourself does not make you a bad daughter or a disinterested mom, it simply makes you a human being who has needs that you can fulfill if you take the time to help yourself.

- Reach out for the help you need. You don't have to make this journey alone. As a caregiver you need to reach out to the people you trust to help you through the difficult times. As one caregiver said, *"I have a friend who is on speed dial. She's kind and insightful and allows me to talk, cry, and fuss all I want. When we finish talking (usually I do most of the talking), I feel a sense of relief and I can go on and do what I have to do. If I have any words of advice to caregivers it would be that each and every one of you needs someone in her life who allows them the freedom and safety to fuss."*

- Pamper yourself. Please don't read this and say, "They have got to be kidding, I don't have a minute to myself." The truth is that just about everyone can take a few minutes a day to do something relaxing. Walk around the block, sit in a tub of bubbles, have a manicure, give yourself a manicure, read a book, buy a hat or hit a bucket of golf balls. It doesn't matter what you do as long as the focus is on YOU.

- Do it your way. The world around you can guide you and help you every step of the way as you take care of your loved ones. You are a unique individual and you will learn, sometimes by trial and error, what works the best for you and your family. Unless your parent is in danger, there is no right or wrong rule of eldercare. Be open to suggestions and let your heart and mind do the rest.

Being a caregiver is an exhausting job and it is just one of the jobs that you do so well. Take care of yourself, remember not only because your family needs you but also because you deserve it.

Protect Yourself from Self-Neglect

You have the ability and power to reach out for what you need for continued strength and confidence. It is time to say NO to self-neglect and YES to taking care of yourself.

- **I will practice self-awareness.** I will listen to my heart and head and take the time I need and want. Once I decide what is best for me, I will practice ways to help myself.
- **I will prioritize.** I will learn how to take one step at a time in order to enhance my quality of life.
- **I will be kind to myself.** I will remind myself that I have self-worth. I will treat myself with the same respect and love as I treat my loved one.

B. SURVIVING SAYING *NO*

Why is it so hard to say NO? What obstacles do you face? Common sense easily tells us that it's in our best interest and the best interest of our families to take care of ourselves while we care for others. Healthy and well-rested caregivers have more energy and are able to think more clearly, which helps them handle problems with greater efficiency.

Caregivers often feel that saying NO means they are abandoning a parent or sibling. In other words, Mom will think you don't love her anymore. That statement is far from true.

We may not recognize that we've done our best. We continue to search for ways we could have done better, should have done better . . . it's called the "shoulda', woulda', coulda' syndrome" and it carries an enormous capacity for guilt. No one can tell you how to feel, and no one can tell you not to feel guilty. You may even carry a little guilt with you all your life, but that shouldn't preclude you from *having* a life.

Eldercare 911 repeats this message in several chapters because it is one of the most important you'll ever receive: *Once you've done your best, no one has the right to ask more of you.*

Take the time to learn how to let the people in your life know how wonderfully strong and capable you are. Sometimes the only way your family will acknowledge your ongoing service to them is if you recognize your amazing efforts first and set limits that serve notice on them: *"I am doing a good job. Instead of making my life more miserable, help me. Or be quiet and let me do my job."* When you mean what you say, they will see your strength and acquiesce to your feelings and needs.

This worksheet will help you get started.

C. WORKSHEET: PROTECTING YOURSELF FROM TOXIC PEOPLE

Caregiving can be a difficult job on the best of days. It becomes even more frustrating when toxic people are involved. Use this worksheet to begin saying NO and to help protect yourself and your quality of life.

The most toxic person in my life is _____.
She/He disrupts my life by doing this: _____

_____

_____

_____

Beginning today I will help myself say NO by setting these two boundaries to help:

❏ Free up my time ❏ Decrease my frustration

❏ Lessen my anger ❏ Regain Control

1._____

_____

_____

_____

2._____

_____

_____

_____

I know that saying NO might be difficult, but I am determined to

❑ Stop the negative effects this toxic behavior has on me.

❑ Acknowledge my strengths and contributions to my family.

❑ Allow myself more than one try to learn how to say NO.

Read these affirmations aloud every day to help keep you strong while you begin setting limits:

Saying NO doesn't mean that I am abandoning my loved one; it means I am setting realistic limits.

Saying NO doesn't mean that I don't care; it means that I am taking care of myself while taking care of someone else.

Saying NO doesn't mean I'm selfish; it means I will no longer let toxic people burden me.

Saying NO means I know that I am doing a good job *within my limits* and I believe my family owes me their recognition as well.

D. MY JOURNAL

Putting thoughts and feelings on paper can help us understand them more clearly. What bothers you? What changes do you want to make? What or who are you grateful for? When you read what you've written, you may see a new pathway to help resolve stressful issues. Use this page as a safe place to express your feelings. For example:

   "I'm getting to the point where I can't stand my brother Tom anymore. He thinks he has all the answers. I might listen to something he said if he'd ever spent even one full day caring for Dad, but he has no concept of reality. I'm sick of him, but what can I do? He's still my brother. Maybe if I explained my feelings he would understand. It's worth a try, because if he still acts like a jerk, I can ignore him without feeling guilty."

_____
_____
_____
_____
_____
_____
_____
_____
_____
_____
_____
_____
_____
_____
_____
_____
_____
_____
_____

E. TIP SHEET

- Recognize that saying NO doesn't mean you are abandoning your parent; it means you understand the need to care for yourself as well.
- Identify your toxic relative's strategy so you can formulate your defense.
- Use the sample responses in this chapter to help create your own way to say NO.
- Once you say NO, do not change your mind or negotiate; change the topic or end the conversation.
- Let your family know you are doing the best you can *within your limits* and you expect them to recognize your hard work.

7

LONG-DISTANCE CAREGIVING

A. WHY YOU NEED A LONG-DISTANCE SUPPORT SYSTEM

"It goes like this: the doctor says mom needs twenty-four-hour supervision; my uncle says she needs a little help with cleaning and cooking, and Dad says don't worry about it, he's got it under control. If the conflicting descriptions of her health weren't bad enough, the part about my demented dad having it 'under control' is enough to scare me silly. He couldn't find his way to the store and home again. So I call the airport, travel three thousand miles, accomplish almost nothing, and come back again out several hundred dollars poorer and dreading the next call. It's hard to believe we landed on the moon and can't fix this."

Pat, Iowa

"If my mother's doctor said, 'Rose, tomorrow morning I'm going to cut off your head,' she would tell me, 'Tomorrow the doctor's giving me something for my headache.' I never know if she's telling me the truth or trying to protect me from what's really

177

happening. Actually, I'm not sure that she remembers enough of what he says to give me the information I want to hear. When she repeats what the doctor said to her, it reminds me of the game 'telephone' that we played as kids. Each person whispers a message to the next person. The last person in the group recites the message out loud, and everyone laughs because the message is always so different from the way it was when the first person whispered it. Each time I call my mother, it's like our own private game of 'telephone.' Only this time I'm not with my friends and I'm not laughing. I'm twelve hundred miles away. I know I'll still be staring at the clock at three AM because I'll be too worried to sleep. It happens every time. I'll call her doctor from the office in the morning, but then I'll have to go out to see a client, and I won't be there when he calls back. I need him to connect what she told me with her actual diagnosis. I have a really bad feeling. Right now, it may only mean taking time off from work (again) and going to visit her so I can see for myself. One day, I assume, her life may depend on it. How am I supposed to do this? I expected to have to help her when she got older, but I'm an accountant, not a mind reader."

Louise, Oregon

You're an accomplished user of a support system if you've relied on a tutorial for your computer, had a service contract for your car or appliances, contracted for day care, or employed a cleaning service, a travel service, or a sitter for your child. You instinctively recognize the benefits of retaining experts to help in certain areas. You hired these services because they save you time and money. They also provide peace of mind. We use support systems to help our lives run more smoothly. In fact, most of us would probably be lost without these everyday helpers.

Elder caregiving support is critical. As one daughter said to the care manager she hired for her mother, "I have car insurance for my car, and I have you for my mother." When you are hundreds or thousands of miles away from your ill parent, you need all the help you can get. Instant access to accurate information and services can help you when you need to intervene quickly. If you don't have a clear picture of your parent's situation, you may not be able to identify and act on all your options. Your ability to make informed decisions will certainly be impaired. What would you do if one of these two common occurrences happened to you?

> "When my mother explained that she didn't send my son a birthday present because she forgot, I was hurt, but I believed her. Now I wonder if there's more to it. She seems to forget things all the time, including recipes that she's baked from memory for years. Last time I visited, we went shopping together, and I could swear she wasn't going to buy her favorite cookies. When I teased her about not putting them in her basket and asked if she was dieting, she gave me a totally blank look and said, 'What cookies, dear?' Last night I called her and told her that I was worried about her constantly forgetting things. She said, 'There's nothing to worry about, dear. The doctor told me I had a little problem with my memory, but that I shouldn't worry about it because it's not Alzheimer's disease.' I don't know whether to believe her or take time off work, park my kids at their friends' houses for a few days, and go help her right away."
>
> *Becky, Indiana*

> "The hospital called to tell me that my father-in-law was brought in by emergency rescue, but by the time I got the message off my voice mail, he had been discharged and was home. When I reached him, he said he was fine. He just felt a little dizzy and the restaurant panicked and called 911. Is he really safe alone? Or do we need to go to him immediately and assess the situation for ourselves?"
>
> *Ruth, Illinois*

If you aren't sure what to do, you are absolutely right! Without more information, it's impossible to correctly evaluate your next move. Reliable reporting can make the difference between a calm telephone call and a last-minute airline ticket or an emergency five-hour drive in the middle of the night. It doesn't matter if you see your parent every month or once a year. If a problem occurs, you'll need the same information and objective assessment of his diagnosis and current status to determine the most effective and efficient way to help.

Long-distance caregivers usually count the telephone among their greatest assets, but it can also create unnecessary fear and confusion. It is helpful as a caregiving tool only if you can rely on the person at the other end of the line for an accurate description of your parent's condition and needs. Many caregivers are faced with uncertainty because they receive conflicting accounts similar to these:

> "My mother and I lived so far from each other that we only visited two or three times during the year, but we talked at least twice each week. We always asked each other, 'What are you making for dinner tonight?' One day I realized she hadn't asked me that question during the last few phone calls. When I asked her, she said something like, 'Same old, same old. I'm tired of cooking. Let's talk about something different.' It seemed reasonable at the time. A month or so later my aunt Sal called, upset because my parents had lost a lot of weight. They always had had enough food in the house for the whole neighborhood, but not anymore. My aunt said she found an old, inedible apple on the counter and some spoiled milk and rotting lunch meat in the refrigerator. There was stale bread and other foods like that. I called my mother, who said, 'Sal's upset over nothing. I told her, the doctor wanted us to lose weight. We're on a diet, so I don't stock a lot of food anymore.' I wasn't sure whether to believe my mother or my aunt. I called my brother. His response was, 'Are you kidding? Mom never missed a meal in her life. She and Dad needed to lose that weight. Good for them.' He seemed to be right. My aunt might have overreacted. I didn't know what to believe, so I didn't do anything. About three months later, adult protective services called and said a neighbor had called them to help. My parents were suffering from dehydration and malnutrition. I had twenty-four hours to get there and set up around-the-clock homecare or move my dad into an assisted living facility and my mother into an Alzheimer's facility. If I didn't, they would

become wards of the state. I went, but I wasted a lot of time before I got there. I didn't even have a phone book to call ahead and make appointments with homecare or their doctor or anyone. I did have the sense of mind to call a geriatric care manager. She called adult protective services, got the report, then got a homecare worker that same day. She met me at my parents' home when I arrived. If I hadn't had her support, I'm not sure I could have coped with what I found. I'll always carry a load of guilt and pain from not acting when my aunt called."

Carol, Oregon

The best time to establish your support network is *before* you need it. That way you'll be able to act quickly when a problem arises. If you are beyond the "before you need it" stage and deep in the middle of caregiving, it's not too late. If you don't have a network that responds when you need it, promise yourself that you are going to try to change that today. It takes patience and time, but the rewards far outweigh the effort. When your network is in place, you will have the names and telephone numbers of professionals near your parent who can quickly respond to any emergency at any time of day or night. They will be able to advise you if the situation is severe enough for you to "come immediately" or if you can stay where you are without an undue amount of anxiety. They will be advocates for your parent and work on your behalf regardless of whether you are nearby or far away.

B. CREATING YOUR LONG-DISTANCE SUPPORT NETWORK

Denise and Lydia shared very different stories with us:

"My father died ten years ago. My mother and I always talked about how lucky we were that we really liked each other and would always be there for each other if one of us had a problem. But when she really needed me, I was almost helpless. My ten-year-old daughter was in the hospital at the same time as my mother. I tried to help my mother without leaving my daughter but I didn't even have a Scottsdale phone book to look up homecare agencies or other senior services. I knew she had expressed some of her wishes in a document, but she mentioned it only once, and I'd never seen it. I assumed she also had other advance directives, but I didn't have a copy of them and neither did the hospital. I'd never met her lawyer and didn't know his name. Not that it mattered. Without her consent, I'm sure he wouldn't have talked to me anyway. Her doctor talked to me, but the hospital wouldn't count my voice in any decisions without my mother's consent. As soon as I could, I flew to Scottsdale but didn't have a key to Mom's apartment and couldn't get in until I found a neighbor who did. I didn't have any of her friends' full names or telephone numbers. As I struggled through this fiasco, I realized that I didn't know enough about her life to help her. The peace of mind I felt knowing that we had each other for support vanished."

Denise, California

"Fortunately for me, my father was a very smart man. After his first heart attack, he insisted that I meet his attorney so I would know what to do if he couldn't take care of things anymore. He also insisted that I meet his and Mom's doctor. I didn't want to talk about it, but he said he didn't care what I wanted. It had nothing to do with me. He needed me involved because the only way he could protect Mom was to make sure I understood all his plans and knew her doctor. If anything happened to him, he wanted to make sure I knew whom to call for support and information. He always took care of the legal and financial details. Mom's job was taking care of him. He didn't want her to have to be burdened with new responsibilities when he died."

Lydia, Alabama

When you begin thinking about your support network, you'll probably find you need help in three key areas. A professional geriatric care manager can help you with all of them, or you may ask for assistance from your parent's friend, neighbor, doctor, or anyone you believe can help. The three areas are:

1. *Information.* To stay informed, you'll need to be able to communicate regularly with someone who has recently seen your parent and who can provide an objective evaluation of whether or not your parent needs assistance.

2. *Assessment.* You may need a geriatric care manager who can assess your parent for his current status and potential risks. Although some professionals conduct telephone assessments, you will have a more accurate picture with an in-person assessment conducted in your parent's normal surroundings. This is a task for a professional. Can your mother walk without risk of falling? Has your father's vision changed enough to make driving unsafe? Has a formerly spotless house become untidy or dirty? Has your mother stopped refilling one of her medications without her doctor's approval? Any one of these changes can be a precursor to a problem that needs medical attention. None of them can be identified over the telephone.

3. *Assistance.* A responsible person who lives in the same area as your parent and who can act on your behalf is essential to your peace of mind. For example, if you need someone to interview a homecare worker or if your father needs a variety of services to provide support for him, a geriatric care manager may be your best option for local assistance.

If your parents are able to participate in building their network of helpers, they may be your first line of support. You have every reason to believe that if you clearly explain why you want their help, they will be happy to actively participate. If asked, *"Whom would you call if you became ill and needed help?"* many parents would answer, *"My children."* Others might answer, *"I don't know."* Let your mother know that you want to be there for her, but you need her help now so that you can be effective at a later time when she needs you. She may not understand that her physicians might want her written consent before they discuss her health with you. She may be surprised to learn that a hospital is free to act without consulting you unless you have legal authority to speak for her and can produce documents to prove it. These are excellent reasons for her to introduce you to her physicians and other professional counselors. If she doesn't want to talk about it or involve you, explain that it's unfair for her to expect your help unless she gives you the knowledge and materials you need to do a good job. Let her know that you don't *want* her to become ill or dependent, but you are being practical. The reality is that the longer your parents live, the more chance they have of becoming ill and dependent on others for at least a short period of time.

Above all, be certain your mother understands that you do not want to take any action now. Everything you do and any documents you create will be used only if and when she is too ill to make decisions on her own behalf. At that point, she will need an advocate. If you don't want the responsibility, or she doesn't want you to have it, then suggest that she appoint another person. If she tells you she doesn't want to burden you or anyone else, gently explain that you will be many times more burdened if you can't help her when she needs you, because you don't have enough information to know her wishes or to make an informed decision. If you need help to find the strength to approach your parent, consider what may happen if you don't:

"My mother was always so independent. It never occurred to me to invade her privacy and ask to meet her lawyer or doctor. While I was waiting for her to come out of surgery, I realized how little I really knew about her life since she moved to Florida. She knew all about mine because I always told her everything. A friend of hers came to the waiting room, and we talked. I told her that my mother had consistently told me everything was fine. Her friend said, 'She didn't want you to worry, she didn't want to be a burden to you.' I must've felt really guilty because I yelled, 'Didn't she think a call in the middle of the night from a hospital announcing that she was in intensive care would burden me? I might have been able to help if I'd known what was going on.' Of course, I should have known something was wrong. There were plenty of signs, but I never pushed her for answers past 'Mom, are you sure you're okay?' I took the easy way out and believed her when she said, 'I'm just a little tired.' I got so used to her being tired, I forgot to notice she had never recovered."

Rene, Nebraska

If your parent is still concerned about privacy, reiterate that you only want her to share the information that you will need if she becomes too ill to help herself—and that you, or whomever she appoints, will use that information only in those same circumstances.

Be specific and practical. Once your mother agrees to help you, don't give her time to change her mind. Make your appointments right away. If your mother is ill, it may be harder to obtain her help, but it's very important to try. If she is ill and refuses your assistance, get help from her physician or hire a geriatric care manager.

Consider these categories for your network.

Geriatric Care Managers

Registered nurses or social workers are trained to work under difficult and uncertain circumstances. Their job is to be advocates for the care receiver by creating a care plan that takes into account healthcare, quality-of-life issues, and financial status. They work with or without a physician's supervision. They work closely with local resources and can usually provide clients with quick access to many types of assistance, including homecare workers, attorneys, home repairs, and government entitlements. Some operate only during normal business hours; others provide twenty-four-hour/seven-day accessibility.

"I'd been with my mother-in-law during most of her stay in the hospital, but eventually I had to go back home to my kids and my job. When I talked to her after she was moved to the rehabilitation facility, she told me that it only took her a few hours to realize that she'd never get well in there. She said, 'I haven't been that frightened in a long time. It smelled, the workers never smiled and had no time for me, and my roommate groaned and complained constantly. Then John walked in. Thank God for him. I knew he'd help me get out of there.' John was her geriatric care manager. My husband and I hired him when the hospital told us she was being discharged. We should've hired him before that. If I had, my mother-in-law might never have had to go through that horrible experience. He talked to Mom and to the administrative people, and then he called me. He confirmed her report and suggested we talk to her insurance company and try to get permission to move her to another rehab facility. I'm embarrassed to say this, but if it hadn't been for John, I might not have believed my mother-in-law's description. I might have assumed she was just upset over being there."

Julie, Texas

Elder Law Attorneys

Because elder law attorneys specialize in assisting older clients, they have an in-depth understanding of various needs, including government programs, advance directives, durable powers of attorney, and guardianship law. Laws and requirements regarding these issues often differ from state to state, so it's best to work with an elder law attorney in the area where your parent lives. They are used to responding to emergency needs and are usually familiar with eldercare resources in their communities. It is unlikely that your parent will have established an association with an elder law attorney, so this contact will be new for all of you. Ask your geriatric care manager, the Area Agency on Aging or Alzheimer's Association in your parent's community, or check with the National Academy of Elder Law Attorneys (www.naela.org) for a list of attorneys located near your parent's home.

"The Alzheimer's Association explained that state laws governed many of the things I had to address with regard to my mother. They suggested that our best choice was an elder law attorney in her area. I had never even heard of an elder law attorney, but I followed their advice. She was great. I got a real education on Arizona law. After we talked to her, we had a better idea of how we needed to proceed to safeguard my mother's future. I think the most impressive thing was her gentleness with my mother. She asked lots of questions, but didn't hurry Mom. She just waited patiently for the answer. She even asked me to leave the room so she could ask questions in private."

Ginger, New Jersey

Other Attorneys

If your parent has established a relationship with other attorneys, you want to meet them. A face-to-face meeting will let them know that you are thoughtful and caring enough to prepare for the future, and will help you feel more comfortable if you need to call them for advice or other services. They will be able to draw up powers of attorney that will release your parent's assets to help care for him. They can also prepare durable powers of attorney, which will give you the authority to make healthcare decisions when your parent is legally unable to do so for himself, and advance directives that instruct you and others as to whether, when, and how your parent wishes to stop treatment.

Physicians

Meeting your mother's physicians is a must. When your mother is ill, these are the people both she and you will turn to for information, guidance, and recommendations on treatment. It is equally important that her physicians know you and can locate you when it is appropriate. Doctors are happy to meet children who can help them keep their patients well. A personal meeting now will help smooth the way for better communication, greater cooperation, and more trust when your parent is ill.

Friends and Neighbors

You want to meet at least one or two of your parent's close friends and neighbors. If your mother becomes ill at home or is hospitalized, her friends can help you a great deal. As Sonia found out, one of them probably has an extra key to her apartment. "*A friend of my mother's called and said my mother was in the hospital. She said she'd meet me at my mother's house when I came in and give me the key. Just let her know when I was arriving. I had never met the woman, but I'd have had a lot worse time without her.*" Your mother's good friend or the neighbor she has coffee with probably knows where most things are in her apartment, where she shops, whom she calls for repairs, and so forth. All of this will come in handy. Her friends and neighbors will also be anxious to find out how she's progressing. You can set up a system to keep one or two of them informed and ask them to call the others. That may cut down on the telephone calls you have to make, which will save you time and allow you a few moments of peace and quiet at a busy time.

Succeeding in creating a support team now can eliminate many hours of anxiety and frustration later. Your ability to reach the people who hold the legal documents and control the finances may make the difference between being able to afford the care your mother needs or having to postpone it until you can pay for it. Bringing in help immediately may make the difference between your parent going to a nursing home or remaining at home. Planning ahead so that you can access the correct resource on the first call may save you considerable time that you need for other obligations or an entire trip.

C. PREPARING FOR YOUR VISIT

Whether this is your first trip or your twentieth, unless it's a last-minute trip triggered by an emergency, plan ahead. Each visit may involve different interventions. You can make the most of your time and accomplish much more if you prioritize the things you have to do before you leave. Being organized may also allow you to spend more quality time with your parent. The hope is that when it is time for you to return back home, you will have a feeling of comfort and peace of mind.

If you plan to stay a few days or several weeks, some of the most significant people in your network will be the family you leave at home. Your son may need extra time and special attention to understand clearly why you will not be there for his birthday or his team's championship game. Your partner may resent that you will be absent for a critically important business event or during your anniversary. This is a time to open your heart. Explain what happened to your parent and why you have to be there. Tell them how badly you feel about leaving them and how much you will miss them. Explain to your children that you are helping your parent just as they would help you. Tell them it's important to you that they understand why you have to go. Involve your family in your crisis so that they won't feel left out. Ask for their help in taking over some of your chores while you are gone so that when you return, you will be able to spend all your time with them instead of catching up on things left undone.

We've discussed how vital it is to meet the professionals involved in your parent's life. This caregiver's experience emphasizes the point:

"I hadn't seen my father in three or four months. I was shocked. He looked much thinner. His eyes had lost their twinkle, and he seemed to have lost his enthusiasm for everything. He'd just say, 'Not right now, sweetheart. I'm a little tired.' I checked the garage, and I don't think he'd been in his workshop in ages. He used to build things continuously. Half the people on the block are using something he made for them. I asked him if he still played cards every week, and he said, 'Sure. I've played cards for thirty years,' but I didn't believe him. When we went to temple Friday night, I really got frightened. My father used to sing so loud and so off-key, he threw half the congregation off. He was like that with everything. His enthusiasm made us all tired! But this time he just sort of mouthed the words. I sat up half the night trying to figure out what to do. It wasn't an emergency, so I had no hope of reaching his doctor on the weekend. It certainly wasn't an emergency room case, so going to the hospital for help wasn't an option. I rationalized that Dad was fine, just getting older, and I left. It didn't take much longer for him to end up in the hospital. He'd developed diabetes, and no one knew. Luckily, he's under control now, but he could have died. What if he had passed out while he was driving and killed someone? Or what if he hadn't passed out at all and we still didn't know he was ill? He might have lost his sight or even his foot. It didn't need to be that way. I learned my lesson. For my father-in-law, my husband and I recently had a get-acquainted visit with his doctor. He told us not to hesitate to call him if we ever felt that my father-in-law needed medical attention. That's the way it should have been with my father."

Sara Beth, South Carolina

These few simple steps can help eliminate a substantial amount of frustration:

- If your visit is preplanned, consider this a golden opportunity. Call as far in advance as possible for an appointment, and meet the professionals your father depends on and others you may want to retain. Be flexible in the times you can meet, and be on time for your appointment. Have your questions ready before the meeting starts. Bring a pad and pen to write down the answers. Most professionals work on a time-based fee-for-service arrangement. To avoid unpleasant surprises, ask if you will be charged for the time spent in the meeting.
- If you have time before you leave, contact the Area Agency on Aging, Alzheimer's Association, or other appropriate service organizations closest to where your parent lives. They can provide you with information regarding eldercare services in your parent's community. You can call ahead and set up appointments with homecare agencies, visit day care centers, surviving spouse support groups and counseling, or other support services you expect to need.
- If your parent is hospitalized, call and make an appointment with the physician, nurse, or social worker in charge of your parent's care before you visit. This will go a long way toward helping to assure that you get the answers you need to act on your parent's behalf. Do not go empty-handed. Write your questions out before the meeting and be prepared to make notes of the answers. If you have hired a geriatric care manager, ask her to accompany you to the meeting. Her experience has taken her through situations just like yours many times before. It's her job to know how to make certain that your parent receives all the help the system can possibly provide. She may be able to steer you toward services that are covered by government benefits or your parent's insurance. Her input can be invaluable.
- Start a simple, easy-to-access file before you go. Keep a pad in your purse or use your computer to help you keep track of contact names, telephone numbers, and all the essential information you will gather as you talk to everyone involved. Carry this file with you so that you can refer back to it wherever and whenever you need. Having all this data at your fingertips may radically reduce your stress and make your job much easier.
- If your parent is ill, it's even more important to surround him with

people he loves. Consider bringing photographs you can leave with him, or a videocassette tape of your siblings, children, or grandchildren. Spending time together talking about good times will make your visit more enjoyable.

During Your Visit

Take time to collect all the data you will need to follow up and feel more in control when you return home. If you made the trip because of a crisis or emergency, you can successfully use some of these suggestions to help you focus on what you need to do to help reestablish as much control as possible. No matter how long or short the trip is, use the time to your advantage by following these few steps:

- Prepare a list of information, as much as you can find, regarding your parent's medical diagnosis and the names, addresses, and telephone numbers of her primary care physician as well as any treating specialists.
- Include all medical, long-term care, life, and homeowner's insurance policy names, policy numbers, addresses, telephone numbers, and contacts. List all local emergency contacts.
- If your parent has a private caregiver, include the name of the company, the caregiver's name, and the supervisor's name.
- Try to find out if someone has a key to your mother's house or apartment, and write down the name and telephone number of that person.
- Obtain a local telephone directory from your parent's community. Take it home with you so you will have instant access to the names, telephone numbers, and locations of physicians, pharmacies, hospitals, and community agencies.
- Evaluate your parent's home for risk/safety factors that apply to your parent as she functions today. (Chapter 3 includes a complete safety check.)

Don't be upset if you don't have everything you want right away. You may have to do a little digging and research. But when you are in your parent's home, you will have the opportunity to search for the information you need to complete your list.

You may need to accomplish other specific tasks, and take care of new medical, social, or living situations and circumstances. For example, you may want to review and update all of the important information you have, and add newly diagnosed medical conditions or recently prescribed medications. If your parent is living alone in her own home and now requires homecare, contact at least two or three agencies, compare the costs, the experience level of the workers, and the availability of services. (You can find helpful information and worksheets about hiring a homecare worker in chapter 11.) Try to obtain a referral to a specific agency from a geriatric professional, a family member in the community, or your parent's friend. If your parent is in the hospital, meet with the physicians and any other professionals involved in your parent's care. You'll want to talk about discharge planning and the options you have to keep your parent comfortable and safe at home or in an assisted living or nursing facility. Think about hiring a geriatric care manager who will visit your parent on a regular basis in your absence and keep in close contact with you. These ongoing preparations and connections are designed to help you feel more in control, which may help reduce your stress and anxiety levels.

After Your Visit

After your visit, try to organize the new information you acquired during your stay with your parent. Be particularly aware of changes in your parent's status:

- Is Mom less able to function in her environment?
- Can she no longer care for herself independently?
- Have her eating or grooming habits changed for the worse?
- Have her physical surroundings fallen into disrepair and do they present a safety risk?
- Would Mom have trouble safely evacuating in an emergency such as a fire?

If you answered *yes* to any of these questions, it may be time to consider relocating Mom. Chapter 3 will help you clearly evaluate the risks and safety issues involved and help you make this important and difficult decision.

Even if your parent's status has not changed, you may experience some uncomfortable feelings such as anxiety, sadness, and loss. Remember that these feelings should be less intense because you've become more informed, prepared, and connected during this visit than ever before. The information that you gathered and the preparations and contacts that you made should help give you a sense of control and serve you well when you are hundreds or thousands of miles away.

You can help yourself stay calm by staying connected.

- Develop a level of trust by keeping in contact with healthcare professionals and caregivers you've chosen as your support system.
- Speak to your parent's physician on a regular basis, and take every opportunity to update the healthcare information in your file.
- Decide how often you and your parents will speak on the telephone and try to adhere to that schedule. If they become used to talking to you once or twice a week, they will enjoy speaking to you and look forward to that routine.
- If you notice a change in your parent's behavior, make a mental note to be especially vigilant during your next conversation. If the unusual behavior persists, alert your parent's doctor. Call another member of your support team and ask her to visit your parent and provide you with a full report.

During this visit, you gave yourself two wonderful gifts: updated, important information and good connections with people you can talk to before you hit the panic button. Be pleased with yourself because you were able to accomplish so much on your trip. Now, you feel more in control and know that when the next crisis comes, you will be prepared and not have to face it alone.

D. WORKSHEET: ORGANIZING FOR LONG-DISTANCE CAREGIVING

Long-distance caregiving is difficult under the best of circumstances, but you can reduce your stress and be more effective if you work toward organizing the information you need and establishing a local support system in your parent's area.

Don't be discouraged by the amount of information you need, just take it one step at a time and do your best.

This worksheet will help you take the first step.

1. ❑ I have (❑ I need) a release from my parent authorizing her professional advisors to share ❑ healthcare information ❑ financial information with me.

2. ❑ I already have my network.   ❑ I need to create my network.
   I would like to talk to:

❑ Private geriatric care manager   ❑ My parent's physicians

❑ Elder law attorney   ❑ My parent's friends and neighbors

❑ Attorney for _____ ❑ _____

❑ Community orgs.: _____

_____

_____

To do: _____

3. ❑ I have created (❑ I need to create) a list of telephone numbers I can use to tell me what the situation is in case of an emergency.

❑ My parent's physician(s)   ❑ My parent's neighbor(s)

❑ A reputable homecare agency   ❑ My parent's attorney(s)

❑ Two of my parent's good friends

To do: _____

4. On my next visit, I will:

❑ Bring a list of items I need to discuss with Mom and her advisers.

❑ Bring home a telephone book from Mom's community.

❑ Ask Mom to sign a medical records release form so that her I can discuss her needs with her physician.

❑ Get the name and phone number of anyone who has a key to her house and make sure I have one as well.

❑ Talk to my mother about her current healthcare status.

❑ Find out if Mom has advance directives and a will and talk with her about the importance of completing those documents.

❑ Talk to my mother about a durable power of attorney for healthcare and finances for use only if she becomes incapacitated.

❑ Ask her to introduce me to all her professional advisers.

❑ Schedule time for a safety check of mom's home (see chapter 3).

❑ Talk to Mom about obtaining a Personal Emergency Response System for her safety.

❑ Talk to Mom about obtaining a Safe Return Bracelet for Dad in case he wanders away and can't remember where he lives.

❑ Talk to Mom about what she thinks would make her life easier or safer and put those safeguards in place before I leave.

❑ Work with Mom to be certain she can locate important documents and make copies of them for my files: social security and Medicare/other health insurance ID cards, card, titles, deeds, driver's license; advance directives, will; home, health, life, and auto insurance policies; savings, investment, or loan records.

To do: _____

5. When I schedule my next visit, I will explain my parent's needs to my family so that they will understand the need for my absence and why I'm directing my attention to someone else.

To do: _____

❑ I have made (❑ need to make) arrangements for my family in the event I have to leave suddenly:

❑ My children will be cared for by _____.

❑ My family will remain at home. Their meals, supervision, and other needs will be provided by _____.

❑ My pets will be cared for by _____.

❑ Everyone involved has my cell phone number.

6. ❑ I have (❑ have not) alerted my supervisor that I may need to use my personal days to visit my parents.

For more information, review this chapter.

WORKSHEET: IMPORTANT TELEPHONE NUMBERS

Creating a list of telephone numbers for people who are important for your parent's well-being is a must for every caregiver. Having these numbers at your fingertips will prove invaluable for helping you save time and remain calm in emergencies.

In an emergency, always call 911 first.

1. Family members to contact in an emergency:

Name _____ Tel. _____

Name _____ Tel. _____

Name _____ Tel. _____

2. Physicians:

Name _____ Tel. _____

Name _____ Tel. _____

Name _____ Tel. _____

3. Pharmacy:

Name _____ Tel. _____

4. Neighbors:

Name _____ Tel. _____

Name _____ Tel. _____

Name _____ Tel. _____

5. Friends:

Name _____ Tel. _____

Name _____ Tel. _____

Name _____ Tel. _____

6. Other (geriatric care manager, elder law attorney, financial adviser, bank, transportation service, homecare agency or worker, grocery store, plumber, home repair contractor, or others):

Title _____ Name _____ Tel. _____

Title _____ Name _____ Tel. _____

Title _____ Name _____ Tel. _____

Title _____ Name _____ Tel. _____

Title _____ Name _____ Tel. _____

Title _____ Name _____ Tel. _____

Title _____ Name _____ Tel. _____

Title _____ Name _____ Tel. _____

Title _____ Name _____ Tel. _____

Title _____ Name _____ Tel. _____

E. MY JOURNAL

Expressing our thoughts on paper often helps see our feelings more clearly and that makes it easier to arrive at solutions to our problems. What bothers you? What changes do you want to make? What or whom are you grateful for? Who are angry at? When you read what you've written, you may see a new pathway to help resolve stressful issues. Use this page as a safe place to express your feelings. For example:

"If I have to travel three thousand miles one more time for a false alarm, I'm going to lose my job and maybe my husband. There must be a way to stop this madness, but I'm clueless. That's the answer, I guess. I need to learn the ABCs of long-distance caregiving. I wonder if the American Stroke Association can give me some tips?"

"Mom is very sick in critical care. I am so grateful that we got all her documents together last year. I have copies of everything and a list of where she stored the originals. Oh God, I hope she didn't move them. This

situation could go from horrible to 'shoot me now' if I have to rummage through her belongings searching for an insurance policy or something else."

_____
_____
_____
_____
_____
_____
_____
_____
_____
_____
_____
_____
_____
_____
_____
_____
_____
_____
_____
_____
_____
_____
_____
_____
_____
_____
_____
_____
_____
_____

_____
_____
_____
_____
_____
_____
_____
_____
_____
_____
_____
_____
_____
_____
_____
_____
_____
_____
_____
_____

F. TIP SHEET

- Use the Organizing for Long-Distance Caregiving worksheet to help create a support network where Mom lives.
- Start a "Mom" file and keep it updated with support network information and legal, financial, and medical documents and needs.
- Talk to my family about my responsibilities and the potential for an emergency trip.
- Talk to my supervisor about using my personal time for an emergency trip.
- Consider alternative housing and/or relocation if Mom needs more help than I can give her from here.

8

WORKING CAREGIVERS: A BALANCING ACT

A. FINDING A BALANCE IN YOUR LIFE

"I sometimes feel as if I can't breathe. My heart is racing, my hands are shaking, and my body feels as if it's in a vice. Why do I feel this way? It's really very simple: everybody needs me and I feel like I am all alone. One day I actually tried to run away from home only to find that my head and thoughts come with me wherever I go. Funny thing about thoughts and feelings, they are very hard to turn off. I need to find a way to make my life better."

Nancy, Pennsylvania

"My life is one big question mark. I never know what's going to happen next. I can't believe that a friend actually called me on Wednesday and asked me to meet her on Saturday. I told her I can't book anything that far in advance. She asked me if I was kidding, and I said to her, 'believe it.' My father was diagnosed with Alzheimer's and I was promoted to store manager. I don't plan anything, because anything can happen at anytime."

Mary, New Hampshire

"I am an only child and my father relies on me for everything. I have my own small business and I have to be available for my clients. My father calls my office and nags my secretary until I get on the phone. I admit I can't do it all and I really don't want to. I'm sorry for him, I really am, but I cannot be his entertainment, cook, and literal bottle washer. I want a life. I deserve a life."

Sam, Washington, DC

Mary, Nancy, and Sam are not alone. Many of you are living on a tightrope. The line is thin and the rope is wobbly as you try to do everything you can and not fall. The effort it takes to stay on the rope can often result in your heart racing, your hands shaking, or anxiety over what will happen next. How long can your body, mind, and spirit go on before you simply fall off the rope? The answer is clear: working caregivers need help and support from family members as well as geriatric specialists in order to lead well-balanced lives.

You may have time-consuming jobs, and children, spouses, or significant others who want and need you. Along comes your new role as a caregiver for an aging parent, grandparent, aunt, or uncle. Just when you think that you can't do any more than you are doing, you manage to fit one more thing into an already shrinking day. A caregiver said, *"There are days when I can't sleep or eat because I'm too tired. I know that sounds strange. My body is exhausted, yet my mind continues to create more and more lists."*

Taking control of your life is not easy, but we know that you can do it. Remember that you are extraordinarily gifted. It shows by the way you take care of everyone around you. So many of you share one thing in common; you forget about the most important person in the caregiver experience: you. As you learn to balance your personal and work life, remember that you have the right to take care of yourself and enjoy the benefits you find in having peace of mind.

Spouse or Significant Other

In the 1940s and 50s the family was primarily composed of a mother, father, and two or more children. Parental roles appeared clear: Dad worked outside the home and Mom took care of the house and children. This was what we experienced as children and this was what we expected. Today, there are many configurations that make up a wonderful, complete family, including the classic two-parent household in which Mom is a homemaker or working outside the home, single-parent homes, homosexual couples, as well as second and third marriages, and combined families. Our understanding of the word "family" is different, but one thing remains true: the relationship between the adults is extremely important to the foundation of the family. To remain healthy in body and mind, adults need other adults for companionship, love, socialization, and friendship. Keeping your adult relationship alive, fulfilling, and peaceful adds to the health and well-being of your children. As a working caregiver, this relationship is critical to provide you with a balance in your life. Try to make time for yourself and your partner; it will be worthwhile for all of you.

Ask yourself the following questions:

1. Do I often feel too busy to spend time with my spouse or significant other?
2. Do I often feel tired and agitated?
3. Do I find myself snapping at my significant other over petty issues?
4. Do I put the needs of my parents, children, and/or boss over the needs of my significant other?
5. Do I feel as if I am avoiding my loved one because there is less and less we seem to have in common?
6. Do I work long hours and never seem to have a full day off?

If you said *yes* to one or more of these questions you may want to begin mending your relationship. This is not easy to do, but it will be worth it for both of you. As you begin the process of building a better relationship for the future, keep in mind that making changes will help you regain a more balanced and less stressful life. Try one idea at a time and use the suggestions below that work the best for you.

- Set aside a specific time to talk to your spouse or significant other about what is going on in your lives. Some couples may live together; others may live apart but see one another often. No matter what your particular circumstance you may be surprised to learn that many couples really don't understand what the other person copes with on a daily basis.

- Ask for help. You carry so many burdens alone that you may have forgotten three very simple words: *I need help!* Once you say them, you will be surprised at how good you feel. First steps are always the hardest, but often the most satisfactory.

- Talk about a specific activity you can do together. One caregiver wrote, "*My husband loves to play golf; I hate it. I do like miniature golf and I thought we could play together. My husband was thrilled because he was playing a game he enjoys, and I was having a good time. Most importantly it brought us together.*" Another caregiver shared this idea. "*When we were first married my wife and I enjoyed our Saturday night dates. Children and work took over our lives and we lost our time together. We finally decided to bring back the Saturday night date. I feel like a kid again.*"

- It doesn't have to be sports or cards; just set aside time to watch old movies or cook a meal together. Select one mutually enjoyable activity and have fun. You both deserve it.

- Avoid the pitfalls that come with making promises you likely can't keep. You can do this by not overextending what you can do and what you are actually willing to do. Promising your spouse a night on the town every weekend may be more then you can handle. Start small and begin with a promise of doing something together once every few weeks. If that works out well for a period of time, try to schedule an evening out on a more regular basis. If you're worried about spending money, try to do things you enjoy that are inexpensive, such as visiting museums, going to a movie, and walking in the park.

Many of you forget how important it is to laugh and play. Instinctively, children understand and crave the joy of playtime and laughter. The child in each of you needs a little pampering in order to cope with all the adult things you do.

At the beginning of this chapter we talked about a "caregiver tightrope" that creates a difficult balancing act for caregivers. If you and your spouse or significant other takes the time to laugh and play, you will find that a balance in your life will come naturally. As you begin to feel some relief from the stress in your life, you will begin to function better and more efficiently in your many jobs.

Your Children

> "I love my kids and hate myself for saying this, but they just ask too much of me. I'm a single parent and I work hard. When I come home in the evening I expect my teenaged children to clean up after themselves and even make an attempt at cooking a meal. I'm so tired after fighting with my mother, who thinks I'm the only one who can take her to the pharmacy or grocery store. I know she's old and sick, but I'm sick and tired of struggling every day."
>
> *Kathy, New Jersey*

> "You would think once your children are teenagers they would be self-sufficient, at least to some degree. My wife died three years ago and I'm on my own taking care of my twin sons, myself, and my dad. Dad is eighty-one and he had a stroke. He lives in an assisted living facility near my home, so I visit very often. You'd think that would be enough, but invariably every day one of my kids has a school or social crisis. I know women say they feel tugged in twenty directions, but move over ladies, the men are not far behind."
>
> *Frank, Connecticut*

Being a parent is a tough job. Being the daughter or son of an aging parent is a tough job. If you weigh the burden of both responsibilities you can begin to understand why you drag your feet, and you feel exhausted, anxious, angry, and frustrated.

Even very young children sense when a parent is sad, hurt, or angry. We are not suggesting that you discuss specific medical issues with a very young child, but we do hope that you will take a good look at each of your children as individuals. Think about their age and level of understanding and then to the best of your knowledge and ability try to answer the questions they ask. If you are not comfortable answering your child's questions, you may consider asking a favorite teacher, guidance counselor, or social worker to help you find the best way and words to talk to your child.

Many baby boomers have teenagers living at home and they know instinctively when something is wrong. At times they may feel ignored and isolated because no one includes them in the conversation. A young woman named Ellen said, *"When I was away at school I worried all the time about my grandfather. I knew he was sick, but if I asked my mom she would say, 'Everything is great, just great.' I know my mom, she can't hide her feelings. One day Dad called me and said my grandfather died. I cried, not for him so much, but for both of us. My family didn't give us the chance to say good-bye."*

A caregiver said, *"My sixteen-year-old daughter, Debbie, wants to know why I'm so sad all the time. I don't want to burden her with the fact that my mom was diagnosed with pulmonary disease and she may not live very long. That's not her problem; it's mine."*

Wrong. Caregiving is a family issue. Remember, it's Ellen's grandfather and Debbie's grandmother too, not just your father or mother. In an effort to protect your children you sometimes forget the fact that your children deserve the right to know when life is particularly difficult and trying for you. Often our stressors come across as anger at our children, when in fact they have nothing to do with the immediate problems. Teens may not always express how they feel, but as one fifteen-year-old boy said, *"If I knew what was actually going on, maybe I could have helped."* Conversely, there are many tweens and teens that live their lives in a teenage bubble and do not take an interest in family problems. No matter where your teen falls on the family interest scale he or she has the right to be part of the solution. Some may willingly be a part of the solution, some may be an added burden, and others may fall in the middle by being helpful and understanding at times, and difficult and temperamental at other times. No matter what happens, you need to start talking to each other. There is so much powerful family energy when you keep an open door and communicate with your children. The power lies in words that express feelings, concern, understanding, and hope. Try using special words that are age appropriate and teach your children the importance of family communication. Talking together as a family helps to unburden each and every member.

Remember that a child of any age wants to know and feel that Mom and Dad are all right. Didn't you feel better while growing up when your Mom and Dad were having a good day? Some children will be very receptive and others will shrug their shoulders. Talk to your children and help them to help you reduce your caregiver burden. You have nothing to lose and everything to gain. Try any of these reassuring icebreakers when you feel it is the right time to speak to your child. Children of all ages can be very unpredictable. Don't be surprised if you don't get the response you hoped for the first time around. Try again and keep in mind that you are simply opening a door and planting a seed toward better communication.

You could begin with:

1. "I know I missed your baseball game but I have been very busy taking care of grandma. She was recently diagnosed with a disease called Alzheimer's and it affects her memory. I've been very busy because she has to see so many new doctors. This is very upsetting to me. If you have any questions I'll try my best to answer them. I could use your help with grocery shopping so that I can spend more time with her and you right now. Can you help me?"

2. "You know how Mom and I keep going into the den and closing the door? We tried very hard not to involve you because we didn't want to burden you with our problems. But we really need your help. Grandpa needs heart surgery and grandma can't stay alone. We want her to stay with us for a few weeks, but we need you to share your room with her. Can you help us make her feel more comfortable?"

3. "I know you're angry with me because I have been working double shifts and spending the weekends cooking for Grandma. I can't do too much about my job right now, but if you could help me with the cooking we can get things done twice as fast. I'd really like to spend more time with you. How about getting some easy recipes from a cooking Web site and we can experiment together?"

4. "I know that you have felt neglected lately and I haven't been around much. But I know that you overheard me on the telephone with Grandma's and Grandpa's doctors this morning. They are very sick and we have to move them to a nursing home. I really

need your help packing and decorating their rooms. Maybe you can make a collage of family pictures for the walls. What do you think? Can we work together on this?"

Giving your child a way in which to help you will decrease your burden and will give him a wonderful sense of being a part of something that is very important to the family. Talking together also teaches your child the importance of communication and family ties. These life lessons will be useful throughout your child's life. In time, less stress at home equals a more efficient day at work. Balancing your life will become easier as you learn to ask for help from your entire family.

Your Parents

> "There comes a time in every working woman's life when she needs some peace and quiet. I don't get it. Doesn't my mother realize that I cannot discuss her problems day in and day out while I'm managing a store? Who does she think I am? What does she think I am, super woman? I have got to stop her from calling me repeatedly during the day."
>
> *Linnie, Maine*

> "My father has dementia. There, I said it. I hate to admit that he can't do anything for himself any longer, but the truth is, he can't. I work from home and you guessed it, he lives with me. I'm the son you read about in those sad magazine headlines . . . SON HAS NO LIFE, WORKS TEN HOURS A DAY, TAKES CARE OF AGING FATHER. I'm pathetic. Everyone says to me, 'Get a life Bobby, get a life.' Between my dad and my work, there is no life."
>
> *Bobby, Pennsylvania*

Bobby and Linnie are struggling to keep their lives together. Each one is burdened by a job and a parent who needs constant attention. This is a journey none of you could have anticipated, and no one would ask for. Yet here you are, a working caregiver trying to balance all of your responsibilities.

Let's look at two typical days of a working caregiver. The first scenario is about a caregiver whose parent lives with her and the second scenario is about a caregiver whose father resides in a nursing home. It is time for these caregivers to change their routines and ease their balancing act.

Scenario 1:

Maggie is a forty-nine-year-old married woman working for a large corporation thirty-five miles from her home. She has an eighteen-year-old son who lives at an out-of-town college. Maggie wakes up every morning at five AM. She bathes her mother and dresses her for the day. Unfortunately, her mom refuses to allow the home attendant to bathe her. Maggie shops once a week for groceries and cooks all day Sunday for the week. Her husband doesn't know the first thing about a kitchen or a grocery store and he's made it clear that he doesn't want to know. The home health aide arrives at her house at seven thirty AM and Maggie drives to work. Maggie is the head of security and she is on her feet most of the day. The home health aide calls her at least twice a day. During the day Maggie contacts her mother's doctors and pharmacist. She has one sister who couldn't care less about Maggie's stress level or her mother's care. Maggie leaves work at five PM and drives home. Along the way she picks up milk and bread, and enters the front door at six PM. The home health aide prepares dinner for her mother, but her mother refuses to eat it. She asked her husband to defrost the frozen lasagna but he couldn't find it in the freezer. Dinner is ready for all at eight thirty. Maggie tucks Mom in her bed and hopes that she sleeps through the night. Bedtime for Maggie is as soon as her head lightly touches the pillow.

Here are three suggestions to help Maggie:

1. Increase the homecare hours by an extra hour in the morning and an hour at night. Talk to the homecare agency about the home health aide. Maggie's mom may be refusing to be bathed because the home health aide is not gentle enough or her mom has other issues regarding her personal care. If there really isn't a problem, she may allow the aide to bathe her if Maggie is in the house. Increasing the home health aide's hours at the end of the day will give Maggie a little more time to unwind. She could also ask the home health aide to pick up a few groceries during the day when she takes her mother outdoors for a walk.

2. Before Maggie can delegate any task to her husband she should take the time to explain to him about her busy and often difficult day. Though she works very hard, she should be clear that her job is very demanding and she has a keen sense of responsibility. Once she lays the groundwork, Maggie may feel more comfortable asking for the help she needs. Although she said her husband doesn't know how to "defrost a lasagna," he may be able to help her out in other ways. For example, Maggie's husband may be able to call her mom's doctors or the pharmacist. Maggie can explain the problem to her husband over dinner, provide him with the telephone numbers, and then he can relate the information to her when they have time together.

3. Ask the home health aide to heat up the dinner. The home health aide is not responsible to cook the meal, but if she is asked she will probably heat the food and set the dinner table.

Scenario 2:

John is a sixty-year-old widower. He is an insulin-dependent diabetic whose doctor told him to slow down at least a dozen times. He is an attorney for a small private law firm. John enjoys his work, but he is always tired. His father lives in a nursing home twenty minutes away and John visits him every day. The nursing home is reputable, but John just doesn't trust anyone with his father's care. His brother and sister visit Dad once or twice a week, since they are a caring and close family. John has a thirty-eight-year-old daughter and three grandchildren. Between his job and his dad he never sees his daughter or grandchildren. As a matter of fact, John's youngest granddaughter asked his daughter if "Grandpa is in heaven with Grandma." This statement says it all. Here are three suggestions to help John:

1. Stop and listen to your doctor. Visiting every day is not only unnecessary, but it is detrimental to John's physical and emotional well-being. Since his brother and sister visit once or twice a week, John could ask them to report back to him after their visits.

2. Trust is important for peace of mind. As a concerned caregiver, John researched and talked to many people about nursing homes. He educated himself about what to expect. John needs to begin to build a trusting relationship. The first step for John is to talk to a

staff member involved in his dad's care such as a nurse or social worker. Begin to build a relationship with that person and, in time, ask for help. This is not a blind trust and John should continue to monitor his dad's condition. John may find that he can rely on other people to help care for his father and in turn reduce the burden on himself.

3. Working caregivers need time to play and enjoy life. John will begin to feel better once he agrees that his siblings can be reliable reporters and they can report to him once or twice a week about his dad's condition. He will also begin to recognize which staff members are helpful and most capable of taking care of his dad. With a little time on his hands, John will find the time to spend with his daughter and his grandchildren.

Working caregivers like Maggie and John could be you. Allowing your caregiving responsibilities to interfere with every aspect in your life is not helpful to you and it is not helpful to your parent. As you learn to place limits on your family and yourself, and you begin to look at new ways of reducing the stress in your life, you will find that you can work, you can play, and yes, you can take care of your parent.

The Workplace

"You may not like your job and you may have trouble with your kids and then you visit your mother and all of the buttons get pushed. But I have an overwhelming sense of responsibility to my job and my mother and my kids. They are all driving me crazy."

Gayle, Washington, DC

"I want to work, I really want to work. I escape from the pain of thinking about two parents who need me more and more each day. But sometimes when I'm here at work, I'm not. I try hard not to focus on them for short intervals—that's my game. I asked my friend, 'How do you escape?' She said, 'I don't. I just don't know how to.'"

Sally, Florida

So many working caregivers suffer because the work world is often a very tough and unforgiving place. Profits, deadlines, and task projections are all part of a working caregiver's day. Whether your work is physical or cerebral you have a job to complete within a specific time period. Everyone is accountable to someone else and who you are accountable to may make all the difference in your work experience. Some supervisors or employers understand that an employee with family problems may require time off for caregiver-related issues. Other employers stand firm and will not allow a minute of time to detract from the workday. Then there are employers and supervisors who actually fall in the middle. These men and women understand how difficult it is for a working caregiver to juggle all of his responsibilities and they are willing and anxious to help you find a balance. One employer said, *"I am the winner if I can help a staff member out if he has problems at home. If he is less stressed, he works harder and more competently."*

The following four suggestions come from caregivers. By considering their jobs and responsibilities, they have determined the best way to help themselves. As you read each suggestion keep in mind your own situation. Try to use what works for you, modify what you think needs to change, and, most important, give yourself a chance.

1. Meet with the boss. *"My old boss was awful. I actually cried at work and I was mortified. My new boss was kinder so I thought to myself it's time to talk to him. I have to explain what I need. I can't keep visiting my mother at seven PM every night. Maybe if I come in an hour early and leave an hour early I can be home by seven. I made an appointment with my boss and he agreed. He explained to me that he was very aware of the fact that some caregivers need a 'flextime schedule.' He told me it didn't matter to him when I worked, it was only important to him that I finished my assignments in a timely manner. One hour difference in the morning and one hour difference at the end of the day reduced the stress and gave me more time for myself."*

2. Use your knowledge. *"I was so confused by everything I had to do. I began working again after being home for ten years. I raised two children on my own and I needed the money and stimulation. Here I was back in the work force again. My desk at work was a mess.*

I felt completely disorganized in the office. On the other hand my files at home were immaculate. I had my parents' medical and insurance papers alphabetized and in order. Their life was in order and mine was in chaos. One day I was reading an article about getting your life organized and it was as if a lightbulb went off in my brain. It was time for me to use the skills I already have and bring them to the office. I devised a way of organizing my workspace and time by writing a list. I always make lists at home to keep track of everything from groceries to reordering my mom's medications. I wrote the list at the end of the workday and when I came to work in the morning I reviewed what I had to do for the day. The first thing on my list said, 'Clean desk.' It was a start and it provided me with a balance in my life that I never had before. I could actually be a working caregiver."

3. Define the boundaries. *"They all want a tiny piece of me. No one is excluded from this list. My children, husband, parents, brother, and boss. One day I'm sitting at my desk and I realized that I spent two hours on the phone with my dad talking about nothing, ten minutes on the phone with my husband arguing about dinner, and thirty minutes discussing my son's college entrance exam. Amazing how I killed half a workday and of course didn't do my work. All of a sudden it hit me that nothing that happened today was an emergency. Well, if it's not an emergency it doesn't have to be discussed during working hours. That's when I decided to set limits. I told my dad that anything other then a medical emergency has to wait until after five PM. I talked to my husband about being in charge of dinner two or three nights a week since he is home earlier than I am. He agreed—reluctantly—but I'll take it as an agreement. My son said he really needs help with his college preparatory materials and we discussed how to schedule time over the weekend. He moaned about missing a soccer game on Sunday and I ignored the moans."*

4. *Think about yourself. "I found a way to work and take care of my parents, I meditate. This may not be a solution for all of you, but it works for me and many other men and women. I work in an office every day. In order to maintain a feeling of peace I spend some time every morning in a quiet room and I meditate. It helps*

*clear my mind, centers me, and allows thoughts to come in.
Instead of reacting to the thoughts I concentrate on my breathing
and a loving kindness fills me that helps me to cope with my life.
I simply escape. I know the benefits of meditation. I know some
people prefer a vigorous workout in the gym, but I enjoy the tranquility of my quiet time. Balance comes from within and meditation allows me to enjoy that balance."*

A caregiver from New York said, *"I put my sneakers on at lunch hour
and take a vigorous walk or I spend time at the gym. The gym is a few
blocks from the office and I can even take a quick shower before I go back
to work. That is my one-hour escape and it gives me a sense of well-being."*

As a working caregiver you know the challenges you face every day.
Your job, family, and your parents add layers of responsibility to your
already stressful life. Finding a balance that works for you will take time
and through a process of elimination. Try the suggestions of our caregivers. Use what works for you. As you learn to create a balance between
work and other responsibilities you will find your own inner peace.

Your Needs

In order to help you remember how important you are in this complex
journey called caregiving we would like you to keep in mind six words:
I WILL TAKE CARE OF MYSELF. These thoughts are for your consideration. As you read these ideas keep in mind what seems important to
you and allow yourself to make these your own. When you find yourself
struggling through a particularly difficult day, think about the words that
impressed you or left you feeling good. Leave a copy on your desk or
dresser, take a deep breath, and read them again.

I WILL:

- Take care of myself because I am worth the effort.
- Allow myself time for play and laughter to soothe my body, mind,
  and spirit.
- Know when it is time to rest, relax, and revive myself.
- Engage my family and friends to help me when I feel I need the
  support.

- Care for myself as well as I care for my family and friends.
- Answer one question every morning: How can I be good to myself today?
- Revive the child in me by doing something playful and enjoyable as often as I can.
- Eat nutritious foods to help keep my body and mind in balance.
- Only say *yes* when I want to and learn to say *no* when it is not the right time.
- Find the time to enjoy my family and friends.
- Make each day a little better than the day before by taking a few minutes to appreciate my own company.
- Yawn and stretch and take the time to rest when I feel tired.
- Satisfy myself by doing one good thing for myself every day
- Eat chocolate. It's good for the body, mind, and spirit.
- Learn to respect myself as so many others respect and admire me.
- Find my inner voice and allow myself to express my feelings, needs, and concerns.

B. MY JOURNAL

Use this journal as a safe place to express your thoughts and feelings. Putting thoughts and feelings on paper helps you see them more clearly. What changes do you want to make? How can you make things easier? When you read what you've written, you may see a new pathway to help resolve stressful issues. For example:

"*I wish I could find a way to make time for myself. I feel so deprived, frustrated, and angry. . . .*"

"*It is very difficult for me to ask for help, but I know I can't keep up this pace anymore. It's time to start getting the help I need. . . .*"

_____

_____

_____

_____

_____

_____

_____

_____

_____

_____

_____

_____

_____

_____

_____

_____

_____

_____

_____

_____

_____

_____

_____

C. TIP SHEET

- Make time for your spouse or significant other in order to help maintain a good, healthy relationship.
- Communicate with your children and set aside time to talk about their day as well as yours.
- Decide how much time you need and when you will need it and then talk to your boss about flex time or time off to take care of yourself and your family responsibilities.
- Learn how to depend on friends, family, and hired caregivers to help you take care of your parents.
- Help yourself stay strong and healthy by eating right, exercising, and taking a few minutes every day to be good to yourself.

9

FINDING AND USING HELP AND SERVICES

A. WHAT'S THE RIGHT SUPPORT SYSTEM FOR YOU?

"Have you ever tried calling for help? Some people try to help, but most just blow you off. You tell your story eight times and you end up with higher blood pressure and the last place on a waiting list longer than your lifetime. Don't waste your time. It's easier to do it yourself."

Kathryn, Florida

No, it's not. It's much harder to do it yourself. The next time you feel frustrated or angry enough to slam down the phone and give up when you're trying to get an answer or access a service, think about this: It's better to learn how to get help than to fall into the trap of trying to do it all yourself. The nature of the job of elder caregiving is that as your parent ages, your duties will increase. If you try to go it alone and forego help, you may seriously jeopardize your parent's and your own quality of life. You will probably have increasingly less time to enjoy your partner, children, or friends. Less time to pursue a career or nurture good mental health. And less time to pamper your soul with other purely personal pleasures such as a golf or tennis game, manicure or a warm relaxing bath.

Eldercare and healthcare services present a dilemma: even though they are two of America's largest and fastest-growing business categories, the supply of qualified professionals and effective services is still too small to meet the demand. While waiting for more trained geriatric physicians, nurses, social workers, and other advocates, we often find ourselves depending on people who may mean well but do not have the time and often do not have the knowledge to help us. We end up frustrated, angry, and resentful. As more than one caregiver has told us, *"What you get depends on who answers the phone."* Our frustration mounts, and when we don't think we can take any more, we just give up. It doesn't have to be that way.

Caregivers who work on the *"I can't get the help I need; nothing will ever change"* premise usually end up as their own worst enemy. Day after day these caregivers create their own negative self-fulfilling prophecies. If you keep finding roadblocks instead of support, it's time to assess your strategy and make some changes.

Consider your mind-set. You may be justifiably angry if you can't send your parent to day care without outside transportation and the only program in your area doesn't supply that service. You may not be able to drive your father and pick him up because of a conflict with your work schedule or your children's school schedule. You can probably find a solution, but first you have to change your mind-set. Being angry blocks the creativity you need to work out tough problems like this one. Even worse, negative thinking feeds poor results. It adds layer upon layer of "de"-constructive (as opposed to "con"-structive) thoughts and feelings, creating mountains of frustration. Eventually you find yourself unable to resolve even the simplest issue. You're trapped in a negative cycle.

If you are struggling to get assistance or to find a solution, take a break from trying. Talk to a friend about another subject, laugh with someone, and spend your energy trying to change the recording in your head. Your goal is to replace unhelpful thoughts like *"What's the use, I can't get help"* with positive ones like *"I can do this. I can get the help I need. Look at everything else I've accomplished in my life. I deserve this help and I'm going to find it."* Once you start to think in a self-supportive and determined manner, you'll have a much better chance of reaching your goal. You will be on the road to regaining control.

B. IDENTIFYING YOUR NEEDS

One of the most important steps in obtaining help is learning how to identify your needs and wants. Before you make the first call for assistance, do what you do with every other project: start at the beginning and read the instructions. Here they are.

It's easier to find the support system that will meet your needs when you have a clear picture of what you're trying to accomplish. Create a list of the services you feel will help improve your life and your parent's care. Number the items in order of importance. Keep it simple, but be specific. Include quality-of-life needs and remember that your own respite time is critical for continued caregiving success. A sample list might go something like this: (1) Transportation to the doctor for Dad, (2) Day care three days each week for Dad, (3) Someone to fill in Tuesday nights so I can take a class, (4) Help with Dad's grocery shopping.

Next, select the most urgent need and think only about this one need. Organize your thoughts by writing down the answers to these three questions: How often will I need this assistance? How much time will it take? And how much, if anything, am I able to pay? Then do the same thing for each need on your list. These four examples will help you.

1. Transportation to the doctor.

- The transportation costs must be affordable to Mom. Find a service that charges on a sliding scale based on what Mom can afford or (hopefully) what insurance covers.
- Mom's appointment is two weeks from Thursday. I need this resolved by at least ten days before that date. My deadline is: (date)
- Mom will need a wheelchair van that we can reserve ahead of time to pick us up at a specific time and bring us back to her house. I will follow in my car.
- I'll need to ask for references and schedule time to check them. I want to make certain the company is reliable.

2. Day care three days each week.

- Dad will function better and be happier in a program that caters to Parkinson's disease and has a physician or RN (registered nurse) on the premises.
- He needs transportation to pick him up and bring him back home. He uses his wheelchair to get from the house to the van, and then into the day care facility, so we need a van with a wheelchair lift. They also should be willing to help him take his walker with him so he can use it while he's at day care.
- We need a program that charges on a sliding scale based on what Dad can afford to pay, or one that doesn't charge at all. (Note: call Parkinson's Association for referrals.)

3. Someone to fill in Tuesday nights so I can take a class.

- I need someone to stay with Mom from six thirty to nine thirty PM, which includes my travel time.
- I'll need this for four Tuesdays: March 1, 8, 15, and 22.
- The companion should be comfortable talking to Mom, watching TV with her, and just keeping her company so she won't feel lonely.
- I'll take care of Mom's dinner before I leave, and she'll be finished by the time the companion arrives.
- The companion will not handle medications or need to do anything that is "hands-on" care.
- I'll be back in time to help Mom get ready for bed.
- I don't expect any problems, but I have a whole book of information for emergencies to leave with the person who stays with her.
- I'll carry a beeper or cell phone in case the companion needs me.
- I would prefer a family member or a neighbor. I'm not comfortable with a homecare worker or a stranger. (Note: Mom likes my nephew James. I wonder if he would like to earn some extra money? I can pay him $50 total for all four nights. Or maybe I can get Betty from next door to do it without payment. She likes Mom a lot.)

4. Help with grocery shopping.

- I'd like someone to alternate with me every other week so I can have some respite from this chore.
- The food can be brought to my house.
- I will make a specific list for the shopper to follow.
- It takes only about twenty to twenty-five minutes to do his shopping.
- I will change the day of the week to accommodate the person, but it needs to be on the same day each week so I'm sure Dad always has food in the house.
- I can pay $10 for this. (Note: the neighbor's teenage daughter might want to make some extra spending money!)
- I wonder if I can use the $10 to buy this service from a store that does that shopping for me and delivers? Maybe I can just fax, e-mail, or call in the list.

Third, make a list of all possible resources that can help fill your needs. Consider your family, friends, community groups, medical professionals, church or synagogue, as well as certified eldercare professionals, including professional respite care. If your parent has relatively good cognitive skills, add him to your list of potential resources. Don't let past turndowns influence you. Now that you are a "positive" thinker and you are organized enough to be explicit in your requests, you should get better results. Asking for "someone to fill in so I can take a class" often produces a negative response because the request sounds vague and open-ended. Asking for someone to relieve you from six thirty to nine thirty PM on specific dates makes it easier for potential helpers to understand the relatively small amount of time you are asking for and say yes to at least one or two nights. "I don't have time" (to help with grocery shopping) is a quick and easy response. Imagine how hard it would be for a family member to turn down a request for "only twenty-five minutes every other week" because you "really need help."

If you are working on obtaining a designated time for relief such as every Tuesday night for two, four, or six weeks, you're best off trying for continuity. If you can find one person who is willing to substitute for you every week, you and your parent will have to adjust to only one new face or personality, and you'll have to orient only one new person to your routine. Realistically, it may be easier to find assistance if you enlist several people because each person will have a smaller time investment. If three helpers were rotating weeks, then each person would assist only twice over a six-week period. This seems like a very reasonable request. What if the worst scenario happens and you have to use a different person every week? Say "thank you" to each helper and do it. Your need for relief is more important than continuity for this relatively short period of time each week.

Try to keep your expectations realistic when you think about what people will do for you. Avoid asking for help with tasks that you know are problematic. If your mother is incontinent, don't ask her friend or your husband to get involved in a situation where they might have to change her diaper. If she doesn't wear a diaper, think twice about whether your helper will appreciate witnessing or being expected to cope with an accidental urination on the floor or on a chair. To help avoid this occurrence, be sure to take her to the toilet before you leave.

If your father has been diagnosed with moderate or severe dementia symptoms, don't tell your helper that it's her responsibility to feed your father dinner at five thirty PM regardless of whether he wants to eat or not. Even if your neighbor says she'll do it, it will probably be the last time she agrees to help you. If you expect a problem with dinner, find another solution. Feed your parent before you go out or leave plates of nutritious finger food throughout the house. Try carrot sticks, pieces of cheese, celery, apple slices, grapes, orange sections, cut up pieces of chicken, or other foods you know your parent likes. (Before you initiate this type of feeding, however, be certain to check with your parent's physician for possible problems with swallowing or choking, or for other health issues that may make this solution inappropriate. This is not appropriate with illnesses that require regular, measured food intake.) There is a good chance your parent will nibble the entire time you are gone, and your helper will not be caught with the uncomfortable choice between reporting that she didn't follow your instructions or making your parent unhappy by forcing him to eat.

Another consideration when asking for help from friends or family members is the message you send with your own body language. If you have a small tape recorder, practice asking your sister to help you, and listen to your voice on tape. Record yourself, and then stand in front of a mirror. Watch your face and listen closely to your tone of voice. If you resent that your sister hasn't done more for your mother, your voice probably sounds tight and angry. Your lips may be pursed, your shoulders tight, and your whole body tense. Loosen up before you ask. Instead of focusing on what this person hasn't done for you, close your eyes and visualize the benefits of succeeding. As hard as this might sound, it is one of the best ways to help yourself reach your goal. If all else fails, play a game of "pretend." Many professionals use this special technique when they work with their most difficult clients. They overcome their negative body language and tone of voice by pretending the client is someone else, usually a friend or customer who is easy to get along with. When salespeople play this game of pretend, they actually become less tense, their voices lose clipped or angry sounds, so what the client sees is a relaxed person with a smile on her lips and in her eyes. Your body language can make a difference in whether or not you achieve your goal.

Adult Day Care Programs

> "My mother has Alzheimer's disease, and she really doesn't participate in many activities. I will never forget the look on her face when she heard the pianist play songs from the 1930s and 1940s. She stood up in the middle of a group of people and began to dance. Her eyes sparkled as if she remembered something. I'm sure she did. My dad always played the piano, and she sang so many beautiful songs. I'll never forget her face. I think she remembered him."
>
> *Lorna, Michigan*

> "After the stroke, Dad was in a wheelchair. He was always such an active man. He used to play tennis, golf, and even a little softball. One day he told me that his life was over and he wanted to die. His doctor recommended a geriatric psychiatrist. He prescribed an antidepressant and suggested a medical-model day care program. The doctor said it was affiliated with the local hospital. Dad agreed to try it for a few weeks. What happened is amazing! He looks forward to going out three times a week, and

he is the star in wheelchair exercises. I am very grateful to have my Dad back."

Sue, Ohio

If you are a family caregiver or if your parent lives with a hired caregiver, day care is one of the most important support programs you can use to improve both your parent's and your own quality of life. It can provide your parent with many of the ingredients we all need to lead a well-balanced life: mentally and physically stimulating activities, opportunities to make new friends, and social interaction with peers who can understand and help with our personal problems. It may provide you with a brief respite and a feeling of satisfaction that your parent can still delight in some of life's pleasures. Both Sue's and Lorna's moments of realization came when they understood that although an illness robbed their mothers of short-term memory and independence, they still had the potential to hold on to old memories and enjoy a few brief moments in the day.

"I found a great program for my dad that is affiliated with his church. When I brought him into the recreation room, a very nice volunteer took his hand. He looked nervous, but she said, 'Don't worry, your daughter will see you very soon.' I took off in my car as if someone just gave me wings."

Penny, South Carolina

When Penny "flew" away from the respite program, she was acknowledging the fact that as a caregiver your wings sometimes feel clipped and you cannot move. Day care provides you with the ability to spend time in a clothing store or at a movie, or with just enough time to enjoy a cup of coffee. Your parent has the opportunity to socialize with his peers in a caring, safe, and secure environment.

Day care is also another good example of when not to give up too soon, even though that may be your first instinct. Many day care programs have long waiting lists and some seem almost impossible to access, particularly those that charge on a sliding scale based on what your parent or your family is able to pay. Instead of calling to find out when they might have a spot open for your parent, try this.

When you begin to think about day care, make a list of your parent's problems and what type of care he needs during the day, the availability of programs within your parent's community, and the cost of the programs. How many days each week and how many hours each day will serve you best? Do you also need transportation to and from the day care facility? Are you looking for a sliding scale payment policy? Does your parent's condition necessitate medical personnel at the site? Is your parent a candidate for a more social day care program or a medical-model day care program?

Social-Model Day Care Programs

The social model is appropriate for your parent if she has a diagnosis of Alzheimer's disease or a related dementia, or if she suffers from depression or anxiety. Most social-model day care programs will accept your parent only if she is ambulatory, continent, and does not have any serious conditions that will impede her from participating in the program. Generally no medical staff is available, so if your mother requires a portable oxygen tank or insulin injections during the day, she is probably not eligible.

The purpose of day care is to provide stimulating programs, socialization with peers, and support from a trained professional and volunteer staff. The program usually meets in a social service agency, church or synagogue, school, or senior or community center a few times each week. The cost varies from a small contribution to a set weekly fee. Some programs offer a sliding scale fee based on your parent's income. Transportation is sometimes included in the cost of the program or it is available for a fee. Many programs do not have transportation.

Social and recreational activities include exercise programs, music, word games, arts and crafts, dancing, and current events. Many parents enjoy spending the time with new friends and a caring, supportive staff.

> "The social worker asked for volunteers to help out on a trip to the botanical gardens. The trip was long, but we sang songs and listened to music. When we arrived, a well-informed tour guide gave us a lovely tour of the grounds. My mother and her friend kept touching the flowers and trying to pick a bouquet. The guide must have experienced the problem in the past, so she

had a flower for each client. My mother was so happy, and she and her friend held hands. What a great day. She could never have this type of experience anywhere else."

Evelyn, Maine

Medical-Model Day Care Programs

A medical-model day care program addresses the needs of a physically frail and cognitively impaired population. The program often meets in a geriatric clinic, nursing home, or community center. The professional staff consists of social workers, nurses, and physical, occupational, and recreational therapists. In many instances, a master's-level social worker or a registered nurse directs the program.

Your parent may be a candidate for a medical-model day care program if she requires ongoing medical monitoring, such as blood pressure checks or insulin injections, or she uses a wheelchair due to a serious medical condition such as Parkinson's disease, stroke, or a cardiac disease. Many of the clients also suffer from mild to moderate dementia.

The socialization and recreational programs are similar to the ones offered in the social-model day care program. Sometimes the activities require modifications to meet the needs and challenges of a frailer population.

"Everyone is so kind to my mother. She sits in her wheelchair, and someone is always holding her hand or talking to her about her friends and family. She does wheelchair exercises for her legs, goes to physical therapy twice each week, and gets a really good hot lunch. She looks forward to the three days she spends with 'the girls.' The girls are trained nurses and social workers who really care about people. It's a special place."

Marie, Virginia

"I couldn't believe it. My father ran away from home in his electric wheelchair. I don't know what gets into him, but I panicked. I called the day care program that is down the block from his apartment and told the nurse that Dad ran away and he might be on his way to the program. The nurse and social worker ran out of the building and sure enough, they saw Dad at full speed racing down a hill toward the day care center. When they caught up to the wheelchair, one directed traffic and the other finally convinced my dad to stop. Then they brought him inside safe and sound. That is true dedication."

Sylvia, New York

Once you've made your list of your parent's and your needs, it's time to take action. Try these steps to locate and evaluate the most appropriate program for your parent. Because you will be very specific regarding your needs, one of these resources may be able to unlock a door that you couldn't open yourself. Every time someone tells you help is unavailable, repeat these sentences: "I appreciate the time you've spent with me. Could you possibly give me another few minutes of your time and think of someone you could refer me to who might be able to help me?" More often than not, you'll get another name and phone number. When you call that person, be sure to open the conversation with "Miss (Name) at the Area Agency on Aging referred me to you. She felt you might be able to help me find day care for my mother on Tuesdays, Wednesdays, and Thursdays." Mastering the referral process will bring you one step closer to accomplishing your goal.

- Contact the local Alzheimer's, Parkinson's, or Heart Association, or contact the Area Agency on Aging, hospitals, or geriatric clinics for day care programs in your parent's community. Try a local telephone directory for senior programs. Contact local schools, churches, synagogues, and senior centers for information.
- Try to visit and observe two programs if they are available. This will provide you with a comparison of staff, environment, programs, meals, and transportation.
- Talk to the staff. Ask them about their credentials, training, and volunteer screening procedures. Most volunteers are carefully screened and trained by a licensed social worker.
- Observe the staff members' interactions with the clients. Do they seem warm and friendly? Do the clients seem happy and well cared for?

"My father doesn't remember anything, and he seemed so depressed. He paced in his apartment day after day, and was rude to home health aides and any family member who tried to help him. I heard about a day care program at the local senior center, so Dad and I went in to look around. There was music playing and people just sitting around talking and laughing. Suddenly, ten little children about three and four years old marched into the room. The director said that it was an intergenerational program, and that each child 'adopted' a grandma or grandpa the week my father visited the program. Dad really seemed to enjoy it, and he joined the program a few times each week. That was over a year ago. I am so grateful for the program and the wonderful people who take care of him."

Betty, Pennsylvania

- Ask for a calendar of events and try to observe the program in action. Programs may sometimes seem childlike, but the harsh reality is that the activities likely meet the needs of your parent. If your parent is healthy and cognitively intact, but in need of social interaction, try a senior citizens' center. Day care is for those individuals who require supervision and/or care.
- Ask the staff how they celebrate birthdays, holidays, and other special events. Do they plan outings? Is there an additional fee?
- Ask about the availability of transportation and the fees. If the program does not provide transportation, think about your options. Can you drive your parent? Is another family member available? Can you hire someone to drive him to the program? Consider these facts when you make your decision.
- Ask the staff about caregiver support groups and counseling for you and your family.
- Walk into a day care program when the music is playing and the people are singing. Look at the faces, and you will see that the right day care program can bring a few hours of happiness into your parent's life, and give you a few hours of free time.

Medical Support

Medical support is often helpful to ease your anxiety and help you plan for the future. As a caregiver, you may find yourself responsible for duties that not too long ago may have been considered so complex that only medical professionals were asked to perform them. It would not be unusual for you to need additional information or training on how best to handle those duties. If you are a long-distance caregiver, you may feel less anxious if you speak with your mother's physician or a nurse for more information regarding her diagnosis and treatment instructions, as well as what plans you should make for her future and yours. (You'll find more information on long-distance caregiving in chapter 7.)

You may also find yourself caring for a parent with whom you have a less-than-good relationship, or in fact, don't like at all. This is probably not a situation you want to handle by yourself. Don't walk, run to a mental health counselor. If a mental health counselor is not available, you may want to talk to your doctor for a referral to someone who can help you. This story tells it all:

> "When it became clear that my mother would need my live-in assistance, I began psychotherapy. I know now that my life would have been easier if I had gotten help in dealing with the issues and strained relationships much earlier. My health remained good, but carrying a load of guilt served as a limitation on my fullest participation in life. If you can't manage healthy boundaries that honor your identity and unique journey before caregiving requirements arise, it'll be really tough to do so after the fact. The end result is coping over the years with the sense that you didn't do enough. I have great empathy for those with multiple living parents."
>
> *Dana, Oregon*

Planning is key to successful interaction with all support resources; however, it is almost impossible to create a working relationship with a busy physician without organizing your approach. Have your list of questions ready before you call. Don't expect a doctor to keep calling you back if you aren't available after the first or second try. If you request a return call, give the physician (or other professional) several options for times that you will be available and then be there to answer the call. Have your list, your pen, and plenty of paper ready when you answer the telephone. You'll need to write down the answers to your questions. If you or your parent's doctors feel that a short telephone call will not satisfy your needs, offer to pay for a telephone consultation. It's unrealistic to expect a physician to spend a long period of time on the telephone without compensation for her time. Don't try to guess or to work this out alone. Family caregivers often need the advice of medical and mental health professionals to help manage their parents' care. You have accepted an enormous responsibility, and you deserve the same amount of help and attention and the same quality of life you are trying to obtain for your parent.

Family Support

Family support comes in many ways. Being asked to contribute often alleviates tension in the household by making family members feel more involved. They also develop a better understanding of your parent's needs and why your time is so limited. Your son, daughter, and husband can help you; so can your siblings, cousins, aunts, uncles, and grandchildren. In fact, even your parent can provide support. No contribution is too small; every bit of help frees up another few minutes of your time, and that helps lower your stress level.

> "Sam and my father were always fond of each other. They joked with each other all the time, got together on holidays to create menus full of their special dishes, and even argued about politics. When Dad got sick, Sam felt helpless. I was overwhelmed and stressed to the limit. He offered to help, but it seemed easier for me to just do it myself than to figure out how or where he could fit in. Another caregiver in my support group asked me if I'd thought about putting Sam's hobbies or special skills to use. That got me thinking. Sam cuts our son's hair, and he's really good at it. That's where we started. He began cutting my father's hair. They both loved it. They became even closer. Sam feels like

he's contributing, and I don't have to take my father for haircuts anymore. All three of us have benefited. Now, Sam and I are working on our kids. They're afraid of Dad's illness, but we want them to understand that each family member has a responsibility to help other family members. Sam and I think that if we can find them a way to help, the good feeling they get from contributing may grow stronger than their fear."

Joan, California

What do you need? What do you want? Someone to pick up the dry cleaning? Take over dinner one or two nights each week? Do you make daily reassurance calls to your mother?

"I dread that daily phone call. Every day, for the last three years, I wonder, What am I going to say to her today? We didn't have much to say to each other before she got sick. All I really want to say now is 'You okay today?' and hang up. But she wants to talk, and if I get off the phone too fast, I feel guilty all day. So, I spend hours each day figuring out what to talk about. God, it just wears on me."

Louise, Michigan

If you call your mother daily, perhaps one or more members of your family can take over that duty one day a week. Better yet, two or three days a week! Caregivers who call their parent daily report that having someone else call just one or two days each week gives them an enormous feeling of relief and freedom. Very often, family members who have been less than cooperative change their attitude when they actually experience how much energy and patience it takes to continue providing even basic caregiving services. One of the most important components of asking for help is being able to explain *why* you are asking for help. Just tell the truth: "I can't do it all myself anymore. I want more quality time with my family." Sometimes the hardest part of receiving help is asking for it. Try starting your sentence with "I need your help . . ." If you can say that, filling in the rest should be the easy part. (For more information on family support, see chapter 4.)

Community Support

Community support is your best bet for continuing education on your parent's illness. These programs usually are your best resource for services performed at no charge or for fees based on "what the family can afford." Call the local association that represents the illness your parent has: Alzheimer's Association, American Heart Association, Diabetes Association, and so forth. If your parent has no specific illness but has become frail due to advanced age, try the offices nearest your parent for the Area Agency on Aging or the Council on Aging.

> "The Council on Aging was a lifeline for me, particularly when I had to move to Georgia for work and I was not able to find my mother a nursing home there. Prior to calling them, I drove a 150-mile radius around my home, and the places that were acceptable all had 1½- to 2-year waiting lists. Also, I went to several of their support-group meetings when she was living with me and when she initially went into the nursing home, because I experienced a lot of guilt about the nursing home thing."
>
> *Lauren, Ohio*

If you find a less-than-knowledgeable person when you call a community support service, ask to be connected with another person or a supervisor. These organizations exist to serve caregivers and care receivers. Many receive funding based on the number of people they serve. Translation: They are literally waiting for your call! (You'll find a helpful list of organizations and resources in chapter 24.)

Parent Support

Your parent may be your most overlooked resource. If your parent is cognitively or physically able, he can provide some of the help you need. Take a step back and try to assess your parent objectively. Is your father able to make reasonably safe decisions on his own behalf and on behalf of his friends and neighbors? If he is, why not help him help himself? He may remain more independent and autonomous for a longer period of time than he would if you take over and run his life in areas where he can function safely. For example, if your father lives in an area with other people of the same age, he and his friends and neighbors might be able to create a system to check on one another daily, and call for help if there is a problem. Listen to this telephone tree story:

"I used to call my mother every morning to make sure she was okay. She refused to move in with my brother or me. We'd nag her to the point where we ended up in a nasty argument. She'd say, 'Neither of you ever listen to me. I'm fine. I know I'm old, but I'm not sick. Stop trying to make me dependent on you. I have my apartment, I have my friends, and I have my own life. Why would I want to leave it all and live with you? If I need help, I'll call you.' I still don't know why we didn't believe her. I guess my brother and I assumed, very incorrectly in my mother's case, that because she was eighty-three, she was helpless. She told us that she and her friends had worked out a system for their own peace of mind, but we didn't give her enough credit. We assumed that if we didn't create it for her, it couldn't be any good. I'm still embarrassed that I didn't realize that she and her friends were realistic enough to know they needed the protection of a local support system.

"What we eventually found out was that they had set up a safety net using a telephone tree system. They also developed an action plan for problems! Each person in Mom's group has the responsibility of calling one group member every morning. If the person doesn't answer the telephone, the person calls again in an hour, and again one hour later. Getting no answer for all three calls is considered an emergency. Not receiving a call meant the caller had a problem and that was an emergency, too. If no one answered by noon, the whole group went on alert. If a group member wasn't going to be home to receive the call, it was her responsibility to notify the person who would be calling. Each group member had given a key to someone in case of an emergency. One day, my mother's best friend, Frieda, didn't answer any of the three calls. The group called the neighbor with the key. When the neighbor and several group members went to Frieda's apartment, they found her barely conscious. They called 911, then Frieda's doctor, then notified her son and daughter. They had thought of everything, including sharing emergency telephone numbers! After the emergency crew left with Frieda, my mother and another friend took a cab to the hospital to be with her. Then my eighty-three-year-old mother clearly demonstrated what she'd been trying to tell me: she was quite capable of living her own life. She told me not to worry if she didn't answer the phone in the morning. The group didn't want Frieda to be alone, so they were going to take turns watching over her in the hospital until her son got there. They split the day into two-hour periods, and my mother had drawn the early shift. I finally got the message. If I would just fill in when she needed me to help her, she could handle the rest. I'm so proud of her."

Alice, Kentucky

Another caregiver offered this option:

"I call my mother daily. We've always been close, so I manage that pretty well. But some days and weeks I feel as though I just can't make one more call or listen to one more problem. I tried a new approach and said, 'Mom, I need your help for a week.' I asked her if she'd mind calling me every day instead of my calling her every day. I explained that she might reach my voice-mail and I probably wouldn't be able to call her back every day, but I'd know that she was okay. I promised to check in two or three times during the week so that she wouldn't be worried about me. She's happy to help and feels useful being on the caregiving side for a change. We've been using this system on and off for almost a year and we've never had a problem."

Kim, New York

If you have a relationship that makes parent support an option, assess your parent's capabilities and ask for assistance with shopping, cooking, laundry, dinner, telephone calls, or other tasks. Ask your parent for suggestions on how she thinks she can help. Once you begin, you'll think of many ideas to create your own parent support systems.

Significant Other Support

Significant other support is sometimes difficult to obtain, but it is well worth the effort. When you try this, remember that your responsibility involves more than just asking for support. It's vital that you take the time to make a special effort to understand that your partner's position and place in the caregiving system may be very different from yours. Your partner may not really want to take on this responsibility, but might ask if you need help or agree to your request for help. Many of our partners want to help but don't know where or how to begin. Others may be jealous and angry because of the time you've taken from your relationship with them to handle your caregiver duties. Asking for support can help bring your partner back into your busy life and is often a deciding factor in maintaining your relationship. This is particularly true if the time and energy demands of elder caregiving leave very little time for the two of you. If it's too difficult for your partner to care for your parent with you, don't judge him or her too harshly. Sometimes current or past family dynamics make this type of involvement impossible. Your partner may feel burdened with the knowledge that your parent has never approved of your relationship and may simply be unable to provide the kindness and care that was never received. If your partner agrees to lend a hand, this caregiver's experience might help you think of the best way to start:

> "I had a great marriage. Frank and I hardly ever argued; we both loved our kids, we loved our jobs, and we loved each other. Then my mother got sick, and I became a caregiver. After a couple of years, my marriage needed more help than my mother. He thought I spent too much time taking care of her needs and not enough time with him and our kids. We argued all the time. During one fight, I said, 'If you helped me instead of stressing me out more, things would get done faster and I'd have more time for us.' He looked dumbstruck. It sounds so stupid to say this, but it never occurred to either of us to try that. The problem was figuring out what he could do. He and my mother got along

okay, but that's all. They weren't close. We agreed to think about it. I ended up watching everything I did for my mother for the next two weeks until I found something he would be comfortable doing. I asked him to take over the paperwork: banking, check writing, insurance papers. Frank also thought of something else: my mom used to read a lot. Frank reads all the time. He suggested that when I'm doing the shopping, he could read to her. That way we could go over to her house together and come back together—maybe go out for dinner on the way home. This arrangement is still new, and we have to work out the bugs, but at least we're working toward solving the problem together."

Kaye, Texas

C. RESPITE

If there is one absolute in eldercare, it is this: Every caregiver needs respite. These shared experiences will help show you why.

"When my mother and father could no longer live alone, I did what I thought I had to do. I moved in with them. I found myself in a new city, jobless and friendless, just when I needed both the most. I needed a salary for obvious reasons, and I needed the support of my friends back home to shake some sense into me. I needed someone to shake me into reality and get me off the self-destructing 'only-I-can-handle-this' path I'd chosen. Many years later I entered therapy and discovered that the biggest mistake I made was thinking I had to do it all. My need for control almost did me in. I just could not believe that anyone else would or could handle this job as well as I did. I sank deeper and deeper into a world that was too much for me to handle alone, and everything became a major problem. Something as simple as opening the mail would make me want to cry. To this day, I don't handle mail well. It just piles up. Sometimes when I'm thinking about my mother and father, my eyes just well up with tears, and I literally ache with guilt because I'm still not sure that I did everything I could to help them. Then another kind of guilt sets in: I wonder if I did too much. Maybe we'd all have had a better life if I'd gotten counseling while they were alive instead of waiting until they died. You asked if I had one piece of advice or one good coping skill I'd like to share with other caregivers? You bet I do. Get help. There are people who know as much or more about caregiving than you do. They don't have to do it your way; they just have to do it well. Get help from someone who knows which end is up. Go to a professional or an organization that can teach you the two skills you need most: how to take an afternoon or a weekend off and how to accept what you can't change. Those are the keys to quality of life for a caregiver."

Laura, Maine

All of us need a break from our responsibilities to help us relax and relieve some of our stress. We need to clear our minds. It's essential to create quality time to spend with our families, our friends, or by ourselves. This simple act helps replenish our ability to cope with daily tasks and enjoy life. It all boils down to this: You can avoid many physical and emotional problems by remembering to care for yourself while you are caring for others.

Every support system mentioned in this chapter is a form of respite care. A more encompassing form of respite is offered by assisted living facilities and nursing homes that accept your parent as a resident for a few days or a longer period of time. This caregiver's story illustrates how valuable this service can be:

"When my mother was released from the hospital, she needed twenty-four-hour assistance at home. My sister and I both work, and we didn't want the responsibility of us being her only way out of the house. We needed someone who drove so she wouldn't have to stay home until one of us could come over and take her out. We decided on a live-in caregiver. Mother wouldn't tolerate anyone who smoked. We also needed someone who would cook from very specific recipes for her special diet. We interviewed several candidates, but there was always a problem. The discharge planner at the hospital told me about a nursing home that could care for Mother on a short-term basis until we found a suitable caregiver. What a relief! We thought our only other options were three eight-hour shifts of homecare that would have cost twice as much as a live-in homecare worker, or putting her in a nursing home permanently. Once we enrolled her in the nursing home's respite program, we had the luxury of taking our time and finding the right person. It took two weeks."

Margaret, Louisiana

Take the time to clear your mind so that you can try to use positive energy to solve your problems. Remember the basics: First determine what type of support you want, and then search out the assistance you need. Stay flexible and always be ready to accommodate changes. Don't take rejection personally. Keep asking for referrals until you get the help you want and need. You deserve it.

D. WORKSHEET: FINDING AND USING HELP AND SUPPORT

Family, friends, or community resources that have declined help in the past might find it easier to commit to a request for one specific need. Use this worksheet to help identify one thing you want to do (take a class, go away for the week, go out to dinner), how much time you'll need to do it, and who can help you with caregiving during that time. Use a different piece of paper for each need. Keep your worksheets for reference.

1. I want time for (one thing only, please): _____.

2. I think I need this much time: _____.

3. I need this time on these dates: _____.

4. The help I need for my parent while I'm out is (dressing, feeding, companionship, and so on): _____

_____

_____.

5. My prospects for assistance are (when you call, remember to keep your request specific to the type of help you need and when, such as the next two Tuesday nights from 7–9 PM):

A. Name & Tel. _____

    Dates Available _____

B. Name & Tel. _____

    Dates Available _____

C. Name & Tel. _____

    Dates Available _____

D. Name & Tel. _____

    Dates Available _____

WORKSHEET:
PEOPLE IN MY SUPPORT NETWORK

Family and friends are a great source of support for respite, home repair, transportation, visiting, homecare, meals, shopping, or other needs. Use this worksheet to help identify who you think might help you with these or other needs (don't forget your wants!), and to keep a record of the help you've been promised. Use more paper to add additional helpers.

To make the best use of this worksheet, review this chapter.

1.

Name: _____

Address: _____

_____

Telephone: _____

Services Offered: _____

_____

Available Dates: _____

_____

2.

Name: _____

Address: _____

_____

Telephone: _____

Services Offered: _____

_____

Available Dates: _____

_____

WORKSHEET:
IMPORTANT TELEPHONE NUMBERS

Creating a list of telephone numbers for people who are important to your parent's well-being is a must for every caregiver. Having these numbers at your fingertips will add to your peace of mind.

In an emergency, always call 911 first.

1. Family members to contact in an emergency:

Name _____ Tel. _____

Name _____ Tel. _____

Name _____ Tel. _____

2. Physicians:

Name _____ Tel. _____

Name _____ Tel. _____

Name _____ Tel. _____

3. Pharmacy:

Name _____ Tel. _____

4. Neighbors:

Name _____ Tel. _____

Name _____ Tel. _____

5. Friends:

Name _____ Tel. _____

Name _____ Tel. _____

6. Other (geriatric care manager, elder law attorney, financial adviser, bank, transportation service, homecare agency or worker, grocery store, plumber, home repair, or others):

Title _____ Name _____ Tel. _____

Title _____ Name _____ Tel. _____

Title _____ Name _____ Tel. _____

Title _____ Name _____ Tel. _____

Title _____ Name _____ Tel. _____

Title _____ Name _____ Tel. _____

Title _____ Name _____ Tel. _____

Title _____ Name _____ Tel. _____

Title _____ Name _____ Tel. _____

Title _____ Name _____ Tel. _____

E. MY JOURNAL

Use this page as a safe place to express your feelings. Putting thoughts and feelings on paper helps you to see them more clearly. What bothers you? What changes do you want to make? When you read what you have written, you may see a new pathway to help resolve stressful issues. For example:

"*I know we need help with Dad, but it's so hard to figure out what's right for him. I guess it's time for me to see what's available and then I ask for help . . .*"

"*My sister thinks she knows everything but when it comes to Mom she's no help at all. I just want to tell her off, tell her how I feel. I need help, not criticism . . .*"

F. TIP SHEET

- Ask for help to find the right support system and services for your parent.
- Think about what type of help your parent requires, then create a list of specific needs. For example: asking someone to take your parent to the doctor every week or for a walk in the park every other day.
- Review the list with a family member, friend, or professional healthcare provider to help you determine your first steps in getting the help you need.
- Utilize community services such as adult day care programs, senior centers, church and synagogue groups.
- Make sure you take time to take care of yourself. Respite for you is as important as the care that you provide for your parent.

10

HANDLING BURNOUT

A. HOW DO YOU KNOW IF YOU'RE BURNED OUT?

"I'm always exhausted. My day starts and ends with my father's needs. Today I realized it's been years since I was lighthearted enough to hum or sing, or since I just had a fun day with my daughter. I've been crying all day. What have I done to myself and my family?"

Rebecca, Pennsylvania

"I experienced joint deterioration, weight loss, incredible physical and emotional fatigue, insomnia, and drank more. I was angry at not having any mental break from the pressure, and frustrated at the feeling that the experience could go on for years. I know my work suffered. It was impossible to commit time to anything else. The caregiving responsibilities were a factor in the end of my last relationship."

Renee, Florida

B urnout has become so commonplace in caregivers' lives, many accepted it as unavoidable. Don't buy into this fable.

For too many caregivers, the "rewards" of trying to handle a job no one else wants are marriage problems, career limitations, isolation from friends and social events, personal healthcare problems, depression, and an overall feeling of loss of self. If you wake up dreading each day, cry regularly, or feel like you're on a runaway train, you are showing symptoms of burnout.

> "Why do they call it burnout? When a lightbulb burns out, I go to the store and buy another one. What store do I go to for another mother who can take care of herself for a couple of weeks? Or another daughter who can take this load off of me for a while? I'm not 'burned out'; I'm charred beyond all recognition. You'd need my dental records to find the person I used to be. It goes with the territory."
>
> Sandy, Florida

No, it doesn't. Nor is it a matter of trying harder or resolving to "get it done no matter what it takes." You are experiencing a physical and emotional response brought on by adding twenty, forty, sixty, or more hours of caregiving duties to your weekly schedule. That's like adding another full-time job! To make your situation even more frustrating, you may be caring for a parent or stepparent with whom you never enjoyed a good relationship or who hasn't had a kind word for you in years. If your mother suffers from Alzheimer's or another neurological disorder that produces dementia symptoms, you may be caring for someone who no longer even recognizes you.

If you are taking care of your children, taking care of your parents, and trying to juggle a career at the same time, you may be too physically and mentally exhausted to step back and form a clear picture. During those hectic times, it often becomes progressively easier to accept the status quo as inevitable. We imagine that changing our lives will take a lot of work and energy, and regardless of the benefits, we feel we cannot add "one more thing" to do to our already overcrowded schedule. At that point, we are likely to deceive ourselves into believing that no matter how difficult our routine is, it's less disruptive and more manageable than trying to change the way we handle our lives. We continue to fulfill our obligations as best we can and try to provide loving care and emotional support for our parents and our families. In the process, we give up trying to provide care and support for ourselves.

It's easy to understand how dangerous burnout is to your physical, emotional, and financial well-being. It's harder to visualize a different approach and to recognize that burnout is treatable and avoidable. You can improve your life by using the skills you already have to advocate for yourself. It may take some practice, but it's worth it. You can regain control and once again experience all the things that made your life enjoyable: good emotional and physical health, close relationships with family and friends, and an interesting career. These things are worth fighting for.

B. WHAT KIND OF HELP DO YOU NEED?

"We've got it all under control. It's a good thing we do. Who else would do all the things that we do? My husband and I care for my father and mother and his mother. My parents live with us in a couple of rooms we built on to our house; his mom lives across town. All of them need someone to shop for their food and prepare their meals. If you leave it to them to cook their meals, none of them will eat. My parents are from Holland; his are from Italy. Needless to say, they eat totally different types of foods. All of them need their laundry done. My father refuses to wear a shirt or slacks more than once, and my husband's mother is incontinent, but won't get help for it or even admit to it. My husband handles all the financial details and pays their bills for them. Their banks are not the same as the one we use. We both drive them around so they don't have to stay at home all the time. I go to all their doctors' appointments with them. Everyone keeps telling us how lucky our parents are to have wonderful children like us. That's easy for outsiders to say. And we probably used to think that we were only doing what 'family' is supposed to do. I think we stopped having good thoughts about our caregiving jobs years ago. Now, we're just tired. Even if we could find the courage to tell them we can't help them anymore, I'm afraid the guilt would kill us. We feel like there's no end to their needs and our duties. It's like being in prison. Our parents are the bars, and our consciences are the guards. We never have time for ourselves. But at least we have it all covered."

Melinda, Pennsylvania

Whether you and your parent have always enjoyed each other's company or you have an adversarial relationship, if you look deep inside, where you keep your very private feelings, you probably already know the time has come to get help. You may have put off asking for it because you are afraid that others will not maintain your high standards and care for your parent as well as you. You may feel that it is your duty to help your parent, and if you complain, you might be labeled unloving or ungrateful. Unfortunately, depending on your parents and family members, there may be some reality to all those concerns. However, none of them is a good enough reason to continue suffering alone through your commitment, ignoring the impact on your health, family life, career, and future.

Most caregivers want help. Some have succeeded in finding it; but most don't know where to begin to look. Start at the beginning and organize your thoughts. Build on one central piece of information just like you do with other projects, such as decorating a room, getting dressed, or cooking dinner. For example, you may have a taste for pasta, but that's only the first step. You won't have a complete dinner until you identify the rest of the ingredients, find them, and integrate them into a whole meal. Follow the same pattern for getting help. Start with the main part of the project. What do you do for your parent? Do you provide transportation? File medical claims? Prepare meals? Are you the only socialization your parent has? Do you oversee the medications your parent takes? Are you the liaison with your parent's physicians? Do you accompany your parent to doctors' appointments? Are you in charge of home repairs? Are you responsible for financial transactions? Are you the first name on their "emergency call list"? Review your contributions and carefully select one caregiving task you can delegate.

If you can afford private help, it usually provides the most options because of the variety of services available and the immediacy and continuity of service. Community services that are free or based on what your parent can afford may be readily available or may have a waiting list. The actual costs will vary from community to community. Don't be discouraged if your first call or even first three calls don't provide the help you want. This is one of the most important steps you can take to ease your burden. (You will find more information on this in chapters 9, 11, and 24.)

Call your local Area Agency on Aging and ask for the community services expert or the community liaison. (If you can't find the listing in your telephone book, look in chapter 24.) Once you are connected to the right person, state the service you are trying to locate and ask for referrals to independent professionals, or take advantage of community services. If your parent is suffering from a specific disease, use the same strategy with the corresponding organization (heart, cancer, stroke, and other associations). Don't end the conversation without taking at least one step forward toward your goal. If the person can't help you, politely say, "*I appreciate your time. Could you please refer me to someone who might be able to help me?*" Disease-specific associations can be especially important because the service providers they recommend are usually experienced in working with people who have the same symptoms as your parent.

Try to get the names of several service providers and call at least three. In addition to general expertise, be sure to ask about their experience with your parent's problems and your needs. You might find a perfect fit with the first call, but you'll find out more about pricing and services options if you talk to two or three providers. Later, if you or your parent experiences a personality clash or it doesn't work out for other reasons, you will be ready to call another helper with a minimum time investment. If you are hiring an independent professional, ask for and check at least three references. Even if you are the professional's first client, you can check references from prior business associates or community involvement groups. Don't make your choice solely on the recommendation of an elderly person. Older people often enjoy the attention and socialization that outside helpers provide and may give positive references to keep them coming to visit. You cannot successfully hand off a responsibility without a certain amount of peace of mind. Be firm. Do not accept any excuse for a lack of references.

One of the resources caregivers frequently forget to try when they need help is their parents. We often tend to take over many duties that our parents can actually do for themselves.

> "I had just gotten off the phone with my mother. I told her I would pick up the veal for dinner tomorrow night. I began to feel anxious the minute I hung up because she is very specific about the veal she likes, and I have no idea what makes one piece of meat better than another. I muttered, 'Oh God, why can't she get her own veal?' and then it hit me like a lightning bolt: she could! I was so nervous I actually wrote out what I wanted to say so I would get it right. I called her back and said, 'Mom, I know you are very picky about your veal. Would you be more comfortable taking a walk to the store and picking out exactly what you want?' There was a moment's silence, and then she said, 'That would be nice. I'd like that.'"
>
> *Marianne, Tennessee*

Everyone wants to feel useful. Geriatric professionals generally recommend that your parents do as much as they can for themselves. For instance, if your mother is physically able to walk to the grocery store or drugstore to pick up a few items, by all means she should continue doing that chore. If your father is in a wheelchair but he is cognitively intact and still able to balance his checkbook—and he wants to do it—encourage him to continue.

> "When my father was diagnosed with Alzheimer's disease, I gradually began taking over all his responsibilities. I would like to say I didn't want anything to worry him, but the truth is, I just assumed he couldn't handle them anymore. I thought I was doing the right thing. When I finally almost collapsed from exhaustion, I called the Alzheimer's Association. They assessed us both and came up with a whole list of things I was doing that he could do for himself. I feel like a fool. I probably hurt him, and I made my life a living hell. But it never occurred to me that he was still capable of doing anything for himself."
>
> *Millie, West Virginia*

Churches, synagogues, and other places of worship often have volunteer programs to provide transportation, grocery shopping, and companion or sitter services. They may also help with yard maintenance and cleanup. Don't worry if you aren't a member; that is usually not a prerequisite.

Many colleges require community service in their admissions criteria. Call your local high school and speak with the guidance counselor to determine if the school sponsors elderly or community assistance programs.

The yellow pages can be one of a caregiver's best resources; however, it's best never to use this option without thoroughly checking references. Look for someone who has worked with an association that is known for helping elderly clients: the Alzheimer's, Diabetes, Heart, and Parkinson's associations are a good place to start.

Once you have successfully handed over one responsibility, you may want to revisit your list and get help with another one. Don't worry if you find it difficult to trust another person at the beginning. Or, if the first person you hire to help doesn't work out. Think about the positive changes you can experience if you can make it work. Then, try again. (For more information, read chapter 9.)

C. REAPING THE BENEFITS OF RESPITE

"I had sitters come in once a week for four hours while I went out and tended to grocery shopping and did what I had to do. Four hours is not enough. It's a mad rush. You come home, you're just totally wiped out, and then you still have to do your caregiving duties. Four hours twice a week was a godsend. It gives you time to go out, have a leisurely lunch, and maybe go to the library. Do things for yourself. Take your mind off what's going to be facing you when you get home."

Charmaine, Florida

Sometimes finding the courage to give yourself respite is harder than finding the program that works best for you. It can be very difficult to let someone else take over, even for a few hours, and care for your loved one. A good respite program can change your attitude and improve your health. You can improve your quality of life to a more acceptable or enjoyable level. Could you use Saturday mornings to yourself? Would you like to have an entire weekend that is free from caregiving duties to take care of your own needs, spend the time with your husband, or go to your daughter's school play or son's sporting event? Do nothing or do many things, but the point is that you will have the option to do whatever you choose. Respite's only purpose is to give you a break from care-giving. To help ease the pressure on you by providing time off from your duties, use substitute caregivers.

You may worry that things won't be exactly the same as when you handle your parent's needs yourself. That's probably true. They don't have to be. If the change doesn't put your parent at risk for personal safety or health matters, how much will it really matter if your parent eats at five thirty instead of five on Tuesday nights?

Once you've tried respite, you'll wonder how you ever survived without it. It is one of the most efficient and effective methods of adding hours or even days of personal time to your life.

Adult day care is one of the most comprehensive respite plans. Services and costs vary, so investigate thoroughly. If the first one you call is outside your budget, ask for a referral to a program with a sliding scale fee based on what your parent can afford. You may find hot meals, transportation to and from the facility, movies, current events speakers, sing-alongs, and other mental stimulation. Your parent will also have the benefit of socializing with peers. Some programs require a minimum attendance, such as two or three days each week. Many are sponsored by community centers or religious organizations. Most programs also sponsor ongoing caregiver support groups. These groups provide you with information and emotional support. You'll also have an opportunity to gain new friendships with people who are dealing with similar issues. You can read about a variety of day care programs and how to locate them in chapter 6.

For weekends or vacations, contact an assisted living community or nursing home. Many have weekend, weekly, or even longer programs. If your parent has specific disease-related needs, it's a good idea to contact the corresponding organization for a referral to facilities that specialize in that illness. Ask for professional and client references and check them out thoroughly to help create the comfort level you need.

Chapter 6 will give you more information on how to get respite support from the medical community, your family, and even the parent you are caring for.

> "I packed a bag for my mother—actually by the time I got all her stuff together, it was more like a suitcase—and took her to my brother's house. He promised to take over for the weekend so that I could take the first real break I'd had since my mother came to live with me three years ago. He had always inferred that all the problems and chaos were my fault. Of course, he had never had her in his house overnight, let alone for three years, so he didn't know what the hell he was talking about. Just his usual B.S. Anyway, I dropped her off about 8:30 Friday night. I couldn't wait to get home. I filled the bathtub with hot water and bubble bath, put some perfumed candles I'd gotten for presents around the rim of the tub, turned on my favorite music, and finally climbed in about 10:00. I used to love this, but I hadn't been able to relax with Mom in the house. She has dementia, and I never knew what she would do. About 10:30, I heard this pounding on the door. I ignored it, and it got louder and louder. Someone was banging and yelling so loud, I thought there must be a fire next door. I got out of the tub, went to the door, and there was my mother! Suitcase and all! Alone! Mr. Know-It-All brought her back, but couldn't face me, so he ran when I came to the door. I had the 'satisfaction' of knowing he couldn't even last two hours, but my weekend was ruined. After I put Mom to bed, I wondered if I should've talked to him about her attitudes and habits. Maybe he would've tried longer if he had been expecting whatever happened. Maybe he would have agreed to do it again. I cried for hours."
>
> *Leah, Florida*

Wherever your helpers come from, be certain you give them enough information to do the job. Plan to spend some extra time orienting them to your parent's habits and needs so that they will understand their responsibilities and you will know whether or not you have the right person for the job. Think about the length of time and time of day your helper will spend with your parent. Will your parent require a meal? If so, have you left instructions that include what to do if your parent refuses to eat? Do you expect your helper to entertain your parent by reading to him? Does your parent react positively to certain kinds of music? Perhaps you expect your parent to sleep the entire time you are gone and have no interaction with your helper at all. Even so, be sure you leave a telephone number where you can be reached, an alternate name and telephone number for emergencies, and the name and telephone number of your parent's physician. Carrying a pager may make contacting you easier. Planning ahead will help ensure a successful experience for you and your helper. For more detail on the types of information your helpers need, please see chapters 6 and 15.

D. MANAGING YOUR TIME

Time may be your most precious resource and the hardest one to manage, but more effective time management is a critical step in regaining control of your life. Remember the old adage "Take care of the pennies and the dollars will take care of themselves"? When time is as valuable as money, that phrase might change to "Take care of the minutes and the hours will free up themselves." Many caregivers rely on the "consolidation" method to save a few minutes or an hour in a number of areas. They find it easy to master. The time they save allows them to spend more quality time with their children, to read a book, or enjoy a quick nap.

Think about how you spend your caregiving hours. Write down some of the things you do for your mother that you also do for yourself or your family. Compare your list with these timesaving ideas. Once you begin, you will think of other duties you can consolidate.

1. If you handle your parent's financial transactions, move the accounts you deal with most often to your bank and handle the deposits, withdrawals, or payments when you do your own banking. Your mother may object on the grounds that she has been banking at the same location for twenty years, but if she isn't

going to the bank anymore, her complaint isn't really valid. The reality is that she is no longer banking anywhere. You are banking for her, and you no longer have the time to travel to two different banks. Many financial institutions will cooperate by changing statement dates and payment due dates to help you organize your visits so that you can handle both accounts in one trip or make both payments in one envelope.

2. If you are comfortable with the Internet, electronic banking can save you hours of time. Most banks are happy to help customers master the process.

3. If you pay your parent's utility bills, credit card bills, insurance bills, and others, ask the companies to reschedule the due dates to coincide with your own bills. Instead of paying bills twice a month, you can write your parent's checks at the same time you write your own.

4. Look into paying as many bills as you can via the Internet.

5. If you take your mother grocery shopping, you can save time by buying your groceries at the same time. If you go without her, buy groceries for both of you at the same, in the same store. One of you may have to change brands, but that's a small price to pay for saving an hour or two each week. If you go alone, have the store bag the orders separately. If you are worried about keeping your items cold while you deliver your mother's groceries, purchase an inexpensive insulated bag that will keep meats and dairy products cool until you reach home.

6. Many HMOs offer a convenient mail-order prescription service. Or, try moving your parent's prescriptions to a drugstore that delivers so that you don't have to pick them up. Before you make any changes, investigate thoroughly to make certain you don't lose any benefits. If the change is financially agreeable, you or your parent may have to sign a permission form. Then, the new pharmacist will take over and facilitate the change.

7. If you prepare meals for your parent, consider making two extra portions of the meals you prepare at home. Freeze them and transfer them to your mother's freezer when you visit. It won't be long before your mother has a variety of meals stored in her freezer without any extra time investment on your part.

8. If you work outside the home, ask about working electronically from home for one or two days each week. This can free up the time you spend putting on makeup and sitting in traffic. Also, ask about flextime. (For information on how flextime works, see chapter 8.)

One of the most important rules of time management is to not spend time doing things you don't have to do. It takes some practice to master the next two tips, but it's well worth the effort. When you succeed, you'll free up hours of time each week.

1. If you are in the habit of picking up after your husband, children, or parents, stop it right now. Resolve that yesterday was the last time you will perform this service for people who probably have more free time than you have. Explain your burned-out state of mind and your need for their help, and declare that they will be assisting you by putting the things they use back where they belong. When someone leaves shoes, CDs, socks, sporting equipment, or something else in the wrong place, ask the user to put it back where it belongs. If clutter becomes a problem, buy straw, rubber, or cloth mesh baskets (like a laundry basket), put them up against the wall, and toss the items into the baskets. Use one basket for each person. Your family won't change overnight. When you are tempted to give in and resume putting away your family's things, help yourself stick to your new time-management program by thinking about the time you'll eventually save.
2. If someone else cleans your house for you, there is no need to tidy up before the cleaner arrives. That's what you're paying for. What difference does it really make if the cleaner sees how much your house needs cleaning? After all, that's the reason the service exists.

You can find more timesaving suggestions by asking other caregivers to share their best tips. Saving a few minutes here and there can lower your stress level and add up to hours of free time for you to spend with your family or on your own needs.

E. RESTORING YOUR QUALITY OF LIFE

Do you ever wonder whatever happened to your daydreams, or do you wish you had a few minutes alone to think? When was the last time you just closed your eyes and smiled because everything was OK? If it's been a while, it's probably because you've been busy handling one crisis after another, taking care of your day-to-day problems, and everyone else's needs. STOP, if only for a few minutes a day, dream again, and slowly begin to restore your quality of life.

You are the only one who can determine what brings quality to your life. Think about your personal wish list. Some women hope for a new car, a house, or a trip to the Bahamas. Many caregivers often have a different type of wish list. Although you may want the new house, car, or exciting vacation, most often you may just want a few minutes for yourself, or space in your home, apartment, or on the back porch. All it takes is some thought and preparation.

Time is a precious commodity for someone who has many jobs and multiple responsibilities. Space does not have to be measurable in square feet. All you may need is a few minutes in a cozy corner where you can read your favorite magazine or look out of a window, a place that provides you with comfort, a sense of security, and inner peace. This story may help you to think about the need for just a few minutes a day, and a little space you can call your own.

> "I'm in this alone. I am an only child, and my husband and I have no children. Until recently, I loved my life. Now I'm always tired. I don't even have the time to sit down and read a newspaper. I take care of both my parents and my husband. We all live in my apartment. It used to be a lovely place to live. Now, it's overflowing with people, furniture, wheelchairs, commodes, and cases of adult diapers and nutritional drinks that I buy in bulk to save money. Three bedrooms used to seem like a lot of space, but I can't even find a few square feet where I can sit and relax for a few minutes. The doctor says I have to change or I'll end up needing more care than they do."
>
> *Edith, Florida*

There are times when you cannot change your responsibilities, but if you can stand back and look at your life and your duties from a different perspective, you might be able to clear a little time to spend on yourself.

These five steps are not always easy, but they can help you regain some of the quality in your life.

1. Look around your environment and identify a room or corner that you can reserve for yourself. Does it have a window? Does it catch the morning or afternoon sun? It can be in a den, bedroom, attic, or porch. (Edith found a corner in her living room with bright daylight streaming from a large window.)

2. Remove the furniture, knickknacks, old newspapers, and magazines from your area. Try to look at the space the way an artist looks at a blank canvas. Ask yourself, "What would make me happy in this new area? Colors? Furniture? Plants?" (Edith always wanted a lounge chair, so she could rest her feet. She picked up an inexpensive chair at a flea market and draped a homemade afghan across the back. She eventually added a small table with magazines and a tiny vase with one fresh flower.)

3. Decide what you want in your space, and then take the first step to create your personal getaway. For instance, in preparing a quiet workstation, one caregiver cleaned one shelf off one day, polished the furniture another day, and bought a new computer printer during a lunch break. She continued doing a little at a time until the work area was complete. Whether you have the luxury of redesigning an entire room or are working on a small corner, the process should be the same.

4. Sit in your new area for a few minutes to feel how good it is to be surrounded by the things that give you pleasure. Close your eyes. Remember how it feels, so you will want to return again and again. (Edith sat down for a few minutes, and said she cried because it felt so good.)

5. Take the time to take care of yourself. (Edith said that she could never find the time every day to sit down and read, rest, or think. She agreed to try to enjoy her "serenity corner" three or four times each week for fifteen to thirty minutes each time. In order to find the time, she thought about which hours her family napped and

rested. During their rest time, she usually washed the floors. She was very fussy about her floors, but she realized that if she gave up washing the floors once a week, she gained thirty minutes of free time. She then started to think about other ways to add to her free time. She remembered that her neighbor visited her parents and husband about two hours each week. Edith always served coffee and some snacks. She decided since the visit was fairly short, she really could eliminate the refreshments, and excuse herself. She gained another two hours each week to enjoy her private retreat. And so on.) Initially, this simple approach allowed Edith three hours of relaxation time each week. As she began to enjoy her time off, she found more and more ways to take care of herself.

By reviewing all the things you do, as Edith did, you should be able to consolidate some tasks, eliminate other tasks, and free up the time you need and want. Once you create the space and give yourself the time, you will begin to enjoy some simple pleasures. Take an hour to read a book or just a few minutes to reflect and dream. There is no one who deserves it more than you. (For more on information on helping improve your quality of life, read chapters 5 and 9.)

F. TAKING CARE OF YOURSELF

Listen to these three women who have so much in common. They are caregivers for a parent, and they are suffering from physical and/or emotional problems. Like so many other caregivers, they suffer from a myriad of physical symptoms, such as headaches, stomachaches, and back and muscle pain.

"My mental health has deteriorated."

Sheila, Connecticut

"I'm on antidepressants."

Lynnette, Alabama

"I'm on muscle relaxants."

Francine, California

They suffer from anxiety, irritability, depression, and sleep deprivation. Pain, lack of sleep, anxiety, and fear of the next problem or crisis impacts the lives of millions of women.

"I average five hours of sleep on a good night. I am so often sleep-deprived that I can fall asleep at my desk."

Mark, Minnesota

A caregiver who is physically or emotionally ill and stressed to the limit will have more and more difficulties in his role as a caregiver because of physical and mental pain and exhaustion. How can you protect yourself from illness and fatigue? What can you do if you are suffering from physical or emotional problems, or feel trapped and out of control?

"My mother-in-law had refused outside help for years. She kept insisting, 'I have a son and a daughter-in-law, why should I pay strangers?' Looking back on the situation, it's easy to see how she could maintain that position; my husband believed exactly as she did. Only he didn't have to do anything. They both had me. I took care of her needs and his as well, until the day came when I couldn't deal with one more request. I went to my doctor and cried my eyes out. He sent me to the stroke association. They had a family counselor. What a difference that counselor made in my life! She helped me learn how to explain to my husband and mother-in-law that I just couldn't do all the things they thought I should do. I had a job and three kids to care for as well. All I wanted was a few minutes for my own needs. I won't tell you they understood. First they were surprised. My husband said, 'Terry, you're handling everything fine. What's the problem?' Then they were angry. I wanted to hire someone to help with my mother-in-law, and we got into a fight about money. Then they just didn't talk to me. It wasn't easy, but the counselor kept me on track. I'm still doing too much for all of them, but at least now I have a little time for myself."

Teresa, New Jersey

You've done a great job taking care of everyone else; now it is time to nourish and protect your body, mind, and spirit. It's time to take care of you. No matter how you are feeling today, there are steps you can take to help yourself to a better tomorrow.

- Nourish your body by taking care of your physical needs. Have regular medical examinations, gynecological checkup and mammogram or prostate exam, and dental checkups. Take the time to wash your hair, polish your nails, or soak your feet in some warm water. Talk to your doctor about preventative measures such as a flu shot or a change in diet. Listen and watch for your special "triggers" that tell you something is wrong and it is time to see a doctor, such as fatigue, sleeplessness, weight gain or loss, headaches, backaches, pain, and so forth. When you make an appointment with a physician and she recommends that you have further medical tests, follow up as soon as possible. Spend the time to get an accurate diagnosis because many problems and conditions can be reversed.
- Your psychological and emotional well-being is essential to good overall health. Nourish your mind by bringing balance and a sense of well-being into your life. Do something that gives you mental peace. Write in a journal, read a favorite old book, or plant a few flowers. If you feel burdened, tearful, angry, anxious, or depressed, you may want to see a social worker, a registered nurse, or a psychologist to help you work through your feelings. If talking isn't enough to alleviate your symptoms, ask your doctor about the options available to you. (See chapter 15 for more information.)
- Give your spirit the sustenance it needs by surrounding yourself with people you love and people who can return your feelings by providing you with emotional support. Envelop yourself with things that give you joy, such as a bunch of wild flowers, good music, or a funny film. Sit down for just a few minutes and close your eyes. Let your mind drift to any wonderful place that gives

you peace. Envision a beach, a park, or a mountain retreat. As you drift to your special place, enjoy the tranquility of the moment. If thoughts of faraway places are not what relax you, listen to music, or watch an old movie. It really doesn't matter how you feed your spirit; it only matters that you do it.

G. SETTING LIMITS

Many caregivers find themselves in a situation that sends their lives into a tailspin.

"When my husband's father died unexpectedly, my mother-in-law moved smack dab into the middle of my house. During the first few days, it didn't hit me, then I realized that my whole life had changed. The worst thing is that we have no privacy. I feel as though she's watching everything we do and listening to every word we say. How do other people manage this?"

Maryellen, Texas

"My father's totally out of control. He thinks his wish is my command. If he needs something, he expects me to jump into action the minute he mentions it to me. I'm a twenty-four-hour, seven-day-a-week butler, house cleaner, and all-around general servant for him. The rest of the family got tired of his demands a long time ago. No one else will help him anymore. I don't know if I'm more disgusted with him for taking advantage of me like this, or more disgusted with myself for letting him get away with it."

Kirsten, Washington

"There was no one else to help my mother, so I got the job. I mean, my sisters and my brother offered to help, but Mother wouldn't be happy with them. She would have to compromise on too many things. For example, she likes to eat her evening meal at six o'clock on the dot. My sisters were really smart. They said, 'Mother, you are welcome in our homes. We will try to accommodate some of your wishes, but you will have to adjust to our families' ways of doing things as well.' Do you know what my mother had the gall to answer? 'I have eaten my dinner at six o'clock for eighty years, and I will continue to eat my dinner at six o'clock until my dinner-eating days are over.' My sisters held their ground, so she had nowhere to go. Finally, I broke the deadlock by bringing her to my home. She's such a pain in the neck about everything that most of the time it's just easier to give in and give her what she wants. I hate having her here, but now I'm stuck with her."

Cecile, Mississippi

When you feel a loss of control, compounded by the strain and anxiety of a crisis or emergency, you may not think about setting limits. As a matter of fact, that may be the furthest thing from your mind. Once the crisis or emergency is resolved, the situation may seem unmanageable, but that can change.

Setting limits does not mean that you don't care about your or your spouse's parents. Limits simply provide a sense of order, privacy, and control for all of you. The idea that you can change the course of events from something unmanageable to something workable may be difficult to understand. Caregivers who have a problem saying "no," "I don't have time," or "I can't," may have a hard time with this concept. In trying situations, reaching an understanding can be extremely difficult and frustrating. But when you make your feelings known and those involved try to understand one another's situations and needs, you are more likely to reach a compromise.

Still, there are no perfect solutions. If you are the only one who is willing to change, then go ahead and set limits anyway. You may be the only one with something to gain. These three steps will help you achieve success.

1. Set your first limit by compromising on control. Relinquish one responsibility. It may not be permanent. Later on you may want to reconsider, reacquire that duty, or give up another one. You may be surprised at how free and relieved this can make you feel.

2. Talk to your parent about what is bothering you. Try to limit your discussion to one issue at a time.

> "My mother calls all the time, during work hours, or the minute I walk in the door at the end of the day. Doesn't she know I have a job to do? How does she know I'm home? I can't chat during the day, and then I just want a few minutes to myself before I have to make dinner or wash the clothes. I feel bad telling her not to call."
>
> *Robin, South Dakota*

Your parent's generation universally understands the importance of "a day's work." Tell your parent you'd be happy to talk to her, but after work hours. Set a time, and try to adhere to the routine as often as possible. This will give you a chance to unwind, and your parent should be able to relate to your request and appreciate the time you need. If your parent visits unannounced and this is causing you unnecessary distress or is disrupting your family's routine, talk about it. If possible, begin your conversation with something positive. For instance, "Mom, we really enjoy your visits, but since we are all on such different schedules, it would really help if you could give us a call first." If your parent is receptive, great, but you are just as likely to hear, "I am insulted, I guess you just don't want me around." Take a deep breath, count to ten, and say, "Of course we want you, but we need to have some notice so that we can be available to enjoy our time together." If your mom does not want to discuss the situation and she walks away, just let her go for now. You can try again in a few days. Sometimes this approach works, and sometimes it doesn't work right away, or at all. Keep trying; the benefits of any small compromise beat no compromise at all.

3. Reevaluate the situation if there are changes in your family's circumstances or in your parent's physical or cognitive status. Although it is still important to set limits, you may need to readjust your agreement. Suppose your mother finally agreed to telephone you after 5 PM during the week, but she had an accident

and is unable to leave the house for a few weeks. She may need to reach you earlier in the day to call the doctor or the pharmacy. Try to understand that this is probably a temporary situation, and after a few weeks you can go back to your original agreement. If your parent is becoming increasingly forgetful and calls you every hour of the day, you have a different problem and you need a new solution. Your mother may need homecare assistance, and the limits you set are no longer with your mother, but possibly with a home health aide. If your family is assisting with one chore a week and you want help with other chores, talk to them about the situation. Try to reach a new agreement that is acceptable to all of you.

Setting limits is an ongoing process. When things change or your needs change, remember to talk it out, try to reach a compromise, be flexible when necessary, and always reevaluate the situation.

H. MY JOURNAL

Use this page as a safe place to express your feelings. Putting thoughts and feelings on paper helps you to see them more clearly. What bothers you? What changes do you want to make? When you read what you have written, you may see a new way to resolve some very stressful issues. For example:

"I know I don't feel well, but I just can't seem to find the words to explain it. My body aches and my mind just doesn't rest . . ."

"After caring for my mother for five years, I feel like her death has created this hole in my life. No, it's not just her death, it's that I don't know what to do with my life . . ."

_____

_____

_____

_____

_____

_____

_____

_____

_____

_____

_____

_____

_____

_____

_____

_____

_____

_____

_____

_____

_____

_____

_____

_____

_____

I. TIP SHEET

- Avoid burnout by taking care of yourself with the same love and care you show your loved ones.
- Get the help you need from friends, family, and professional health-care providers in order to maintain your quality of life.
- Use time management techniques to make the most out of your day by prioritizing what you do, when you do it, and how you do it.
- Set limits by learning to say NO when you are too tired, stressed, or busy.

HOW TO HIRE A HOMECARE WORKER

A. WHAT ARE YOUR OPTIONS?

"My mother refuses to let a home health aide in the house. I've used every approach I can find, but she won't budge. I think she's afraid of having a stranger in the house and you know what? I would be afraid, too. But what's the alternative? I can't be the one who takes care of her all day. I have a full-time job and three kids. To tell the truth, even if I didn't have other responsibilities, I can't imagine bathing my mother. We just never had that kind of relationship. I'm so stuck you could use me for glue to mend a broken cup."

Barbara, North Carolina

"Everything changed after Jeanine took over. Mom wasn't as negative. She began to laugh again. The doctor said it was a combination of better healthcare, the companionship, and the nutrition. For the first time in years, someone was there to make sure she took her pills and ate three balanced meals each day.

When Jeanine helped her bathe, she was less afraid of falling and hurting herself in the shower. They sorted out the clothes that still fit her, and she began to get dressed and put on makeup every day. They watched soaps together. Jeanine took Mom for walks and to the mall. I think the more she realized she could really depend on Jeanine, the less afraid she got. The better she got, the less anxious I felt. I don't know what we would do if Jeanine left. She's only missed three days in two years. All I can tell you is that Mom was very resistant at first, but I think they have ended up with a great respect and deep liking for each other."

Cecile, California

I f your parent needs help to continue to live at home, you have two options: you or another family member can provide the care your parent needs, or you can hire someone to help you. This isn't an easy decision. Trusting a stranger to care for an ill parent is never easy. It shouldn't be. Think about the process. You hire from a telephone call, or meet in person once for a very few minutes. You expect, or at least hope, that your new helper will be honest, dedicated, patient, dependable, and skillful. You choose her, anticipating that she will handle the problems that arise each day, the ones you haven't the time, the knowledge, or perhaps the desire to deal with. Then you go on with your life and leave this almost totally unknown individual alone with your parent, hoping that she will respect the sanctities of your parent's body and home. It's no wonder that just mentioning the subject is likely to emit groans from so many experienced caregivers.

Because you know so little about the caregiver who you hired, and about the potential for abuse of your trust, or physical or financial abuse of your parent, you may worry and be quite anxious. On an emotional level, you may even be afraid. You have reason to be. Too often these gnawing feelings are on target. When the safety of your parent is at stake, even one bad experience is one too many. When you survey the potential risks, you begin to understand the inherent obstacles in finding the help you need. Your options may not be as numerous as you'd like them to be, but even if you have limited choices, you can still set some guidelines for the type of person you want. It's unrealistic to believe you can eliminate all the problems you are likely to encounter, but a working knowledge of how to plan a homecare program may help ease the process and provide a better experience.

Family Caregivers

> "A lot of people tried to discourage me from taking care of Pop. They said it would ruin my social life, depress me, and wind up making me sick. I can still see my best friend, rolling her eyes, giving me the exasperated look she saves for her kids, and saying, 'I'm telling you, Fran, you're crazy! He's too much for you to handle. If you do this, he'll still be alive long after I've gone to your funeral.' They were right. I shouldn't have done it. But none of them really knew why. If any one of them had sat me down and said, 'Have you considered how many years this is going to take?' I expected it to be hard. But if I'd known I'd be a caregiver for eleven years, I don't think I would have taken on the job."
>
> *Francine, New Jersey*

If you've decided that you or another family member will provide the care, it's important to understand that the process and goals are partially the same as if you had hired a stranger: you want good care with a minimum amount of stress and disruption for everyone involved. To achieve this, you have to be clear on your parent's needs, and then be certain that the family caregiver's capabilities match those needs.

- How long will your father need care? If you don't have an answer, ask his physician for an estimate. If the physician says, "There's no way to know at this point," don't give up. Explain why you need to know, and ask him if he expects your responsibilities to last longer than one year? Two years? Even if your answer is "It could last that long," you now know enough to take action.
- If you aren't prepared to remain a caregiver for "as long as it takes," talk to your family and make sure you have a plan to replace your services. Try not to accept vague assurances such as, "Don't

worry, we'll take care of him when the time comes," or "I'm sure we can convince your sister Caroline to take over when you can't do it anymore." When your potential replacements have had the opportunity to witness the scope of your duties, they may not be eager to jump into your caregiver role.

- Use every resource you can find to make your life easier and your caregiving duties less stressful. Chapter 24 provides a list of caregiver resources. Many services are provided at no charge or on a sliding scale based on your parent's ability to pay.

> "I couldn't afford to hire someone to help us. I didn't want Mom to move in with me because I wasn't sure she would ever leave again. So, I moved in with her. Senior Services would have sent us some help at no charge, but I was so consumed by what was happening that I didn't ask. Maybe I didn't trust them to send someone who would care for her the way I thought I could. Maybe I just didn't want to admit that we didn't have enough money to take care of ourselves. I just don't know. Looking back, it might have made all the difference. By the time my mother was able to walk again, just with a walker, I was so run down and so stressed-out that I was sick. I couldn't sleep. I had no appetite. I tried everything in the store and couldn't stop my headaches. *Every* part of my body ached."
>
> *Anne, Kentucky*

Don't delay. If you are a family caregiver or are planning to be a family caregiver, act now and start easing your load with help from local resources. Take advantage of the educational, networking, and referral opportunities the various organizations provide to help you care for your parent in a manner that is physically and emotionally safe for all of you.

Paid Homecare Workers

It's essential to consider the pros and cons of hiring a private health aide (an independent contractor), an aide from a registry, or a worker from a licensed homecare agency. Medicare will reimburse your parent only for a homecare worker from a licensed Medicare agency. Most insurance companies follow specific Medicare guidelines and reimburse clients only for the same homecare services that Medicare pays for. Don't assume that the agency or the duties they perform qualify for reimbursement by your parent's insurance carrier. Call the insurance company and verify that the company you are considering is approved for payment, and ask how much the company will pay. If you skip this step, your parent may be liable for any amount the insurance company does not reimburse. You can find more information on Medicare reimbursement at the Medicare Web site, http://www.medicare.gov.

Consider the pros and cons of paid homecare:

Pro: The good news is that an independent contractor or an aide from a registry may lower your costs. Some registries may deduct payroll taxes, but only a very few carry liability and workers' compensation insurance for the aide.

Con: The independent aide may not have liability or workers' compensation insurance. This may leave your parent liable for expenses for injuries sustained as a result of the job.

Pro: You may be able to negotiate for additional services that an aide from a licensed agency will not perform. For example, some agencies may refuse to permit an aide to drive a client's car. Others may refuse to let an aide transport a client in a personal vehicle. Some agencies may charge as much as an additional 50 percent for an aide to cook for a second person such as a spouse. Independent aides may agree to perform those services at no charge or for a small fee.

Con: The skills of an independent aide may not be as developed as those of an aide from a licensed agency. Aides who work for a Medicare-licensed agency must update their training annually.

Pro: Aides who work for a Medicare-licensed agency must have regular health checkups to certify that they are free from contagious diseases and physically fit to care for patients.

Con: Independent aides may be working without medical clearance.

Sometimes finances dictate our choice. If you can afford it, choose a licensed agency. If you hire an independent aide, it is even more important to read the recommendations in the rest of this chapter for evaluating your parent's needs, interviewing homecare workers, and supervising homecare workers.

Geriatric Care Managers

Geriatric care managers are professional advocates. They can help you with one aspect of your homecare needs or take over responsibility for setting up the whole program. If you are a long-distance caregiver, or feel you don't have the time or expertise to set up a homecare program, their service might be your best bet. For a referral, call the organization that has expertise in your parent's illness. If your father has had a stroke, call the American Stroke Association; if he has Alzheimer's, call the Alzheimer's Association; and so on. This type of referral may help you reach a professional with training specific to your parent's needs rather than a general practitioner. You can find specific information on the expertise of geriatric care managers and the benefits of working with them in chapter 7.

B. EVALUATING YOUR PARENT'S NEEDS

Regardless of who the caregiver is, he or she cannot function without a clear understanding of your parent's status. Why does your parent need in-home assistance? Does your mother need someone to help her until she regains her strength and recovers from surgery? Is your father coming home from a rehabilitation facility after a stroke? Is your parent chronically ill with declining abilities that make it unsafe for him to remain at home alone? Or is he very frail with a need for assistance and supervision to remain independent? Perhaps bringing services to your mother in her own home is her last remaining chance to stay out of a nursing home? Perhaps your father would prefer a male aide?

Duties and Skill Levels

Write down your father's medical diagnosis and the specific problems that relate to his illness, such as memory loss, incontinence, loss of vision or hearing, inability to walk without assistance, digestive problems, special diets, or others. Be thorough. Specifics are critical, as different illnesses pose different problems for caregivers. If your father has been diagnosed with a disease that affects his vision, he will certainly need a caregiver who has been trained to approach him without frightening him. Another of his needs may be assistance when he travels outside his immediate familiar surroundings. Or he might want someone to read the newspaper to him every morning. That translates into a person who can comfortably read in your father's language. Unless your father can clearly understand the caregiver's pronunciation, you will not have satisfied this need. If your father requires transferring from his bed to a chair, or on and off the commode, that means you'll need someone who understands the mechanics of lifting your father and has the physical strength to do so. Without the necessary training, your father may be at risk for a fall.

Contact your father's physician for more input on his physical needs. Explain that you are in the midst of setting up a homecare plan and would welcome suggestions. The physician may feel that it is unsafe for your father to shower without someone in the room in case he falls. The physician or a nurse may recommend equipment or medication that will help the aide care for your father in a safer manner. Ask for safety tips and if there are specific situations or problems that the doctor wants the homecare worker to look for and report. Is your father's illness one that is associated with a disease-specific organization such as the American Heart Association or the Parkinson's Association? If so, call and ask the community liaison or patient advocate for recommendations and suggestions. There is no charge for this assistance and you'll gain the benefit of other caregivers' experiences with the same illness. If your homecare program already exists, you may pick up some helpful suggestions to make it run more smoothly. If you are a caregiver-to-be, ask about training and a support group. You will be amazed at how much easier your life will be using the general information and helpful tips you'll pick up from both.

Next, write down the caregiving duties you want the worker to perform for your parent. Imagine helping your parent through an entire day. If you were the caregiver, what would you have to do to ensure a safe and pleasant experience? Would you have to help with personal grooming like bathing, shaving, hair styling, applying makeup, laying out clothes, and assisting with dressing? Will the homecare worker need to cook from a special diet? Help your parent get undressed and into bed? Does your parent need help to safely use the bathroom? Or will the worker need to change your parent's diaper several times each day? Will you expect the worker to provide entertainment and companionship for your parent with activities throughout the day? Drive your parent to a restaurant or mall? Accompany your parent to the doctor?

Expectations: Reality Check

> "I just don't get it. What's the big deal? She's cooking for my mother anyway, couldn't she just cook a little bit more for the rest of us? She's there all day. My mother sleeps half the time. How much trouble would it be for her to run a vacuum or toss some clothes in the washing machine while Mom's asleep? Or put a pot on the stove and throw something in it for me and my kids?"
>
> *Stephanie, Maine*

It is unrealistic and unfair to expect to pay a homecare worker to care for one person and ask her to cook, clean, or wash for two or three people. Most workers expect to attend to light housekeeping duties and laundry as they pertain to your parent's activities. Their duties usually include washing, vacuuming, and dusting the areas your parent uses and washing your parent's clothes, bed linens, and towels, as well as your parent's bathroom. Caregivers are rarely, if ever, obligated to look after another family member's needs.

> "My mother was demented and couldn't stay alone, but every day she repeated the same phrase to the social worker at day care: 'I don't like her. I don't want her.' When the social worker finally got to the bottom of it, here's what she found out. My

mother told her, 'I tell her every morning that she has to take down all the drapes and curtains and wash them every day. She never does it. I don't like her. I don't want her.' She would not accept a compromise. She just kept repeating 'I don't like her. I don't want her.'"

Janice, Connecticut

As you create your list of duties, remember that a homecare worker is not a housekeeper or cleaning person. Guidelines vary in different areas, but the following are most of the generally accepted duties homecare workers can legally perform and are trained to perform regardless of whether they are privately hired or from a licensed agency.

- Homecare workers are not responsible for heavy cleaning such as washing windows or curtains. They are not responsible for straightening up, cooking, or taking care of laundry for the rest of the family. If you want the worker to cook for other family members, discuss it with the agency or the worker. Be prepared to pay extra for the service.
- Homecare workers will attend to grocery shopping and meal preparation as it relates to your parent. If you want the worker to shop and cook for you or other family members, negotiate and come to an agreement for payment for extra work.
- It is usually illegal for a certified nurse's aide or home health aide to give medications to patients or to fill pillboxes with medications. Only a licensed nurse or physician may do this. They can, however, assist your parent with self-administered medications. Check with the homecare agency, the Area Agency on Aging, or your state licensing agency for specific guidelines and instructions.
- Homecare workers' duties include partial or total assistance with your parent's personal care and grooming. They can help your parent bathe or shower, choose clothes for the day, help your father shave, or help your mother style her hair and apply makeup.
- If your parent cannot walk without assistance, a homecare worker should know how to safely assist your parent with ambulation to help prevent your parent from falling.

"Even though we had an aide helping her, my mother had fallen or had almost fallen several times while she showered. I didn't think this was supposed to happen, but the aide said she was hard to manage, and I really didn't have any experiences to contradict her. I finally mentioned it at my support group. They told me to get another aide because this one was inept. I called the agency and spoke to them. They supported the aide, so I called another agency and told them the problem. They sent an aide for an interview, and she showed me the difference. She pretended I was my mother, and she walked me into the shower from the front so if I fell, I would fall against her. She caught me easily because she was in front of my fall. She said the other aide was probably standing behind Mom or on her side, so when my mother crashed into the wall or fell, she had a hard time trying to catch her. I hired her on the spot."

Nancy, Texas

- It is the homecare worker's responsibility to maintain a safe environment in the home. "Maintain" assumes that the worker was brought into an already safe environment. For helpful ideas to make your home or your parent's home safe, read section B of chapter 19.
- If transportation is part of your need, do you want the worker to drive your parent's car? Or do you want your parent to ride in the worker's automobile? Neither may be a good idea or even possible. To help you make your decision, ask the agency for its policy on its employees driving clients' cars, or transporting the clients in its employees' cars. If the agency allows this procedure, ask the worker for a driver's license and a current certificate or card that will allow you to verify adequate insurance coverage. If a home health agency is involved, ask the agency for proof of insurance coverage as well. Do not accept verbal assurances.

"I asked the agency to send a homecare worker who could drive my mother on errands and take her to church. The aide had been doing that for weeks. She used my mother's car because it seemed more comfortable for my mother. Then my sister showed up. She asked if I had checked the aide's insurance and driver's license. I said that I hadn't, because I assumed the agency did that. To make a long story short, my sister found out the aide didn't have a driver's license, so she had no insurance. The agency's B.S. response was, 'She told us she did.' It gets worse. English was not the aide's first language, and she had no conception of what most of the traffic signs meant. My sister was crazed. She threw her out. My mother loved her and wanted her back. All I can think of is how many times I put my mother's life at risk and how betrayed I felt after trusting that agency. Meanwhile, my sister's gone back home, and now I'm stuck driving my mother around two days each week. I hate this."

Alicia, Virginia

- If your parent is incontinent or needs assistance to safely use the toilet, the worker should be trained to help.
- If the worker is hired from a licensed homecare agency, she should have instructions to report changes or emergencies to a supervisor who is a licensed healthcare professional, preferably a registered nurse. (You can learn more about the protocol for emergency situations later in this chapter.)

Now that you understand the worker's responsibilities, add up the time you'll require to satisfy the needs on your list. Does your parent need a part-time caregiver for four hours a day, two or three days each week? Eight hours every day? If you find yourself struggling for the answer, ask your parent's physician for his opinion or hire a geriatric care manager to help create a care plan. When you have the time estimate, check to see if your budget allows for the coverage you want or need. Can you afford to pay the worker?

Take a moment to reevaluate the entire picture. Will a homecare worker solve your problems? If you've answered yes, the next step is interviewing the worker.

C. INTERVIEWING THE HOMECARE WORKER

"Everything that can go wrong always does. My mother always accuses the homecare workers of stealing or sitting around and doing nothing. The worker always denies it. The agency says it 'understands' and replaces the worker. But eventually, the agency refuses to send any more workers into 'this abusive situation.' From their point of view, I suppose I can't really blame them. I know my mother's difficult, and I can't imagine spending every day alone with her. But from my point of view, I'm still not sure whether she's just being a pain or whether she was telling the truth."

Juanita, Oklahoma

This is personal. If you are a long-distance caregiver, your parent's safety and your peace of mind may depend on this stranger. If you and your parent live in the same home, you may be leaving the homecare worker alone with your children and all your possessions. Taking the time to interview the worker is a significant first step to helping safeguard everyone you love and everything you own. You or someone you trust must accept the responsibility to interview the candidates and gather as much information as you can to help prevent problems.

Legal and Professional Certifications

If you can afford it, choose a licensed agency. If you hire an independent contractor, these guidelines are doubly important.

Regardless of whether your candidates are independent contractors or employees of a licensed home health agency, there are certain documents that you will want to see before you invest your valuable time examining the rest of the workers' credentials. Because some of these requirements are state-mandated, they may vary.

- A current certificate stating that this person has been certified as a home health aide in your parent's state. This indicates that the person has mastered the accepted techniques for taking care of your parent safely and efficiently. The certification teaches aides how to help prevent skin breakdown (also known as bed sores or decubitae). Your worker will have also been taught to change bed linen while the patient is in the bed, as well as safe and comfortable methods of bathing a person who is bed-bound. The training includes diapering and skin care for incontinent patients and appropriate safety measures for showering or assistance with ambulation (walking).

- Ask the worker to show current healthcare clearance from a board-certified physician confirming that she has been tested and is free of tuberculosis and other communicable diseases. Without this, you may be exposing your parent, your children, or yourself to unnecessary risks. You'll also want to see clearance that your candidates are able to fulfill their duties, that is, to lift your parent or heavy items, and to bend and move appropriately for all the assistance your parent needs. This is critical to your parent's safety. A homecare worker who is unable to support your father's weight may injure him by dragging him instead of lifting him. Or, the worker may not be able to support him if he falls and may inadvertently drop him.

- Your potential caregiver should have a photo identification issued by a governmental or licensing organization. If you hire the person, make a copy for your records. If you wish to be even more thorough, you can use your computer to check the issuing source to verify the identification.

- If your worker comes from a licensed homecare agency, ask the agency for a copy of current documentation showing the agency's state license and Medicare certification. If the agency is not Medicare-certified, Medicare will not pay for the services it provides. Also, ask for proof of current workers' compensation insurance and general liability insurance. Independent contractors rarely have workers' compensation insurance.

- If your agency is not currently licensed by the state your parent lives in or isn't approved by Medicare, your parent's health insurance may not pay for its services. State and Medicare approval require that homecare workers employed by that agency have basic training, health and background checks, and up-to-date certifications. Without those requirements, you do not have assurance that universally accepted standards for health and training have been met. Ask if the workers are employees of the agency or independent contractors.

- Workers' compensation and general liability insurance may be important to help prevent you or your parent from claims if the worker is injured on the job.
- If the worker is an employee of the agency, the government requires the agency to deduct payroll taxes. You'll want a copy of this policy in writing to protect yourself against future claims.
- Medicare-approved homecare agencies are required to perform a state or federal background check on their workers. To be certain your agency has complied with this rule, ask for a copy of the report. If your request is refused on "confidentiality" grounds, explain that you are concerned and anxious about leaving a stranger alone with your parent and your possessions. Suggest that if the worker has nothing to hide, the worker should be happy to give permission for the agency to share a copy of her background clearance.

Do not accept verbal assurances. Ask for copies of the documents described in the preceding bullets.

Training and Experience

Before you call a homecare agency or hire a private worker, take a moment to double-check your assessment of your parent's needs. If you're satisfied with your evaluation, discuss your list of requirements with the agency by phone, fax, or e-mail. Ask to interview workers with the understanding that you'll pay each one for two hours of her time. Remember, they have to travel to and from your home and give up a paid shift to meet you. Two hours is a fair price, and if you can afford it, well worth the money. If your mother is physically well enough and cognitively able to make sound decisions, she should participate in the interview. This pre-employment meeting gives you and your parent an opportunity to choose an employee you both feel comfortable with. You'll also have a chance to assess the worker's ability to communicate with your parent. If it's not feasible for your parent to interview with you, and you can find the time, talk to several candidates, choose two or three who you feel comfortable with, and let your parent make the final decision. Since you will already have found them all acceptable, you won't care which one your mother chooses. She, however, will have a voice in her own care. That may be extremely important to her. Self-determination and independence are meaningful to all of us. Another benefit is that your mother may be more cooperative if she is involved in decisions that concern her care. A warning: If your mother has moderate or advanced dementia, it is not safe for her to exercise control over her healthcare.

It's not a good idea to interview alone. If your parent won't be helpful during the interview, then get other backup. An objective view from an uninvolved friend, relative, or coworker can often help identify benefits and problems that you may miss on your own.

Don't assume the agency has told the worker about your requirements or that a private-hire aide remembers everything you said on the telephone. If you want to avoid misunderstandings later, discuss your list of requirements at the beginning of the interview. If your parent has Parkinson's disease, ask the homecare aide to tell you about other patients she has cared for with Parkinson's, or about specific training she has received, and her knowledge of the disease. Ask the worker to tell you two of the worst experiences she has had caring for patients with problems similar to your parent's, and how she handled them. A homecare aide who has substantial experience with dementia, stroke, hearing or vision impairment, or other illnesses will easily be able to relate these stories. This will give you insight into the worker's hands-on experience.

Talk to your candidates about continuity. You've pre-assessed how long you expect to need services. If your parent will need help three days each week for at least eight to ten weeks, confirm that the aide will be available for those dates. You'll be investing a substantial amount of time and money to make sure your homecare program works smoothly. Every time you have to replace the worker, you'll have to invest your time and money in interviewing and training all over again. If your mother has established a trusting relationship with the aide, she might become upset and less cooperative when she loses that closeness and has to put her care and trust in the hands of a stranger.

When you've found a person who meets your requirements, be certain to ask for and phone her references and tell them exactly why you want to hire the worker. For example: "(Name of worker) gave me your name and telephone number as a reference for her. I am considering hiring her to care for my mother. They will be alone in my house all day. I would appreciate any information you can share about your experiences with her. I will keep what you say strictly confidential." Regardless of how you feel or your impressions, it is important to take the time to follow up with references. What you hear may change your mind entirely or may give you additional peace of mind.

When you are ready to hire, show your intentions as a responsible employer. The final step before hiring is to ask the person what else she needs from you to meet your requirements and provide excellent care for your parent.

D. SUPERVISING HOMECARE WORKERS

"My mother's homecare worker was wonderful. She cooked my mother's favorite foods, and she kept the apartment spotless. As my mother became sicker, she was even more important in her life. My mother didn't go out much, and Sara was such good company for her. Even when my mother got nasty and yelled at her, she stuck with it. She seemed to handle everything. Not like the stories I heard from my friends about one problem after another. She never called me. When I called my mother, we spoke, and she reassured me everything was fine. I always said how lucky we were to find someone who really cared about Mom. I needed someone like her because my mother and I never had a great relationship. I lived almost three thousand miles away. I had plenty of excuses not to get involved, and I took advantage of them all. Sara gave me peace of mind. But everything changed on my last visit. I decided to clean out a couple of closets. I was sleeping in a guest bedroom, so I started there. When I found a man's sock, I thought 'Yuck! I can't believe no one's cleaned this closet since Dad died eight years ago!' Then I found running shoes, a baseball bat, computer books, and a load of other stuff that couldn't have belonged to my dad. I considered the possibility that Mom may have had a secret boyfriend before she got sick. I didn't say anything. I kept looking and found more items in the house that didn't belong to our family. Then I knew. I went through my mother's checkbook and found checks to various stores and one to a travel agency! When I confronted Sara, she cried. Her husband and children lived there. They just moved in without permission from anyone. They used my mom's car; our electricity, heat, and air conditioning; and everything in Mom's house. When I finally unraveled the whole story, I was astounded. Mom was lonely and liked Sara. She was afraid that if Sara left, she'd be alone. So she bought Sara, her husband, and their two children whatever they asked for. They knew we were ripe to be taken advantage of because Mom was alone and I distanced myself from the whole situation. Once they got in, they just took over and got whatever they wanted."

Sheila, New Jersey

Your Responsibilities

If you want your parent to be well cared for, you still have a great deal of work to do. For a really clear view, compare your situation to any employer-employee relationship. For example, imagine a company where the employer hires a person to take charge of a difficult job with serious, perhaps life-altering, consequences for sloppy or incomplete work. The employer says, "Okay, you're hired," and turns the duties, planning, and problem solving over to the newly hired worker without any guidance except a "to do" list. The worker has no helpful files, documentation, or history; the worker doesn't know who the service providers or suppliers are. Without supervision or with only superficial supervision, the homecare worker, a total stranger, is left in charge. There shouldn't be any doubt in your mind that, at best, this is a recipe for a stressful experience or a failure. At worst, it's the road to disaster. Adjust these two recommendations to fit your lifestyle.

1. Keep the lines of communication wide open. Meet with the worker weekly for a status report. It's always a good idea to make a personal

visit and evaluate the house and your parent's appearance with your own eyes. It you are a long-distance caregiver, you'll find the assistance you need to create a local support system in chapter 5. When you visit, vary your routine. Call ahead or arrive unexpectedly; visit in the evening as well as in the morning. The homecare worker will quickly understand that you are an involved caregiver who expects your mother to be treated equally well at all times.

2. Buy a ring-binder notebook and enough tabs to create a separate, easily accessed section for emergencies, doctors, medication schedules, important telephone numbers, menus, activities, transportation, and petty cash and receipts. Some sections might contain only one page, others several. Your objective is to provide your employee with as much information as you can so that she can do the best job possible.

Tab 1: Emergencies. In an emergency, the first number to call is 911. Give the worker the name and telephone number of the first family member to be notified in an emergency, and at least two alternates in the event the first person cannot be reached. If your parent is very ill and you expect to be called, consider carrying a cell phone or a pager. Do not expect the homecare aide to call the entire family. Make that the responsibility of whoever is the primary contact. Be sure your parent's primary care physician is on this list along with his other doctors.

Tab 2: Doctors. Write down the name, address, and telephone number of every one of your parent's physicians. Be sure to clearly state their specialty: primary care, heart, podiatrist, and so forth. Under each name, add simple directions to the doctor's office. This is important information and should be readily available in your parent's home for whoever accompanies your parent to appointments or makes arrangements for transportation. Having this caregiver's book readily available will relieve you of repeating the directions or writing them down each time your parent visits the doctor.

Tab 3: Medications and medication schedules. Ask your parent's pharmacist for a printout of your parent's prescription medications. Add nonprescription tablets or liquids such as aspirin, non-aspirin pain relievers, vitamins, homeopathic remedies, or others. When your parent receives a new medication, ask for a new printout. Having this history will be extremely helpful when your parent visits a new physician or if he experiences side effects from a new medication.

Tab 4: Important telephone numbers. Write down every telephone number the homecare worker might need: taxi, day care, grocery, pharmacy, library, restaurants, senior center, grocery store, repair companies, and others. Having these numbers will help the aide meet your parent's needs more efficiently. Do not give the telephone numbers of companies you prefer to call yourself for financial control or other reasons.

Tab 5: Menus. Help your parent's caregiver by providing lists of foods your parent likes to eat. If you want the foods cooked exactly as you or your mother cooks them, include the recipes. Ask the caregiver if she has a problem cooking from recipes. Type or print them so they are clear and easy to read. Your worker may never have tasted the foods your mother prefers. It's unrealistic to expect her to know how to prepare them in an identical manner without written directions or from a faded, sloppily written, food-stained recipe. If your parent has a special diet, create menus and make sure they are easy to prepare. Don't expect your worker to create a five-star menu every night unless she agreed to do so during the interview. If your mother enjoys take-out food, include menus from the restaurants she likes, but make sure the worker knows you expect a nutritionally balanced diet. Be sure to make provisions for payment with your petty cash account or a charge account at the restaurant. Visit the restaurant and explain your situation. Tell the manager you would like to set up an account and agree on the amount you authorize to be charged each week or each month. Your parent will enjoy dining out, and you will be able to control costs. Food is vital to your parent's physical strength and emotional comfort. It's just as important to the homecare worker. Remind your mother that the aide may be used to different foods and has the right to enjoy them. If the worker "lives in," you will be paying for the worker's foods, so remember to increase your budget to cover this expense. Your attention to this section of your caregiver's book may be the difference in whether or not your parent accepts the homecare worker or complains until you find another one.

Tab 6: Activities. Why make the homecare worker guess which activities your mother might enjoy. You can make your mother's life more pleasant by providing this information to the worker ahead of time. Does your mother play cards? Read books or magazines? Watch certain television programs? Walk for exercise? Stroll for pleasure? Enjoy the challenge of a jigsaw or crossword puzzle? Like to have friends in for coffee? Attend the theater? Got to art exhibits? Surf the Internet? Increase your parent's quality of life by making arrangements so that the aide can continue as many previously enjoyed activities as possible.

Tab 7: Transportation. The homecare worker may live in a different area and may be unfamiliar with roads that are second nature to you. If you expect the aide to accompany your mother on various outings, it's a good idea to provide information about local transportation. Street maps, bus routes, taxi companies, car services, senior service transport, and medical transport are all helpful. List the places you expect her to go with simple, clear directions for getting there and getting back.

Tab 8: Petty cash and receipts. If you expect the worker to shop for groceries, buy take-out food, or pay for transportation, it's important to set up a petty cash system to help avoid misunderstandings. It's simple. Buy a plastic envelope that fits in the binder. Tell the worker to ask for a receipt for every expense, and put all the receipts in the envelope. Pick up the receipts weekly or monthly and balance the remaining cash to the money spent. If you gave the worker $20 and the receipts show that she has spent $12.94, she should have $7.06 remaining in the petty cash fund. Be sure to check the receipts to make sure you have approved—or do approve of—the purchases. And don't forget to replace the $12.94 so the worker will have enough cash for the following week.

E. YOUR RIGHT TO COMPLAIN AND REPLACE THE WORKER

One of the most important aspects of your homecare plan is to understand that your first plan may not work. Your second or third plan may need revisions. Remember, the reason your parent needs care is because something has changed. Don't expect your parent to behave the way he "used to." Expect unpredictable behavior. Elder caregiving will never fit into a tightly wrapped, neat package. You may think you have found a homecare worker who perfectly matches your qualifications, only to find an instant personality clash when you introduce her to your father. A candidate who wants the job may tell you he is confident he can meet your needs, but when it comes time to replace words with actions, you may be very disappointed in his skill level. We have no foolproof methods for assuring appropriate homecare. If the aide you employ doesn't work out, you have two options:

1. Talk to the aide. Sometimes a frank discussion can change the whole picture. Tell the homecare agency or the aide or both how you feel and why. In some cases, the worker may have misunderstood your instructions. Don't be surprised if you find that your parent or another family member issued conflicting directions. You may find your mother has been manipulating the entire situation in hopes of removing the worker and all supervision from her home. If this happens, don't blame the aide. She was likely caught in the middle.
2. Ask the homecare agency for a replacement. Explain your position and be firm. You are under no obligation to accept a worker with inferior skills, a poor attitude, or an inability to communicate clearly because of language difficulties. You don't want and shouldn't accept a worker who is unclean, inappropriately dressed, insists on making multiple phone calls from your parent's residence, invites friends or family to visit at your parent's home, or sleeps at inappropriate times. Do not hesitate to complain. If the worker comes from an agency, it is the agency's job to fire the worker. You have a right to expect a replacement before the worker leaves so that your parent will not be left alone.

Use the worksheets at the end of this chapter to guide you through planning a homecare program. Concentrate on the basics.

- Be certain the agency or the private-hire knows that you want to begin your relationship on a trial basis. Do not commit to long-term employment until you have tested the worker in your parent's home.
- Maintain close supervision of your parent's care. Monitor your parent's reaction to your employee's behavior. Stay alert for changes in your parent or the aide's emotional, mental, or physical attitude.

- Solve problems quickly. Don't be afraid to complain. Discuss your concerns and try to identify the cause of the problem. If you can't resolve your problems, replace the aide.
- Most of all, don't be afraid to revise your plan whenever you have a better idea to improve your life or your parent's life.

F. WORKSHEET: SEVEN HELPFUL TIPS FOR SELECTING A HOMECARE WORKER

Bringing a stranger into your or your parent's home is never easy. Following these guidelines may help you avoid problems. It's also helpful to ask a friend or professional counselor to assist you.

1. Look for and try to use state-licensed or Medicare-certified agencies. This may help ensure that your aide has a current healthcare certificate, background check, and continued training.
2. If you can afford it, pay for two hours of the workers' time for an interview prior to hiring. This will allow you to meet the candidates and determine which one would be the best match for your parent.
3. Ask the homecare worker to tell you about her experiences with patients like your parent. A worker who has had experience with your parent's problems should be able to tell you some of the problems she faced and how she handled them.
4. Be certain you're comfortable with the communication between you and your potential helper. Will your parent be able to understand her when she speaks? Is she well groomed? Did she appear to listen attentively and understand you when you explained your needs?
5. Be clear about what duties you expect the worker to perform and how you will supervise her. Ask her directly if she has agreed to commit to the number of hours, days, and weeks you need her. Do not assume the agency discussed this with her. Continuity is essential to your plan's success.
6. If you're uncomfortable handling this process alone, ask a friend or relative to assist you. For more information on how to hire a homecare worker, review this chapter.

7. When you find the homecare worker who you feel is the best qualified to meet your and your parent's needs, the next step is to telephone the worker's references. Confirming the worker's skills and experience can help keep your parent safe and increase your peace of mind.

WORKSHEET: MY PARENT'S HOMECARE NEEDS

Determining your parent's needs is an important step in creating a homecare program. Do this before you call a paid homecare worker or decide which family member would be the best choice to help your parent.

1. At this point, I feel my parent will need help _____ hours each day, _____ days each week, for the next ___ weeks. I will revise this if my parent's needs change.

2. My parent's medical diagnosis is: _____

_____

3. I want the caregiver to perform the following duties:

_____

_____

_____

4. I have prepared a file for the worker with the following information for my parent:

- At least two names and telephone numbers of people to notify in an emergency
- Medications and schedules
- Allergies
- Activities list

- Petty cash system
- Doctors names, addresses, and telephone numbers
- Other important telephone numbers (pharmacy, etc.)
- List of foods my parent likes to eat, is not allowed to eat
- Local transportation names and telephone numbers

G. MY JOURNAL

Use this page as a safe place to express your feelings and concerns. Putting your thoughts and feelings on paper helps you to see them more clearly. What bothers you? What changes do you want to make? When you read what you have written, you may see a new pathway to help resolve stressful issues. For example:

"My mom was always so independent. I know she doesn't want anyone in her house to help her, but she needs the help. I know too, that I'm not the one who can do it . . ."

"I thought Mom could handle this herself, but I was wrong. All she does is complain about what the aide 'doesn't' do. I guess leaving them alone wasn't a good idea. The only way I'm going to have any peace is to sit down with both of them and decide what the aide is going to do, then make a list so she'll know what we expect . . ."

H. TIP SHEET

- Learn about your homecare options through your local hospital or Area Agency on Aging. Knowing your options will help you provide your parent with the best possible help.
- Evaluate what your parent can and cannot do for herself. If you do not feel capable of assessing the situation, hire a geriatric care manager, social worker, or registered nurse to provide you with an accurate and realistic assessment.
- Interview two to three homecare workers before you decide who will take care of your parent. If your parent is cognitively intact, involve him in the selection process. Make a copy of the aide's certificate and driver's license.
- If possible hire a homecare worker from a licensed, bonded homecare agency to ensure accountability and continuity of service.
- Observe your parent with the home health aide at different times of the day, different days of the week. If you are not comfortable with the home health aide, you have the right and responsibility to replace the worker.

12

MANAGING MEDICAL ISSUES

A. LEARNING TO BE AN ADVOCATE IN THE DOCTOR'S OFFICE

I t's second nature for most of us to be the advocate for our families and ourselves. You may remember checking your son's school menus to make certain that he was receiving nutritionally sound lunches. If you didn't like the menu, you became his advocate by packing a lunch for him. Most of us have left a job for better working conditions somewhere else, or have been our own advocates by speaking to our boss after we were denied a pay raise or promotion. But when it comes to the medical system, we often feel timid and cowed. Instead of asking questions, we grumble. The result is a communications breakdown. When you say, "Thank you, doctor" and leave, the physician rightly believes that you understand and approve of the prescribed treatment. Because you didn't ask the questions you wanted to ask, you neither fully understood nor approved of what course of action was decided: you just assumed that you have no choice. If you learn only one caregiving skill, learn to be your family's and your own advocate in the medical system. It may save your lives.

Most physicians work long hours to keep us healthy. They are usually there when we need them, and it's almost impossible to imagine staying well without them. But what we tell them, our input, and ability to follow directions are critical to their success. Doctors need your help. They know that one solution doesn't work for all patients because each of us is different. They aren't surprised that a medication that helped your mother's friend might not help your mother. In fact, if she's taking several other medications, the interactions among medications may actually harm her. Good physicians do not want you to blindly obey them. They prefer an alert, interested patient or relative who asks questions and shares information. Doctors welcome and appreciate patient advocacy because it helps them do their job more effectively.

Most of our parents were taught exactly the opposite. They were taught that the doctor knew best and it was disrespectful to question or challenge a doctor's diagnosis or directions. They may also sometimes expect the doctor to tell them what's wrong without describing symptoms or all the necessary information. The result is that your mother might not tell the doctor that although the medication helped one problem, it also made her feel dizzy. If she tells the eye doctor that her vision is blurry, she might not tell him it started with a new medication because she may never have reasoned that there is a link between the two. Even if her ophthalmologist asks her directly, "Could you see better before you started taking this medication?" she might not make the connection. You and I might go back to the physician for another appointment and discuss the problem. Your mother is more likely to decide the medication can't help her and simply stop taking it. The doctor will never know she did this. Without that feedback—that self-advocacy—neither the eye doctor nor the physician can provide effective treatment. With it, the doctor might have simply changed the medication to one that worked without debilitating side effects. Instead, your mother would very likely receive a prescription for new glasses that she really didn't need. Lack of reporting, or advocacy, is one of the leading causes of illnesses among the elderly. Any side effect can be potentially dangerous. If a drug leads to a little confusion at the wrong moment for your mother, she could fall and break a hip, or become distracted and cause an auto accident. Either could result in admission to a hospital or nursing home, or even death. (See chapter 17 for more information on dealing with medications.)

ELDERCARE 911

One of the reasons we sometimes find it difficult to be advocates in a medical situation is because some of our parent's attitudes and beliefs were passed on to us as children. Keep your respect for physicians; eliminate your blind acceptance. Start advocating. Take the time to learn about your parent's treatment and the results her doctors expect. If your expectations are different from theirs, communicate that to them. Learn to keep meaningful records. When you accompany your mother to her doctor's appointment, bring her records with you. Otherwise, fax, mail, or deliver the records before her appointment. Your thoroughness will be appreciated.

Most caregiver organizations offer information, support groups, and counseling designed to help you become a more effective advocate. To find one that specializes in your parent's illness, consult chapters 9 and 24. Your ability to listen to a physician, appraise the situation, and speak up when you spot a potential problem is one of the least expensive and most effective insurance policies you can obtain for your parents and yourself. Your parent will be safer, and you'll feel more in control.

B. CHOOSING A DOCTOR

When you take your father to the doctor, you are often going to the physician he has been placing his trust in for years. But what about your confidence? It's important that both of you feel comfortable. Your peace of mind may depend on whether you feel that you can rely on the professional knowledge and expertise of the doctor your parent has chosen. Checking Certifications and professional credentials are one step in generating that confidence.

Board-Certified Physicians

Board-certified physicians are those who have graduated from medical school, completed residency, trained under supervision in a specialty, and passed a qualifying exam given by a medical specialty board—abbreviated BC.[1] Be sure that your parent's physicians meet these standards.

Geriatric Physicians

Geriatricians or geriatric physicians specialize in treating elderly patients. This specialty is important because as we age, our physiological makeup changes. We generally become more dependent on medications, but our liver and kidneys metabolize them differently. Receiving treatment for a knee bruised in a fall might resolve the problem for most of us. For our parents, it might not. We need to know what caused the fall because a simple stumble could easily be a sign of dizziness or confusion brought on by medication, poor eyesight, or other problems. Pain medication prescribed for problems resulting from the fall might actually add to your mother's dizziness, and she might fall again. (For more information on falls, see chapter 2.) Preventing another fall could avoid a possible hospital or nursing home admission and help your parent remain independent longer. Geriatricians are trained to look for underlying reasons and clues. They try to track and treat the root cause of the problem from a different approach. They schedule time to engage the elderly person in conversation. They usually make sure the patient is comfortable and make a deliberate show of respect for the patient's dignity and age. They ask questions slowly and gently with a unique understanding of the elderly patient's special privacy issues.

Specialists

Specialists usually limit their practice to a particular class of patients (elderly) or of illnesses (neurologists, psychiatrists, pulmonologists, dermatologists, podiatrists) or techniques (surgeons). They are qualified in their field by advanced training, and they are certified by a specialty examining board.[2] They are experts and are usually your best resource for a severe illness. Because they are totally immersed in one area, they are more likely to network with other specialists in that field and are usually more aware of new treatments and drug trials. Medical insurance often requires a referral from a primary care physician to a specialist and to take part in a new treatment program.

If you have good reason to believe your father has not received the best treatment available, trust your instincts. Sometimes elders are diagnosed based on ageism: "At his age, what do you expect?"

"My eighty-three-year-old mother had just moved to Florida to be near me. She drove and took care of herself without my help. She found it very difficult to make friends, so she spent much of her time alone in her apartment. She lost a lot of weight. Her new doctor diagnosed her problem as 'depression.' He said it fit the circumstances, with her relocation and loneliness, so we didn't question him. When she kept losing weight, we took her to a geriatric specialist who immediately diagnosed her with cancer. She died six months later. We don't know if she could have been saved if the first doctor had diagnosed her properly."

Jane, Florida

C. PREPARING FOR THE VISIT

When your parents were your age, chances are they prepared for doctor visits by making a note of what day and what time to show up for the appointment. Today, if you want to get the most out of your time with the doctor, you need to gather as much information about your parent's physical and emotional problems, medications, and insurance status as you possibly can before the visit takes place.

"My father's primary care physician wanted him to see a cardiologist immediately. Both doctors were in the same building, just a few offices apart from each other. We literally just walked down the hall and into the cardiac specialist's office. The cardiologist asked for all kinds of information regarding medication changes and test results. I told him the other doctor had them, and I assumed he had sent or faxed the information when he called for the appointment. He looked at me like I had two heads. He must have been wondering what kind of an idiot would come to an emergency appointment like this without background information. To make it worse, my father and I were both so nervous we couldn't remember the names and dosages of all his prescriptions. I rushed down the hall to the other doctor's office to get the information, but it was closed for lunch. The doctor had carved out the time, but couldn't use it because he didn't have the information he needed. He was annoyed. He didn't know my father, so he accurately reported that the patient couldn't remember the names of his medications. So now my father's medical record reads like he has a memory problem."

Marsha, Texas

Gathering Medical and Insurance Information

The doctor you are taking your parent to visit may be one of several physicians caring for your parent. Your parent may have seen a specialist for a totally different problem without mentioning it to her primary care physician because she assumed that the ailment was unrelated to this one. Here's how to find out what is or has been happening.

- First, try to obtain your mother's cooperation. Explain that previous medications and problems might affect the one you are currently trying to diagnose or treat. Ask your mother if you can talk to her doctors and her pharmacist to collect the records her doctor needs. If she agrees, ask her to sign a medical records release form. This form is called a HIPAA (Health Insurance Portability and Account-ability Act) form and gives the professionals involved the authority to talk to you freely. You can find HIPAA forms on the Internet, and at the many doctors' offices, hospitals, and other places involved in medical treatment. Once you have the form, make copies, as you will need to leave one with each medical and insurance profes-sional who shares Mom's information with you.
- Once you get her permission to speak with her physician and others, check her prescription bottles to find the pharmacy she uses. Tell the pharmacist you have a medical records release that you can fax or mail, and ask for a printout of her medication history. If your mother refuses to sign a release, visit the pharmacist, explain your need, and ask for the printout. If the pharmacist refuses to release the information to you without your mother's approval, he will probably agree to send it directly to your mother's physician.

- Next, call the doctors whose names appear on the prescription bottles. Explain that you are gathering your mother's medical history, and ask for a copy of her medical records. There will probably be a small charge for this service. Pick up the records, or ask the physicians to send them to the doctor you are going to visit. Be sure to let them know the date of your appointment and to give them as much notice as possible.

- Finally, make sure your parent is carrying her health insurance card and that the card is current. If you have any doubts, call the insurance company or check the mail for correspondence regarding benefits paid. It's unlikely the insurance company will give you information unless you fax them a copy of the HIPAA form your mother signed.

Bringing Medications and Prescriptions

The truth is that even the safest medications have the possibility of adverse side effects. Most people over the age of sixty-five take several medications, often several times each day. Think about the number of problems our parents have, and then imagine the potency of medications that can help control high blood pressure, low blood pressure, digestive ailments, arthritic problems, coronary diseases, high cholesterol, diabetes, Parkinson's, Alzheimer's disease, or any number of viruses and infections. Add aspirin, vitamins, and numerous other over-the-counter treatments, and it's easy to see why we need to stay alert. Many doctors and pharmacists rely on computers for compatibility information. The potential for negative interactions between four, five, six, or seven prescription medications has grown beyond our ability to control from memory or by simply reading labels. Using general guidelines to help your parents manage and monitor their medications will ultimately help keep them safer.

Meet your parent's pharmacist (see chapter 14). Your parent's pharmacist can be your most accessible source of information and provide you with valuable management tools and suggestions.

If you've been taking a list of medications to your parent's doctors, you've done well. Now, go one step further and take the pharmacy printout and the actual prescription bottles with you. Look on the kitchen counters, in the bathroom and kitchen cabinets, in the refrigerator, and in dresser and nightstand drawers. Regardless of what you find, do not chastise your parent. Just collect the medications and take them with you to your parent's doctor. To help avoid potential errors with technical terms, hand them to the nurse and ask her to copy them into the file.

If the doctor changes your parent's prescription or adds another medication to the list, be your parent's advocate by asking the doctor to please recheck the medications you brought with you to be certain the new medication won't adversely interact with the others and produce any problematic side effects.

When your doctor hands you a prescription, ask questions and write down the answers. When you pick up your prescription at the pharmacy, compare the physician's instructions with the label on the bottle. If you find a discrepancy, call the pharmacist and ask her to check the instructions on the original prescription. If you still have conflicting directions, call the physician for clarification.

Use this list of questions as a guide or take this book with you and read them off, one by one. Be polite, but firm, and take the time you need to get the answers that will keep your parent safe.

1. "How many should my parent take each day, and is there a specific time of day? Morning? Bedtime?" If you feel your parent is unlikely to cooperate because of the number of pills each day or because the times of day seem problematic, ask the physician and the pharmacist for other options. The nurse in the physician's office may have additional recommendations.
2. "Does my parent need to take this with food?" If the prescription is for "one tablet with meals three times a day" and you know your parent doesn't eat breakfast, speak up. You need an option that will allow your parent to get appropriate treatment.
3. "Can my parent take the pill with fruit juice, milk, coffee, or tea instead of water?" Make sure your parent understands the answer and the reason for this direction.
4. "What are the most common side effects?" Ask the physician if she wants to be notified if your parent experiences any of these.
5. "Does combining this medication with the other medications I brought in today present a possibility of adverse medication reactions?" Most caregivers assume the physician has already ruled that out. This is a good time to invoke the advocate's primary

rule: Never assume anything. Ask this question of the physician and the pharmacist for every medication.

6. "Will a glass of wine or a cocktail change the affect or impact of this medication?" Alcohol and medications don't mix. If you aren't going to be able to stop your parent from having a drink before dinner, talk to the physician and the pharmacist for a better understanding of the risks.

7. "Are there any activities that my parent should give up while taking these medications?" Ask how this relates to your parent's ability to drive, garden, walk up or down stairs, use a ladder, work with tools, cook, and other activities.

8. "What if my parent forgets a dose?" Get clear instructions on whether your parent should make up a missed dose when he remembers or skip it and take the medication at the next appropriate time.

9. "If my parent has a problem swallowing these pills, what do you recommend?" If you know this has been a problem in the past, mention it to the doctor, the nurse, or the pharmacist, and ask for a solution.

10. "Is there anything else my mother and I should know about this medication?" Always ask this question. Some of your most important information may come with the answer.

D. ASKING THE RIGHT QUESTIONS AND GETTING THE ANSWERS

How many times have you left the doctor's office and thought of a question you wish you had asked? What about the visits when you asked all the questions you could think of and when you left, you still had no idea what to do next? Or what the future held for you? Asking questions and getting answers that will help you provide better care is a three-part process.

First, write down the questions you believe will help you understand your parent's illness. Take the list with you to the doctor's office. Wait until the doctor is finished examining your parent and finished talking to both of you, and then take out your list and ask the questions that he didn't cover. You may be tempted to save time and try to remember the answers, but taking your parent to the doctor can be a very stressful, even traumatic, experience. This is not a good time to trust your memory. Write the answer down before moving on to the next question.

The second part of the question-and-answer process is making sure you understand the answers. You want the medical explanation, but that's only one piece of the puzzle. You also want practical information, in lay language, as to what this means to your parent and to you. How will this problem change your parent's ability to function? What kind of help will your parent need tomorrow? Six months from now? One year from now? The answers will help you create a plan that will meet your parent's current needs and begin organizing to meet future challenges. Your physician may be able to provide only a portion of the information you need, but she will probably be able to refer you to a local support resource that can answer the rest of your questions.

Finally, don't hesitate to repeat questions if you don't understand the answers. You are the advocate for your parents, and you're working hard to maintain a good quality of life for him and for yourself. The difference in understanding and misunderstanding can affect your parent's health. Most physicians will be happy to answer your questions until you feel comfortable that you have gotten all the information you need. It's your responsibility to be as organized as you can so that you can return the courtesy by not wasting your doctor's time. (Read section F in this chapter.) Use these questions as a guide to write your own, or take this book with you and just read them. Be sure you have paper and a pen to write down the answers.

1. "Is this problem treatable or curable?" Medical science now has treatments for illnesses that were considered fatal only a few years ago.
2. "Please tell us about the treatment program." Understanding the process is critical to planning. Your parent and you may also feel less anxious if you know what to expect.
3. "Will there be any more tests?" Many treatment programs require ongoing tests. It's best to know what's ahead.
4. "Does my mother have other options for treatment in this geographic area?" If the answer is yes, you may want to ask the physician to refer you to a specialist for treatment or for a second opinion.

5. "Are there physicians or hospitals that specialize in this disease in other parts of the country who may have other options for my mother?" Sometimes options are different in other geographic locations. This may be a factor in obtaining the newest, most successful treatment available.
6. "How will my mother's life change during (and after) treatment? Can she still swim every day and play cards?" Be sure to ask if it's safe to continue normal activities such as driving, playing golf, swimming, or other activities your parent currently enjoys.
7. "What side effects can we expect from these medications? Which ones do you want us to report?" Anticipating problems can help you plan around them and deal with them. In addition to the doctor, it's also wise to ask the doctor's nurse and pharmacist about potential side effects
8. "How often will my parent need to see you during treatment?" This question is a planning question. If your parent needs weekly visits, you may have to schedule transportation, time off from work, babysitters, or deal with other organizational needs.
9. "Is my parent safe at home alone?" If your parent needs help, be certain to ask the doctor what help he thinks your parent will need. Some possibilities include twenty-four-hour supervision, help with bathing, meals, dressing, toileting, transportation, or transferring from a bed to a chair.
10. "Is there anything else my mother and I should know about this illness or about the treatment? Is there a book you'd recommend on the subject?" Even if you've covered it all, this may bring gentle and kind words of wisdom and courage from your physician. Words that are well worth asking for.

E. AFTER THE VISIT

If you are satisfied with the diagnosis and the treatment, the next step in good healthcare is one of the hardest: making sure your parent follows the doctor's orders. If you have received a serious diagnosis, or aren't satisfied with the information and treatment your parent's physician recommended, do not hesitate to exercise your right to a second opinion.

Complying with Physicians' Orders

"My mother's cough keeps recurring because she never finishes her medication. As soon as she begins to feel better, she stops taking it and puts the remaining pills in the cabinet. She tells me, 'Nature will take over now.' Since she never finishes the treatment, the cough keeps coming back. But she feels like she's done something wonderful because she knows that when it comes back, she'll have medication left over from the first prescription and won't have to go to the doctor again. She's very proud that she can just open the cabinet and treat herself! No matter what I say, she just won't believe that the only way to finally get rid of her cough is to follow the doctor's orders and take all the pills as prescribed. She's driving me crazy."

Amanda, Idaho

"When the doctor asked me, 'What do you want me to do?' I lost it. I screamed into the phone, 'You're his doctor. Make him listen.' But we both knew he wouldn't. My father would just go on not filling his medication, not going for rehab, and getting worse and worse. I have a new baby, his first grandson, that he can only play with for a couple of minutes at a time because he doesn't have the strength to continue. It would be different if this wasn't treatable, but it is. How do we make him understand that this isn't just about him? We're all paying for his lack of treatment because he can't participate in many activities we want to try. What am I supposed to do? Ignore him and just watch as he gets weaker and weaker?"

Barbara, North Carolina

You've probably nodded your head by now because you've realized your parent isn't the only one ignoring your pleas and resisting treatment. It sometimes takes us weeks or even months of discussing, pleading, and nagging to convince our parent to visit a doctor.

After all this resistance, why are we still surprised when the same reluctant parent never follows through with the physician's instructions?

Many fill prescriptions but never take the medication. Others ignore the order entirely and never bother to fill the prescription even once. Still others fill the prescription once and never refill it, or only refill one portion of the multi-medication program.

Most of our parents called the doctor only for serious problems. Their parents, our grandparents, taught them to treat their own stubbed toes, colds, fevers, sinus infections, warts, and dozens of other problems.

> "My sister and brother and I still laugh at the 'medical treatment' we received as kids. None of us can recall going to a doctor, ever, except for serious issues like chicken pox or to remove our tonsils. My grandmother was a village nurse in Czechoslovakia. She cared for her kids herself, and I guess Mom learned self-sufficiency from her. Also, I think most people in our parents' generation only called the doctor for serious problems. There seemed to be nothing our mother couldn't cure by covering it with some sort of cream, filling us with chicken soup, or making us drink a glass of hot milk with butter. Ga-ag. I still can't think about warm milk without wanting to throw up."
>
> Judith, Florida

Our parents usually had sound, practical reasons for this independent lifestyle. Did they get paid for the time they took off work to visit a doctor? Did they have enough extra money to make up the salary loss and also pay the doctor? In a rural environment, the distance between where your parents lived and the doctor may have been too great to bother for a minor problem. We may still use some of our parents' remedies. But carrying medical self-treatment too far can be very dangerous. Most of our parents need professional medical assistance to successfully treat the many life-altering problems they face as they age.

Finances often affect compliance. Are you sure your parents can afford all the medications their physicians have prescribed? Most parents do not want to be dependent on their children for financial help.

> "When I took my mother's medicine to the pharmacist for a refill, he asked about another medication. I told him that I knew nothing

about it, but I'd ask my mother. He told me she needed the other one because it offset the dizziness caused by this one. I was dumb-struck. She'd fallen twice in the last week but refused to go back to the doctor. I went right over to her house and asked her. 'It didn't do anything. It was the other one I needed.' When I started yelling at her for not filling both, she told me, 'I couldn't afford them both, so I figured out which one I needed most, and that's the one I refilled.' I knew then that she didn't go back to the doctor because she couldn't afford the medicine. She'd have to explain that to the doctor, and she was too proud to even consider doing that. If I hadn't offered to help her that one day, I'd never have known and God knows what would have happened to her."

Celia, Wisconsin

Some pharmaceutical companies provide free prescription medications to patients who cannot afford them. The prescriptions are dispensed through physicians. Each manufacturer may have its own criteria for eligibility.

If you think your parent might qualify for this program, ask your parent's physicians for assistance or call the local Area Agency on Aging and the illness-specific organization that relates to your parent's problem (the American Heart, Parkinson's, or Alzheimer's organizations, and others). You can also call the company that manufactures the drug(s) your parent needs or ask your pharmacist. The Internet is always an excellent option to search for the companies that participate in this type of program and the drugs that are covered. Try the Web site for the Pharmaceutical Research and Manufacturers of America, http://www.phrma.org. Look for the Directory of the Prescription Drug Patient Assistance Programs.

Getting a Second Opinion

If you feel you would benefit from more information, don't hesitate to make an appointment for a second opinion. An examination by a second physician may present options for different or additional treatments, including new medication trials. If the diagnosis is the same as the first physician's, you will have peace of mind knowing that you've done everything you can to help your parent.

Most insurance coverage allows for a second opinion in the case of a serious illness. Call your parent's provider and ask for your options, or ask your parent's primary care physician to please obtain authorization for you. If the company denies your request, you have other options. Retain a geriatric care manager or insurance claims professional who specializes in getting referrals or getting claims approved. It could be well worth your while.

> "I came home one afternoon and my father said, 'I can't feel my right foot.' It was totally numb. The neurologist did several tests and said it was some sort of a virus that would run its course in time. He diagnosed foot drop and said my father needed a brace to walk and to protect his foot. I got a referral to a different neurologist for a second opinion. He couldn't find anything definitive, either. I was scared to death. How could something strong enough to make his foot go numb have no name? Then two of his fingers went numb. I could hardly breathe. I took him to a third doctor who added one more test to the blood workup she ordered and found the answer: he had arsenic poisoning! I went on the Internet and found a similar situation where a woman deteriorated to almost vegetable status before someone found the answer."
>
> *Barbara, Florida*

(For more information on your right to a second opinion, read sections B and E in chapter 15.)

Returning for New Treatment Options

> "Whenever I ask my father how he feels, he answers, 'Fine.' He could be having a heart attack when I ask him, and he wouldn't admit it. The problem is, he answers the same way to his doctor. He's in terrible pain, but when the doctor asks him how he feels, he answers, 'Not bad, thank you.' He's been that way his whole life. He considers functioning with pain a mark of pride and honor, and I want to strangle him for not getting the treatment that's

available. I don't understand why he'd rather suffer, and he doesn't understand why we keep nagging him. I know he's just making it worse. I never know how sick he really is. It frightens me."

Ken, Florida

"I knew there was a new treatment for my mother's problem. It had been out for over two years. I threatened to not call anymore, to stop coming over, to stop taking her out to dinner, to stop bringing her granddaughter for visits, and heaven only knows what else if she didn't go back to the doctor and see if the medication would help her. She ignored me, and I never did any of those things. One day she said, 'I made an appointment with the doctor.' After I got done telling her how happy I was and how proud of her I was, I made the mistake of asking her what changed her mind. I should've known better. After all I've been through, after years of torment, her exact words were, 'Oh, I saw something on television.' It took every ounce of control and effort I could muster to hold my tongue. Can you understand this? I can't."

Marianne, Georgia

There are many reasons for refusing another visit. Your mother may not want to suffer through another disappointment of being told she cannot be helped, she may not want you to know how bad her problem is, or she may not want to admit to herself that she is seriously ill. All of those really add up to fear and denial. What can you do? Realistically, there are times when you can't do anything. All the pleas, threats, promises, and tears add up to the same staunch refusal. But sometimes a different strategy will help. These examples may help you think of others based on your parent's habits and needs.

- Try approaching the problem from a different entrance point. For example, in addition to her main problem, your mother may have a problem with a toe. For the moment, forget her arthritis and focus on getting her to a doctor to treat the toe. Talk about how much more comfortable she'll be walking around. Or how much safer she'll be just taking a bath or standing in the shower. If you can convince her to go to the doctor for a minor ailment, take the doctor into your confidence before the appointment and ask for help with the major problem while you are there.

- Everyone wants to save money. If your mother is treating herself with over-the-counter medications, remind her that she might be able to save money if she had a prescription that was covered by insurance. This will require a doctor's visit for the prescription.
- If your father has used the same wheelchair for years, it may no longer fit him properly, and he may be uncomfortable. Check his insurance benefits to see if he's eligible for a new one. If he is, ask him if he wants an appointment for a prescription. (Note: Don't automatically accept a denial of this benefit from dad's insurance company. Call again on a different day, check the policy carefully yourself, or ask the equipment supplier to check for you.)

F. UNDERSTANDING PATIENTS' RIGHTS AND RESPONSIBILITIES

The next time you visit a doctor, look at the walls and you are almost certain to see a patient bill of rights. Be sure to read it. This document assures you of certain considerations and protections from the doctor and the entire staff. Understanding your rights can make your experience more comfortable and more informative. The number of rights often varies from office to office, but the basics remain the same.[3]

As a patient, you have the right to:

- Respect and courtesy from the entire staff.
- Privacy and confidentiality regarding your records.
- Complete disclosure to you of all the information in your file.
- Clear and understandable written or spoken explanations of illnesses, medications, and other treatments.
- Express a complaint and receive a prompt response.
- Receive effective relief from pain.
- Review all cost for treatments regardless of payment source.

"Rights" are a two-way street. If you expect your healthcare providers to abide by and protect your rights, you must acknowledge that they have many of the same rights you do. They want you to participate. They believe you will have a much better relationship if you acknowledge your responsibility to get involved and understand your care. Their list of your responsibilities will vary from office to office, but these are the basics.[4]

As a patient, your responsibilities include:

- Respect and courtesy toward the entire staff.
- Asking questions, appraising options, and making informed decisions.
- Reporting on the effectiveness of treatment provided, including pain relief.
- Providing full and accurate information regarding your medical history and insurance.
- Following the prescribed treatment plan unless you formally refuse it.
- Understanding what your medications are for and how to take them.
- Paying bills promptly.

G. WORKSHEET: QUESTIONS TO ASK YOUR DOCTOR (AND WHAT TO DO WITH THE ANSWERS)

Most caregivers will benefit from taking an active role in their parent's healthcare. These questions will help you understand your parent's diagnosis and prognosis, and may help you organize for the future.

1. What is my parent's formal (exact) diagnosis? Are there any additional tests usually recommended to confirm this diagnosis?

_____

_____

_____

2. What is the short-term (and long-term) outlook for people my parent's age with this condition?

_____

_____

_____

3. What is the treatment? How long will it take? How incapacitating will it be?

_____

_____

_____

4. What are side effects of the medications? Have you reviewed my parent's current medications for adverse drug reactions?

_____

_____

_____

What to Do with the Answers:

1. Prioritize: What do you need to do today? Tomorrow? This week? Next week?
2. Ask your parent's insurance carrier for approval for a second opinion. In most cases, it's a good idea not to ask your parent's current doctor for a referral to the physician you use for a second opinion.
3. Identify potential lifestyle changes: What changes will this make in your current activities? In your parent's current activities?

4. Identify potential needs: What do you need for your parent's healthcare? To maintain your parent's and your own quality of life?
5. For more information on communicating with physicians, review this chapter.

WORKSHEET:
IMPORTANT TELEPHONE NUMBERS

Creating a list of telephone numbers for people who are important to your parent's well-being is a must for every caregiver.

In an emergency, always call 911 first.

1. Family members to contact in an emergency:

Name _____ Tel. _____

Name _____ Tel. _____

Name _____ Tel. _____

2. Physicians:

Name _____ Tel. _____

Name _____ Tel. _____

Name _____ Tel. _____

3. Pharmacy:

Name _____ Tel. _____

4. Neighbors:

Name _____ Tel. _____

Name _____ Tel. _____

5. Friends:

Name _____ Tel. _____

Name _____ Tel. _____

6. Other (geriatric care manager, elder law attorney, financial adviser, bank, transportation service, homecare agency or worker, grocery store, plumber, home repair, or others):

Title _____ Name _____ Tel. _____

Title _____ Name _____ Tel. _____

Title _____ Name _____ Tel. _____

Title _____ Name _____ Tel. _____

Title _____ Name _____ Tel. _____

Title _____ Name _____ Tel. _____

Title _____ Name _____ Tel. _____

Title _____ Name _____ Tel. _____

Title _____ Name _____ Tel. _____

Title _____ Name _____ Tel. _____

H. MY JOURNAL

Use this page as a safe place to express your feelings. Putting thoughts and feelings on paper helps you to see them more clearly. What bothers you? What changes do you want to make? When you read what you have written, you may see a new pathway to help resolve stressful issues. For example:

"I was always so insecure. Now that my dad needs me to talk to his doctors I have to learn how to speak up . . ."

"I am 54 years old and Dad has so many medical problems in addition to his Parkinson's disease I'm not sure I can handle all this alone. I'm either going to have to be very organized or get help, and organization isn't what I do best. I won't get help from my family. Maybe I'll call the Parkinson's Association tomorrow and see if they can help me . . ."

_____

_____

_____

_____

_____

_____

_____

_____

_____

_____

_____

_____

_____

_____

_____

_____

_____

_____

_____

_____

_____

_____

_____

_____

_____

_____

_____

_____

_____

_____

_____

I. TIP SHEET

- Ask your parent for permission to speak to his physician and when it is possible join your parent at the doctor's office during a regular medical checkup.
- Choose the best doctor for your parent's condition or illness. Sometimes your parent may require his primary care physician and sometimes he may need a specialist to diagnose and treat his medical problem.
- Prepare a list of questions for the doctor when you accompany your parent to a medical examination or a hospital visit.
- Bring all medication in its original containers when your parent has a medical examination or an emergency trip to the hospital. This helps avoid mistakes regarding the type and dosage of each medication.
- Stay on top of managing medical issues by keeping accurate records of medical appointments, names and addresses of physicians, medications, and changes in your parent's condition. If you become overwhelmed, get help.

13

IN CASE OF AN EMERGENCY

"I've been a caregiver all of my life. I took care of my younger brothers and sisters, my children, my husband, and now my parents. I think you develop this instinct that lets you know when something is very wrong. My parents are not well. My mom has dementia and my dad is so frail that a strong wind could knock him down. I know the telephone and particularly the cell phone are great inventions...but I hate them. Every time one rings my heart races, and I have a feeling of dread. Every day seems to bring another emergency."

Jenny, New Jersey

"My mother had an emergency, so I ran out the door and forgot my purse. When I reached the car in the garage of my building, I realized I forgot the car keys. I went back to my apartment, got the keys and my purse, and ran out the door again. I drove blindly to the hospital only to find out that my mom ate too much sauerkraut. I was ready to scream. I am slowly killing myself to keep her alive. There has to be a better way."

Nancy, California

A. REACTING TO AN EMERGENCY

Jenny and Nancy describe feelings that each one of us has felt at one time or another. When the telephone rings you may have an extreme physical reaction such as a pounding and racing heartbeat or a feeling of nausea. Or it could be something as simple and frustrating as forgetting your keys. One caregiver said she just starts to cry. Crying is a great release for tension and frustration. Another said exercise helps decrease his stress and anxiety.

What we know for sure is that everyone is different and each of you has your own reaction to the ring of the telephone. For some of you, it may be a feeling of panic. Your mind races with questions: What do I do? Whom do I call? How can I help if I can't think straight? Other caregivers may experience a completely different reaction. They may quickly and without hesitation turn to their trusty emergency response system known to us as "crisis mode." What is "crisis mode"? It is a time when your body and mind snap to attention. You immediately reach inside yourself to find a solution to the latest problem. Is this instinctive or is it a technique you can learn? We believe we all can learn this technique in part to help you through the tough times. Read on to learn how to help yourself and your loved ones.

How to Avoid Panic and Unnecessary Aggravation

Panic and aggravation are two emotions that we actually can't avoid. What the title of this segment could say is: Panic and Aggravation: "We All Have It and Here's What We Can Do About It." The reality is that at some time or other each of you will feel panicked and aggravated about something or someone. The following steps will help you face the crisis, assess the problem, and react. Will you do it without feeling emotional pain? Probably not, but you will feel more in control and we hope you will accomplish what you need to do.

Think of these suggestions as your "guide to better emergency management."

1. Keep a pad and pen next to the telephone, count to ten, and take a slow, deep breath before you answer it. Yes, whenever it rings.

2. Listen carefully before you respond to the caller. Here is a possible call you may receive. "Jane this is Dr. Smith. I am calling from XYZ Hospital's emergency room. Your mom fell and she is unconscious, but her vital signs are good." What do you hear? Instinctively, you hear the words, "doctor," "emergency," and "unconscious" because your mind immediately goes to the worst-case scenario. Listen again. "Jane, this is Dr. Smith. I am calling from XYZ Hospital's emergency room. Your mom fell and she is unconscious, but her vital signs are good." What did he actually say? Mom fell, she's unconscious, but her vital signs are good. This is extremely important information. The last few words—although you might like to hear them first—provide you with very significant and reassuring information. Listening helps to avoid panic.

3. Ask questions. How often have you said or heard someone else say, "I have a stupid question." And just as often the response is, "No question is stupid." The reality is that no question that is important to you is stupid or insignificant. Before the next emergency strikes, prepare a list of questions to help your mind stay focused. Keep a copy of these questions in your wallet or by your telephone next to the pad. For example:

   - How serious is my mother's condition?
   - Does my mother require a blood transfusion?
   - Have you contacted my mother's primary care physician or any other specialist involved in her care?
   - Should I come right over to the hospital? (If you live out of town, you may want to ask: How soon should I make arrangements to visit my mother?)
   - Does my mother require a companion or certified nursing assistant?
   - May I have a number to reach you directly?
   - Will another physician be caring for my mother later in the day? What is her name and how can I reach her?

- What is the name and telephone number of the emergency room social worker?
- How long will my mother be in the hospital?

4. Sit down for a few minutes and try to digest what you just heard. Prepare a few notes. Is there someone you should contact immediately? Is there someone who will provide you with support and a kind word?

5. Reach out to family and friends as soon as possible. Support from people you love and trust will help you stay calm and decrease some of the aggravation. Hopefully, you will receive the validation you deserve from your support system, and they will provide you with the time and interest to vent your concerns.

6. Decide when and how you are going to go to the hospital. If you live nearby and you want to drive, ask yourself if you are calm and clear enough to drive. If not, call a car service, taxi, family member, or friend to drive you. *Just be aware that driving while panicked is dangerous to yourself and others.* Be careful.

7. Be sure you have everything you need: purse or wallet, money, keys, eyeglasses, your parent's health insurance information, lists of questions for the doctor, telephone numbers of family and friends. For future reference, place an erasable board in your kitchen, office, or bedroom and call it IN CASE OF AN EMERGENCY. List the above items on the board as a reminder. Refer to the board as needed.

8. Leave a note for your children or spouse if you cannot reach them by telephone. This is to help avoid your family from panicking when they do not find you at home. Be specific and clear but try to avoid words such as "critical," or "dying." For example: Dear Family, Grandma Jean is not feeling well and she is at the emergency room in XYZ Hospital. The doctor says she will be fine but I went to the hospital to check on her. I will call you from the hospital about 6 PM tonight. Dinner is in the refrigerator. Love, Mom

Because you have taken very specific steps to help decrease your feelings of panic you will be less aggravated and more able to cope with the emergency and the emergency room chaos.

How to Handle Emergency Room Chaos

As Gerry from Massachusetts said, *"The smell and sound of an emergency room is awful. When I walked into the waiting area I heard screaming children. The receptionist told me that the hospital did not have an area specifically for children. As bad as the noise was for me, I can only imagine how deafening it was for my dad. He had been rushed to the hospital after falling down five steps in his house. His neighbor saw the front door open and found my dad. When I was in the emergency room I didn't know where to turn first or who to talk to. I really just wanted to run out and hide."*

The emergency room is often a cacophony of noises, smells, voices, and emotions. There is a sense of apprehension that fills each room and cubicle. There is a hustle and bustle unlike any other place because everyone in the emergency room has an important job to do. Lives depend on it.

Can you learn how to walk into an emergency room and not be overwhelmed by your surroundings? Yes. The following information will help you understand the working dynamics of most emergency rooms.

1. Who is the receptionist? The receptionist is sometimes referred to as the "greeter." She is the first person you will probably talk to when you arrive at the emergency room. If you are the patient or you are bringing in your parent or loved one to the emergency room, you will be asked to sign a sheet of paper with your name or the patient's name and the time you arrived.

2. Whom will I see next? Most likely, unless it is a life-threatening situation you and your loved one will meet with the individuals who will ask you about your mother's medical insurance plan. You will have to produce up-to-date insurance cards and a copy will be made of each card. If your mother has been a patient at the hospital in the past, her personal and medical information will probably appear on the computer. You will be asked to verify all of the information such as the date of birth, address, phone number, etc. If your mother is a new patient she will be asked to fill out several forms or answer questions verbally in order to provide the hospital

with her specific information. If she is unable to answer the questions, you will fill out the forms and answer the questions. Try to remain patient and calm. This is simply hospital procedure.

3. What does "triage" mean? Triage is a system designed to help the staff decide who needs help immediately and who can wait. For example, if someone arrives with chest pains and another person arrives at the same time with a sprained ankle, the person with the chest pains will be seen first by a physician. A patient who arrives by ambulance often has priority over one who walks in to the emergency room.

4. What does a triage nurse do? A triage nurse will ask you what is wrong and what brings you to the emergency room. If you are with your parent and she is unable to communicate for herself she will then ask you questions. The triage nurse will check and record your parent's vital signs and then ask both of you to wait in the waiting room or reception area until they call you in to see the doctor.

5. What is an attending doctor? An attending doctor is the person who examines your parent in the emergency room. She will order specific tests if necessary and you will be able to ask her questions. You may also request her to contact your parent's primary care physician if the primary care physician is not aware that your parent is in the emergency room.

6. Which nurse is assigned to your parent? Many emergency rooms have registered nurses and nursing assistants. Your parent will have a nurse assigned to care for her from the moment she is in a bed in the emergency room. At changes in shift a new nurse will be assigned to your parent.

7. What does a physician's assistant do? Many hospitals have physician's assistants to help the doctors in a very busy emergency room. These men and women are highly trained and qualified to answer your questions and to perform many medical procedures.

8. Will I meet a social worker? Most likely you will not meet a social worker immediately, unless your parent will be discharged within a few hours from the hospital. The role of the emergency room social worker is to help you contact family members and physicians, and to act as an intermediary between you and a very busy

staff. Her role also includes preparing you and your parent for a safe discharge from the hospital. (Review section C in this chapter for more information about discharge planning.)

Once you know what to expect and whom you should expect to meet in the emergency room, it may begin to seem less turbulent and overwhelming and then you can concentrate on the most important person in the room: your parent.

B. COPING WITH A LENGTHY HOSPITALIZATION

Jack from California said, *"Days fade into weeks and weeks into months when Mom is hospitalized for depression and anxiety. It is so difficult to see her in that setting. She always looks so unhappy and I wish that I could take her home. I know I can't. Dealing with these long hospital stays drains me mentally and physically. I am so short-tempered. I can't concentrate on my work because I'm just not myself. I wish I could figure out a way to protect myself from this pain."*

There is nothing more draining than visiting a loved one in the hospital day after day. A caregiver said, *"I don't know why I'm so exhausted, I just sit there all day and look at my dad sleeping."*

Physical fatigue, compounded by emotional exhaustion will bring any strong healthy man to his knees. Family members will remind you, the caretaker, over and over again how important you are to your parent and that you have to take care of yourself. As one caregiver said, *"I wanted to scream because I was constantly reminded that if I got sick, who would take care of my dad. It didn't help me; it only placed more pressure on me to be by his side."*

Most of you will not take the time to eat properly or have normal sleep patterns. As you sit by the bedside of a loved one, your mind may fill with memories of a wonderful life lived, or a life that had too many problems and too much pain. You may experience a roller coaster of emotions that you can't express because it is just not the right time. The emotions may become overwhelming and you may feel very alone. But you are not alone. Try to read all of these suggestions and select the ones that you think will help you cope with a lengthy hospitalization.

1. Ask the front desk at the hospital for the visiting hour schedule. If your parent is in the emergency room, that specific area of the hospital will have one schedule. If your parent requires intensive care that will probably be a more limited schedule. If your parent is taken to a medical floor versus a surgical floor that may also have different schedules.

2. Try to adjust your day around the visiting hours. It is very frustrating to arrive at 8:00 PM when visiting hours are over at 7:00 PM. Some hospitals are more lenient about visiting before or after hours. If you have a scheduling problem, speak to the social worker and ask him to help you make special visiting arrangements.

3. Ask your family and friends to relieve you for an hour or two if you are on a vigilant watch at your parent's bedside. Taking even a short break will give you time to clear your mind.

4. Hire a private duty, certified nursing assistant to provide companionship for your parent and calm her fear as well as yours. Check with the hospital's nursing office for information and criteria regarding help from outside agencies. Most often the hospital will require someone from a licensed, bonded agency. The aide will be asked to report to the nursing station with her credentials, which may include the results of a recent medical examination. (See chapter 17 for more information.)

5. Talk to your family or friends about your concerns. Venting your feelings during this time will ease some of your burden. Margo from Maine said, *"While my mom was ill, my best friend was on speed dial. I called her just to hear her tell me that I am doing a good job, or that she was sending me a hug. It got me through the really tough days. I was stronger for her friendship and support."* Don't be afraid to ask for help.

6. Reach out to your mom's medical doctor and specialists involved in her case. Make the call if you have any questions regarding her care.

7. If the doctor does not return your call in a timely manner, contact his office and ask the receptionist to make an appointment to speak to him about your mom's care. If you have difficulty communicating with any physician in the hospital, speak to the patient advocate and ask for the help you need.

8. Prioritize your busy schedule during this time. Many of you may be able to or may be entitled to take time off from work. Make an appointment with your boss or the human resource department in your office to learn about your options.

9. Eat nourishing foods. It is very easy to fall into poor eating habits when you are under an inordinate amount of stress. Try, try, try to eat well-balanced meals. Eating fast foods and snacks will not provide you with enough energy to get you through the day.

10. Sleep provides the body, mind, and spirit with a time to recuperate from the stressors of the day. Often caregivers ask, "Sleep, what's that?" It is one of the things you can do for yourself, no matter where you are. For example: when you are in the hospital for many hours and you find yourself by the bedside late at night, ask the nursing staff if you can have a comfortable chair to sleep on for a few hours. Often the chairs they use during the day for patients are unoccupied at night and many have a reclining feature.

11. Wear comfortable, wash-and-wear clothes when you are visiting your parent. It is easier to put your feet up in sweatpants than in a skirt and more comfortable to walk around the hospital in sneakers rather than in high heels.

12. Visiting a loved one in the hospital is physically and emotionally draining, as well as time-consuming. Take the time to feed your body, mind, and spirit. Use some or all of our suggestions to help you help yourself.

C. WHAT IS A HOSPITAL DISCHARGE PLAN AND WHY DO I NEED IT?

"As my mother's condition got better all she could think about was going home. I tried to explain to her that home was not the best option at that time. She couldn't understand why she had to go to a rehabilitation facility for a few weeks until the day she stood up and tried to walk a few steps alone. She was weak and exhausted and it was only then that she admitted that going home would have to wait."

Marc, California

Hospitals have rules and regulations. Some of these rules and regulations are mandated by the state and others are specifically crafted by the individual institution. One thing that all hospitals share in common is the importance and necessity of a safe discharge plan. A safe discharge plan is a plan that allows the patient to leave the hospital in a safe manner. This is to protect both the patient and the hospital. The hospital does not want a patient to become a liability because of a poor discharge plan.

This example describes a well-thought-out discharge plan that protects the safety and well-being of the client.

Marcia's mom is an eighty-nine-year-old woman with a history of cancer and cardiac disease. She is alert and has minimal short-term memory loss. Marcia's mom lived independently, although she had a cleaning service once every other week. She wore an emergency response system button at all times and was cognizant enough to test the button once a month. Her groceries were delivered and Marcia or her sister visited her weekly. Marcia is a healthcare professional and knows the ins and outs of the system; therefore, she takes care of all medical issues pertaining to her mom.

Her mom was hospitalized for bilateral pneumonia and a secondary colon infection. Marcia's mom was critically ill and her future was uncertain. After several weeks of intense antibiotic therapy her mom responded. She was very weak and frail but ready for discharge from the hospital. Here is a step-by-step description of the discharge plan process.

1. The primary care physician wrote orders for the hospital staff stating that Marcia's mom was ready for discharge.
2. An interdisciplinary meeting was held among the physicians, nursing, social work, and physical therapy staff.
3. The decision was made for Marcia's mom to transfer to a rehabilitation program at a local nursing facility for a few weeks for strength training.
4. Marcia was informed about the decision and she was very pleased, but her mother was not happy or even remotely interested in going to a rehabilitation facility.
5. Marcia's mom was considered competent to make her own decisions, but she needed the expertise of her doctor and the hospital

staff to convince her that rehabilitation was necessary and important for her future well-being.

6. Marcia's mom consented and she spent three weeks in the rehabilitation facility. The discharge plan from the facility to her home was to continue physical therapy at her home twice a week and to have care twenty-four hours a day, seven days a week for several weeks.

7. After three weeks Marcia reduced the in-home care to one eight-hour shift, seven days a week for an indefinite period of time.

It is not unusual for family members to disagree over the discharge plan suggested by the hospital. Ask for a meeting with your mom's physician and the hospital staff involved if you find yourself in a situation where you and your family disagree with the hospital discharge plan.

Ask yourself the following questions before you and your family assume the care of your parent after discharge from the hospital.

1. Where will mom live during the recuperation period?
2. Who will be responsible for her care during the day and at night?
3. Do we need a hospital bed, commode, wheelchair, walker, cane, raised toilet seat, or other assistive devices?
4. Do we have a back-up plan if one of us cannot fulfill his or her responsibilities?
5. Ask to meet with the social worker in charge of your mom's case and talk to her about these issues. She will be able to advise you about assistive devices and possible private homecare agencies.

You always need a Plan B when you are undertaking such a big responsibility. Think about your options, such as hiring a home health aide if you need the assistance, or contact the Area Agency on Aging for additional referrals. Although these problems may seem new and worrisome to you, they are often simple and routine to healthcare professionals.

Most important, a safe discharge plan should always provide your parent with the best possible options for a full and speedy recovery and provide the family with peace of mind.

D. SHORT-TERM AND LONG-TERM LIVING ARRANGEMENTS

There are so many reasons you may have to consider alternative living arrangements for your parent. Many of the reasons are not health or age related. They may be as mundane as a leaky roof or a flooded basement in your parent's home. If you can imagine an emergency, it can likely happen. As you read the three following scenarios you will begin to understand the importance of planning ahead.

Scenario 1: *When Jack's dad called him and said the roof caved in, Jack thought he was kidding. When he went to the house and he saw the roof lying on the living room floor, he knew his eighty-seven-year-old dad was going to have to find somewhere else to live.*

Jack lived in a small one-bedroom apartment and he really didn't have the room for his dad. They never got along and he truthfully didn't want to live with him even if he had the room. Jack needed to find an assisted living facility that would accept his dad for a short term.

Scenario 2: *Ina's seventy-six-year-old mom lived alone. One rainy day she slipped on the sidewalk and fractured her shoulder and arm. She spent two weeks in the hospital and a month in a rehabilitation facility. Ina's mom wanted to go home, but she was afraid. She expressed her feelings to Ina, saying that for a while she would feel safer in an assisted living facility. Ina was surprised because her mom was always so independent. However, she wanted to do what was best for her mom and she began to investigate possible alternative living arrangements. Ina was then surprised to find that she had to deal with waiting lists and financial requirements.*

Scenario 3: *Suzanne's dad required hospitalization. It was clear to Suzanne and the doctors that because of her dad's dementia and cardiac problems, he would need long-term care in a nursing facility. The hospital social worker provided Suzanne with a list of forty nursing homes and told her to select five. Suzanne knew nothing about nursing homes. She did not know how to judge them or what to do. She wanted to do what was best for her dad, but she had no idea what "best" meant in this situation.*

A time may come when your parent will need short- or long-term alternative housing. If an emergency strikes and you don't feel prepared to handle the situation, try some of these steps to help you.

- Meet with the social worker involved in your parent's case to discuss the options. If your mom is cognitively intact, include her in the meeting.
- Talk about your mom's needs and wants as well as the locations of the facilities and the cost of care.
- Ask the social worker for referrals to a few different facilities. If you find that the hospital social worker is reluctant to make a referral because of hospital policy, contact the National Association of Geriatric Care Managers at www.caremanager.org for a referral to a private care manager in your community. A private geriatric care manager charges a fee for service, and provides you with an assessment, ongoing care and management, as well as referrals and support. You may also contact your local Agency for Aging for referrals.
- Visit at least two or three facilities, talk to the staff, and then make a decision based on the reputation of the facility, cost, and location.
- To avoid the stress and strain of last-minute emergency intervention, plan ahead whenever you can. If your parent is living alone, you might want to do the following:
  - ° Research two or three assisted living facilities. Ask for referrals and utilize the Internet for specific information about a facility.
  - ° Contact the facilities and plan a tour at your convenience.
  - ° Always record the name and telephone number of the contact you make for future reference.
  - ° Keep the information in a handy folder. You will be better prepared in the event of an emergency housing situation.

(See chapter 19 for further information on alternative housing arrangements.)

E. WEATHER EMERGENCIES

"Mom and Dad lived in a hurricane area on the second floor of a two-story apartment building. We were on the telephone and the last thing I heard was a crash and my mom screaming. I couldn't reach them by telephone, but I had their neighbor's cell phone. I called, and got through. He said when he looked out the window a huge tree fell and blocked off my parents' doorway. He said that they waved to him from the window. As soon as the storm ended he contacted the rescue workers to free my parents from their apartment. What a nightmare."

Gayle, Texas

Weather is the one thing that you can't always plan for, even if you find yourself glued to the television or radio. Weather patterns change and a light rain can become a storm and a snow flurry can become ten feet of packed ice.

Many parents live alone and many of them live far away from you and other family members. Your mom may live in an area that is prone to hurricanes, earthquakes, or tornados, or one that suffers from ice storms several times each year. It's important to plan ahead for unexpected emergencies brought on by inclement weather or other unforeseen disasters.

You are very busy keeping up with everything you do for everyone. As you think about planning for emergencies, allow this information to guide and relieve your mind. You don't have to do everything at once; prepare a little at a time. If your parent is cognitively intact, ask him to help you with the preparations. If your parent suffers from dementia and she is cared for by a homecare worker, advise the homecare worker about all of your plans, and involve her in the planning. If mom lives in an assisted living facility or a nursing home ask the facility about their disaster plan. Request a written copy of the plan as well as contact information in the event of an emergency. Here's how you start to create your personal emergency plan.

- Decide on a safe haven for your parent. Your parent may live near a shelter, or if there is an advance weather warning you may want to move him to a friend's or relative's house out of harm's way. If these options are not appropriate check hotels that are in a safe zone. A hotel is a good option because your parent will have easy access to food and support staff.
- Investigate transportation options for your parent. If possible, make transportation plans in advance and provide your parent or the homecare worker with all of the information. Put all information in writing and leave it posted in a prominent place in the kitchen or bedroom.

- Provide your cognitively impaired parent with an identification bracelet. This can be purchased on the Internet or through the Alzheimer's Association. If your parent becomes confused in a new and different environment, the bracelet will have the number for the Alzheimer's Safe Return registry or your telephone number.
- Speak to your parent's companion or home health aide. Be sure that the aide is willing and able to remain with your parent during an emergency. If the aide is unable to remain with your parent, contact the agency and ask for an aide who will stay with your parent.
- It is very important for your parent's safety and well-being not to be alone in the event of a weather emergency.
- This list provides some of the supplies that you may need in the event of a weather emergency. Use the list as a guideline and tailor the list to meet your parent's individual needs.
- Provide at least a two-week supply of prescription medications such as diabetes medications; oxygen and oxygen supplies; and over-the-counter medications, such as aspirins, laxatives, cold remedies, and dental supplies.
- Purchase a two-week's supply of nonperishable foods. Include any specialty foods and dietary supplements your parent requires. Be sure that there is bottled water on hand for drinking and if necessary for grooming.
- Gather and organize official documents, such as medical records, insurance cards, checkbook, a credit card, legal documents such as a healthcare proxy or living will, as well as a few hundred dollars in cash. Place all of these items in a watertight locked box or plastic container. If your parent is able, have them check the locked box every few months to make sure that everything is in place and up-to-date. If your parent is unable to check the contents of the locked box, take time every few months and check the box for yourself.
- Consider these items and add whatever else your parent may need for his comfort and well-being. Flash light, batteries, radio, cell phone and charger, manual can opener, hand sanitizer, hand lotion, sunscreen, garbage bags, sanitizing wipes, insect repellent, rain or snow gear, hats, gloves, raincoat, boots, deck of cards, checkers or chess, knitting or sewing supplies, other hobbies and clothing for seven to ten days.

- Remember your mom's pet. If possible, remove the pet to a safe haven such as an animal boarding house or a shelter. If the pet is going to remain with your parent prepare a two-week supply of food, medications, and water. Your parent's pet may also need bowls, leashes, favorite toys, and a pet carrier and bed.

During the storm it is essential for your parent to remain in a safe place with a friend or relative. If possible, contact your parent by telephone to assure her that you are well. Keep in mind that if you can't communicate, you have done your best to protect your parent under very difficult circumstances.

Once the storm is over and your parent is home, take the time to replenish any supplies that were used during this emergency so that he'll be prepared in the event of another emergency.

Emergencies happen. Sometimes you know it is imminent and sometimes it strikes you by surprise. By taking some of these precautions in advance you will feel more prepared and better able to cope with the next emergency when it happens.

F. PROTECTING YOURSELF IN AN EMERGENCY

We know that you will do your best to take care of your parent in an emergency. We also know that you might forget how important it is to protect yourself from the aggravation, anxiety, and fatigue that accompany additional stress in your life.

Taking care of yourself in an emergency is simply remembering that you need to plan ahead, rest when you can, and learn how to delegate some of your responsibilities to other family members or friends.

- Make lists that are always "works in progress." This means that you may have different lists for different types of emergencies. For example, if you are in the midst of a medical emergency with your mom, your list should contain doctors' names, addresses, telephone numbers, pharmacies, and hospital contacts. If you're preparing for a weather emergency the same list will require additional information, such as a reminder about medications, food and water supplies, and personal hygiene needs. Change and update the list as needed in order to be prepared.

- Never underestimate the power of a good nap. Ellen from Missouri stated: *"My grandfather always said that the human body was made to take a nap during the day."* Ellen's grandfather is right. Resting for ten or fifteen minutes will rejuvenate and refresh you. Take a time-out for yourself whenever you can, especially if you are in the midst of a stressful family, weather, or personal emergency.

- Give it up! *Allow* yourself to give up some of the responsibility you carry on your shoulders day after day. Particularly in the event of any type of emergency caregivers who feel as though they must solve all of the problems suffer deeply for their high expectations. No one expects you to fix everything yourself. Ask and then allow a family member or friend to help you. Ask and then allow your spouse to pack the emergency suitcase or shop for supplies. Give it up! Once you learn how to delegate some responsibilities to other people you will feel lighter and freer to do what you have to do.

All emergencies require resourcefulness and thought before, during, and after the emergency. Helping your parent through this time is exhausting and time consuming. Give yourself a break and try not to do it all alone. Asking for help from family and friends provides you with a little more strength, and a little more time to take care of yourself.

G. MY JOURNAL

Use this page as a safe place to express your feelings and concerns. Putting thoughts and feelings on paper helps us see them more clearly. What bothers you? What changes do you want to make? When you read what you've written, you may see a new pathway to help resolve stressful issues. For example:

"My mom is sick all the time. It's so hard to watch her suffer. I want to help her, but I know that there is nothing left for me to do . . ."

"Life is chaotic with one emergency after another. Maybe writing down my feelings will relieve me of some of the tension. It's about time for me to take care of myself . . ."

_____
_____
_____
_____
_____
_____
_____
_____
_____
_____
_____
_____
_____
_____
_____
_____
_____

H. TIP SHEET

- Avoid panic and aggravation by planning ahead so you can act quickly and confidently in the event of an emergency.
- Keep a handy list of your parent's medications and the telephone numbers for his physicians and pharmacy. Update the list on a regular basis.
- Prepare yourself for lengthy hospitalizations. Adjust your schedule around visiting hours, take breaks during your visit to prevent fatigue, eat well-balanced meals, and hire a home health aide or certified nursing assistant to relieve you for a few hours a day.
- Learn as much as you can about hospital discharge plan options by speaking to the hospital staff and your parent's physician.
- Take care of yourself in the event of an emergency. Rest when you can and learn how to delegate some of your responsibilities to family and friends.

14

OVERSEEING MEDICATIONS

A. ADMINISTERING MEDICATIONS

"I visit my dad once a week and I always look in his pillbox. Most of the time I find things in order, however one day I saw what looked like an extra pill. When I took the pill out of the container I realized that it had been cut in half. I said, 'Dad what happened to your heart pill, it's cut in half?' He answered, 'I feel better, so I figured I can take half and save some money.' Needless to say I went crazy and told him that he was putting his life in jeopardy. He laughed and said, 'It's my life.' Don't you just want to scream?"

Jackie, Maine

Are you responsible for administering medications? Do you prepare the pillbox for another caregiver to administer to your parent? Even the most experienced caregivers who administer medication to a parent find unfamiliar names of medications, various dosage requirements, and at times confusing instructions. This is a serious problem. No matter what your level of involvement, be aware that there are medical reasons that medications have specific instructions.

A caregiver related this story that gives a new meaning to the words "should not be placed in a microwave oven." A home health aide took care of her mother every day from nine AM to four PM. The aide always prepared dinner and left it on a dish in the refrigerator. At five or six PM the elderly woman placed the dish in the microwave oven to heat. To the daughter's surprise, the home attendant also left several of the woman's pills on the same dish. The food and pills melted together in the microwave oven. When her mother became ill, the daughter made an appointment with the doctor, who couldn't explain the illness. Finally, a care manager diagnosed the problem. Fortunately, the daughter discovered this uncommon use of a microwave oven before it was too late, and her mother recovered. She realized that in this instance the home health aide innocently created a serious problem when she left the pills on the dinner plate.

Some family caregivers feel as if they need a nursing degree to properly do the job of administering and monitoring their parent's medications. Other caregivers just need a little structure and direction to give them confidence and a feeling of control. Try the following steps to avoid serious medication problems and complications.

- Read and follow directions carefully. If something does not seem right to you, you are probably correct. Contact the physician or the pharmacist immediately for a clarification of the directions. Write instructions clearly and in large print.
- Follow label directions carefully. Often there are small labels that may read "take with water," "finish all medication," and so forth. Carefully follow the directions, and if you are unclear or confused by the directions, immediately contact the physician or the pharmacist.
- Keep all medications in the original labeled containers in a cool, dry area if possible. One pharmacist recommended the linen closet to store many medications because it is usually cool and dry, as opposed to medicine cabinets are in the bathroom, which tend to be damp. He recommended that you do not keep medicines near the kitchen or bathroom sink. In his experience, pills find their way down the drain very easily. Replacing lost medication is costly.

- Do not try to save shelf space and consolidate pills into one container. Pills often have the same shape or color. If you consolidate the pills, you may create unnecessary confusion when you administer the medication.
- If you transfer the medication to a daily or weekly pillbox, be sure the exact dosage is available. If you plan on using a medication machine to dispense the medications, be sure that everyone involved in your parent's care understands the directions and the use of the device. Before you purchase any type of machine, speak to the pharmacist about this type of equipment. It is not suitable for everyone.
- Do not administer medication over a sink. If the pill slips out of your parent's mouth or hand, it may fall down the drain.
- Use a programmable watch if your parent is still capable of taking her own medication. If your parent has mild memory impairment and takes only one or two medications each day, the watch serves as a handy, simple reminder. Talk to your parent about the idea because some parents may find the watch alarm annoying. If your parent agrees to it, the alarm is set to ring at the specific time your parent needs to take her medication. Ask your pharmacist where you can purchase this type of watch. When you purchase the watch, the pharmacist can probably assist you with setting up the system.
- Keep all medications on a written list, and clearly display the list on the refrigerator, in the inside door of the medicine cabinet, or in the linen closet. Use a dark marker or pen, and write in large, printed letters. Some caregivers create a medication list on the computer so that they can easily adjust the size and color of the print. Displaying a complete list of medications is very important and helpful to emergency service personnel in the event your parent has a medical emergency.
- Always wear your eyeglasses when you administer prescription medications, over-the-counter pills, or homeopathic treatments. You cannot be certain what you are administering if you can't see the label or bottle clearly.
- Remind your parent to wear his glasses or use his magnifying glass when he takes any type of medication in order to avoid unnecessary mistakes.

- Turn the light on in the room when you administer medication even if you think you know where the pills are in the dark. Encourage your dad to do the same if he is in charge of his own medication.
- Try to take your time to think about what you are doing in order to avoid accidental overdoses or misuse of medications. If your parent is capable of self-medicating and he does, refer to the above list and write a few simple reminders near his medication box or bottles. Prevention is the key to a keeping your parent safe and well.

Keeping Track of Medications

Knowing when, how, and what medications are administered is a big responsibility for any caregiver. Some parents may take as many as ten, twenty, or more pills every day. One caregiver said that her mother took so many pills each day she often felt that she needed a degree in pharmacology. Trying to keep track of unfamiliar medications or even how many vitamins your parent takes is time consuming and mentally exhausting. Can you keep track of medications when the dosages sometimes increase or decrease or there are many pill changes? The answer is yes, but it is critical to consider that this is one area of caregiving in which you should not rely on your memory.

After several attempts at keeping lists and trying to remember names and numbers, one caregiver created a simple index-card file system. Her eighty-year-old mother was very ill, and she had been prescribed several medications, as well as vitamin therapy. On a regular basis, the frail woman had one doctor's appointment after another. The daughter found that she needed an easily organized method to keep track of all of her mother's medications and medication changes. She used a small metal index-card box and dividers labeled with the alphabet, A–Z. Each card contained the name of the prescription, the dosage, how many times a day and what time of day the pill is taken, the doctor's name and telephone number, and the pharmacist's name and telephone number. Each time they went to the doctor together, she took all of the medication in the original containers. The doctor or nurse then had the opportunity to record the information in her mother's chart and review all of the medications at the same time. By bringing all of the medications to each doctor, she helped to keep everyone apprised of what the other physicians prescribed. She immediately indicated any medication changes on the appropriate card in the card file. She said that this method provided her with a sense of control.

You may want to use a notebook that comfortably fits into your purse or briefcase. Or you may prefer a computer file to keep track of the same information. Check your computer software for a form that may serve your purpose. Punch holes into the computer printout and slip the pages into a loose-leaf binder. When you go to the doctor, remove the most recent page, make any changes, and return it to the binder.

You have so many things to do and remember. Select a system that works best for you and use it to your advantage.

B. DEVELOPING A RELATIONSHIP WITH THE PHARMACIST

Years ago, our parents had their prescriptions filled at a local pharmacy. Most of the time the owner of the store was the pharmacist. Sometimes they referred to this business as a "mom-and-pop store." "Pop" was the pharmacist and "Mom" was his wife. She worked at the cash register and provided advice to the female customers. The pharmacy sold medications, medical aids such as bandages and antiseptic ointments, personal hygiene items, and maybe a box or two of chocolates. The pharmacist knew every family member and his or her ailment. Discussions between the pharmacist and a customer may have taken place in the middle of the store with little regard for the patient's right to or need for privacy.

Times have changed. Being a pharmacist is no longer a male-dominated profession, and women are evident in increasing numbers. The small "pharmacy-only" type of business is becoming obsolete. All across our country, a medication may be sold in a chain store that sells everything from jam and bread to small appliances and picture frames. In the past, a ledger or card file may have sufficed for a pharmacist's medication records. Today, computers play an enormous role in keeping track of medications, alerting the pharmacist to medication interactions, and to filling prescriptions in a timely manner. Many pharmacies respect a patient's right to privacy and confidentiality by providing a corner of the pharmacy department where a client can ask questions in private. As one pharmacist said in regard to the changing role of the pharmacist, "We are not just here to sell drugs, we are here to make sure that people get better. We want to help people understand how important it is to tell the doctor and pharmacist everything they are taking. For example, one of the most frequent problems is the interaction of medication with certain vitamins. People don't think vitamins are important, but everything you take gives us important information."

Communicating with the pharmacist is essential for everyone's good health:

- Introduce yourself to the pharmacist. If you are a long-distance caregiver, contact your parent's pharmacist by telephone or possibly e-mail and tell him who you are and how you are involved in your parent's care. Give him your name, telephone number, and address.
- If the pharmacy employs several pharmacists, be sure that a pharmacist records all the information in your parent's file. Once the information is in the system, you will feel more comfortable because everyone involved in the pharmacy will be aware of your parent's medications.
- Keep the pharmacist apprised of all medications, over-the-counter treatments, herbal remedies, and vitamins your parent is taking. It is vital to provide accurate, up-to-date information in order for the pharmacist to help you help your parent.
- Ask questions. Immediately contact the doctor or the pharmacist if the directions on any prescription medications, over-the-counter medicines, herbal supplements, or vitamins are unclear to you. In some physicians' offices, there are trained personnel who deal with prescription information and renewals.
- Immediately contact the pharmacist or your dad's physician if you are not familiar with the name of the medication on the label of the bottle. Sometimes the doctor prescribes a generic brand of a medication and you and your parent are not aware of his decision. If you have any concerns or doubts, verify the information with the pharmacist or doctor so that you are aware that your parent is receiving the proper medication and the appropriate dosage.
- The same medication that is manufactured by two different companies may come in different shapes, sizes, and colors. Check with

the pharmacist or the doctor if your parent receives an old familiar medication in a different shape. Be safe, not sorry.
- Provide the doctor with the name, address, and telephone number of the pharmacy. In the event of an emergency, this information may save time and unnecessary aggravation. If you have an alternate pharmacy, maybe one that is open twenty-four hours a day, seven days a week, you may want to add that to the information.

As you develop a trusting relationship with the pharmacist and her staff, you and your parent will begin to feel more secure and supported. In time, these secure feelings will provide you with added confidence in the services that the pharmacist provides. Trust and confidence in the people who help you help your parents give you a sense of control.

C. PAIN MANAGEMENT

Not long ago, people accepted pain as a natural part of living or getting older. This is not the case today. The advances in medical research and the wonders of science bring us new medications and treatment options every day that help make most pain manageable.

Pain management can reduce the amount of pain your parent experiences from an illness or injury. Your parent may suffer from a chronic illness such as arthritis or from complications because of a broken hip or arm. The pain may be intermittent or constant. No matter where the pain emanates from or the duration of the pain, your parent does not have to suffer. You don't have to feel helpless like this caregiver.

"My mother fell and fractured her arm. She had surgery on the arm. Weeks later, she was still in excruciating pain. The doctor told her to see how she felt in one year. One year! That is the cruelest thing I ever heard. But the doctor told her to wait and see, and she was determined not to question him. One evening during dinner, she hit her arm on the table and her head fell into the dinner plate. Once she caught her breath, she said, 'It only happens when I bump it, but I'm very careful.'"

Betty, Virginia

If you don't know why your parent is in pain, contact your parent's primary care physician for an appointment for a complete physical examination. For instance, if your parent has pain in her leg and the primary doctor is unclear why this is happening, she may recommend specific medical and laboratory tests, or refer your parent to a specialist. All of this takes time. If you think this situation is serious and cannot wait for an appointment, you are probably right. Call 911 for immediate assistance from your local emergency services. Once your parent's physician makes a definitive diagnosis or confirms the diagnosis of an existing problem, request a meeting in his office to discuss all of the available treatment options. Be sure to inform the doctor about all of the prescription medications, over-the-counter medications, herbal remedies, and vitamins your parent is currently taking. The doctor may offer one type of approach to alleviate the pain or a combination of treatments. Pain management may include medication, intravenous therapy provided by a doctor or a registered nurse, physical or occupational therapy, diet changes, or a simple daily home-exercise program. The following questions may help you help your parent make the best decision to find the right pain relief treatment.

1. How quickly will my parent find relief?
2. Are there any side effects to this treatment? What are the side effects?
3. Is this treatment or medication covered by insurance? If not, how expensive is the treatment? If the cost is very high, is there an alternative to this treatment that will also be beneficial?
4. Are there any drug trials that may be suitable for my parent?
5. How long will my parent have to take this medication or follow the treatment plan?
6. Does my parent require laboratory tests or any other type of monitoring? If so, how often? Is it covered by insurance?
7. What is the prognosis for this type of problem? Will my parent always require some form of pain management?

Once a course of treatment is determined, it is important to follow the doctor's instructions in order to maximize the benefits of the treatment plan. There is usually a good reason for the different steps in a treatment plan. For example, a treatment plan may include pain medication and physical therapy three times a week. One caregiver said that her mother could not understand why she continued to have serious pain in her leg after weeks and weeks of physical therapy. The daughter decided to contact the physical therapist. The therapist told her all about the treatment plan. In addition to physical therapy, her mother had exercises to do every morning as well as a prescription medication. When the daughter asked her mother about the treatment plan, she said that the medication was too expensive, and she did not have time for the daily morning exercise routine.

If you are uncomfortable with the treatment plan, or it just does not make sense to you, ask the doctor questions. If you still feel dissatisfied with the answers, you and your parent are entitled to a second opinion. Sometimes a second opinion will bring new treatment options to your attention and a completely different way of looking at a problem. Anne from Wisconsin said, "*My mother suffered from chronic back and hip pain. She insisted that her doctor of thirty-eight years was the only one with the right answers. He told her it was arthritis and old age. He could never do anything wrong, so she accepted what he said. Finally, my brother and I convinced her that he may not be right and there may be a better answer. We went for a second opinion and found out that my mother had a hip problem that could be alleviated with surgery. She had the surgery and she's back to her old tricks.*"

D. MISUSE OF MEDICATIONS

"We called the ambulance because she looked so pale and still. My mother takes so many pills each day. We didn't know that she was taking too many of one medication and not enough of another. When we looked at the pill bottles, we were shocked. I picked all of these pills up within a day or two of each other. Some bottles were empty after only two weeks, and two bottles were missing only a couple of pills. Was she trying to hurt herself?"

Laurie, Florida

Like so many unsuspecting caregivers, this woman was shocked by the way her mother misused a variety of medications. After a complete physical and psychiatric examination, the doctors confirmed that her mother was suffering from memory impairment. The doctor believed that her mother made a mistake, and the misuse of the medication was not intentional. Fortunately, this mistake ended happily, and the woman survived her ordeal.

The misuse of medication is often an accident waiting to happen to people who suffer from memory and cognitive impairment. Taking too many pills, not taking enough medication, or not taking the medication in a timely or appropriately manner may lead to various physical, emotional, and psychiatric complications. Listen to the story of this caregiver:

"My eighty-three-year-old mother lives alone in a small private house. I live four miles away, and I try to visit once a week. Mom was always well dressed and groomed, but for the past several months, I noticed changes in her appearance. Not only did she appear unkempt, but she was also thinner, frailer, and lethargic. I made an appointment with my mother's primary care physician. After a complete physical examination, he referred us to a geriatric psychiatrist. The psychiatrist diagnosed Mom as suffering from clinical depression. He prescribed an antidepressant often used in the treatment of depression among the elderly. The doctor informed us that given a little time she should begin to feel better. He told us not to expect miracles, but that in a few weeks she should have more energy and feel brighter. I felt satisfied with the diagnosis and treatment plan. I tried not to dwell on the situation, and I assumed that my mother was taking the medication. I also assumed that my mother was following up with monthly visits to the psychiatrist. After a few months, I didn't notice any positive changes in my mother. I finally asked her if she was taking the medication, and she said she was taking it. I knew something was very wrong, and I asked to see the bottle of antidepressants. When I followed her into the bedroom, I found the unopened bottle of pills in a dresser drawer. Mom never took one antidepressant.

"I realized that my mother could no longer make important

decisions for herself or live alone. I hired a home health aide to assist with her care, but she continued to be noncompliant with medications. Within a few months, I moved her to an assisted living community where she receives medication monitoring and other essential services."

Connie, Connecticut

The misuse of medication can be a life-threatening problem. If your parent is cognitively impaired, or suffers from memory loss, or psychiatric or emotional problems, she may inadvertently misuse her medications. Your parent may need someone to administer her medication at home, or in an assisted living or nursing facility. If your parent is capable of administering her own medications, but her first language is not English, the directions may be unclear. Some of the other reasons medications are misused include simple mistakes regarding dosage, misunderstanding or misinterpreting directions, and denial of the need for medication. You can avoid some of the pitfalls of medication misuse and mismanagement by trying these few guidelines.

- Assess your parent's ability to administer her medication. As a caregiver from New Jersey said, *"Do you think I know if Dad takes his medication? He says he takes it. I guess he does."* If you feel you are not able to make the assessment, contact the doctor, a social worker, or a registered nurse for a professional assessment.
- Make sure that all of the instructions are clear and legible. If your parent does not speak English, or English is not his primary language, be sure that he understands the instructions. Interpreting the directions and writing them in your parent's native language will help ensure proper administration of the medication.
- Make periodic inspections of bottles and pill containers. Look in the medicine cabinet, kitchen cabinet, dresser drawers, and closets. Old shoeboxes and hatboxes are good hiding places for medication bottles. Discard old, out-of-date, and expired medications. If you find a medication that was prescribed a few months or years ago, check with the doctor to see if the medication is necessary at this time. Do the same "housecleaning" for over-the-counter medications, vitamins, and herbal remedies.

- Contact your parent's doctor or the pharmacist if you have a question or concern.
- Call 911 if your parent is in immediate danger due to ingesting the wrong medication or a medication overdose.
- The misuse of medication is not uncommon and it is frightening when it occurs. However, it is essential for you to remain as calm as possible, learn as much as you can about the situation, and then take the necessary steps in order to avoid future mistakes and medical emergencies.

E. ABUSE AND DEPENDENCY

The idea that your parent is abusing medication or is dependent on a pill for his happiness or comfort is a disturbing idea for any adult child. Some of the causes include the accidental misuse of medication, and psychiatric and emotional problems. When your parent is cognitively intact, the abuse or dependency may be the result of a deliberate attempt to reduce pain, anxiety, or depression. Inadvertently, your parent may think if one pill helps alleviate some of the discomfort, two pills may be better. If your parent is cognitively impaired, the abuse of medication may be the result of the inappropriate use of a medication. For example, your father may take too many pills because he did not understand the directions, he forgot that he already took the pill, or he may take a combination of pills that are contraindicated. Medications that are "contraindicated" should not be used or taken at the same time. Unfortunately, many times the abuse of the medication is obvious. Your parent may have developed some very serious medical problems that may even require hospitalization.

If you suspect a problem with medication abuse or dependency, try not to hit the panic button. Your parent needs medical intervention immediately to assess the situation. The doctor will probably conduct a complete physical examination and order several laboratory tests. After the results of all the testing are complete, the doctor will be able to determine if your parent has any serious conditions due to the drug abuse. She will make recommendations for treatment and suggest hospitalization if it is necessary. For instance, Zack lived in his own home, and he suffered from chronic depression and anxiety. Unfortunately, Zack did not enjoy a close relationship with his children. They resided in another state, and they saw their father only a few times a year. During a telephone conversation, they noticed that Zack slurred his words and sounded somewhat incoherent. Zack went to the emergency room at the local hospital. Initially, the doctors thought he suffered a stroke. After a full physical examination and appropriate tests, the doctor informed the family that Zack mixed his prescription medication with alcohol. Zack spent several months in the hospital. After several medication adjustments, counseling, and group therapy, it was time for him to go home. The family realized that Zack could no longer live alone. The doctors and the family agreed that Zack would be safer in an appropriate assisted living facility where he could receive medication monitoring in a controlled setting.

The signs of abuse and dependency are not always clear. If you suspect that something is wrong, don't spend time worrying about what-ifs.

"Our father is a chronic alcoholic, and our mother suffers from dementia. Because of a poor family history, my brother, sister-in-law, and I felt that we could not help our parents, although we tried on several occasions. When we didn't hear from them for several weeks, we felt a sense of responsibility, and we contacted a geriatric care manager for assistance. The four of us went to our parents' apartment, and the building manager let us in. Our father was lying on the bed in a drunken stupor, and our demented mother was sitting on the couch with several opened bottles of pills on her lap. The care manager called 911 and contacted the physician whose name and number appeared on the label of the medication. Eventually, our mother required a nursing home and our father entered a geriatric detoxification program."

Brenda, Virginia

"There she was on the floor, dirty and disheveled. When Dad died Mom began to drink. She added vodka to her juice and thought we didn't know. A few months later my younger sister died from an overdose and her son died in a car accident. We thought Mom would just give up and die, but she didn't. She just stepped up the drinking until she collapsed. I guess you can say it was slow death by alcohol. The day we found her on the floor we knew it was now or never. She was hospitalized for several weeks and then we arranged for her to receive ongoing care in a nursing facility.

Annie, Massachusetts

Try these six steps to help you help your parent.

1. Take action. If you think there is a serious problem, there very well may be one. If you are not available, or this is not something you want to do, it's OK. Get the help you need by speaking to your parent's doctor(s) or a geriatric care manager.
2. Discuss any changes you observe with your parent. This is not easy for anyone. If you think you can do it, ask the questions clearly. For example, "Dad, we noticed that you are sleeping more than you used to," or "Dad, we noticed that you are slurring your words, have you been to the doctor?" If you are not comfortable with the answers, or if you have any doubts, make an appointment with the doctor as soon as possible. If you don't think you can ask the questions, ask for help from a family friend, your parent's doctor, or your sibling.
3. Contact your parent's doctor about your suspicions. Due to confidentiality issues the doctor may not talk to you without your parent's consent. If your parent refuses to give you his consent then provide the doctor with what you know in writing so that the information can be filed in your dad's chart. Hopefully during your dad's next visit to the doctor, he will attempt to discuss these issues with him.
4. Reach out to the pharmacist for insights about your parent's medication regimen. Get as much information as you can in regard to the type of medication your parent is taking and if he is filling the prescription at the pharmacy in a timely manner or trying to fill the prescription too often.
5. Be supportive and not judgmental. Your parent may feel embarrassed by this problem if it is accidental or by choice. You can help

alleviate some of those feelings by saying things like "I understand and we will get you the help you need," or "I'm here for you
and we can get through anything together."

6. Take a deep breath and deal with it one day at a time. This problem
is not going to go away quickly, and it may return. Patience, vigilance, and ongoing reassessment should help you feel in control,
even in a situation that at times may seem out of control.

F. OVER-THE-COUNTER AND ALTERNATIVE MEDICATIONS

> "I didn't understand why my mother was always complaining
> about stomach pains. Her home health aide told me what she
> ate and drank and the doctor tested her for every possible gas-
> trointestinal condition. One day when I was visiting my mother,
> she asked me to find her eyeglasses. I went into her bedroom
> and rummaged through a few drawers. I couldn't believe my
> eyes. She had boxes and boxes of chocolate-flavored laxatives. I
> said 'Mom, what were you thinking eating all of these laxatives?'
> She smiled and said, 'It tastes good.' Who would have imagined
> that she would use laxatives as a treat?"
>
> *Renee, Arizona*

As you walk through a modern pharmacy, look at the wide variety of nonprescription medications in colorful, appealing packaging, each bottle or
tube promising "the cure" for one ailment or another. The number of
items is staggering, and it is often difficult to make any decision, much
less the right decision. Something as simple as choosing a vitamin supplement can be perplexing for your parent.

> "I took my mother, who is recently widowed, to the vitamin
> counter of a large pharmacy at ten o'clock at night. The store was
> open twenty-four hours a day, seven days a week. My mother was
> looking for 'just the right vitamins that Daddy used to buy.' I
> pointed out several brands and read the contents of several vit-

amin bottles out loud. My mother just couldn't make up her mind. After one hour and thirty minutes, I threw my hands up in the air and a bottle of vitamins into the basket, and I said, 'That's it, it's these vitamins or nothing.' My mother was so calm, and I just wanted to scream louder. 'I don't know why you are so impatient with me,' she said. I shouted back, 'Mom, it's almost midnight.'"

Joanne, New Jersey

Although this is an extreme example of "over-the-counter confusion," it does exemplify a problem that many of the elderly experience. If your parent is taking medication prescribed by a doctor, it is imperative that you speak to the doctor or the pharmacist before purchasing any over-the-counter medications, vitamins, or herbal remedies. The accurate facts that you provide to the doctor or the pharmacist may help your parent avoid an adverse drug reaction.

You can find herbal remedies and supplements in drugstores and health food markets. Your parent may select from a variety of drinks, teas, creams, ointments, and foods. Many times she can speak to the pharmacist who is knowledgeable about the different products. Most likely a sales-person is probably not aware of the other medications or over-the-counter remedies that your parent is taking and the possible drug interactions. Some herbal supplements and remedies taken with certain medications may cause a dangerous drug reaction. Not all products and medications will cause a problem, but it is important to be cautious and aware. Several years ago a daughter decided to give her mother several herbal treatments in the form of pills, drinks, and powder supplements. At the impressive age of ninety-five, her mother required several medications prescribed by the doctor. The daughter did not tell the doctor about her herbal treatments. She said in retrospect that it wasn't a secret; she just thought it was not important because you could buy all of the products without a prescription. Over a period of several months, her mother became ill and required hospitalization. When the emergency room doctor asked about medications, the daughter told him about everything including the herbal remedies. The doctor discovered that the ingredients in one of the potent medications and the ingredients in several of the herbal remedies were the same. In essence, her mother received a triple dose of a very strong medication.

How can you help to protect your parent against an adverse drug reaction when there are so many tempting choices, and the promise of better health?

- Communicate to your parent the importance of checking with his doctor or the pharmacist before buying any over-the-counter or herbal products. Let your parent know that he should not buy a product unless he clears it with the doctor or discusses it with the pharmacist.
- Be vigilant. If your parent is cognitively impaired, be sure that all of his caregivers are aware of all the medications he takes. Tell the caregivers to notify you immediately if they find any new or different medications, vitamins, drinks, or foods.
- Read all directions carefully and ask questions. If you are not satisfied with the answers, do not buy the product until you feel satisfied that it is a safe purchase for your parent.
- Keep all prescription medications, over-the-counter medications, and herbal remedies in a safe place. If your parent suffers from cognitive impairment or memory loss, everyone involved in your parent's care should be aware of the location of all medications and any other products. It is a necessary precaution to keep these things out of sight and reach. Some caregivers use a lock box or a lock on the cabinet door.

The improper use of medication is dangerous and can even be deadly. The proper use of medication can bring a better quality to your parent's life, and in many cases save her life. Precautions, vigilance, and a little common sense go a long way in ensuring that your parent is safe and healthy.

G. WORKSHEET: TIPS FOR OVERSEEING MEDICATIONS

If you administer and oversee your parent's medications, it is vital to be aware that the proper use of medication may enhance your parent's life, while the misuse of medication may have dire consequences.

1. Make sure you have the following information:

   Name of pharmacy(s): _____

   Telephone number(s): _____

   Name of physician(s): _____

   Telephone number(s): _____

2. Keep an accurate, up-to-date list of all prescription medications, over-the-counter remedies, vitamin pills, and homeopathic products in a convenient place such as on the refrigerator door or inside a medicine cabinet.

3. Read and follow all label directions carefully. If the directions are not clear, contact your parent's physician or the pharmacist for a complete explanation. Write down all of the directions for accuracy.

4. Keep all medications in the original containers in a cool, dry area if possible.

5. If your parent is cognitively impaired, be sure that all types of medications are out of reach and out of sight.

6. If you transfer pills to a pillbox or container, be sure that the exact dosage of each pill is placed in the pillbox or container.

7. Develop a relationship with the pharmacist. Introduce yourself by telephone or in person. Be sure that all of your parent's medication information is on file.

8. Provide your parent's physician with the name, address, and telephone number of your parent's pharmacy.

9. Review this chapter for more information about administering and overseeing your parent's medications.

H. TIP SHEET

- Be certain that anyone who administers medication to your parent is aware of the name of the pill, its size and shape, and the appropriate dosage.
- Introduce yourself to your parent's pharmacist by telephone or in person. The pharmacist will assist you with any questions or problems.
- Immediately contact your parent's physician if you suspect misuse of any prescription, over-the-counter, or homeopathic medications.
- Help your parent *before* a medical emergency occurs by watching for the signs of medication abuse or dependency.
- Keep a list of all of your parent's current medications and remember to take the medication in its original container to doctor or hospital visits.

15

DEALING WITH SERIOUS ILLNESS

A. INSISTING ON AN ACCURATE DIAGNOSIS

"My father was diagnosed with Chronic Obstructive Pulmonary Disease (COPD) but wasn't responding well to treatment. Fortunately, my friend is a geriatric nurse. She told me, 'Something is wrong. He was vital three weeks ago and now he can't walk a block. COPD has a slow progression, it doesn't incapacitate someone in three weeks. You need a second opinion.' It took us two months to get an appointment but when we saw the specialist, he looked at the same exact test results the original doctor had and guess what he found? My father had very minor, non-incapacitating COPD, but it was being exacerbated by asthma! Do you believe his doctor missed something that simple?! Dad's fine now because we know what to do when an attack starts."

J. B., Florida

"I'm worried all the time. My father is just not aware or in touch with his own needs. I just wish I had his cooperation, then we could find out what's wrong."

Martha, New York

352

It would be impossible to overestimate the value of an accurate diagnosis. Just like this caregiver, you cannot create a realistic or appropriate plan to help your parent without one. An early diagnosis of many illnesses often leads to a cure and a complete recovery.

Sometimes recovery from a debilitating disease or chronic illness is not possible, but with an accurate diagnosis, many of the problems may be controlled. When you understand and control the effects of an illness, you are helping to maintain your parent's quality of life.

Medical advances have made many previously terminal diseases treatable, controllable, and curable. A wrong diagnosis or a lack of a diagnosis may result in a missed chance for a normal, full life. What holds your parent back from finding out what is really wrong? Educated fear. A parent who is alive at eighty or ninety years old has seen many of his friends and family members die from a variety of illnesses. Your parent probably shared many of the pains and heartaches of his close friends and relatives. Your parent probably knows the signs and symptoms of many diseases. Even if your parent is suffering from one or more of these symptoms, she may feel that if she doesn't give it an identity or a name, it doesn't exist. In short, she is in denial. Years ago people never talked about diseases like cancer. It was the family secret often whispered about and referred to as the "C word." It probably made people feel safer, even untouchable. Family members would never talk about a relative suffering from a mental illness, either. The lack of understanding and education for such illnesses as depression or schizophrenia left some people improperly diagnosed and treated. Because of this, families were misinformed about their loved ones' problems, and many people may have unnecessarily spent years in mental institutions.

Some parents may see illness and disease as a part of growing older. Age is not an excuse from your parent or anyone else for a lack of medical attention. "What do you expect at her age?" is not a diagnosis; it is ageism and it's wrong. How do you overcome years of avoidance, fear, and denial? How do you help your parent seek appropriate treatment and possibly a cure? Follow these guidelines for an accurate diagnosis.

- Begin by asking your parent how she feels and if she is noticing any physical, emotional, or cognitive changes. The problem may be obvious such as excessive weight loss or a change in sleeping habits. Your parent may have a problem that you are not aware of such as headaches, or subtle changes in vision or hearing. Once you begin the dialogue, urge your parent to make an appointment with her primary care physician. Preferably, your parent's physician specializes in the care of the elderly and is a board-certified geriatric specialist.

- If you cannot be there, try to have someone responsible with your parent when the doctor questions him. Provide as much accurate medical history as you can. Some caregivers find it more efficient to write the information and hand it to the doctor. Make sure the doctor takes the time to read your information. If he slips it into the chart, insist that he reviews the information before questioning your parent. If your parent suffers from dementia, notify the doctor in advance of the visit.

- Ask your parent and relatives about any medical problems in your family. Pay special attention to major illnesses, chronic complaints, recurring diseases, or accidents. Think about and ask your family members which relatives had diabetes, heart disease, and cancer. Don't neglect emotional and psychiatric problems such as depression or anxiety. Ask about hospitalizations or if someone in the family secretly "went away" for a long period of time.

> "I never knew that my aunt suffered from chronic depression. I remember hearing the whispers and learning that my aunt simply 'went away,' and when she returned, no one said a word. This was the family secret. When her mother approached her eightieth birthday, she was hospitalized for depression. Looking back on my mother's life, I realized that my mother was also depressed many times. The family didn't acknowledge it; they didn't talk about my aunt, so it didn't happen. Finally, I put the pieces together and realized that my mother suffered her whole life, only to find help and relief at eighty."
>
> *Katherine, Nevada*

- Try to develop an accounting of the dates your parent was in the hospital, the reason for the hospitalization, and the length of stay. If your parent is not an accurate historian, ask a relative who is a contemporary of your parent to fill in the blanks. If there is no one capable of providing the information, contact your parent's physicians or the local hospital. Ask your parent to sign a medical records release form. You can get a copy of this form from the physician or hospital. Physicians, pharmacists, and other healthcare professionals may require a copy of this before they can release information about your parent's medical history or talk to you about your parent. The medical records office should be able to provide you with the necessary information. Ask if there is a fee and the amount for copying records. In your research, don't neglect automobile accidents or any other traumatic incident.

- Many years ago an elderly woman was suffering from dementia that was never diagnosed. The family believed that the change in the woman's behavior was something new. A nurse and social worker specializing in geriatrics suspected that something happened to this woman a long time ago to possibly create the problem. After looking into her medical background and hospitalizations, it was apparent that the woman suffered from a rare type of dementia. In its early stages, it was not noticeable to her friends and family. Many years after the diagnosis, the problems became evident. The woman became increasingly confused and belligerent. With the accurate medical history provided by the nurse and social worker, the doctor suggested a course of treatment. With this new information, the family was able to prepare for her care.

- Make a complete list of all present and past medications. Save yourself time and energy by asking for a computer printout at the pharmacy. Include all homeopathic treatments, vitamins, herbal remedies, and over-the-counter medications. If you are uncertain about the prescription medication information, it should be available at the pharmacy. Check all medicine and kitchen cabinets and closets in your parent's home for additional hidden or misplaced medications. (See chapter 9 for more suggestions and information on medication management.)

- Encourage your parent not to accept a serious diagnosis of a chronic or terminal illness without comprehensive testing to confirm the cause of the symptoms. Keep her calm by talking to her about the tests. Assure your parent that hospitals conduct many tests in an out-patient setting. Provide her with as much information as she wants or can absorb. If the test is pain free, let her know, but you can also gently prepare her if she may have some discomfort. Talk to the doctor about pain medication, if necessary. Without the benefits of test results, your parent may be generically treated for symptoms that could be present in many diseases. Confusion, failing memory, and other dementia symptoms are prime examples. These are symptoms of a variety of diseases, many of which are treatable, controllable, or reversible if diagnosed early. Be cautious and wise. Get a second opinion for a completely new look at your parent's problem.

Although getting an accurate diagnosis may seem like a daunting task, you can do it. Try to enlist the help of your family or friends. Any information you can provide to the doctors is generally welcomed and useful. If you begin this important step today, you'll waste less time, save money, and have more success helping your parent plan for the future.

B. MANAGING MAJOR ILLNESS

The treatment and outcomes of many major illnesses have changed in the past few decades. The words "long life" mean something very different than they did thirty or forty years ago when life expectancy was shorter and the quality of life was uncertain. The amazing contributions of the medical community may extend your parent's life for decades. Illnesses such as coronary artery disease, diabetes, Parkinson's disease, cancer, and pulmonary problems are no longer seen as death sentences. Who would have imagined forty or fifty years ago that doctors could sustain life on a coronary bypass machine and graft new arteries onto the heart? How could anyone have imagined that robotic limbs would bring movement back to paralyzed arms and legs? Or that the latest in eye surgery might restore your parent's vision, and help her to see her favorite television show or enjoy the face of a beautiful grandchild.

The world of medical science is changing and expanding every day and that should bring all of us hope for tomorrow. But you and your parent will not benefit from the advances of technology and medicine if you don't look beyond the first opinion or treatment plan. A caregiver from a small town in the West said that her mother received a diagnosis of lung cancer. The doctor said she had six months to live. Friends and family questioned how the doctor could be so definitive about his prognosis. They encouraged her to take her mother to a major teaching hospital. After her mother underwent tests, the caregiver learned that her mother was a candidate for a new chemotherapy treatment. Her mother received the treatment and enjoyed a better and longer quality of life.

Another caregiver jokingly said that her father "always had selective hearing." The family was convinced that Dad heard only what he wanted to hear. The truth is that his hearing was so impaired that he seemed confused all the time. When the family finally realized that this was the problem, they had his hearing tested, and he was fitted with an appropriate hearing aid. Although he still sometimes had "selective hearing," he no longer seemed confused.

When the diagnosis is a major illness, you can help your parent live comfortably and safely with the illness, and not prematurely die because of avoidance, fear, denial, or misconceptions. Use this information to help you begin talking with your parent:

- Your parent may have a long history with the doctor who diagnosed his condition, so he may be uncomfortable questioning the doctor's opinion. Be sensitive to your parent's feelings about his doctor. Start by affirming your parent's connection to the doctor. For example, "Dad, I know that you have been a patient of Dr. X's for thirty years, and I know how fond you are of him." Wait for a response. Your parent will probably agree with you. Then you can say, "It would make me feel better to be sure about the diagnosis. Would you mind seeing another doctor to confirm Dr. X's opinion and maybe give us some alternative treatment options?" Wait for a response. If he responds positively, then the battle is won. But if he is negative about making any changes, you can continue by saying, "How about thinking about it, and we can talk more tomorrow." Once you plant a seed, hopefully it will give your parent something to think about. Bring up the subject again in a day or two. Let your parent know that you realize how difficult this is for him, and how vital a second opinion is for everyone's peace of mind.

- Talk to your parent about his current lifestyle, and review this information with his doctor. Lifestyle issues that may need attention include smoking cigarettes, cigars, or a pipe; drinking alcohol; poor diet; and little or no exercise. For instance, if your seventy-five-year-old father began smoking and drinking at an early age, or if your diabetic mother insists on baking and eating chocolate cakes, it will take a great deal of encouragement and support to make even the smallest changes. Always check with the doctor before suggesting any changes in lifestyle to your parent. For the parent who smokes, ask the doctor about an appropriate treatment for nicotine addiction. If your parent has a poor diet, or is not aware what constitutes a proper diet, talk to the doctor about a referral to a nutritionist. If your mother thinks walking from the television room to the bedroom is exercise, encourage her to talk to the doctor about an exercise program. Many senior centers sponsor exercise and swim programs. If your parent drinks excessively, he may need the support of an organization such as Alcoholics Anonymous. If your efforts don't seem to work, don't be too disappointed. Although you try to do the best you can, it may be impossible for him to change because of a sense of entitlement, and the comfort of old habits.

- Treatment for most major illnesses is changing day to day. As new research trials, surgical procedures, and approved medications join the front line of the medical community, location should not determine your parent's treatment. If you and your parent do not feel that the treatment he is receiving in his community is beneficial, you have the option and opportunity to find the best treatment you can elsewhere. Large teaching and research hospitals are often on the forefront of the latest techniques. In the past few years, caregivers reported that by exploring the Internet, they have found hospitals and clinics that specialize in their parent's needs. Always check the source of the information. It is important to keep in mind that the best treatment is only as good as your parent's willingness to comply with the treatment plan. Lack of compliance to a medication regime, or failure to follow up with visits to a hospital or clinic, will undermine even the best plan.

When you encourage your parent to seek the best options available and support his compliance to a thoughtful and appropriate treatment plan, you may be giving him the fortitude to keep trying and helping him sustain his will to live.

The Importance of a Second Opinion

Peace of mind is sometimes the best medicine for you and your parent. If your parent receives a diagnosis of a serious disease, don't hesitate to ask for a second opinion. When possible, consider a doctor outside your physician's circle of colleagues or geographic area. New eyes may see new problems and solutions. The important thing is for all of you to be sure that the diagnosis is correct. Time may not be on your side if your parent faces a life-threatening emergency. You and your parent may find yourselves agreeing to medication or a surgical procedure before you have the opportunity to obtain a second opinion. If you or your parent still wants a second opinion, talk about it after the emergency situation stabilizes.

The ability to look at a problem with a different perspective has to do with the doctor's training and specialty, and your parent's history. As a doctor once said in regard to making a difficult diagnosis, "Sometimes our instincts are even better than our medicine." A feeling of trust and safety is paramount in any relationship with a doctor. But try not to confuse trust with unrealistic worship. Your parent probably grew up with the belief that whatever the doctor said or did was correct. He would likely never question the wisdom of the doctor's opinion or, for that matter, change doctors. But modern times, education, and a better understanding of people leads us to the reality: Just like everyone else, doctors are human beings. As providers of a remarkable service, most doctors use their skills with care and compassion. If you find that the doctor does not meet your needs or expectations, you should find someone else. A different doctor, a second or third opinion, may make the difference between adequate care or excellent care. Whatever you and your parent decide, you do have a choice. You and your parent are in control.

Researching Treatment Options

Research and teaching hospitals are on the cutting edge of new discoveries every day. As you read this section, there is a probability that the medical community is introducing something new to the public. What does this mean for you and your parent? It means that you and your parent have choices to make and a better chance of finding the right treatment.

- Talk to your parent about the possibility of different treatment options. Ask him how he feels about the prospect of trying something new. If he agrees and he is capable, your parent may be one of the best researchers. Many seniors are computer savvy, and they may still enjoy a trip to the library. Your goal is to help him find new treatments for his condition, but in the process, you are also empowering him by asking him to make an investment in his own future. If your parent is not able to help you, just let him know that you are trying to find the best way to help him.
- Contact a disease-related organization, such as the Alzheimer's Association or the American Heart Association, for the latest information and medical breakthroughs. These organizations are there to help you find what you need for your parent. Contact hospitals in your community and in other locations that specialize in your parent's particular problem.
- Explore the Internet for some of the latest research information on a particular condition. Before you make any decisions based on what you've learned on the Internet, be sure that the information comes from a qualified source. Try to find a second source to validate what you learned.
- Speak to the primary care physician or specialists involved in your parent's care. Most doctors will be happy to refer you to other doctors and resources if it will benefit your parent. The nursing staff in the doctor's office may be an excellent source for information and innovative programs.
- Let friends and family know that you are looking for new treatment options. Some of the best resources come from talking to other people.

"The way I found an unusual treatment program for my seventy-five-year-old father was just by making telephone calls. One telephone contact led to another and another. Finally, one of the contacts seemed just right. I spoke to a social worker in the facility's clinic. The social worker listened intently to me, but she told me that this particular facility was not appropriate. I was ready to give up my search, when the social worker described a wonderful program located fifty miles outside the city in a beautiful countryside community. The social worker told me that it was the facility where she placed her own father five years ago. Tenacity and a little luck helped me find exactly what my father needed."

Angela, Pennsylvania

- Spend time researching television, radio, magazines, newspapers, and the Internet for healthcare issues. New perspectives may stimulate you to think about a problem in a different light.

No matter how you decide to research treatment options, keep in mind that the more you learn and understand, the better informed you and your parent will be to make the best decisions.

C. COPING WITH SPECIFIC CONDITIONS

As a unique individual, you likely cope with problems in your own way. For instance, some caregivers can help their parents with hands-on physical care, such as bathing or incontinence care. Other caregivers know that they cannot handle these responsibilities, and they may ask for help from family members or professional aides. As one caregiver came to realize, each time her mother was diagnosed with another condition, *"My mom's illness seems to take on a life of its own."* For example, a parent with insulin-dependent diabetes may need your assistance with daily injections. A parent who undergoes dialysis treatments may require an extremely rigid diet that requires extra thought and preparation. Another may suffer from cognitive impairment and memory loss, which requires you to have a great deal of patience and creativity to get you through the day.

Often the things you don't understand are the things that upset you the most. Knowledge about each condition should help decrease some of your anxiety. You will feel better prepared to ask appropriate and useful questions. You may be more receptive to learn from geriatric professionals who specialize in your parent's condition, such as social workers, nurses, and doctors. You will be more open to talk to family and friends who may have had a similar experience. Every condition is different, and every caregiver is different. With education, support, and understanding, you will do the best you can for your parent.

D. DEPRESSION AND ANXIETY

"My father stopped eating, and he was losing weight. The doctor ran one medical test after another, but he couldn't find anything physically wrong with him. Dad did seem sad to all of us, and sometimes he was so nervous he couldn't sit still. I remember the time we took him out for his birthday dinner and all he wanted to do was go home. What's happening to him?"

Kate, California

Trying to understand what is happening to your parent can be difficult at best. Caregivers often describe the situation as painful and heart-wrenching. Your parent may be depressed and anxious due to many losses and changes in his life. For example, your parent may begin to feel increasingly lonely and vulnerable as he experiences changes due to family and friends moving away or dying. Personal physical loss due to an illness, accident, or the aging process may create additional fear and uncertainty. Fear of dependency may leave your parent feeling anxious or depressed.

Try to remember your parent when he was younger. Think about all he used to do, and then on some level you will begin to understand the overwhelming fear and helplessness your parent feels, knowing that nothing is the same. Your mother may have enjoyed years tending to a flower garden, suddenly to find that when she bends by the flowerbed, her back aches with pain. If your father was an avid reader, he may struggle to read any size print even with corrective glasses. Try to understand that these losses don't diminish; they grow day after day. Your parent may feel the loss day after day. Years ago on a family trip, an eighty-year-old gentleman purchased a number of boxes of greeting cards. When his niece looked into the cart, she was amazed and somewhat bewildered. She found fifteen boxes of cards, clearly marked "sympathy cards." She asked her uncle the obvious question, "Why would you buy only sympathy cards?" He nonchalantly responded, "At my age you never have enough." By purchasing the cards, he was expressing some of his deep feelings about loss.

Suffering from depression or anxiety is nothing for your parent to be ashamed of or embarrassed about. In the past, mental illness was unfortunately one of those dreaded family secrets that no one talked about and everyone tried to ignore. Because of old learned behavior, it may be very difficult for your parent to express her feelings and concerns. One bright eighty-five-year-old woman who was treated for depression found it so hard to articulate her feelings. Day after day, week after week, she said, "I would have, I should have, and I could have." Initially, it was the only way she found to express the regrets she experienced in her life. After being treated for depression, she was able to express her feelings and complete the thoughts that seemed to haunt her for so many years.

Everyone feels sad and anxious at times. But when sadness and anxiety interfere with daily living and simple pleasures, it is time to get help. Your parent may find it difficult to express her feelings, so it is important for you, your family, and other caregivers to understand the signs and symptoms of depression. These signs and symptoms are generally severe and ongoing.[1] They include:

1. Depressed, irritable, or anxious
2. Crying spells or an inability to cry
3. Lack of self-confidence, low self-esteem, self-reproach
4. Poor concentration and memory
5. Loss of interest in usual activities, loss of attachments, social withdrawal
6. Hopelessness, helplessness, increased dependency
7. Recurrent thoughts of death
8. Suicidal thoughts (rare but serious when present)
9. Fatigue

10. Agitation
11. Anorexia and weight loss
12. Insomnia

More serious or psychotic symptoms include:

13. Delusions of worthlessness and sinfulness
14. Delusions of ill health
15. Delusions of poverty
16. Hallucinations

If your parent is experiencing any of these symptoms, make an appointment with her physician for a medical examination. Inform the doctor about all of your parent's medications, vitamin therapy, or homeopathic remedies. Be sure to let the doctor know the changes you observed as well as your concerns. He will probably want to rule out other medical conditions, then refer your parent to a psychiatrist for an evaluation. Depending on the severity of the symptoms, your parent may require medication or hospitalization.

If your parent expresses suicidal thoughts, a plan to kill herself, or any of the other more serious symptoms, go to your local hospital emergency room or call 911. This is a medical emergency and your parent needs help immediately. Do not wait for a medical appointment.

Doctors often prescribe medication to treat depression and anxiety. As one geriatric doctor said regarding the use of medications, "We go low and slow with the elderly." "Low" refers to the amount of the medication in each dose, and "slow" refers to the fact that the doctor probably will introduce medications slowly to see how your parent reacts. Sometimes it takes several different prescriptions until the doctor finds the right medication or combination of medications. For any treatment to be effective, it takes monitoring and patience.

> "I took my father to the doctor on a regular basis, approximately every three months. The doctor prescribed an antidepressant for Dad because he was suffering from depression and anxiety in response to the loss of my mom and brother. I was aware that the medication could take several weeks to become effective. I

visited Dad on a regular basis and asked him if he was taking the medication. He promised me that he was taking the pills every day. Weeks went by and Dad lost more and more weight, his clothes were dirty, and he was tearful. Dad was refilling the medication in a timely manner, but he was throwing the pills down the sink. Because of his noncompliance he was hospitalized, but fortunately he recovered."

Sybil, New York

Talk to your parent if he suffers from depression and anxiety. With an accurate diagnosis and treatment, your parent may be able to resume a full and meaningful life.

E. DEMENTIA

"When they told me he had dementia, I cried. Months and years went by, and he changed from someone who laughed and played to someone I didn't recognize. Every time I left him, I cried. Then he died, and I didn't cry. It was anticlimactic, because for so many years I mourned the loss of the person I loved. Death was a relief for all of us. Does that sound unkind?"

Maryanne, Illinois

Not only does it not sound unkind, it sounds like the deep, sad feelings experienced by many caregivers. This caregiver's loss began a long time ago as she watched her father lose himself in a terrible, confusing illness. The vast majority of caregivers seem to find that dementia is one of the most difficult diagnoses to accept. Often they report that when a parent has a heart attack, stroke, or a broken hip, they feel they can do something about it. The caregiver looks toward medical care, time, and healing to turn things around and bring her parent back. Dementia is not a disease. It is a group of symptoms that are characteristic of certain diseases or conditions. Alzheimer's disease is a progressive, neurological brain disorder, and is the primary cause of dementia in people over the age of sixty-five. (See chapter 12 for specific facts and information about this illness.) As one geriatric nurse practitioner said, "It's a downward spiral. You may be able to maintain your parent for periods at a time, but eventually the disease progresses."

While medical science has made many encouraging breakthroughs in this area, many caregivers live today with the reality that dementia care is difficult and time consuming. These suggestions will help you cope and care for your parent.

- Get an accurate diagnosis. An accurate diagnosis is necessary to help you plan for the care your parent will need, such as day care, homecare, medications, or appropriate living arrangements.
- Be honest with yourself. Ask yourself these questions: Can I handle this situation? Do I need someone else to help me, such as my family, friends, a social worker, a nurse, or a home health aide? Knowing that you need help is one thing, accepting the help is something else. Accepting your own limitations is not a weakness. It is a strength to know what you can and cannot do for your parent. (See chapters 5, 6, and 10 for more information.)
- Learn all you can about dementia. Check with your local Area Agency on Aging for information about support groups and educational seminars on the subject of dementia. Local hospitals, clinics, and disease-related organizations such as the Alzheimer's Association are excellent resources. Check the resources in chapter 24, your local newspaper, magazines, and the Internet for the latest medical news and research data.
- Investigate day care as an option for your parent. Day care provides appropriate activities for your parent to help maintain the quality of his life. Day care provides a meeting place for you to share your concerns with trained geriatric professionals. It is also a wonderful environment for your parent to socialize with people he can feel comfortable with and relate to. (See chapter 9 to learn more about the best support systems for you.)
- Laughter is sometimes the best medicine. Caregivers often find solace in sharing stories and frustrations. The closeness felt by the brotherhood and sisterhood of caregivers often brings a combination of laughter and tears. As one caregiver said, "Sometimes I think if I didn't laugh, all I'd do is cry." When another caregiver asked what

happened, she said, "My father is always losing his teeth. I find them in the garbage can, under the bed, everywhere except in his mouth. One day I called over to the day care program because I just couldn't find them. The social worker told me to try two places: the freezer and the refrigerator. I looked in the freezer and they weren't there, so I looked in the refrigerator. Believe it or not, they were in the refrigerator." The other caregiver shrugged and said, "What's the big deal?" The woman laughed and said, "I just made a ham for dinner, and I put it in the refrigerator uncovered. I guess my father decided to take a bite, but he left his teeth behind stuck to the ham."

> "My mother loved hot dogs. During a family barbecue, she asked for 'one of those.' She finished a hot dog on a bun with mustard and sauerkraut. After five minutes, Mom walked back to the barbecue pit and said, 'I want one of those.' I gently said, 'Mom, you just ate a hot dog.' Without missing a second, my mother said, 'If I did, I guess it was good.'"
>
> *Bobbi, North Carolina*

- Go with the flow. The many faces of dementia include changes in personality and a decline in the ability to do everyday tasks, such as bathing, dressing, or shaving. Trying to fight the situation leaves both of you exhausted and even angry.

> "When my ninety-year-old mother reached the stage where she could no longer handle a knife, fork, or spoon, I had to get very creative so that she would eat her meals. I simply made small, easy-to-handle finger sandwiches for each meal. By doing this for every meal, my mother regained some independence, and I really began to feel more at ease and in control."
>
> *Linda, Massachusetts*

Dementia is a terrible illness with many complications. It is also terrible to neglect yourself. Take the advice of this caregiver, "I finally figured it out. My mother needs me. If I'm sick, what is she going to do? I still take care of her, but I take care of me, too."

F. AGITATED, HOSTILE, AND
AGGRESSIVE BEHAVIOR

For two years a very gentle man belonged to a day care program. His family gratefully brought him to the center five mornings each week for a five-hour program. One day during a caregiver support group, his wife of fifty years began to cry. She unbuttoned the top of her shirt, revealing violent bruises. She told the group that all of a sudden her husband began beating her. At first she said it was the first time this happened. After a while she admitted that the favorite day care participant cruelly beat her day after day. The members of the group responded with tears and words of support. It was as if some form of permission was granted to the rest of the group because suddenly one caregiver reported that her mother spit at her every time she tried to shower her. Another caregiver tearfully admitted that her eighty-three-year-old mother was hitting her ninety-year-old father. As one caregiver said, "This is terrible. Is this going to happen to my father?"

The answer to her question is yes and no. Yes, this is a terrible problem for family members to deal with, and no, agitated, hostile, and aggressive behavior does not manifest itself in everyone. Generally, a parent who was aggressive in business, controlling at home, but still loving and caring may develop this type of behavior. This frightening behavior is simply an exacerbation of the way your parent may have functioned and behaved. He may feel angry, fearful, or uncertain but have difficulty expressing himself. The words become violent expressions and the frustration takes the form of punches. During a day care program session, a confused but very docile ninety-eight-pound man wanted to leave the building. He ran out the door and down the hall. The nurse in charge ran after him and caught up to him at the front door of the building. He turned, grabbed her wrist, and pulled tightly. It took several people to restrain this tiny man because something probably upset him and he wanted to leave. Because of his dementia, he found it difficult to express himself with words. The only way he could show his anger was by resorting to a physical attack on the nurse. His anger and strength overwhelmed the staff.

This type of behavior is painful and frightening for most people to observe or experience. Adult children sometimes feel the sting of the angry words and the pain of physical assaults as if they were small children again. One woman cried, "I thought she could never hurt me again." The impact can be so strong that it makes caregivers feel helpless and defenseless. You are not helpless. This behavior has a cause, and it is not an attack on you, although it may feel that way at times. It is most likely the result of a medical, emotional, or psychiatric problem. It is important to try to understand why the behavior occurs in order for you to find the best way to deal with the situation. As you work toward reaching a better understanding, you will see things more clearly. Hopefully, in time you will feel more confident to help your parent and yourself.

- Look at the situation and ask yourself these important questions. As you review the questions, you will begin to understand that there is a reason for the problem and it is not you.

    1. Is this behavior new?
    2. Is this behavior the result of a serious illness?
    3. Is my parent becoming more confused?
    4. Did the doctor prescribe a new medication that is not agreeing with my parent or is he having a poor interaction because of another medication?
    5. Does my parent have an undiagnosed psychiatric problem?
    6. Is my parent in physical pain and unable to express herself in any other way?

- Make an appointment with your parent's physician immediately. Let the doctor know that you see changes that frighten you and your parent. Talk about your parent's actions. You may feel a little uncomfortable, but this is not the time to be shy. This is nothing new to the doctor. Be honest and candid so that he can help you and your parent.
- If the doctor suggests further testing to find the cause of the problem, discuss it with your parent. If your parent has severe dementia, talk to the doctor about the benefits of the test results before you make the final decision.
- Contact the insurance company to find out if they cover the rec-

ommended tests. If not, contact the provider of the tests and inquire about the out-of-pocket expenses.

- Discuss the possibility and practicality of medication, counseling, or other treatment options for your parent. Be sure the doctor is aware of all of your parent's medications.
- Once treatment begins, take note of any positive changes. If you do not see any changes, notify the doctor. It may take several trials with different medications to make a difference. As your parent takes the medication, observe her habits. Is she falling or tripping? Does she seem more confused? Inform the doctor of any changes you observe because the doctor may want to adjust the medication.
- The feelings you have because of this situation may make dealing with everyday problems even more difficult. If your parent receives appropriate treatment for the behavioral problems, most likely the situation will become less stressful, but probably will not go away completely. If you approach your parent in a non-threatening manner, being conscious of your tone of voice and your body language, you will help ease the situation.
- Speak calmly when you ask your parent a question or for her cooperation to do something. For example, "Mom, it's time to take a shower." Your mother may not want to take a shower, and she may begin to cry. Instead of arguing with her, have her sit or lie down in a safe place. After twenty or thirty minutes, approach the subject again. If she still refuses, offer to help her with a bed bath. Allow her to do as much as she can for herself. You can always try the shower the next day. If you don't have much time, immediately offer a warm sponge bath as an alternative. If that doesn't work, simply try giving her clean underwear. Sometimes you just have to accept small accomplishments.
- Don't use quick, harsh physical movements such as grabbing your parent's arm. Try to gently touch her arm and direct her to a chair or another room. As you walk with your parent, talk to her slowly, clearly, and in short sentences. Give only one direction at a time in order to decrease confusion and agitation.

With medical intervention and a better understanding of why this is happening, you should be able to continue being a loving caregiver for your parent. If you continue to feel overwhelmed or hurt by the situation, inquire about a caregiver support group or private counseling. You never have to feel alone.

G. ACQUIRED IMMUNE DEFICIENCY SYNDROME, OR AIDS, IN THE ELDERLY

Reaching an understanding and a level of acceptance that sex can be a part of your parent's life may be difficult. You may not like to think about your parent as a sexually active adult. It may conjure up the same type of unsettling feelings you have when you think about your teenage son or daughter involved in an intimate relationship. The reality is that sex is a part of the lives of many older adults, and avoiding or ignoring the situation will not make it go away. The truth is that "older Americans often lead active, vigorous lives in which unsafe sexual activity may occur. Thought to be at a low risk and with no need for pregnancy prevention, the elderly are least likely to practice HIV-preventive measures. Another issue is the disproportionate number of elderly women to men, and it is not unusual for an older man to have multiple sexual partners. Heterosexual women are one of the fastest growing groups of AIDS patients nationwide, and this trend is similarly observed in the older female population. Although the risk of contracting HIV through a blood transfusion has declined, it appears that "the other risk categories have subsequently increased maintaining the same incidence of the disease."[2]

Unsafe sex may be one of the reasons AIDS is a fact of life in our parent's generation, but age discrimination also plays a role in the misdiagnosis of this disease in the elderly. Healthcare professionals often assume that our parents are not sexually active, or that if they are involved in a relationship, it is monogamous. Many years ago a sixty-seven-year-old grandmother of two was receiving treatment for anxiety and depression. During the treatment process, she revealed her exploits with a number of men. After a while, the therapist lost count and began assigning a number for each affair. When the therapist asked the woman if she practiced safe sex, the woman replied, "No. Why, do you think I'm going to get pregnant?" The therapist said she realized that pregnancy was not an issue, but did the woman think about AIDS or other sexually transmitted diseases? The woman appeared perplexed and said, "That's for teenagers." A few months later, the woman arrived at her therapy session in tears. She had not contracted HIV, but she had a serious medical condition transmitted by having unprotected sex.

The difficulty of diagnosing AIDS in the elderly has a great deal to do with misconceptions about the lifestyles of the elderly and the difficulty of properly diagnosing AIDS in the elderly. Memory loss, fatigue, and weight loss can easily be symptomatic of many other age-related diseases. Because medical professionals must consider all the possibilities before making a definitive diagnosis, your parent may not be diagnosed early enough because of these unrealistic assumptions. And as with many diseases, early detection is the strongest ally to fight the disease and begin medical treatment.

Unlike many other tough topics, such as finances, alternative living arrangements, or homecare, your parent's sex life is out of bounds for discussion because it is a private, personal, and emotional topic. It can also be a deadly practice for your unsuspecting parent. Approaching this topic from an objective perspective without prying, or being judgmental, is not easy. You can do it. Here's how you can approach this subject with your parent and healthcare professionals.

- Talk to your parent if you suspect that she is involved in a sexual relationship. Be prepared with literature that you can obtain from your local hospital, physician, or AIDS resource centers as well as the Internet.
- Begin your conversation with, "Mom, I guess you and John are more than just friends?" Wait for an answer. If she says yes, say, "I am a little worried about you because even though I know having a baby isn't an issue, there are sexually transmitted diseases like AIDS that you can contract from unprotected sex." If your mother gets angry, don't press the subject any further for now. Leave a brochure or some other information about HIV and AIDS on the table, and give her a hug. You can always try again after she has a chance to look over the materials. If she answers, "We use condoms," tell her you're glad she's taking care of herself. If you think you have opened communication to comfortably talk about the subject, go for it. Discuss the importance of safe sex no matter the age. Even if she thinks her relationship is monogamous, it is important to practice

safe sex because she or her partner may have had previous sexual partners. Tell her if she feels uncomfortable talking to you, she should have this discussion with her internist or gynecologist.

- Contact your parent's physician if you know that this is one subject that you cannot approach. Explain to the doctor that you are concerned, and ask him to talk to your parent and provide her with educational materials. If the doctor has concerns or suspicions about the origin of some of your parent's symptoms, ask him if he thinks an HIV test is appropriate.
- Contact your local hospital or healthcare department to learn about educational seminars for you and your parent. Education provides your parent with important information to keep her healthy and vital. Honest and open communication allows you and your parent the opportunity to understand how each other feels. The combination of education and communication may not only keep your parent well, but it may even save her life.

H. WORKSHEET: GETTING AN ACCURATE DIAGNOSIS

The importance of an accurate diagnosis is essential to your parent's health and well-being. Without an accurate diagnosis, your parent may be treated for the wrong problem or go entirely without treatment. Use these steps to help you help your parent obtain an accurate diagnosis.

1. Gather as much information as you can about your family's medical history. Try to include all illnesses, unexplained maladies, and surgeries.
2. Make special note of any illnesses that appear in more than one generation of the family or in one member of the family.
3. Ask your parent's pharmacist for an update of your parent's drug history for the last six months to a year. If you have any questions, review the list of medications with the pharmacist. Make a few copies of the list.
4. Ask your parent's physician to write down your parent's diagnosis, and ask for any literature on the subject.

5. Ask your parent's physician what tests he performed to confirm the diagnosis. Ask for the names and telephone numbers of any specialists involved in your parent's diagnosis or treatment. Ask the specialists for the same information.

6. Show the pharmacy printout to your parent's physician. Ask the doctor if the diagnosis was made with complete knowledge of your parent's medication history.

7. Ask your parent's physician and any specialists involved in his care for a copy of his medical record, test results, films, and any other pertinent information. Some physicians' offices charge a fee for this service.

8. Get a second opinion if you and your parent do not feel comfortable or convinced that the diagnosis is accurate. It's very important to select a board-certified physician in the specific illness or a physician who is board-certified in geriatrics.

9. If you want a referral to a board-certified geriatrician, ask trusted friends, colleagues, and illness-specific resources such as the American Heart Association or the Alzheimer's Association.

10. When your parent gets a second opinion, be sure to provide all medical records and an accurate family history to the physician. Bring all medications in the original container with a copy of the pharmacy printout.

11. Chapter 13 will provide you with more information on coping and dealing with these difficult issues.

WORKSHEET:
IMPORTANT TELEPHONE NUMBERS

Creating a list of telephone numbers for people who are important to your parent's well-being is a must for every caregiver. Having these numbers at your fingertips will save you time and lower your stress.

In an emergency, always call 911 first.

1. Family members to contact in an emergency:

Name _____ Tel. _____

Name _____ Tel. _____

Name _____ Tel. _____

 2. Physicians:

Name _____ Tel. _____

Name _____ Tel. _____

Name _____ Tel. _____

 3. Pharmacy:

Name _____ Tel. _____

 4. Neighbors:

Name _____ Tel. _____

Name _____ Tel. _____

 5. Friends:

Name _____ Tel. _____

Name _____ Tel. _____

 6. Other (geriatric care manager, elder law attorney, financial adviser, bank, transportation service, homecare agency or worker, grocery store, plumber, home repair, or others):

Title _____ Name _____ Tel. _____

Title _____ Name _____ Tel. _____

Title _____ Name _____ Tel. _____

Title _____ Name _____ Tel. _____

Title _____ Name _____ Tel. _____

Title _____ Name _____ Tel. _____

Title _____ Name _____ Tel. _____

Title _____ Name _____ Tel. _____

Title _____ Name _____ Tel. _____

Title _____ Name _____ Tel. _____

I. MY JOURNAL

Use this page as a safe place to express your feelings. Putting thoughts and feelings on paper helps us to see them more clearly. What bothers you? What changes do you want to make? When you read what you've written, you may see a new pathway to help resolve stressful issues. For example:

"*I feel as if I spend every day in a doctor's office with my father. I know he needs me, but I'm so tired . . .*"

"*When I heard the word Alzheimer's my heart sank and I thought I would throw up. But there it was and here I am caring for my mom who needs more then ever before. This is very painful . . .*"

_____

_____

_____

_____

_____

_____

_____

_____

_____

_____

_____

_____

_____

_____

_____

_____

_____

_____

_____

_____

_____

_____

_____

_____

J. TIP SHEET

- Insist on an accurate diagnosis to help you create a workable and realistic plan of care for your parent.
- Be open to new treatment methods to help your parent live life to the fullest.
- Educate yourself about your parent's condition or illness in order to help her maintain the best quality of life.
- Prioritize what you need to do for your parent. Use your organizational skills to keep track of doctor appointments, medication changes, and specialized care and treatments.
- Go with the flow. Parents who suffer from a serious illness have good days and bad days. Try to enjoy the better days together and ask for help from friends and family when you need it.

16

COPING WITH ALZHEIMER'S DISEASE

"My father visits Mom every day in the nursing home. He stays there for hours. I think he has to in order to survive. I'm convinced that even when she doesn't recognize him, visiting her and doing things for her is the only thing that keeps him from dying of guilt or a broken heart or maybe both."

Paul, Oklahoma

"My mother lives with me, but she doesn't always know me. Sometimes her behavior is so bizarre that I don't know her either, and then I'm the caregiver for a total stranger. My sisters say she belongs in a nursing home. They're right; she could live another ten years. I'll die of exhaustion or a broken heart long before she does. But I still can't put her there."

Lenore, Texas

"My dad's been in an Alzheimer's support group for years. I asked him why he still goes to the group meetings a year after mom died and he said, 'I just can't give her up.'"

Rene, New Hampshire

A. FACTS ABOUT THE DISEASE

If you suspect your parent is a victim of Alzheimer's disease, you are not alone. This disease is truly democratic, crossing all socioeconomic borders, and affecting men and women almost equally. "One in ten persons over sixty-five and nearly half of those over eighty-five have Alzheimer's disease."[1] While Alzheimer's remains incurable, treatment options offer hope for slowing or halting the progression of the disease.

Whether you and other family members are actively involved in caring for your parent or visit him periodically, all of you will benefit from a thorough understanding of the disease and the medical advances and treatments available. Early detection of developing symptoms, followed by an accurate and definitive diagnosis and post-diagnosis planning, are key to successfully treating and coping with Alzheimer's. Unfortunately, both we and our parents usually become so frightened when we see signs of memory loss and confusion that we tend to deny that it exists. For example, your mother may tell you she's trying to lose weight, or your father may tell you he overdrew his checking account because he forgot to write in a check. The realities may be that your mother is losing weight because she forgets to eat or becomes confused when she tries to remember how to cook a meal, and your father is having trouble with arithmetic. When we deny something is wrong and pretend that everything is fine, we are usually instinctively trying to protect ourselves from pain or guilt. Denial may feel safer and more comfortable, but with Alzheimer's, denial can be self-defeating and dangerous. Denial may help your parent remain at risk for additional illness and accidents, and may prevent treatment. This is a time for action. If you suspect your parent has Alzheimer's disease, call your local Alzheimer's organization, tell their representatives your fears, that you are going to intervene, and you would like their help.

> "My advice to other caregivers is to find an organization that remembers that you need as much help as your loved one with Alzheimer's. All diseases are hell, but this one is the worst and no one should try to handle it alone."
>
> *Marty, Ohio*

Many elderly people suffer from some form of dementia, which means that their cognitive and intellectual functioning is compromised due to physiological causes. Alzheimer's disease (AD) is a progressive neurological brain disorder and is the primary cause of dementia in people over sixty-five years of age. All AD patients suffer a continuing cognitive decline, becoming progressively less able to think clearly, perform sequential tasks, remember accurately, or reason appropriately. In addition to loss of intellectual functioning, your parent with AD may exhibit changes in personality, mood, and behavior, and develop problems such as wandering, depression, belligerence, incontinence, constant agitation, combative behavior, and sleeplessness. Sleeplessness often presents itself as an inability to discern day from night. Your parent may take long naps during the day and wander around the house at night, disrupting the household and creating a situation that requires supervision twenty-four hours a day, seven days a week. The rate of decline and severity of symptoms varies from person to person.

The first signs you may notice are changes in your parent's ability to make safe or sound decisions regarding medical care, paying bills, or financial matters. There may be a decline in your parent's ability to perform routine tasks such as grooming, grocery shopping, cooking, turning off the stove, or locking the door. A caregiver from New York described it this way: *"One day it all seemed to change. My mother looked dirty. The woman who always dressed well wore the same pair of jeans and the same shirt for over a week. She looked thin and frail and even when I brought her food, it stayed in the refrigerator for days."* Your parent may sometimes seem disoriented, forget words, have difficulty in learning, or be unable to concentrate, read the time on a clock, write a letter, or recognize a friend. You may notice a decreased interest in hobbies and social or religious activities. As frightening as these symptoms may be, they do not automatically constitute a diagnosis of Alzheimer's disease.

B. TESTING AND DIAGNOSIS

Ageism and its assumption that age + forgetfulness = Alzheimer's often prevents needed treatment for diseases other than Alzheimer's disease in which dementia symptoms may be present. Alzheimer's cannot be diagnosed solely on the basis of a single traditional medical examination, one psychological test, or a series of forgetful episodes. A diagnosis can be rendered only after a complete medical evaluation has ruled out the many different diseases and conditions other than Alzheimer's that can produce dementia symptoms. These diseases include: ALS (Lou Gehrig's disease), Huntington's, Parkinson's, Diffuse Lewey Body, depression, hydrocephalus, nutritional deficiencies, thyroid disorders, head injuries, and adverse drug reactions, to name just a few. An incorrect diagnosis may condemn a parent to a life of confusion, fear, and dependency, and subject the caregiver and the caregiver's family to unneeded physical, emotional, and financial stress.

Alzheimer's testing is generally administered in an outpatient setting under the supervision of a board-certified neurologist specializing in dementia. As science understands AD better, simplified testing will become available. Currently, the procedure includes extensive neurological and psychological testing, a variety of laboratory tests (blood, EKG, chest x-ray),* and scans (MRI, PET, CT),† gathering data to create a detailed patient history, and a complete physical examination. These tests are outpatient procedures, usually scheduled over three to four appointments. After all the testing has been completed, a final visit entails a frank discussion with the supervising neurologist about the diagnosis, treatment plan, prognosis, and referrals for assistance with caregiving. The information gathered at this meeting will assist you in planning for future needs: caregiving, housing, medical care, support groups, family education, and training, as well as with necessary legal and financial details.

> "Dad's doctor kept telling us that Dad's only problem was that he was 'getting old.' I finally got him to a neurologist who did some tests and diagnosed him with early Alzheimer's. I almost screamed 'do the tests again, you're wrong!' But I knew in my heart he was right. He also said, 'I can help you if you do what I tell you. Bill, you have to go to day care, and Ceil, you have to go to a support group.' When I got up the courage to go to my first support group meeting, Dad blocked the door and said, 'You're

---

*EKG = electrocardiogram.

†MRI = magnetic resonance imaging; PET scan = positron emission tomography; and CT scan = computed tomography.

not going anywhere. There's nothing wrong with me.' About a half dozen group members said the same thing happened to them. There's nothing normal about Alzheimer's disease, but talking to others with the same problems normalizes it somewhat because it reduces your feelings of being out there alone."

Jan, Minnesota

If you receive no more than a diagnosis, ask for referrals to professionals who can help you with the rest, or call your local Alzheimer's community organization for referrals.

C. TREATMENT OPTIONS

Alzheimer's disease is irreversible, but not without help or hope. Because current treatment options center around medications designed to halt or slow the progression of the disease, early detection carries the best chance for effective medication, for your parent's continued independence, and for maintenance of an acceptable quality of life. Entering into a treatment program may help your parent maintain or even improve a current cognitive level for a period of time. The goal is to maintain that improved functioning level until the next generation of medication becomes available. At that time, the new generation of medications may take over and achieve the same results for another few years. And again. And again. The opportunity to receive cutting-edge treatment is usually found in neurological practices that specialize in Alzheimer's or in clinics called "memory disorder centers." You can obtain a list of these through your local Alzheimer's support organization. (See chapter 24 for more information.)

D. THE EFFECTS ON YOUR FAMILY

Perhaps more than with most other diseases of the elderly, education, support groups, and ongoing training make a documented difference in the effect of the disease on your family life and personal quality of life. The reason is simple: regardless of whether your parent is at home or in a nursing home, almost every established and routine activity of daily living, including how you communicate, will change as the disease progresses. Many caregivers expressed this same sentiment:

> "This is a special kind of hell. My mother, who lives in my home, and who I love and spend hours caring for every day, doesn't know me anymore. She calls me by her sister's or mother's name. She doesn't remember me as her daughter. I keep saying, 'Mom, it's me, Dale.' She just stares at me. Through me, really. I might as well be telling her I'm George Washington. She has no idea who Dale is. I just keep crying. I've never known such pain before."
>
> *Dale, North Carolina*

Education is also important for improving your skills as a caregiver and making sure both your and your parent's well-being is maintained.

Because the disease impairs and eventually destroys memory, the longer your parent has the disease, the less recollection she will have of everything. As incomprehensible as it seems, literally nothing is excluded from this loss: family, friends, home, events, possessions, addresses, telephone numbers, places, and even the most basic skills. Starting with the most recent events and the most recently learned skills and trailing backward in time, all will be forgotten eventually.

E. WHAT TO EXPECT AS THE DISEASE PROGRESSES

The course of Alzheimer's disease can vary significantly with each individual. However, some changes are more typical and so you can reasonably expect to experience them. Educating yourself to the flow of Alzheimer's can help you communicate better with your parent, your family and friends, and your parent's physician.

Alzheimer's disease systematically destroys your parent's ability to use and rely on the critical skills and cognitive functions we develop from infancy through adulthood and take for granted, such as memory, orientation to time and place, judgment that allows us to discern right from wrong or safe from harmful, and problem solving. Your parent will lose the instincts and memories that are needed to function safely and appropriately in all areas of living: driving, self-medicating, eating, writing, reading, cooking, interacting socially, cleaning, playing sports, grooming, and making financial or legal transactions. The list is endless. The loss is all-encompassing.

What to Expect in the Three Stages of Alzheimer's Disease

Use the box to the left of each symptom to check those that apply to your parent. Check all that apply. Feel free to check off symptoms in more than one stage. This information can help you create plans to keep your own mental, physical, and financial future intact. Taking this list to your parent's physician will provide her with an insider's clear written account of your parent's behavior and abilities. The physician will be more able to prescribe appropriate lifestyle and medication changes that may help improve the entire family's quality of life.

Changes Commonly Experienced in Stage I

In the early stages of AD, you can expect your parent to show consistent, increasing memory loss, especially about recent events. You'll notice minor difficulties in handling everyday matters, less interest in hobbies, some disorientation to time and place, and perhaps a need for prompting to keep appointments or continue an established personal care or household routine. If your parent plays card games needing strong memory skills for counting cards and suits, that may become progressively more difficult. Because safe driving entails remembering how to start, brake, steer, reverse, park, read road signs, obey speed limits, and use landmarks and clues to get from one point to another, driving for a parent with AD is always considered extremely dangerous for him and for all others on the roads and streets.

Although Stage I is called the "mild" stage, it is actually one of the most difficult periods of the disease process for you and your parent. Most people in Stage I AD realize that they are losing control and fight back by denying the existence of the problem. Their children also find it easier to deny the disease and attribute problems to "getting older." These combined denials mean delayed diagnosis and treatment, often putting the person with AD at more risk. An early diagnosis by a board-certified neurologist specializing in AD can result in Mom's receiving medications that may help slow the progression of the disease. Treatment at an early stage gives Mom the potential to retain a higher functioning level for a longer period of time.

Short-Term Memory Loss, Confusion, Focus

- ❑ My parent is beginning to forget recent experiences such as appointments made yesterday or last week.
- ❑ She has trouble with new experiences such as a new telephone number or area code, or meeting someone new.
- ❑ My parent sometimes has trouble finding familiar places like her home or mine, the grocery store, and the doctor's office.
- ❑ My parent finds it difficult to follow sequential directions like recipes, projects, or greetings, such as *"come in, take your coat off, sit down."*
- ❑ My parent has a shorter attention span and sometimes finds it difficult to focus on specific tasks or finish activities.

Speech/Conversation

- ❑ My parent has had word-finding problems and has filled in the sentence with a nonrelated word or made-up words that sound like gibberish to cover the difficulty.
- ❑ My parent seems to be talking less. (This may help avoid having to find words or making another embarrassing mistake.)

Initiative/Self-Care

- ❑ My parent has difficulties with decisions on menus or selecting clothing to wear.
- ❑ My parent has begun to make inappropriate driving decisions.
- ❑ My parent has begun to make inappropriate financial decisions.
- ❑ My parent has lost interest in hobbies, friends, and other activities.
- ❑ My parent is not as well groomed as she used to be.
- ❑ My parent doesn't appear to bathe as often as she used to.

Personality/Mood Changes

❑ My parent has mood swings that he didn't have before.

❑ My parent makes excuses to avoid friends and family.

❑ My parent has become depressed.

❑ My parent has experienced a reversal in personalities from kind to nasty, outgoing to reclusive, gentle to sharp-tongued, or other obvious and significant changes.

As your parent draws closer to Stage II, you'll notice significant memory loss. The AD patient will have retained fewer and fewer memories, will be more severely disorientated about time and place, will have great difficulty in problem solving, and will be unable to handle social relationships or function independently except for simple tasks. Your parent will need an increasing level of assistance with dressing, grooming, preparing meals, taking medications, handling most household activities, driving, or making sound decisions regarding personal safety and finance.

Changes Commonly Experienced in Stage II

Memory and cognitive ability continue to deteriorate in Stage II, which make supervision and assistance a primary need. Preparations for this stage include considerations for twenty-four-hour assistance, transportation, housing, financial and legal matters, and long-term care.

Medical assistance and caregiver respite are mandatory for your parent's safety and yours, and to control your quality of life.

Increased Confusion

❑ My parent has difficulty remembering to lock the door.

❑ My parent cannot remember how to call me if she needs help.

❑ My parent cannot formulate complete thoughts and sentences.

❑ My parent cannot read.

❑ My parent may mix up identities or forget names and identities (daughter, son, grandchild, friends, and deceased relatives).

❑ My parent doesn't recognize or remember the use of objects like a chair or bed.

❑ My parent shows frustration at not being able to understand or at not being understood.

Speech/Actions

❑ My parent repeats questions or statements many times.

❑ My parent makes repetitive motions.

❑ My parent paces in circles or wanders from room to room.

❑ My parent often becomes unmanageable in the afternoons or evenings with verbal outbursts or physical activities such as masturbating, disrobing in public, or running away.

❑ My parent makes up stories to fill in memory gaps.

Hygiene Changes

❑ My parent refuses to bathe or becomes fearful and agitated when we bathe her.

❑ My parent wants to wear the same pieces of clothing for extended periods of time without washing them.

❑ My parent is incontinent.

Sleep/Paranoia/Fear

❑ My parent sometimes or always sleeps during the day and stays awake at night.

❑ My parent has accused us of trying to kill her or stealing her money.

❑ My parent is sometimes aggressive or combative and has tried to kick, hit, scratch, or bite other people.

Safety Risks

❑ My parent lives alone and gets lost when he goes outside his home.

❑ My parent no longer understands what poison is or does.

❑ My parent is unsure of himself on stairs or balconies.
❑ My parent's balance is off and he is at risk for a trip or fall.
❑ My parent can no longer dial my number on the phone. (Try this test: hand your parent the telephone and say, "Dial my number, Mom.")
❑ My parent could no longer evacuate in a fire.
❑ My parent could no longer remember how to call 911 in an emergency.

At the more severe levels of impairment, your parent may not remember you, your siblings, or a spouse. It will no longer be safe to leave your parent alone. Your parent will require twenty-four-hour supervision and total assistance with all activities of daily living such as eating, bathing, dressing, and toileting.

Changes Commonly Experienced in Stage III

> "Mom is only sixty-eight years old, but she is at the end stage of AD. I want to spend as much time with her as I can, but it's very hard to see her this way. Sometimes she cries for the baby son she lost forty years ago. A nurse who visits Mom once a week suggested we give her a baby doll to hold. Her home health aide said that when Mom becomes upset or agitated, she gives her the doll and Mom rocks it to sleep in her arms. I'm a 6'1", 220 lb. marine, but sometimes I wish I was that baby doll."
>
> *Paul, South Carolina*

Stage III is also known as "end-stage" Alzheimer's, because it signifies the final years of the disease. At the end of this stage, your parent will pass away. Assistance from a counselor at your local Alzheimer's organization and hospice, and a physician specializing in Alzheimer's disease and related dementias can help you and your parent enormously during this very difficult time.

Assistance

❏ My parent needs total assistance with transferring from bed to chair, eating, walking, and every activity of daily living.
❏ My parent has difficulty swallowing.
❏ My parent refuses to eat.

Memory

❏ My parent no longer recognizes himself or family members.

Speech

❏ My parent rarely or never communicates.

Body and Functions

❏ My parent sleeps most of the time.
❏ My parent has had a significant weight loss.
❏ My parent's skin bruises or tears easily
❏ My parent is completely incontinent of bowel and bladder.

One of the results of society's continuously expanding Alzheimer's knowledge is that AD is a long-term disease. Patients may survive as long as twenty years from diagnosis to death—meaning you may find yourself in the position of caregiver for two years or two decades. Caring for a loved one with dementia is considered one of the most difficult jobs in the caregiving spectrum. The financial losses, loss of quality of life, and loss of *self* make it vital to get help.

Ongoing support and caregiver education can help avoid or minimize the effects of depression and loss of quality of life by supplying you with the information you need to understand the illness and make informed decisions. You can begin your search for assistance in chapter 24.

F. ORGANIZING TO HANDLE MILD MEMORY IMPAIRMENT

Simple planning and organization can alleviate some of the frustrations resulting from mild memory impairment. For example, create a system to help keep the number of lost or misplaced items to a minimum. Many times you can use your own life experience as a source of solutions. What do you do with your house keys so they are easy to locate? Where do you look for your messages? If you yourself are totally disorganized, don't give up. Get help from a professional. Recognize when your first solution doesn't work, and try another one. Your life will be a lot calmer and your parent will be a lot happier once simple frustrations are alleviated. Here are some useful examples.

1. If your parent sometimes forgets which apartment door or which bedroom door is the right one, decorate your parent's door with an object that is in high contrast to the door for easy viewing. Both AD and normal aging can affect vision, so be sure to use a large decoration with a strong contrasting color, and be certain there is enough light for your parent to see it. Some caregivers use a pretty wreath, a dried floral arrangement, a contrasting unusual door-knocker, a picture of the room's occupant, or the occupant's name in large, colorful, and easy-to-read letters.

2. Post a large calendar in a prominent place and fill in doctor appointments, birthdays, and other dates. This can help remind a mildly impaired parent of important occasions and give her a sense of control.

3. Place a sign on the inside of the front door reading LOCK THIS DOOR or DON'T LOCK THIS DOOR to help remind a mildly impaired parent to perform this essential safety step.

4. Install a telephone with extra large, lighted numbers, programmed for use by pressing the photo of the person your parent wants to call. This will relieve your parent of the need to remember telephone numbers. Check with your local Alzheimer's organization or telephone equipment company to locate this and other helpful equipment.

5. For a moderately or mildly impaired parent, reframe or label photos with identifying notes: "Norm and me in Acapulco," "My friend Helen," "My grandchildren Derek, Kim, and Tommy," and so forth.

6. Place a basket in plain view for mildly impaired parents to drop keys, eyeglasses, and loose change in the same spot every day. This helps alleviate some of the problems of misplacing these items. Be sure to put a sign on the basket: keys, eyeglasses, and change.

7. Place a notepad by the telephone and in the kitchen for a mildly impaired parent to record "to do" or grocery lists. "Things to Do" or "Grocery List" or another title that will give your parent a clue to the pad's use should be in a large, dark type. Black ink on white paper is the best contrast and the easiest to see; black ink on yellow paper the next best.

G. PRIMARY COMMUNICATION TIPS AND COPING SKILLS

"We argued every day. Mom said something that was completely wrong or ridiculous and I always managed to correct her. The stress of communicating with her became almost unbearable. Her geriatric doctor made a wonderful suggestion. He said, 'Go with the flow.' He said if Mom says it's time to eat, tell her she is right. Before she has a chance to think about it, I distract her and point out a family picture or a flower in the garden. She forgets about eating, and we move on to the next thing. One day she couldn't stop thinking about her dog, Jack, who died ten years ago. I remembered what the doctor said, and instead of screaming at her that Jack's dead and gone, I suggested we try to find him in the yard. By the time we got her coat on, she forgot why we were going outside. It doesn't always work, but coping with her in this way makes it easier on both of us."

Denise, New York

"I was just about at the end of my rope when I walked into the Alzheimer's care group in my city and the nurse took me by the hand. She talked to me for an hour, and then came to my house to see my wife. She was the first person I met who worried about me, the caregiver. What a difference she made in my life."

Sam, California

Very few tasks are more stressful for a family member than being an Alzheimer's caregiver. As you and your family find it more difficult to care for or communicate with your parent, you may be more apt to be angry and frustrated. At the more advanced stages of the disease, you may be caring for someone you've known for fifty years, but who doesn't recognize you in return. Your mother may look at you innocently, call you by the wrong name, and begin to tell you about her daughter whom she calls by the name of your grandmother. Your father, with whom you've had a lifelong close relationship and who adored his grandchildren, may ask you who you are and tell you he's sorry he didn't have children. It's easy to understand why depression is so prevalent in Alzheimer's families. It's also easy to understand the anger you might feel when a parent asks the same question repeatedly even though you answered it seven times in the last five minutes, walks away in response to a request to "sit down, Mom," or even becomes aggressive and actually strikes you with no warning and for what appears to be no reason at all. There is a reason for all these actions and reactions.

We learn by association and memory. When your parent's memory fails, your parent may no longer remember the names of beloved family members, pets, friends, his home address, telephone numbers, eating and personal grooming habits, and all the rest of a lifetime's learning and memory storage. Your parent doesn't remember asking the same question repeatedly (or even once before), may not remember what "sit down, Mom" means, and may act aggressively out of fear, confusion, frustration that she is unable to communicate with you, or simply because that's a symptom of Alzheimer's disease. Because you can't "see" the impaired cognitive function of your parent's brain, your parent may look perfectly healthy. It's difficult for caregivers with normal memory function to imagine living with no memories of as recent a time span as five minutes ago.

A major cause of tension is the lack of understanding of how to handle routine tasks such as dressing, eating, or family gatherings so that problems are minimized.

> "Do you have any idea how much easier my life would have been if I'd known the simple stuff at the beginning? Like, 'it doesn't matter what clothes she sleeps in as long as she's happy when she goes to bed. It doesn't matter if she doesn't wear clothes.' What you want is a peaceful evening."
>
> *John, Oklahoma*

> "It's always the little things that drive you crazy. When we traveled overnight to my daughter's house I forgot the plastic sheet we use in case Paul wets the bed. I was so nervous in the motel I couldn't sleep a wink. When I told my support group, they laughed and told me whenever that happens they just take off the plastic shower curtain and cover the bed with it!"
>
> *Lynne, Kansas*

Specific Alzheimer's training and coping techniques are critical to controlling stress levels. Without specific training, usually available from your local Alzheimer's organization or Area Agency on Aging (see chapter 24 for a list of organizations and resources), you may not understand that the reason your parent continues to ask the same question over and over again is because she has no memory of having asked it the first time. You may not realize that angry, hostile behavior from your parent when you insist on a bath may be because your parent has forgotten what water is, and she may be frightened. Your parent, who practiced modesty for eighty-five years, may be embarrassed to undress in front of a daughter or anyone else.

As your parent's memory and skills decrease, it's important that your knowledge of AD and your coping skills increase. The primary rule is: the more confused your parent feels, the more difficulty you will have communicating and accomplishing even the simplest task. These twelve suggestions will help keep both you and your parent on a more even emotional plane, and that will make routine tasks simpler.

Remember Your Own Needs

Get help. Involve your family. Involve healthcare advocates. Involve your physician. Get involved with your local Alzheimer's support groups. (See chapter 24 for a guide to resources.) Involve your clergy. Alzheimer's disease is the wrong illness with which to become (or to stay) isolated, independent, or alone. The best way to help your parent is to help yourself. Ask the neurologist who performs the testing and presents the diagnosis for a list of resources in your community. Ask the representatives of these resource organizations for assistance, and keep asking until you find the type of help that meets your needs. Stay in contact with the AD community throughout the duration of the illness. Staying current with new research and coping techniques may allow your parent to participate in new treatment options. Also request referrals to the appropriate professionals who will help you obtain the information to make informed decisions as you plan for the future.

"I feel the support I've been getting is beneficial, but the burden still falls on me. I would recommend anything and everything, the more the better."

Sharon, Maine

"Peace of mind is the greatest gift you can give anyone."

Annette, Connecticut

Accept the Disease

People with Alzheimer's often become less inhibited. They do and say things that can cause us great anxiety because they embarrass us in front of friends and in public places. The caregiver who shared this lesson said it all:

"I never knew what my father was going to say or do. It didn't matter if we were in a restaurant, on a walk, or at the doctor's office. I was always so tense I could hardly breathe. Once, in a mall, he looked at a woman and blurted out, 'Don't you own a girdle? You look awful in that dress.' Another time, in a restaurant, he picked up his chicken breast, smeared it with gravy, put it in his shirt pocket, and patted it down until it seeped through his shirt. I finally learned how to handle it. Now, I just look at whomever he insulted or anyone who's staring at us, smile, and say, 'He's got Alzheimer's disease.' Once I stopped keeping the secret, I relaxed. It took me too long to realize that there is no shame in being ill."

Arlene, Florida

Many Alzheimer's organizations offer a small card that easily fits in your pocket, wallet, or purse. The card is designed to hand to those you think your parent may have offended. It simply says, "My loved one has Alzheimer's disease." If you've experience behavior issues in public, call your local organization today and ask for cards.

Don't Take Outbursts Personally

Your parent has not changed from a loving parent (or a nonloving but reasonably rational person) into a spiteful monster and your parent isn't trying to get back at you. Personality changes like anger, irrational outbursts, and aggressive behavior are part of this disease. Anxiety, fear, and frustration precipitate many aggressive outbursts. Affirmation, distraction, and humor are the best tools for you to use to deal with these disturbances.

For example: You know your father has no plans and no visitors are scheduled; however, he suddenly walks up to you and angrily says, *"Tom was supposed to pick me up and he's late!"* Remember, your father actually believes Tom is late, and he is angry. You might smile, nod your head up and down in affirmation, point to another room in your house, and respond, *"Oh, he called and said he was going to be late, but he'd pick you up in there."* You have every chance that by the time your father reaches the other room, something else will attract his attention, he will forget about Tom, and his anger will disappear. You have just successfully used affirmation and distraction to diffuse your father's anger.

A more dangerous example is Mary's tale: *"I had no warning. All of sudden he just lashed out and hit me. I'm afraid to go home. How can I*

care for him if I'm afraid of him? I don't know what to do." Sometimes
the only way to calm your parent down in a situation like this is to briefly
leave the room for a few minutes. Again, your parent will likely forget the
outburst very quickly unless the trigger is still in place. After the outburst
is over, call your parent's physician and ask for help.

> "The way I look at it, we're not just working with a disease; we're
> treating behavior problems. Caring for someone with
> Alzheimer's without treatment for her behavior is so stressful it'll
> kill you. If your doctor doesn't understand or can't help you with
> that, move on and find another doctor."
>
> *Jack, Oregon*

When your parent seems disturbed, try to identify what triggered the
disturbance. It may be a high-pitched siren, an inability to understand
your request, fear of a stranger, or frustration over a complicated menu.
Sometimes the confused person is not only angry, but may be anxious as
well. When Fred, a retired seventy-five-year-old farmer with AD, was
hospitalized, the nurses found him more anxious at lunchtime than any
other time of day. Every time he looked out the window, he became
increasingly angry and upset, and refused to eat. The staff was puzzled
because they couldn't distract him. One day they realized that when Fred
looked out the window, he saw the lawn furniture and thought he was
looking at his cows. They thought about the problem and came up with a
solution to relieve his anxiety. The next day when he refused to eat, the
nurse acknowledged his feelings and told him not to worry because they
had arranged for someone to take care of his cows. Fred was clearly
relieved, and he happily went to lunch.[2]
    You won't be able to identify or avoid all the triggers, but if you keep
a list of stressful situations, you may be able to avoid them, develop ways
to deal with them, and slowly reduce the number of outbursts.

Keep Your Requests Simple

The more you prompt and use orienting words and physical expressions,
the less confused your parent will be. Because Alzheimer's destroys

memory, your parent will find it progressively more difficult to remember the correct response to off-the-cuff requests or commands, and almost impossible to respond to slang expressions. Speak clearly and simply. Use language with identifying words and prompting actions to help your parent understand your request. An unclear request like *"Have a seat"* changes entirely when you touch the chair and say, *"Sit here."* Another example of unclear language is this double command with sequential tasks: *"Take your sweater off and get ready for dinner."* You'll have better results by walking over to your mother, smiling, and saying, *"Let me help you take your sweater off,"* and gently helping her. Then point to or touch the chair where you want your parent to sit and say, *"Sit here."* Continue, one request at a time, until you've accomplished your goal. Use the same command each time. Do not change *"Sit here"* to *"Sit down in this chair."* Your parent has to try very hard to understand any command and do what you ask. If you change the words, your parent will have to start all over again, trying to understand what you want.

Beware of Your Physical Attitude

Alzheimer's does not prevent your parent from sensing fear, anger, hostility, tension, or other negative feelings in other people. These feelings may be recognizable to your parent in the way you stand (shoulders hunched, fists clasped, lips taut, body or voice tense); in your speech (clipped and terse), loud voice, hissed words; and in physical displays or actions (slamming doors, phones, objects, waving hands, your red face, and your eyes blazing with rage). Any of these can easily create fear and confusion. Your parent will recognize your anger, but will not know why you're angry. He will become anxious and will be afraid of you. Reactions may range from tears to striking out at you; certainly all communication will be destroyed, and you will not accomplish whatever you started. The stronger the feelings that you send, the more extreme your parent's reaction will be.

> "I didn't understand why Dad got so upset when we introduced him to his new home health aide. He became aggressive and angry, and he said terrible things to her. At first I thought it was the fact that someone new was in his house, but then I realized

exactly what had changed. His old aide was very soft spoken and gentle. The new aide was very personable and made us feel good, but she was much too loud and aggressive for Dad. We talked to her about toning down a little, but in a short time we all realized that she was not the one for this job. When we screened the new aide, we asked her to talk to Dad and spend the afternoon with us. She was calm, and he reacted favorably to her. You live and learn."

Hilda, Florida

If you feel your frustration boiling over, or if your stress factor has reached overload, make arrangements for a break. A short respite period, even an afternoon off, may help.

Use Strategies When Eating Out

If you go out for dinner, don't expect your parent to understand a long list of specials and a multi-option menu. All of those unfamiliar choices in an unfamiliar room will simply bring on confusion, which may turn into fear, which may turn into anger or stubborn rejection of the food or you. Order for your parent by saying, "Dad, I know you like chicken for dinner. I'll order that for you." If your parent insists on ordering, start the ordering cycle with your parent. This may help eliminate the anxiety of waiting to order.

Avoid Crowds

You may not notice or think twice about crowds in restaurants, shopping malls, and other public places, but they may seem frightening, confusing, or overwhelming to an AD patient. Help your parent to focus on what you are saying by eliminating all other points of interest. Alzheimer's disease causes increasing problems with focus and concentration, and anything that competes for attention is certain to make understanding and communication more difficult. Try to frequent crowded places at off hours: for example, restaurants before and after peak dining hours, and malls early, late, or at the dinner hour. Your parent should be less anxious and more at ease, which will enable both of you to enjoy the outing more.

Unfortunately, no matter how well planned an outing is, there are always exceptions. A caregiver in Florida reported taking her father to the doctor. This doctor and the staff were skilled in treating patients with dementia, her appointments were always scheduled for midmorning, the doctor usually saw them immediately, and she rarely had problems during these visits. On one memorable occasion, the physician was late, and Arlene and her father had to wait. Her father kept staring at a heavyset woman in another chair. The woman finally smiled and said, *"Hello. It's a beautiful day today, isn't it?"* Arlene's father answered, *"Hello yourself, you've gotten pretty fat!"* Arlene said she apologized and took her father out for a walk. She felt guilty because she was embarrassed and ashamed of her father.

We suggest two words: "accept" and "admit." Uncensored speech and relaxed inhibitions are often a part of the disease process. Admitting to the people around you that your father has AD and accepting the fact that his behavior is sometimes part of the illness may help you place your parent's socially unacceptable behavior in the proper context. It is sometimes difficult not to feel that this type of "acting-out" behavior is not payback for something you did forty years ago, but it isn't. It is not retribution, and it is not happening to you because your parent wants to hurt you or punish you. It is just one aspect of a very difficult and complex disease process. If this type of behavior becomes increasingly difficult for you and your parent, ask your geriatrician, neurologist, or geriatric psychiatrist for assistance.

Make Appointments for Midmorning

A part of AD is what is known as sun-downing syndrome, in which the patient is especially prone to act out aggressions, fantasies, or abusive or other uncontrollable behaviors in the mid-afternoon to early evening hours. Even if there is no sun-downing syndrome present, your parent may just be fresher in the morning. Try to make medical, shopping, and other appointments during midmorning, when AD patients are usually more alert and rested, and have more ability to concentrate.

Make Sure Professional Healthcare Workers Are Savvy about AD

Physical exams, psychiatric tests, CT scans, blood tests, dental work, homecare workers, and even a simple blood pressure reading require special knowledge when working with an Alzheimer's patient. Your parent may have trouble comprehending a standard explanation of the test and may become frightened or even combative. The experience may be traumatic enough to throw off the results of the test, or worse, your parent may become anxious enough to elevate a current level of confusion. When you make the appointment, ask if the physician, nurses, and technicians are experienced in working with AD patients. If not, ask your local Alzheimer's organization for a referral to another professional. It usually takes experience to keep an AD patient calm and comforted while a dentist is treating a toothache or while a technician is drawing blood. If you hire a professional homecare worker or companion, ask about previous Alzheimer's experience. What was the worst experience the homecare worker had, and how did she handle it? This will give you an idea of how knowledgeable the worker is. (See chapter 11 for tips on selecting a homecare worker.) If you doubt your ability to assess the professional's skills, ask someone more knowledgeable to help you.

"Mom needed some dental work. Her regular dentist refused to handle the situation, because the last few visits were pretty tough on both of them because she kicked the dentist and tried to bite him. We called the Alzheimer's Association and asked for a referral to a dentist who can handle Mom's problems. They provided us with the name of a dentist who spent time talking to Mom, learning about her medical conditions and her medications. Once she had a complete picture, she examined Mom's teeth and said that she needed to give Mom anesthesia in order to do the work. She said she would speak to Mom's doctors to determine if this was possible and then she would schedule an appointment. Mom received medical clearance, and the dentist took care of her teeth. We really appreciated the fact that she did not dismiss Mom's needs, and found the best way to deal with them."

Faye, Pennsylvania

"While I was relating Dad's increasingly aggressive behavior, the doctor looked at me disapprovingly and said, 'The only thing you've done in the last five minutes is criticize your father. I don't see any of the problems you mentioned.' Did he really expect to see three months worth of problems with an Alzheimer's patient in the four or five minutes he spent with Dad?! Right then I knew we had the wrong doctor."

Deena, Kentucky

Build in Routines and Encourage Pleasurable Activities

For an AD parent who lacks memory, eating or dressing may be new experiences each day. You can help your parent feel less anxious and more secure if you create a routine and schedule the same morning, afternoon, and evening activities at roughly the same times every day. As the disease progresses, your parent's ability to participate will be limited, but you can adjust and simplify accordingly. For example: take shorter morning walks; confine gardening activities to one plant, one flower pot, and a small bag of soil; and limit helping with housekeeping to folding two or three laundry items. As short-term memory fades, memories of enjoyable events from earlier years take on added importance. Religious services learned as a child remain comforting; music enjoyed decades ago may bring pleasure because the words and tunes, stored in long-term memory, will still be familiar. Looking at photographs of earlier family life and memory boxes filled with your parent's favorite items are good for stimulating memory. Whether your parent is at home or in a nursing home, feeling appreciated and a part of the family remains critically important. When possible, try to involve your parent in pleasurable activities you both can enjoy together: walking, listening to music, talking, or singing songs. Include your parent in the family's routine as much as possible to make him feel comfortable and loved.

Use Day Care Programs

"To this day my father thinks he's a volunteer for 'those who need help' at the day care center. He thinks they asked him to come sing. Otherwise I'd never have gotten him there. The idea came from my support group. I couldn't make it without their help. Now I have a few free days each week and he has peers to talk to. We're both happier."

Jenny, Iowa

Dementia-specific or Alzheimer's-specific day care programs can be invaluable for an AD parent and caregiver. Many are subsidized by grants that allow users to pay on a sliding scale, many are free, and some provide transportation. One to three days (or more) each week can help provide stimulating social and mental activities for your parent. For you, it may just provide enough freedom and time off from caregiving duties to make a substantial difference in your life and your family's life.

"There is no greater joy or pleasure than seeing my dad dance and sing and laugh. When he began to lose his memory and say and do inappropriate things, his healthy friends dropped him as if he had the plague. I always wanted to say, 'It's not contagious.' But he was left alone. Now he goes to day care and this wonderful man has come back to life. I know that some people don't do as well in a social setting, but this is made for Dad's personality. He just needed a place that accepted him for who he is today."

Ted, Montana

Take Appropriate Safety Measures

Act now. Don't wait for an accident before you take simple safety measures. Intervene at the first sign of impairment.

- Remove scatter and throw rugs and make sure all electrical cords are out of walking areas. An AD parent is many times more likely to take shuffling steps, trip, and fall.
- Call a professional to install railings on stairs and grab bars in the bath or shower so your parent can use them to balance and to avoid falls.

- Add more lamps or change bulbs to a higher wattage if current systems can tolerate the increase. Your parent will need bright lighting to avoid tripping or bumping into table edges.
- Place night-lights throughout the house to help avoid stumbling or falling if your parent wanders during the night. Pay particular attention to stairways.
- Place a safety gate on stairways. Make certain someone is available to open the gate in case of an emergency.
- If your parent wanders, raise the lock on outside-access doors above your parent's reach or Velcro a cloth the same color as the wall over the doorknob. This will make the doorknob almost invisible and keep your parent from opening the door. Do not try either of these or block exits unless your parent has twenty-four-hour supervision to help evacuate in an emergency.
- Make certain chairs are heavy enough to stay put if your parent suddenly "plops" down; many kitchen or dining room chairs can skid out or tip backward and cause a fall.
- As the level of impairment increases, be certain balconies and walkways are only accessible under supervision.
- Secure all medications, even over-the-counter remedies such as aspirin, laxatives, and vitamins.
- Firearms and chemicals, including household cleaning products or insect sprays, should be stored out of reach in locked cabinets.

H. REMEMBER YOUR BODY, MIND, AND SPIRIT

Sylvia's story may help you. Sylvia spent many years taking care of her father with AD, and although she tended to all his needs and wants, she always managed to take care of herself as well. How did she find the time? Where did she get the willpower? She explained it very well. *"I do my back exercises every morning. If my back hurts, I can't help him."* Sylvia brought her father to day care four days a week; this allowed her to continue her weekly trips to the beauty parlor, and even treat herself to a Wednesday afternoon show or movie with her friends once or twice a month. *"Each and every day I see another piece of my father slipping away—his memories, his skills, and his ability to do the things he used to do. Taking a break from caregiving while he's in day care and focusing on other topics with my friends helps me to step back a little and clear my mind. Then I can remember him as he was when he played the piano, when we could have a conversation, and when he remembered me as his daughter. Those are the memories I want to keep forever."*

With an Alzheimer's parent, you will experience many profound losses. You can help yourself. Like Sylvia, try to keep your special memories in your heart and nourish them by remembering to care for your own mind, body, and spirit.

I. PLANNING FOR THE FUTURE

Trust and estate and elder law attorneys, as well as geriatric professionals, stress the importance of planning for the future. Key topics include financial and legal issues, healthcare arrangements, and the known or stated wants and needs of your parent. Because the laws regarding legal, financial, and healthcare issues may vary from state to state, it's a good idea to retain an expert advisor in your parent's home state. Check with the professionals in your community for a referral.

- Wants and Needs: Designate a private time when you can talk to involved family members. If your parent is able to participate, try to include him in the discussion. Set the ground rules at the beginning for openness, honesty, and listening quietly so that each person can speak freely without fear of angering others. Discuss living arrangements: Will your parent stay home, move into an assisted living community, or enter a skilled nursing home? If homecare is advisable, who will hire, supervise, and pay for the worker? Which family members will become caregivers, and what responsibilities will each have? If alternative living is desirable, what will happen to the family home and everything inside? What type of funeral arrangements do your parents have or want? Check with your financial advisor or attorney about the desirability of pre-paying for this service. Take notes and make certain everyone receives a copy of the decisions that come out of this meeting.
- Legal and Financial Issues: Depending on your parent's condition,

suggest that he review existing legal and financial documents with an attorney or financial advisor. Or make an appointment with a trust and estate attorney or an elder law attorney to discuss the need for and the drafting of pertinent legal documents such as a power of attorney, durable power of attorney, living will, healthcare proxy, trust, last will and testament, and when necessary, guardianship documents. Gather and organize as many legal and financial documents as you can prior to the appointment. Some of the documents may not be readily available: your mother may have no idea where your father kept them, or she may have misplaced them or put them in a "safe" place that she no longer remembers.

"By the time we took over, my mother was totally out of it. My father had MS and was too sick to be of much help. Mom's friends and sisters told us she had been putting away money for years in case of an emergency. Mom never told them where the money was, and we were lucky if she remembered who we were, let alone what money was. That was thirty-five years ago. My sister, brother, and I still talk about that money. We still wonder whether or not it ever existed and if it did, how much did we lose?"

Harriet, Wyoming

Geriatric professionals understand the difficulty of organizing documents and may be able to obtain some of the information they need by speaking to your parent's lawyer, accountant, or bank officer.

- Healthcare Matters: The reality of AD is that at some time in the course of the illness, your parent will need care. It may begin as part-time in-home care and may eventually advance to in-home or nursing home custodial care: twenty-four-hour/seven-day care and assistance with all daily needs, from family, nurses, nurses aides, or physicians. The types of care that are available and the costs for care vary from state to state and community to community. You will need to understand what type of insurance your parent has, the exact coverage, the amount of the benefits, the period of time that is covered (days, weeks, months, years, lifetime?), and how to activate the benefits. Get help from a geriatric professional who specializes in these matters. Making life-altering plans and decisions can be frustrating during the best of times. Take these three steps to help alleviate some of the stress and worry:

1. Gather as much medical, legal, and financial information as you can.
2. Discuss your needs and wants with a professional.
3. Continue asking questions until you clearly understand your options.

Now make your decision knowing that whatever lies ahead, you were thoughtful, diligent, and in the end, you chose the best plan for your parent, your family, and for yourself.

J. MY JOURNAL

Expressing our thoughts on paper often helps see our feelings more clearly and that makes it easier to arrive at solutions to our problems. What bothers you? What changes do you want to make? What or who are you grateful for? When you read what you've written, you may see a new pathway to help resolve stressful issues. Use this page as a safe place to express your feelings. For example:

"Since Mom's been in the nursing home Dad is a shell of himself. I feel guilty for pushing him to do it, but he's sick too and I couldn't take care of both of them in my home. I hate feeling like this and I'm angry at him for making me feel this way . . ."

"My mother was an architect. Now she stares at me wondering who I am and I wonder if she's going to welcome me or be afraid of me. I'm so lost. I called for help today and I'm seeing a counselor tomorrow. I hope it works. I need relief from this anguish."

_____

_____

_____

K. TIP SHEET

- Do not try to solve every problem alone. Alzheimer's is a long journey and you'll need help along the way.
- Make sure your parent sees a board-certified physician specializing in Alzheimer's disease.
- Join an AD support group. It's soothing and healing to share problems with others who face the same issues.
- Use day care programs to give you respite and keep your parent active within a peer group.
- Improve your mental and physical health by educating yourself on your parent's disease at your local Alzheimer's disease organization.

17

WHEN HOSPITALIZATION IS NECESSARY

A. FACING YOUR FEARS

"A calm, detached voice said, 'This is the emergency room at Community Hospital. Your father was just brought in.' Time stood still. It wasn't just the regular fear you feel when someone you love goes to the emergency room. This was different. A feeling of the end came over me. I knew he'd never come out alive. He was eighty-nine and so frail. Never before or since have I felt as helpless as I did at that moment."

Brenda, South Dakota

When a partner or a child enters the hospital, we may be frightened, but most of us hope for the best and expect medical science to prevail. Less optimistic feelings often arise when an elderly parent enters the hospital. It doesn't matter how strong or self-sufficient you are. It doesn't matter if your mother has been hospitalized many times because of a chronic illness or if you were totally surprised because you believed she was in relatively good health. You instinctively begin to subconsciously wonder if this is the beginning of the end. We dread the potential loss of a parent and loss of control that we may experience. Doctors often confirm our feelings when they tell us, "At her age, the operation is too risky," or "At his age, I'm not sure he's strong enough to fight this." Sometimes we appreciate their wisdom and understand that they are trying to help us face reality. But there are other times when reality, if left unchallenged, translates into a certain death sentence, and we feel the need to proceed regardless of the obstacles.

> "She had blocked arteries, her heart was enlarged, and she was seventy-eight years old. I guess because of the severity of her illness and her age, she didn't look good from a medical standpoint. The first surgeon whom we consulted declined to operate because he felt that she didn't have a very good chance of surviving the surgery or of having a decent quality of life after the surgery. My sister and brother and I decided that we were going to give my mother every opportunity, so we decided that we wanted to pursue this surgery even though her chances didn't look good. I had been through my own open-heart surgery about four months earlier. I contacted that surgeon because I felt that he was very good. My sister said that because he knew me, he agreed to go ahead and perform the surgery. He did advise us that she had only a marginal chance of coming through the surgery. However, we decided that she deserved every opportunity to live, and we told him that the alternative was not acceptable. That's why she had the surgery. She wasn't able to go in right away. They had to prepare her and build up some of her functions. Her hospital stay was six weeks, not the normal five- to six-day stay for open-heart surgery. It was a long, slow, painful recovery, but she's a fighter. She made it."
>
> *Belinda, Florida*

Our feelings of frustration and helplessness may be exacerbated in a hospital where the personnel are sometimes too busy or too overworked to communicate effectively. "The doctor just left" or "She was here earlier" may be the only information we receive. Visiting hours may not mesh with our work schedules and other responsibilities. We may have pressing obligations that constrict our ability to spend as much time as we'd like visiting in the hospital.

Nothing will totally eradicate reality. There are times when we have to accept the fear and frustration and just do the best we can. There are times when we have to accept that medical science cannot make us all well. However, whether your parent's hospital stay is two days or six months, you can make a difference if you understand your options and your rights as your parent's advocate.

B. CHOOSING THE RIGHT HOSPITAL

"My mother called 911, then she called me. The next day when I called in to let my supervisor know I wouldn't be in to work, she told me how lucky we were. It turned out that the ambulance took my father to the hospital that has the top neurological surgeon in the city on its staff. If they'd asked me, I would've said 'Take him to the one that's closest to my mother.' How would I know which hospital has the best doctor for what he needs? Who thinks of these things before you need them?"

Lauren, California

If your parent's hospitalization is elective or preplanned, ask your physician if you have a choice of hospitals. If your parents live in a town where there is only one hospital, you may feel you have no choice and be tempted to skip the advice in this section of the chapter. Before you do, however, read Lee's story:

"My father's physician saw a suspicious spot on a yearly routine x-ray and referred him to a local surgeon. The surgeon sent him to the local hospital for some tests. When my father called me, he had this plan all worked out. The surgeon would take a biopsy on the operating table. If the test showed a malignancy, the surgeon would continue the operation and remove the cancer right then and there. No second opinion, no concern about the degree of difficulty the operation might entail, no nothing! My father didn't think he needed a second opinion because he trusted the primary care physician he'd been seeing for twenty years. He said this doctor had always referred him to 'good people.' I was terribly uneasy. The next day I called the physician. It turns out the town didn't have a surgical oncologist. He knew my mother was ill, so he decided to send my father to an excellent general surgeon who had handled these problems before. He thought it would save mother the discomfort of making the trip to a city where my dad could be treated by a specialist. He never suggested that my father get a second opinion. Now my father had become adamant about staying home for this surgery. I took the next plane out. It took me nearly two days of almost around-the-clock begging and pleading before he agreed to come back with me and see a specialist at a large university hospital. The new tests reported the same tumor, but the hospital's cancer specialists didn't feel my dad needed surgery. They wanted to try treating him with chemotherapy. Six months later, there was no sign of the tumor. Every time I think of my seventy-eight-year-old father undergoing major surgery and my mother caring for him through a long recovery, I get chills. He still goes to the same doctor. If he feels even slightly out of sorts, I automatically begin mentally rearranging my life and preparing to bring him back here for another opinion."

Lee, Massachusetts

There are two overall reasons for you and your parent to take an active part in choosing a hospital. The first consideration is medical. All hospitals do not provide equal care. For example, if your mother needs a coronary bypass, the benefits of choosing a hospital with a specialization in that field are significant. The hospital with the cardiac specialty may have several physicians with extensive experience in treating your parent's illness. If needed, your parent's physician can have a conference with the other specialists and treat your mother using the combined knowledge of the entire group. Your parent may have the advantage of being treated with cutting-edge technology or an experimental technique that is being tested in a limited number of hospitals. The nurses and the supporting staff may be more familiar with the problems associated with your parent's diagnosis. This makes it easier for them to teach you coping skills and offer instructions that will help your parent recover faster. You and your family may be able to lower your stress by attending educational seminars and caregiver workshops to learn more about your mother's diagnosis. You may have an opportunity to network with other caregivers in a support group whose needs are similar to yours.

"When my father was ready to leave the hospital, he and my mother got standard discharge instructions. You know, 'Don't lift anything for twenty-four hours; call the doctor right away if you have a problem.' My parents live in a small town, and although the care my father received was good, I wasn't comfortable. I felt a specialist with more extensive experience might have been a better choice, but the nearest one was about one hundred miles away and my mother flatly refused to leave home. Two months later, he was still having problems, and the doctor wanted to readmit him to the same hospital. I convinced my parents to talk to their doctor about a referral to the specialist I found. I picked up both my father and mother, drove them to the appointment, and sat in on the conference after the examination. What a difference! He wanted to rerun the tests, but he felt my father's problem appeared pretty routine. There was a relatively new medication that he should have been given the first time he was in the hospital. It had only been in use for about four months, but it was available then. He said the tests would give us more definitive answers, but he didn't expect any surprises. He also said that the hospital's rehab team would teach Dad safety techniques so that he could continue to do some of the things he liked to do. Unless the tests proved him wrong, at this point, it didn't look like Dad would have any further limitations. You could just see the relief on my mother's face. The previous doctors just told him to 'try' and if it caused him discomfort, forget it and take up another hobby. Then he said the nurse would talk to us some more. The first thing she did was take my mother's hand and say, 'It's normal to worry, but the doctor deals with this every day. You're in good hands.' She said the doctor wanted to see us again in two weeks, but after that visit, we'd only have to come every three or four months. In between, he would work with my dad's primary care physician to make it more convenient. Then she said, 'Now, I'll answer any questions you have.' Until that moment, I'd been trying to figure out how to take all that time off and still keep my job. Right then I had the feeling that everything was going to be okay.'"

Lucy, New Mexico

The second reason to talk to your doctor about the most appropriate hospital is convenience. Does your mother drive? If your father goes to the hospital, will she be able to visit him? If your mother enters the hospital, will her friends be able to visit? Why accept treatment in an inconvenient location if you can be cared for equally well in a more suitably located hospital? These two caregivers experienced the same problem.

"I couldn't believe my father was in a hospital so out of the way that the cost of a cab was close to $30 each way. So my mother, who is none too healthy herself, took two buses to get there. If the buses were on time, it took her over an hour each way; if they were late or traffic was heavy, it could take more than two hours. It was winter, so she had to wait for the bus in the freezing cold or worse, sleety rain. What a disaster. It's a wonder she didn't end up in the hospital herself!"

Suzy, Nebraska

"My mother seemed to get more depressed daily. The doctor said she was recovering physically, but she became quieter and more withdrawn every time I saw her. At first the nurses said that it was nothing to worry about; it was normal for her to act that way. She'd had a major scare, and it would take time for her to feel like her old self. After a week, there was still no improvement, and we all began to worry. Then I got an idea. I called her best friend, Edith. None of my mother's friends drove, and it had been so cold out that they hadn't been able to come to the hospital by bus. They sent cards, but it wasn't the same. I sent a cab for Edith and told her to pick up one more friend along the way. I told her I'd pay for the cab when they got to the hospital; just to tell me when they were coming. They were there two hours later! These women had shared every joy and every problem for the past fifty years, and all of them were suffering because they couldn't be together during my mother's time of need. I tell you, when Edith and Fran came through that door, my mother's face lit up like a million-watt light bulb. It was just what she needed. I did the cab thing again two more times, and then she went home. They don't make a medicine that could replace the love and companionship she needed to get her through this. I'm her daughter and I know she loves me, but she 'shares' with them. She can tell them her fears, talk about her aches and pains, or about dying; most of all, she can laugh with them. You would blush if you heard the jokes these supposedly 'old ladies' made about what they 'could do' with her 'doll-baby' doctor."

Rita, Montana

Take the time to talk with your parents and let them know they have choices. You will all benefit from a better understanding of your options.

If your parent enters the hospital through the emergency room, you probably won't have a choice. He will most likely be brought to the nearest trauma center. Once your parent is stabilized, the physicians in charge may want to admit him to the hospital. At that point, you can ask your parent's physician whether or not this is the best hospital to provide treatment for your parent's specific diagnosis. You can also investigate on your own by calling specific organizations that relate to your parent's problem such as the American Heart Association, the Diabetes Association, the American Stroke Association, and others. Chapter 24 can help you locate the organization that can best serve your needs. The Internet is an excellent resource for locating hospitals that specialize in different treatments. Enter the diagnosis or treatment (log on to Google, enter "hospitals specializing in heart bypass surgery," and review the resources that match your needs).

C. BEING PREPARED

Instant information can be the key to quick and effective treatment. During an emergency, your parent might not be able to gather information that the hospital needs or answer the critical questions that help medical professionals perform to their best ability. Emergency rescue technicians, physicians, and nurses will need to know, for example, if your parent is allergic to any medications or foods, what medications your parent currently takes, including the doses and frequency. Quick access to your mother's physician and her medical records could save her life. They cannot call you unless they know your name and telephone number. One of the simplest ways to avoid a potential tragedy is with a program like the "Vial of Life," which is offered in many communities throughout the United States under a variety of names.

If your parents are emotionally and physically capable of working on this project with you, discuss it with them and offer to help prepare a packet of information that will accompany them if they should go to the hospital. If your parent suffers from dementia or another problem that makes participation difficult, do it yourself. For a preplanned hospitalization, your parent can simply pick up the packet and take it to the hospital. In an emergency situation, fire rescue, emergency medical, and ambulance personnel may be trained to look at the window closest to the front door or on the refrigerator door for a Vial of Life notification. These frequently asked questions might help explain how Vial of Life or a similar packet can work for your parent and for you.

Q. What is Vial of Life?

A. Vial of Life was created to help in medical emergencies. Rescue personnel often need to act immediately, so there may not be time to stop and gather critical information regarding the patient. Your parent may be too ill to answer questions about his medical history, and family members may not be available. If the emergency occurs in your parent's home, Vial of Life gives rescue personnel immediate access to the information that can help save your parent's life.

Q. How does it work?

A. It's a two-part program usually sponsored by a local fire department, senior service organization, pharmacy, hospital, private community-service-oriented company, or other type of organization. Each sponsor has its own version. Many of these programs are called Vial of Life, but the one in your parent's community may have a different name. Most provide a form for your parent to complete, two magnetic stickers that say VIAL OF LIFE PARTICIPANT, and a plastic bottle or clear plastic bag. The form will ask for your parent's name and address, the person to call in an emergency, and the names and telephone numbers of the physicians involved in your parent's care. The form may request that your parent attach copies of a living will or healthcare proxy (if they exist), a Do Not Resuscitate (DNR) order, or other pertinent documents. It will probably ask for your parent's usual blood pressure along with a list of current medications and medical conditions. All of this will be on one page, front and back. The form is folded and inserted into the plastic bottle with copies of the documents mentioned. Do not insert the original documents; always use copies. The bottle is placed on the top shelf or in the door of the refrigerator or freezer. Your parent will be asked to place one of the magnetic stickers on the window of the front door, the window nearest the front door, or the door that the fire department or rescue personnel are most likely to use. The other sticker should be placed on the outside of the refrigerator door.

Q. Shouldn't I place the sticker in the room I usually sit in like the TV room or my bedroom?

A. No. In communities with Vial of Life programs, rescue personnel are usually trained to check the front of your refrigerator. The refrigerator was chosen because everyone has one and it's comparatively easy to locate.

Q. Doesn't the information in the vial become outdated pretty quickly? My mother has four doctors who prescribe and change medications regularly.

A. Yes. When you present this program to your parent, stress the point that for the Vial of Life to be safe and effective, the information has to be kept current. Outdated information can potentially put your parent's life at risk.

Q. How much does participation cost?
A. There is no charge for the Vial of Life. It is free.

Q. How do I find one in my parent's community?
A. Call the Area Agency on Aging, the fire department, your parent's pharmacy, a senior center, the Alzheimer's Association or American Heart Association, or a nearby hospital. These numbers are easily found in the telephone book. Chapter 24 lists telephone numbers for the national headquarters of many organizations. They can direct you to the office nearest your parent's home.

Q. What can I do if my parent's community doesn't have this program?
A. Try to locate Vial of Life in your community or on the Internet. When you have a sample, prepare your own. When you post your notice on the front door, you'll have to give an emergency information location such as "in refrigerator." On the refrigerator door, you can post the words "emergency information inside."

One more tip: It's important that whoever places the emergency call to 911 remembers to alert the operator that your parent has this information and gives the location. Whenever possible, it's also vital to alert the rescue personnel when they arrive.

D. EMERGENCY ADMISSIONS

If you are with your parent when a life-threatening situation occurs, you have only one thing to do: find the telephone and call 911. If you receive a call telling you an emergency has occurred, you have only one course of action: ask if the caller has called 911. If he hasn't, tell him to hang up and call 911, or hang up and do it yourself.
When you call 911:

- Be prepared to give the operator your parent's full name, address, and telephone number. If you don't have full information, call anyway and give as much information as you can.

- Give the operator the name and telephone number of your parent's personal physician. This enables the rescue team to find out vital information about your parent's medical history to help determine treatment.
- If your parent has a Vial of Life, a hospital packet, or other similar emergency information prepared and ready for a situation like this, inform the 911 operator of its location.
- Ask which hospital your parent will be taken to.

The quicker your parent is treated and stabilized, the better chance he has for survival and recovery. Only a trained medical professional can accomplish that. Driving your parent to the emergency room in your car only adds more risk to the situation. Your parent may become unconscious, may have a heart attack or a seizure, or may actually die on the way. Even if nothing else happens to your parent, you may be delayed in traffic or have an accident, your car can break down, a tire can blow out, or you may have to stop for gas. Every minute spent without attention from a medical professional gives your parent the opportunity to deteriorate further.

Once you know emergency rescue services are on the way:

- Notify your parent's physician as soon as possible and ask him to follow up and stay on the case. If he tells you that he cannot care for your parent because he doesn't practice at that hospital, ask him to recommend a physician who does. That will help you avoid being randomly assigned to the first available physician.
- Double-check to be certain that the hospital has the name and telephone number of your parent's physician so that they can obtain the medical information they need. Advise them that you've asked your parent's physician to stay on the case or that you would like the physician referred by your parent's physician to take over.
- Notify other family members. Elect one person to act as a liaison with the hospital and report back to everyone else. Trauma centers can be very hectic places. It's best to avoid having each family member call for information independently.

Once your parent reaches the hospital and is in the hands of skilled medical personnel, try to clear your head and consider your next steps. If your father is being admitted to the hospital:

- Find out the name of the admitting doctor. Try to talk to him for a full explanation of why your father is being admitted. Ask for a written copy of the diagnosis.
- Talk to admissions, a social worker, or the patient advocate regarding the room and roommate before a room is assigned.

> "My father got run over. He was crossing the street, and a car pulled out from behind a parked car and slammed right into him. After hours in the emergency room, he was sent to the only room they had available. It was on a critical care floor. When a room opened up on a more appropriate floor, they moved him. I didn't ask any questions. It never occurred to me to ask who his roommate would be. It took me about ten minutes to get the picture and another ten to go berserk. His roommate either talked or moaned continuously. He never once kept quiet, except to take another breath. I guess he was demented. I don't know. I felt sorry for the man, but how was my father supposed to get any rest with this continuous noise? They said they had no other room. The patient advocate told me that if I had objected before the move, they would've waited for another room. How exactly, I asked her, was I supposed to know that? I finally called his doctor and asked him to intercede. They moved him, but it took two days. Would you believe I ended up buying earplugs for both of us? We just couldn't take it."
>
> *Jack, South Carolina*

- The admitting representative may ask you for copies of your parent's insurance cards, advance directives, or other documents. Most of the information they need is in the Vial of Life or hospital packet the emergency technicians brought to the hospital with your parent. If there was no hospital packet, the information is probably in his medical file and available via fax or e-mail from his physician's office.

If your mother is not being admitted to the hospital, these issues will need your immediate attention:

- How will she get home?

"My mother had been complaining of pain for weeks, but she refused to call her doctor. The other night the pain got so intense, she couldn't stand it. She did the right thing. She called 911. The hospital treated her and released her. Unbelievable as it seems, they put a ninety-one-year-old woman full of painkillers and antibiotics in a cab and sent her on her way alone—at three o'clock in the morning!"

Diane, Michigan

- Will she need help at home? If so, why? What kind of services will she need, how long will she need them?
- Are these services covered by her insurance? If not, why?
- Did the hospital discharge planner order the in-home assistance or will that be your responsibility?
- Ask for a copy of her written diagnosis.
- If you have any other questions, ask them. The patient's bill of rights clearly states that it is the hospital staff's obligation to provide accurate, understandable information in a courteous manner.

E. PREPLANNED ADMISSIONS

The admissions process can be smooth or it can be a lengthy, frustrating experience. Most preplanned admissions enter the hospital early the same day or the evening before a procedure. If the hospital is busy, there may be a backlog in admitting. You may be able to reduce your waiting time by making an appointment to take care of the admissions process a day or two earlier during off-peak hours. The admissions person may also have more time to spend on your special requests. If your parent's room is being assigned at this point, she may have a choice in the room that's assigned to her. Ask how many beds are in the room and about your parent's roommate. If you think your parent would be happier with the bed by the window, now is the time to ask for it. If the hospital has a spirit-lifting view like an ocean or a park, you may be able to choose a room on that side. If your parent is very anxious, a room near the nurse's station may provide her with some comfort. If you receive consistently negative responses to your questions, check to see if the person you are talking to has the authority to grant your requests. If not, find out who does and ask the appropriate person.

Your parent may be called for routine tests prior to admission. These may include blood tests, blood pressure measurements, and others that are pertinent to her care. It's a good idea to ask if your parent needs to fast before the tests, and whether or not she should take her medications at her regular times. Reconfirm the fasting and medication instructions with her doctor.

Your mother will be asked for pertinent documents and information during the admissions process. The hospital will photocopy the documents and return them. Someone should be prepared to take them home. Do not leave any of the originals at the hospital.

The hospital will ask for:

- The name, address, and phone number of her referring physician and her primary care physician.
- The name, address, and phone number of the person she wants notified in case of an emergency.
- Her Social Security card. (The hospital will make a photocopy and return the card.)
- Her insurance cards. (The hospital will make a photocopy and return the cards.) Without proof of insurance, your mother may be asked to sign a document stating that she will pay the hospital for its services.
- A copy (not the original) of her living will, healthcare proxy designation, and all other advance directive documents.
- A copy of her durable power of attorney.
- A list of current medications and dosages. Bring the actual pharmacy bottles instead of a list. Ask if she should take her medications before she actually checks in and whether or not she should bring them with her.
- Information on allergies to foods or medicines.
- During this process, you should:
  ○ Ask about visiting hours. If they are inconvenient for you because of work hours or other obligations, ask for special permission to come at other times.

ELDERCARE 911

° Ask for a copy of the patient's bill of rights. Read it. It will help you understand what your parent is entitled to during her hospital stay.

° Ask to meet the patient advocate. This alerts the staff that you are an educated, concerned family caregiver.

F. WHAT TO TAKE ALONG, WHAT TO LEAVE AT HOME

Instinct often helps us to pack what is necessary when we're about to leave the house. When we leave the house, we automatically check to see that we have enough money, a driver's license, a wallet, a purse, perhaps a charge card, house keys, or even car keys. None of these personal items belong in a hospital room. Help your parent's hospital visit go as smoothly as possible by following the instructions you'll receive during preadmissions testing or in the mail. If you are helping your parent pack a bag to take to the hospital, follow these guidelines:

- Do not bring money or jewelry. Most people are honest and try to do a good job, but there is a risk that someone may take advantage of your parent's empty room when she is in the lab or in surgery, or even while she is asleep. Play it safe. Bring twenty dollars (twenty one-dollar bills) and leave all other valuables at home.
- If the hospital has asked you to bring your parent's medications with you, alert her nurse that you have them with you.
- Take at least one family photo. Having your family's photo near can be extraordinarily comforting during stressful times.
- Take books, magazines, hobbies, games, and similar items that can help pass the time.
- Take a robe. Be aware, however, that hospital requirements may mandate that patients wear only items issued in the hospital.
- Do not take a cell phone. It interferes with hospital equipment.
- If you take food or snacks, be certain to ask the nurse if your parent may keep them. The physician may be regulating or tracking your parent's food intake.
- Do not take alcoholic beverages. Alcohol and medications can be a

lethal combination. The hospital has the right to confiscate the alcohol and may even ask you to leave if you persist in bringing in more.
- Take patience and flexibility. Leave your temper at home. Patients and their families often spend a lot of time waiting for doctors, nurses, and tests. If you have a problem, discuss it with the nurse in a quiet and respectful manner. If you cannot resolve your problem, discuss it with the patient advocate. Yelling at a busy nurse or patient advocate may only make matters worse.

G. DURING YOUR PARENT'S HOSPITALIZATION

"My view of being in a hospital is that on a good day, it's similar to landing on another planet where you not only don't speak the language, you haven't got any idea what the language is. You get the same answer to most questions. Ask 'When will the doctor be here?' or 'How long will my mother be gone for her test?' and you're likely to hear, 'We don't know.' That's on a good day. On a bad day, you just get a shrug signifying the same thought."

Mary, Illinois

A hospital is a large community. To operate smoothly, it must run on a system. In a system everyone and everything has its place, and people often become just one of the thousands of pieces in the overall mix.

Once your parent is in her room, how you assume the role of advocate is key to a successful visit. Courtesy and cooperation can make your life easier, even in the busiest hospitals. Keeping current on your parent's status can help lower your stress and anxiety levels.

Find out when the doctor makes her rounds, and be there when she arrives. Don't complain if it's 6:00 AM. No matter how frustrated you feel she is not trying to avoid you. Doctors often make their rounds early so that they can see patients in their offices or perform operations during the day. Ask her to take a few minutes to explain the diagnosis and treatment. Find out what she hopes to accomplish. The doctor will appreciate your involvement and concern.

- If you still have questions, ask your parent's nurse for the answers. Many nurses are skilled in translating complicated medical issues into easily understood terms. Nurses are also a good source for practical caregiving tips.
- Write down the name of the medical problem and research it in the library or on the Internet. If you don't have time, ask a family member or friend to do it for you. Ask the doctor or nurse about anything you don't understand.
- If you still don't understand, repeat the entire process. You cannot help your parent unless you understand what she needs and why.
- Talk to your mother's nurses and get to know them. They are often overworked and unappreciated. If you personalize your communication by remembering their names, smiling, or asking about their lives, you'll be establishing a relationship that will help you and your family through this trying time.
- A little kindness can go a long way toward making your mother's stay more pleasant. If your parent is staying for longer than a day or two and you an afford it, bring a box of cookies or candy to the nurses' desk to thank them for their attention to your mother. This doesn't have to be expensive. A $3 or $4 bag of cookies from the grocery store shows your thoughtfulness and gratitude.
- Be cheerful and optimistic, but do not pretend that everything is fine if it isn't. Your parent may be concerned that the doctors aren't telling her everything. You don't want her to feel the same way about you. She needs at least one person to trust.
- Pay attention to your parent. Listen and take her concerns seriously. Your parent needs an advocate, not an adversary.
- If your parent is in the hospital for "observation" or "tests" and something changes, ask to speak to her doctor. Try to avoid surgeries or other potentially life-altering processes without confirming the need. Ask the doctor if your parent will be in danger if you take the time to obtain a second opinion.

"My father had been in intensive care for five days. The nurse told me they were treating him prophylactically, just dealing with the symptoms and watching him because they didn't know why he was so sick. The next thing I knew, someone came in to draw blood. I asked why, and the tech said, 'We need it for surgery.' You could've heard a pin drop in the room. Neither my mother nor I, nor my father, had been informed of pending surgery. I said, 'There must be some mistake. No one has told us he was having surgery.' She left and came back a few minutes later with a nurse who confirmed that my dad was going to have surgery the next day. She said the latest tests showed a blockage. They were going to go in and remove it. We were terrified. How serious an operation was this? What were the odds of survival? What was the recuperation time? We asked her to please find the doctor and tell him that we needed to talk to him. He explained that he would have to crack open his ribs. That was a very long and sleepless night. I thought of everything I had never said and how much I loved him. I wondered if he could emotionally survive a painful six-month recovery. The next morning I brought my children to the hospital to kiss their grandfather—just in case. My mother looked like she was going to need intensive care any minute. Then the doctor came bouncing in and announced, 'Good news, I'm not going to operate. I scheduled the operation based on what the lab technician told me he saw in the films. I saw the films for the first time this morning. That's an old wound. It's not the cause of your problem.' I was torn between two reactions: one was joy. But I also wanted to kill him for scheduling surgery and putting us through this before personally looking at the films. More than anyone, I blamed myself for agreeing to an unnecessary operation when I clearly had time to secure a second opinion."

Selena, North Dakota

- Try not to leave a parent who is confused, has memory problems, or who has been diagnosed with dementia alone in the hospital at night. If your parent wakes during the night, he may be confused and frightened by the unfamiliar surroundings. It wouldn't be unusual for you to have to remind him where he is or even who he is. Organize shifts for family members to stay with your parent or hire a certified nurse's aide. It's important to be there to reorient him, calm his fears, and reassure him.

- If possible, bring in friends and family for short stays during the day.
- When visiting, bring only good news about family and friends. Problems that your parent cannot handle from a hospital may make him anxious and may impair the healing process.
- Remember, the patient needs quiet time to rest. Bring a book to read so that you will have something to do if your parent wants to sleep or rest without conversation, the television, or other noise.

H. PLANNING FOR DISCHARGE

"My mother was recovering from a triple bypass. She was doing well, but still couldn't walk without assistance. She lived alone, and I knew that we'd need help when she left the hospital, but I planned on waiting until she was ready to go. I thought it would be better that way because then I could see what kind of help she needed. I mean, how could I order help without giving them a date to start? All of sudden, at three in the afternoon, the social services department notified me that my mother was being discharged the next morning. They told me she would be going to a rehabilitation facility for a few weeks until she got stronger. I said that was fine with me. The next day they moved my mother, and I drove over in my car. The rehabilitation facility was the most disgusting place I've ever seen. The smell was unbearable. There were people lying in their own feces and urine. There were flies on food that was left on trays in the rooms and in the hallways. There were urine-soaked bedsheets and hospital gowns piled along the walls in the hallways. I told the ambulance drivers to turn around and take my mother back. They refused. I panicked. I wouldn't let my dog stay that in that place, and I sure as hell wasn't going to let them dump my mother there. I called a care manager I had spoken to about a month before. Her first words were, 'I thought the state closed that place down.' She called the social worker in the hospital, who told her the nursing home was the insurance company's choice. The care manager suggested I contact my mother's insurance company immediately, and request placement in another facility. They told me that this nursing home was exactly what her policy covered. The others were more expensive and required additional coverage. The care manager and I placed a call together, this time to a supervisor. We described the conditions and the care manager presented the facts and risks to my mother in medical terminology. The care manager said that as a licensed professional (she was a registered nurse), she had an obligation to report the insurance company and the facility to the state insurance commissioner and to Adult Protective Services. I said I didn't have a license, but I had an obligation to my mother. I told her she could move my mother right now or the next call I made would be to the newspapers and television stations. My mother was out of there and in an appropriate facility within two hours. Thank God for the care manager. I doubt that anyone ever got well in that place. I'm not sure what would have killed me or her the quickest, the unsanitary conditions or despair."

Karen, Texas

Make it a point to visit the discharge planner or social work department in the hospital as soon as possible. It's unfortunate, but it's also reality that your visibility serves notice that you are watching over your mother's welfare. This often results in better treatment for your parent.

- Ask the discharge planner to let you know what your options are before he makes definitive plans for your parent.
- Make the discharge planner aware that if your parent is being transferred to a nursing home or rehabilitation facility, you want to approve the facility prior to the transfer.
- Note that you need enough lead time to request a change if you aren't happy with the facility.
- Look in chapter 20 for a helpful checklist that you can take with you to assess the facility. This will help you make a more informed decision.
- If you can afford it, hire a geriatric care manager to guide you through choosing a rehabilitation facility or nursing home. These

professionals are often aware of which facility has the best treatment options.

- If you aren't satisfied with your choices, ask the discharge planner to negotiate with your parent's insurance company on your behalf. If you've retained a care manager, she can also help.
- If your parent is lucky enough to return home, work with the discharge planner to prepare the home for a safe and comfortable recovery. Discuss the services your parent will need before he leaves. Ask if securing the services is part of the discharge-planning process or if you are expected to handle those details.
- Ask which services your parent's insurance has agreed to pay for. Your parent will be responsible for the rest.

I. LEAVING THE HOSPITAL

The most important thing you can do for your father when he leaves the hospital is to prepare his home for his arrival. If he is moving into your home, the details might be different, but the concept is the same. He will be exhilarated to be out of the hospital and tired from the anticipation and travel. He may also be afraid that if he suddenly needs medical assistance, it won't be there because he's no longer in the hospital. It wouldn't be surprising if you had the same feelings. In fact, you may be even more anxious because you also have a new caregiving responsibility. Your children may be curious or afraid. Your mother may be worried and add to the confusion by trying to be overly helpful. The homecare worker may not show up. Or, the homecare worker may be on time, but when you meet her, she is everything you hoped she wouldn't be. Some of this is inevitable. It's simply going to happen, which makes it all the more important for you to think the homecoming process through and eliminate problems that you can take care of in advance.

- Do not take your parent home without first taking the time to organize yourself and the services you'll need for care as best you can.

"One of the most crucial things I'd tell other caregivers is that you can't plan for everything, but you need some organization in your life. Anybody who tries to do this without taking the time to get organized just isn't going to make it. There are so many little things that come up during the day that can sidetrack you. Maybe the weather causes problems in getting your mother to the doctor. Maybe the therapist doesn't show up. You have to have enough food in the house so that when it comes time to prepare the meal, you don't have to worry about stopping everything and going out to get milk. You have to have a routine and a plan for every day when you're caring for a sick person. It's essential for you, but it's also very important to have a schedule for the person you are taking care of. Sick people feel very vulnerable. You've got to give them the comfort that comes with knowing what's going to come next. They need that to feel safe and secure in their surroundings."

Belinda, Florida

- If you can afford it, hire a professional care manager to coordinate the discharge with the hospital planner. The care manager will confer with you, visit your father's home (or yours), and confer with the hospital planner. After the care manager assesses the situation, she will present a care plan and a cost estimate for your approval. If you agree, she will make some or all of the arrangements. You'll be free to tend to other matters. You can find detailed information on how a private geriatric care manager can help you set up and maintain a successful homecare program in chapter 11.
- If you cannot afford to hire a professional or cannot find one in the area where your parents live, you have another option. Ask for an appointment to sit down and work out all the details with the social worker in the hospital. Ask for guidance and direction. If the social worker refuses your request or isn't cooperative, contact the patient advocate and explain your situation.
- Make sure your parent's home has been recently cleaned, including the clothing your parent wears. Be especially careful with bed-sheets, blankets, and towels. Hire a service if you can. Safeguard your parent from accidental infections caused by germs in dusty or unclean areas. It may be necessary to confirm the state of the home

with a personal visit. This is a delicate area. Be careful not to insult your parent or hurt his feelings.

- Make sure the foods in the refrigerator are fresh and appropriate. If you are unsure, check with a doctor or nurse.
- Contact friends and neighbors and ask them to choose one representative to call on the telephone and one to visit in person each day. Your parent will know his friends are thinking of him without having the telephone ring twenty times a day, which can be detrimental to recovery.
- Homecoming can be a wonderful time. It can also be strange and frightening. Every step of the process presents another opportunity for confusion and chaos. Organize. Be flexible. Expect problems, but learn to lessen their impact by anticipating them before they arise.

J. WORKSHEET: TEN TIPS FOR PREPLANNED OR EMERGENCY HOSPITALIZATIONS

Staying in control when your parent enters the hospital can help alleviate some of your fear and stress. These ten tips are a good start.

1. In case of an emergency, always call 911 before calling anyone else. Driving your parent to the emergency room in your car will only add more risk to the situation. After calling 911, call your parent's physician as soon as possible. This rule remains the same whether you are with your parent or in another location.
2. Obtain a Vial of Life packet and follow the instructions that come with it. This may help emergency rescue technicians stabilize your parent faster in an emergency.
3. If your parent's stay at a hospital is preplanned, ask your doctor if you have a choice of hospitals. Choose the one that has the most expertise in the treatment your parent needs. You can also consider whether or not the location is convenient for visiting.
4. If your parent's admission is preplanned, ask for an appointment in off-peak hours to take care of all the details of the admissions process. This may help save time and reduce your parent's and your own stress.

5. Do not bring money or jewelry to the hospital. Bring twenty one-dollar bills and leave all other valuables at home.

6. Do not bring a cell phone unless you have asked for the hospital's policy. It may interfere with hospital equipment.

7. Stay in touch with your parent's physician by finding out when she makes her rounds. Be there when she arrives.

8. Except in life-threatening situations, try to avoid sudden surgeries or potentially life-altering processes without confirming the need. Ask the doctor if your parent will be in danger if you take the time to obtain a second opinion.

9. If your parent is confused or has memory problems, try not to leave him alone in the hospital at night. If he wakes up during the night, he may not remember where he is, and he may become frightened and more confused by the unfamiliar surroundings.

10. To find out what to do when your parent enters the hospital, review this chapter.

K. MY JOURNAL

Expressing our thoughts on paper often helps us see our feelings more clearly and that makes it easier to arrive at solutions to our problems. What bothers you? What changes do you want to make? What or who are you grateful for? When you read what you've written, you may see a new pathway to help resolve stressful issues. Use this page as a safe place to express your feelings. For example:

"Every time Mom goes into the hospital it gets harder and harder to manage all the details. Last time she ended up at the other end of town. I'm going to talk to her doctor and get our choices straight . . ."

"My father is coming home from the hospital in a few days and I'm not sure what he'll need. Suzanne told me to talk to the discharge planner or social worker to get some help so I can start getting prepared . . ."

_____

_____

_____

_____

_____

_____

_____

_____

_____

_____

_____

_____

_____

_____

_____

_____

_____

_____

_____

_____

_____

_____

L. TIP SHEET

- In emergencies, always call 911 *before* calling anyone else.
- Be prepared for emergencies by learning about the hospitals in your parent's community.
- For preplanned hospitalizations, talk with your parent's physician and the hospital to learn more about specific admission and treatment procedures.
- Ask the hospital social worker or admissions department for a copy of the Patient's Bill of Rights. Review this chapter so that you're clear on your responsibilities as well.
- When your parent is ready for discharge, speak to the hospital social worker, case manager, or discharge planner to be certain your parent has a safe discharge plan that you understand and agree to.

DETECTING AND DEALING WITH ELDER ABUSE

A. THE REALITIES OF ELDER ABUSE

"The thought of someone hurting or humiliating my eighty-nine-year-old mother makes me ill. To me it is like hurting a defense-less baby. I thought I was hiring a caring woman to take care of her. I felt certain that Mom would be safe and comfortable. I was so wrong. I am an educated, savvy woman and I should have known something wasn't right, but I just didn't pick up the signs. I hope one day I can forgive myself."

Pamela, Pennsylvania

"I am a fifty-year-old man. My seventy-five-year-old dad has been in a coma for one year. During that time he has been in a nursing home. I picked it myself and then my sister put her stamp of approval on it. What we didn't know is that our dad was seldom bathed or turned over and he developed these sores on his body. The doctor I hired to examine him said he has 'bed sores.' Bed sores from lack of care. How can licensed professionals

433

treat incapacitated people with such a lack of respect and human kindness? Doesn't anyone care anymore?"

Larry, Washington

Elder abuse is a problem that does not discriminate. Physical, emotional, psychological, institutional, and financial abuse crosses all demographic lines. Neglecting or denying its existence leads to unnecessary suffering, unimaginable physical and emotional pain, and in the worst-case scenario, even death. The abuser may be a family member or a hired caregiver who exercises power and control over your physically frail or cognitively impaired parent. At times, your parent's cry for help goes unheard if she is unable to communicate effectively. Your parent may suffer in silence due to a fear of abandonment by her caretaker, fear of harsher abuse, or feelings of powerlessness.

As an involved caregiver, you do everything possible to ensure that your parent is receiving the best possible care. But you may not always recognize the signs and symptoms of elder abuse. It is sometimes difficult to detect the pain your parent feels from a repeated onslaught of unkind or offensive verbal attacks by a hired or family caregiver, because in such cases there are no physical bruises. Nothing is more devastating or disappointing than discovering that your parent is the victim of abuse and the person you believed would take care of your parent is unworthy of your trust.

"I was looking for someone like me, someone who cared about her. When I hired the home health aide she seemed so kind; I thought she would love my mother. Love is the furthest emotion she felt for my mother. I didn't know what was going on, but one of my mother's neighbors called me. She said that sometimes she would hear her call my mother terrible names or my mother would cry for hours. I am so grateful that her neighbor decided to let me know."

Jackie, Pennsylvania

Another daughter admitted, "*I feel so ashamed, I don't mean to do it, but he is constantly asking the same question over and over again.*

Finally, I tell him to shut up and I throw him in his room. I actually throw him in the room and close the door. I just wish he would go away."

At times, emotions may run high and it is difficult for a family member to remain objective and keep her feelings under control. A shouting match or physical assault may easily be the result of emotional and mental fatigue, physical exhaustion, and repressed anger.

A caregiver in this position finds herself wishing and hoping for relief. At times, the only thing she wants is for the guilt and sadness to go away. In her heart she knows that wishing doesn't make it happen. If you are a caregiver struggling with this serious dilemma, take an honest look at your own feelings and behaviors. If you hit your parent once, you will probably do it again. This is an emergency. You need help now before the situation escalates out of control.

1. Immediately step away from the job and have a hired caregiver or family member take over. It may be a temporary or permanent measure. You may come to understand that even if you have the best intentions, you are not the best person to care for your parent.
2. Confide in a family member or friend. Unburdening yourself to someone you trust and who believes in you is an important step.
3. Make an appointment with your doctor or a geriatric professional such as a social worker or nurse who may refer you for counseling or an anger management class.
4. Take the time to get the help you need, then decide if you can or want to do this job.

If you believe your parent's safety is in question from a hired caregiver, remove your parent from the danger and report the problem to the appropriate authorities, such as the police or the protective service agency in your parent's community. See the Adult Protective Services (in some areas this may be called Protective Services for Adults or a similar name) in this chapter for detailed information on protective services. If you do not believe your parent is in immediate danger you may want to try to gather as much information as you can about the situation before making any decisions about his care.

- Listen to your parent. If your parent is cognitively alert and aware, talk to him about your concerns. Give your parent the freedom to express his concerns by saying that you can help change things and make his life better if you know what is wrong. Support your parent by acknowledging his feelings about making a change in his hired caregiver. For instance, sometimes a parent will tolerate a situation because the idea of changing the situation increases his anxiety. Talk about change as a positive step toward better and safer care.

- Observe your parent. If your parent has difficulty communicating verbally pay attention to her body language. How does she behave when the hired caregiver enters the room? Does she seem tense or weepy? Sometimes talking about the caregiver to your parent will elicit some type of response even from someone with cognitive impairment and loss of language. One caregiver used hand holding as her cue. Every time she visited her mother in the nursing home she would take her mom's hand and say, *"I'm leaving now. Will you be OK?"* Initially, her mother did not respond, but after a few times she seemed to understand and she held her daughter's hand very tightly. The daughter did a little investigating and found that just one of the evening caregivers was rough with her mother during dinner. She discreetly asked the staff questions and she immediately replaced the caregiver. Another caregiver decided to revert to her father's native language. Although her father had difficulty processing words and thoughts, he was very clear about speaking his native tongue. Since his daughter knew the language and she was aware that the caregiver did not, she asked her father questions in his native language and he responded. This communication helped her to learn more about his care and his concerns. Eventually, she realized that the home health aide was not appropriate for her father's needs and she replaced her with someone more understanding.

- Communicate with the people who take care of your parent and always act on the side of caution. If you have any concerns about the care your parent is receiving, don't wait for a crisis. Report the problem to whoever is in charge of the hired caregiver.

- If a homecare agency has authority over an inappropriate caregiver, contact the nursing or home health aide supervisor and provide her with as much information as you can. Keep a written record of any concerns and observations you make.

- If your parent is in a hospital, notify the supervisor and the director of nursing. They will take your concerns seriously. Ask them to find alternate nursing care on the same floor or if possible ask them to move your mother to a different floor. Consider hiring a home health aide to keep your mother company if the hospital cannot accommodate you in a timely manner. A private caregiver will provide you with information and peace of mind.

- If your parent is in an assisted living community or nursing home, report the problem to the director of nursing and the manager of the facility. Ask for an immediate room change or change of caregivers. If you feel your parent can no longer be cared for in her present living situation, remove your parent as soon as possible. Sometimes there is a fear of reprisal against your parent if you report a questionable situation. If you think this is a problem, then your parent is not in the right situation for him and it is time for a change. (See chapter 19 to learn more about your options.)

Finding Help in Your Community

"My stepfather tried to take my mother's money, her home, and her life. I needed help. Because my mother lived in a small suburban town, the local police helped me to stop him from destroying her life. It took time, but eventually we got her away from him. One day he just left and went back to his hometown. A year later someone called us and said he died in his barn. Isn't that fitting?"

Gloria, Massachusetts

Your ability to find the help you need depends upon your parent's geographic location, the availability of services, and the type of assistance your parent requires. If your parent lives in a quiet, rural community they may not have a specific agency to assist with elder abuse issues. Your only option may be to contact the police or Area Agency on Aging. If your parent resides in a large city, the likelihood is that there is a specific agency devoted to protecting the elderly. In an emergency contact 911 for assistance, or promptly remove your parent from the situation. Regardless of the type of abuse, your parent may require immediate medical or psychiatric intervention.

For all other situations try these options to finding help in your parent's community.

- Contact the local police or district attorney's office for information regarding elder abuse programs in your parent's community. As a service police departments often present lectures to senior citizens at a local library or community center on how to avoid financial abuse, the latest scams, and how to live safely in the community. For instance, a caregiver reported that during a recent charity campaign in her mother's town, scam artists contacted elderly citizens asking for contributions to the cause. Fortunately, the police alerted the elderly citizens before they lost their money to the thieves.

- Check with the local Area Agency on Aging to learn if there is a specific agency that deals with elder abuse issues in your parent's community. Ask about reporting procedures and how long it takes for an investigation to take place. In some situations there is an extensive waiting list. Let the agency know if the situation cannot wait. In some circumstances they may have a crisis team available for immediate intervention.

- Call your parent's physician and provide him with as much detail as you can about your suspicions, such as unexplained bruises on your mother's arms and legs, excessive weight loss, or chronically poor grooming. Arrange for your parent to have a complete medical and psychiatric evaluation. With the doctor's support, report your suspicions and concerns to the appropriate agency. You may need a written medical report from the doctor to document your claim. Ask the doctor if she is willing to write the document and what, if any, is the fee for the report.

- Contact local hospitals and geriatric clinics for information on specific programs or committees available to help identify, prevent, and stop elder abuse.

You may not always be able to protect your parent from abuse or neglect. But once you know or suspect there is a problem you can find the help you need to change the situation and make it safe and secure.

Protective Services for Adults

As your parents age you may begin to recognize their frailty and vulnerability. It is scary and uncomfortable for many of you to think about your father and mother in this state. Your elderly parent may endure abuse and neglect in the same way a small, powerless child does. Just as our society recognizes the need to protect our children, we understand our duty to protect the rights and lives of our elderly.

The role of protective service for adults is to ensure the safety and quality of life of all adults. The local Area Agency on Aging may provide you with the exact name and location of the services in your parent's community. These service providers generally work in tandem with the local police. The role of the agency is to investigate any allegation of abuse or neglect brought to their attention by any member of a community, including geriatric and healthcare professionals, family members, neighbors, and friends. This type of agency also deals with the welfare of an elderly person who does not have a family, lives alone, or is unable to care for herself due to a physical, emotional, or psychiatric condition.

For example, an eighty-seven-year-old woman lived alone for twenty years. Until recently she took care of herself. One day the local adult protection agency received a telephone call from someone in the woman's apartment house. The caller reported that a strange odor emanated from the apartment. When the police and social worker arrived, they found an accumulation of garbage in every room. The woman was disheveled and dirty. The only room that was clean was her husband's room. She kept the room as a shrine to his memory. The woman received a complete physical and psychiatric examination. The doctors believed that she required psychiatric care and she moved to an appropriate facility.

There are times when the adult protective services agency finds that the allegations are unfounded.

"I don't live near my father, so I don't see him very often. I had some suspicions that my father was the victim of physical abuse at the hands of his hired homecare worker. I reported the situation to the nurse in charge of my father's case. I told her that my father's neighbors contacted me to report some kind of banging noises in the apartment. The neighbor also reported that no one ever saw my father out in the park or anywhere else outside of his apartment. The complaint surprised the nurse, because every time she visited the home everything appeared under control. Because of the bizarre allegations she immediately contacted the local adult protective service. When the police and social worker arrived unannounced, the frightened home health aide let them into the apartment. They spoke to the aide, and examined the elderly, bedridden gentleman. They learned that the banging noise emanated from a small, apartment size washing machine and dryer. The reason my father did not go to the park is because his apartment has a large, comfortable terrace where the home health aide grew flowers. As often as possible she managed to transfer him from the bed to a wheelchair and he spent several enjoyable hours each week on the terrace. The social worker dismissed the allegations of abuse as unfounded. She then contacted the home health aide's supervisor and me and she said, 'I just want you to know that when I'm his age, I hope someone takes as good care of me.' Case dismissed. I was so relieved."

Nancy, New Mexico

At times an investigation proves conclusively that your parent is the victim of abuse or neglect. It does not matter if the abuser is a hired home health aide, hospital or nursing home worker, or a family caregiver. The abuser may find herself without a job and in the custody of the police.

Your parent deserves the right to enjoy freedom from fear, abuse, and neglect. Sometimes you are not the appropriate person to help him. Intervention by geriatric and/or healthcare professionals is necessary and available. If you think something is wrong, go with your instincts. Don't be afraid to report a problem and provide as much information as you can. You can help protect your parent and stop the abuse.

Guardians

"A guardian is one who has the legal authority and duty to care for another person or property especially because of the other's infancy, incapacity, or disability. A guardian may be appointed either for all purposes or for specific purposes."[1]

If your parent's judgment becomes impaired and he can no longer make appropriate decisions, he may need a guardian. The legal procedure for appointing a guardian is time-consuming, expensive, and often creates serious family conflicts. There is an old expression, *"One mother can take care of ten children, but ten children cannot take care of one mother."* If a family has made an attempt but cannot resolve issues pertaining to such things as finances, healthcare needs, and living arrangements, they may contact an elder law or family attorney. The attorney will explain the court procedure. To avoid any surprises, prior to meeting with the attorney ask for a written statement of fees.

To assume the role of guardian, you and your parent have to appear in court and prove to the judge that your parent is unable to make decisions for himself. The process is painful for an adult child, because she has to declare in court that her parent is no longer capable of making decisions. It is often devastating for a parent to hear these accusations. The judge may find that you and a family member or two other family members are the appropriate person(s) for the role of guardian, or he may conclude that an independent guardian(s) are more suitable. An independent guardian is not a family member.

As the definition of guardian states, *"a guardian may be appointed wither for all purposes or for specific purposes."*[2] This means that one person may take care of your parent's finances, while another guardian(s) is appointed to take care of healthcare issues.

Your father is diagnosed with Alzheimer's disease. You and your sister are his full-time caregivers, and the situation is becoming increasingly difficult. You and your sister are fighting all the time about money issues, housing, and daily caregiving tasks. The situation escalates out of control and your sister accuses you of stealing your father's money. She says she can prove that when you bought him a new television, you bought two other sets for your children. The accusations seem endless. Although your father does not understand the complexities of the problem, he knows that there is something wrong between his two children. Your sister decides to take you to court. Both of you hire attorneys, and the judge appoints an attorney to represent and protect your father's rights and interests. The judge requests that you and your sister settle your dispute, and he explains that if you cannot reach an agreement he will appoint an independent guardian. Although you and your sister try, you cannot resolve your differences. The judge appoints an experienced attorney to handle your father's financial and personal needs.

The procedure is long and arduous, but sometimes it is the only appropriate action to take to protect the rights and quality of life of your parent.

B. PHYSICAL ABUSE

There is no way to describe the sadness and heartache felt by a caregiver when she thinks or learns that her parent is the victim of physical abuse. Caregivers often feel a sense of overwhelming anger and grief at the thought of something like this happening to their parent. There is an urgency to do something about it right away. Sometimes your good judgment has to take precedence over volcanic emotions. How can you cope with the possibility of your parent's being a victim of abuse? This is a two-sided question because at times the evidence is unmistakably clear, such as in the situation described by these two caregivers. At other times what may seem like abuse is not abuse. The situation has a logical and reasonable explanation.

> "My father is very sick and frail. He always seemed scared, but I thought it was because of his illness. But my instincts told me something was wrong. My good friend told me that I should put a video camera in Dad's bedroom. The hidden camera seemed so underhanded, but I did it anyway. The home health aide slapped my dad every time he changed him. Maybe my dad can't tell us, but we have the proof."
>
> *Marion, Rhode Island*

Sometimes the situation is not so clear and an emotional caregiver overreacts. Listen to this caregiver's story.

> "We were so sure that the woman hit her. She had bruises on her left arm and leg all the time. When we hired a new caregiver, the bruises didn't stop. We felt so confused and uncertain about what was happening to our mother. Finally, a nurse pointed out to us that mom's bed has side rails. Her skin is paper thin and when she bumps into the rails she bruises herself. We were so upset because we accused a hired caregiver of something she didn't do. My mother loved her first caregiver, and she was with her for three years. We turned our mother's life upside down without thinking or asking any questions."
>
> *Brenda, New Mexico*

Physical abuse is a reality in the lives of many frail and elderly men and women. It is also possible that at times what appears as physical abuse may have a reasonable explanation. How can you protect your parent and not allow your emotions to get in the way of making the most informed decisions?

- If you think your parent is in danger, remove her from the situation. Do not wait to assess or evaluate the situation. Once your parent is safe, gather as much information as you can. If the situations warrants, contact the police.
- Provide your parent with support and reassurance. It may be difficult and time-consuming but if possible, you or a family member may want to spend some extra time with your parent while he adjusts to a new nursing facility or homecare worker.
- Insist that your parent have a complete physical and psychological examination, preferably by a board-certified geriatric specialist who will probably be more attuned and sensitive to your parent's fears and feelings. Ask the doctor to assess your parent's injuries and to determine if they are the result of physical abuse or if the origin of the injuries could be from another source.
- Try to visit your parent on different days and various times of the

day. When your parent receives good care in his home or in a facility, the staff does not care when or what time you visit. Unannounced visits are only threatening when there is something to hide.

- Contact the local hospital or social service regarding seminars dealing with detecting and coping with elder abuse.

Physical abuse often leaves physical and emotional scars. It may be difficult for you and your parent to recover from the trauma. Because this is an extremely emotional issue you may want and need to talk to your doctor, a social worker, or a psychologist about your feelings. If your parent is able to verbally express his feelings he may benefit from the same type of intervention. If your parent is unable to communicate his feelings due to cognitive impairment or loss of language, he needs to feel the support of professionals, family, and friends. Help him to remember how good kindness feels by a gentle touch on the arm or a kiss on the cheek. With genuine support he may regain the ability to feel safe and protected.

C. FAMILIAL ABUSE

Familial abuse happens in the homes of the rich and the poor in the form of physical, emotional, psychological, and financial abuse. Family members feel betrayed and the damage to the family unit is often impossible to repair. The picture we hold dear of a loving, caring, and secure family is shattered when abuse, neglect, and betrayal are a part of the family scene. Trust turns to mistrust, love to hate, and a sense of well-being to a feeling of vulnerability. It often defies our understanding how one family member can hurt another. Parents abuse children, husbands batter wives, wives batter husbands, and adult children neglect, hit, and abuse frail elderly parents.

What triggers familial abuse? For some of you, force and fists may be the only way you know how to cope with your problems. For others, it is greed for money, property, and power. Whatever it is, it is against the law and you and if you and your family engage in it, you need help.

Listen to the story of these two women. Each experienced familial abuse in a different way; yet each woman felt sad, grief stricken, and experienced a breach of faith that was difficult to comprehend.

"I felt so betrayed. My older brother told my mother that her house wasn't worth very much and that he wanted to buy it from her. He told her that he needed a place for his family to live, and that she could stay with them until they found a new place for her. He gave her almost nothing for the house and when his family moved in, he immediately placed her in a horrible facility. He just threw her away."

Caroline, New Hampshire

If you are one of several adult children, your parent may feel the influence of one child more than another. An adult child with a strong or threatening personality may secretly use intimidation to influence your parent. For example, a daughter described the relationship that her brother had with their father.

"My brother is physically big and overpowering. My dad is frail, thin, and he never had a strong personality. My mother was tough and she told him what to do. I guess I'm more like my dad; I don't like to confront anyone. I didn't know what my brother was up to until after my dad died. I knew they had some money, a couple of hundred thousand dollars. My parents always kept their money in a lot of different bank accounts and they kept the bankbooks in a dresser drawer. My brother knew where they were too. When Dad died I went to the drawer only to find a few dollars left in each bankbook, a hundred here, five hundred there. Somehow, he took all of the money out of the accounts. In the past two years, my dad physically and mentally deteriorated. I told my husband and together we talked to my brother. Do you know what he said? 'Dad wanted me to have the money, because he said you didn't need it.' My father would never say that, never. He was afraid of my brother and I can't even begin to guess how my brother got the money away from him. I cry every time I think about it. The tears are not for his money, they are for an old man who probably lived the past two years of his life in terror."

Susan, Georgia

What can you do to help protect you, your parents, and your family from suffering the anguish of familial abuse? This section is repeated because it is so important.

- If you think your parent is in imminent physical danger, do not wait. Remove your parent from the danger. If the situation warrants, contact the police.
- Be alert and aware of your family's interactions and relationships. If you suspect that an abusive act is taking place or is going to take place, such as financial abuse, you may not want to confront the family member alone. Contact an adult protective service agency in your parent's community and ask for advice, or you can contact an elder or family law attorney who specializes in these issues.
- Talk to your parent if he is cognitively capable of helping you. Try to learn as much as you can about his meetings with your brothers, sisters, aunts, or uncles. Ask a lot of questions. If your parent is cognitively impaired and suffers from Alzheimer's or a related dementia, be aware of relatives who spend too much time alone with your parent. Be wary of any uninvolved relatives who want too much financial, legal, or medical information about your parent.
- Contact a geriatric care manager to assess the home and family situation. An objective assessment of the situation can help calm your fears or confirm your concerns.

Many of you grew up in families that stayed together no matter the consequences or outcomes. You considered the family sacrosanct. When one member of the family hurts, the entire family is affected. Some of you will successfully recover from this assault, while others will not. Try to remember that you are just one member of the family. It is not your sole responsibility to make things better and heal all of the wounds.

(See section D in chapter 1 for more information.) Do what you can, when you can, because that is all you *can* do.

D. FINANCIAL ABUSE

Financial abuse is an underhanded and deceitful way of taking advantage of your parent. It may change his quality of life. Even if his life savings amounts to a few thousand dollars, he probably was counting on it to give him a sense of security and comfort. In some cases a parent feels his only legacy is to leave the little money he has to help make his children's life better.

The elderly may be the target of scam artists, unscrupulous legal and financial professionals, an adult child who steals money from a savings account or pawns a piece of antique jewelry, or a homecare worker who forges a signature on a check. No matter how your parent is robbed or who robs him, it is illegal.

Frances finally admitted that it was increasingly difficult for her to handle her checkbook. She asked both of her sons to help her out. They had a family meeting and they decided that her older son would handle the finances and the younger son would assist with grocery shopping and things like that. After the family meeting, they met with an elder law attorney, who drew up the papers assigning the older son with the Financial Power of Attorney. This document gave him legal authority to handle his mother's finances and withdraw money from her checking or savings accounts for her benefit. He took his responsibility seriously and provided his mother and brother with a monthly financial statement. For about two months he did not provide either of them with updated financial information. Why? Apparently, he borrowed ten thousand dollars of his mother's money to pay off his son's gambling debt.

Another example of financial abuse occurred to a demented, eighty-three-year-old man. He lived with a male home health aide. His daughter, Megan, interviewed the aide and checked several references. During the first few weeks the family was pleased with the care the man received. One day she noticed that there were several checks missing from her dad's checkbook. When she went to the bank, she asked for an updated printout of her father's account. It indicated that three checks in the amount of one thousand dollars each were missing from his account. As soon as she received the canceled checks with her father's forged signature she contacted the homecare agency and the police. When the police reached her father's apartment they found him alone. The home health aide had simply fled.

It is not an easy thing to do, but it is necessary to report this crime. If you have knowledge that your parent is the victim of financial abuse by a family member or stranger, report the situation to the authorities. If a home health aide is involved, you should report the incident to the home-care agency as well. By following up and reporting the situation you can help stop this from happening to someone else's unsuspecting parent.

E. HOMECARE ABUSE

It is said that the truth is sometimes much stranger than fiction. *When the police received the telephone call saying that there was an emergency, the furthest thing from anyone's mind was "a missing girdle." Two burly police officers arrived at the home of Mrs. Y., who was hysterical and whose home health aide was perplexed. Mrs. Y., a confused and disoriented, tearful and frantic eighty-eight-year-old reported that the aide stole her girdle. The kind police officers asked for a description and later acknowledged that the description was more than they needed to know. The aide denied the charges, but since they received an emergency call, the officers were required to write a report. Somewhere in the U S A, in an unnamed police precinct there is a full report about a missing girdle. Sadly, the girdle remains "missing or stolen by person or persons unknown."*

This story is not indicative of homecare abuse that makes us angry or sad, but it does reveals something about the type of problems faced when a home health aide is caring for your parent. Basically, anything can and does happen.

In general, homecare workers follow a specific plan of care for your parent based on medical and nursing instructions. The worker's job is to make sure that your parent is clean, well nourished, and receives his medication in a timely manner. Most of the time they do their job conscientiously and with a respectful regard for your parent and you. Problems may go undetected when your parent lives alone with the homecare worker, or if she suffers from cognitive impairment and has difficulty communicating. Here are several things to look for when you visit your parent to help you detect homecare abuse:

- Talk to your parent in private. You can ask the homecare worker to do the grocery shopping or laundry while you visit with your parent.
- Ask her questions about the worker. For example, "Mom, how do you like Mary?" If your mom can verbally respond, give her time to think about it and answer. If she has difficulty with language or finding words to complete her thoughts, ask her if you can check her arms, legs, back, and feet. Look for abrasions and bruises.
- Check the refrigerator. Take note if you prepared a broiled chicken last week and the chicken is still in the refrigerator. Look for spoiled food or food left uncovered. One caregiver found a freezer filled with rotting meat because the home health aide did not properly cover the food and prepare it for the freezer. If anyone cooks something, put a date on the package before you place it in the refrigerator or freezer.
- Check the medicine cabinet and pill bottles and containers. Be sure that your parent is receiving his medication by comparing the number of pills left in the pill bottles or containers to the number of days left in the month. Check for outdated medications or medications that have to be renewed. If you have any questions regarding medications, contact the doctor or the pharmacist. The pharmacist is an important ally in helping to keep track of medication dosages and changes. (Chapter 14 discusses the role of the pharmacist and how he can help you and your parents.)
- Visit at different times of the day and different days of the week. Ask a neighbor, friend, or family member to stop by to visit your parent unannounced, and see how the worker handles the unexpected visitor.
- Ask the homecare agency for updated nursing reports about your parent's condition.

F. SOCIAL ABUSE OF DRUGS AND ALCOHOL

"I walked into her apartment and it smelled. When I walked past the living room and saw the bottles all over the floor I knew something awful happened. I opened the door to her bedroom and I found my eighty-year-old mother, naked, alone, and drunk."

Cynthia, Maine

"He started with one pill for anxiety and one for depression. Then he had chronic back pain and he took two more pills. We didn't know he hoarded medication and then took the pills all together. He's no different from my son. My son gets it on the street and my dad gets it from the pharmacy, but they both do the same thing. They take pills to deaden some kind of pain inside them. It makes me sick to think about it."

Claudia, Illinois

You may be in disbelief and you may not want to think about it, but abuse of alcohol and drugs is a problem for some of your parents. Your parent may feel the need to drink or take drugs to try to forget the sorrow of losing a spouse, family members, and friends. He may want to deaden the sadness and grief he feels every morning because of feeling alone and isolated. When reality hits hard, he sees that his life is changing, and moving too quickly. *"I don't know why, I don't do much all day, but after I turned eighty the days seemed to go faster."*

The parent who was a social drinker in his forties and enjoyed good health may not have felt the effects of too many drinks. Forty years later he is not only older, but he takes several medications and his body reacts differently to alcohol. Many prescriptions, over the counter and homeopathic medications, and other treatments are extremely dangerous when mixed with alcohol. This potent combination of medications and alcohol may cause serious medical problems, even death. As a result of alcohol abuse, your parent may develop a medical condition known as Korsakoff's psychosis, which is known for producing dementia-like symptoms.

If your parent is alcohol or drug dependent she may require hospitalization in a geriatric detoxification program in order to receive appropriate treatment from geriatric specialists. During this process the medical staff may try to help her withdraw from the drugs and alcohol and regulate her medications. This step may be necessary before you and your parent can make any appropriate lifestyle changes, such as moving into an assisted living facility or living at home with homecare.

A parent who drinks too much or abuses pills has a problem and needs help even if he denies that he has a problem or if he makes excuses for his actions and behavior. One caregiver said, *"My father always drank too much and there is nothing that will stop him.*" She may be right; and like many things you try to do for your parent you may not be able to change this situation, but here are a few steps to try:

- Talk to your parent before you do anything. Your parent may be angry or embarrassed by the conversation. Let him know that you want to help. If you need help approaching this subject or if you don't think you are the best person to help him, contact the local Alcoholics Anonymous group in your parent's community for guidance and educational materials.
- Encourage him to talk to his doctor about alcohol and his medications.
- If your parent suffers from dementia, you do not have as many options. He may be ingesting alcohol or unknowingly taking too many pills. Talk to his doctor about hospitalization or treatment programs specifically for someone who suffers from dementia.

G. REBUILDING TRUST AND FORGIVING YOURSELF

There is nothing more comforting for a caregiver than to believe that you can trust the person who takes care of your parent. You feel reassured when you know that your parent is in the hands of someone who is a consummate professional, kind and caring. The feeling this provides allows your mind to enjoy a sense of tranquility and your body to rest easy. This sense of peace allows you to function more effectively when you work or when you spend time with your family and friends. When you visit your parent, you can see how well she looks and you sense her comfort with the caregiver.

Listen to this caregiver's story. Although this incident occurred in someone's home, the incident is similar to situations that may occur in an assisted living facility or nursing home.

"My mother was always very fussy about how she looked. Until a few years ago, she never left her house without her makeup. We knew something was very wrong when our mother did not coordinate her clothes, shoes, and pocketbooks. I know it sounds silly, but that was the way mother did things. When I interviewed home health aides I did the silliest thing. I made them look in her closet and select an outfit for her to wear. Of course it wasn't the most important criteria for me, but it was important. I finally found just the right person. She came very highly recommended and she had a sense of style. I know mother is not well, confused, whatever, but she still looks in the mirror and smiles."

Victoria, Connecticut

For several months this daughter enjoyed a wonderful relationship with the caregiver. She realized that her mother's condition was deteriorating, but the hired caregiver seemed to manage. One day something happened to change everything. The daughter arrived in the early afternoon to visit her mother. When she entered the apartment, she felt a sense of disbelief. Apparently, the home health aide hit her mother with such fury that her mother fell and hit her head. Victoria called 911 and her mother was hospitalized for a head injury, and received treatment for bruises on her face. The home health aide made excuses, but Victoria knew that when she talked to her mother she would learn the truth. Although her mother suffered from a mild dementia, she clearly told her daughter that the woman pushed her because she "had an accident and soiled her clean slacks." Victoria's trust was shattered. After the incident she found it impossible to trust anyone, not even herself.

A seemingly beautiful and trusting relationship can break apart and collapse the day the home health aide doesn't control her temper. Since you are the adult child, you may immediately blame yourself. Blaming yourself does not change the situation or make it better. It only adds to the agony. As a caregiver from Maine said, "*I never thought I would see that woman, that horrible woman, shoving food down my mother's throat. My mother was gagging and crying and she kept telling her to be quiet. I hired that woman. It is my fault that she was mistreated.*" If you discover that your parent has gone through such horrendous episodes, please keep in mind the following:

- Forgive yourself, even though you are probably questioning yourself and your ability to care for your parent. Try to understand that you did nothing wrong when you selected the homecare worker. It is important to remember that you hired the home health aide or placed your parent in a facility with the best of intentions. You did the best you could for your mother. Sometimes when we are in the midst of this type of situation we forget one very significant thought and that is that people and places do not come with a tag that reads *"guaranteed for life."*

- Give yourself time to heal. For some of you, your confidence will return quickly and you will let go of the past. You will draw on life's lessons to help you heal and begin to forgive yourself. For others, it may take longer and you will need the support of your family, friends, and professionals.

- Try again. For instance, if your parent needs a new home health aide, review the process you used the first time. Did you ask for references? Did you meet the home health aide in person before she started the job? Did you speak to past employers? Rebuild your confidence by asking a friend, family member, or a geriatric professional to give you guidance through the screening process. Involve your parent as much as possible. Ask the home health aide to spend a few days with you and your parent. Observe the interactions between them. Ask your parent how she feels about this person. If your parent is cognitively impaired, look at the expressions on her face, and the way she acts when you say good-bye. (See chapter 11 for specific information on screening and hiring homecare workers.)

- Keep an open mind and an eye open. Learn from the past when you do hire a new home health aide or transfer your parent to a new facility. The mistakes of the past do not have to dictate the future. Your parent can and will be safe because of your caring and vigilance. It is time to give yourself a break.

Take the time you need to trust yourself again. Once you make a decision, you will know that it is the best decision you can make.

H. AGEISM

"My mother is eighty-seven years old and she is capable and bright. She needed a breast biopsy. We went to the outpatient clinic at the hospital to check in for the procedure. The young woman at the desk said, 'What is her name?' I said, 'Ask her.' My mother started to laugh. But when the woman said, 'How old is she?' I went wild. I said, 'My mother is standing here; talk to her, not me. She can hear, speak, and understand everything you say.' After my outburst the woman spoke to my mother, but she spoke to her slowly, you know, the way people sometimes speak to someone who does not understand English. I finally said, 'Who is your supervisor? You really don't know how to talk to an elderly patient.' My mother smiled and said, 'It's OK, I know I'm good.'"

Sally, New Jersey

The young hospital worker is not that unusual. Healthcare professionals, family, and friends are often under a misconception. Because someone is old does not mean that he lost his ability to think, feel, respond, or understand. People are living longer, healthier, and more productive lives than ever before. Accepting age as a part of life, not just an end to life, helps you to understand that age is a number, not a disease.

A ninety-year-old gentleman resided in an assisted living community. He suffered from mild dementia but otherwise he was healthy. He thrived in the supportive environment and participated in many group activities. During a few current event sessions, the social worker called on him to respond to her question. Several times he just sat there and he did not respond. The social worker thought that her star participant was not feeling well. After the session she sat next to him and he said he was feeling fine. The next day the same thing happened. She spoke to the nurse, who said maybe he had a mini-stroke, or he was becoming more demented. The nurse called his daughter, and she frantically called the doctor. The doctor examined him and ordered several diagnostic tests. A day before the scheduled tests the man actively participated in the current events discussion. The baffled social worker said that she thought he had a miraculous recovery. The truth is he lost his hearing aid and then found it in his room. After he found it, he could hear again and effectively participate in the program. No one—the social worker, nurse, doctor, or daughter—thought to ask him about his hearing aid. Just because he is a ninety-year-old man, everyone assumed that his health was failing.

As the children of aging parents you may find yourself making the same assumptions, often forgetting that if your parent is capable of making independent decisions for himself, then it doesn't matter if he is sixty-two or ninety-two years old.

> "My grandfather was a writer and he retired at sixty-five years old but worked in his field until he was ninety-two. When my parents finally realized that he could not live on his own any longer, they found a beautiful senior community for him. My grandpa never took a pill in his life. The day he checked into the facility the medical staff was shocked. They said that there must be some mistake—he *has* to take some medication."
>
> *Maryellen, Texas*

The active, healthy elderly fight the stereotypes of grandpa in a rocking chair and grandma knitting a sweater. They play golf and tennis, run track, or they go back to work after retirement as teachers, mentors, and consultants. Age brings a rich history, vast experience, and boundless wisdom, and for many elderly a more complete and better sense of self. Looking in the mirror one elderly woman said, "*I look pretty good, I can walk to the store, get my hair done, and take a bath. And I still make a good pot roast with carrots and potatoes. Not bad. I know who I am and I can do what I want. I deserve it. I'm eighty-seven.*"

I. WORKSHEET: WHAT TO DO WHEN YOU SUSPECT ABUSE

The situation is unthinkable, but your parent may be the victim of abuse. If you suspect that your parent is being abused or neglected, here are some important steps to take.

1. If you believe your parent is in an emergency situation, do not wait; call 911.
2. If you believe your parent is in imminent danger, remove your parent from the situation immediately.

3. If you are the abuser, step away from your job as caregiver and ask a trusted family member or friend to help you and your parent.

4. Talk to your parent if he is cognitively alert and capable of verbally communicating. Give your parent every opportunity to express his feelings and concerns about any of his caregivers.

5. Observe your parent if he is cognitively impaired and has difficulty communicating. If he resides in a facility how does he respond around the staff? If he has a hired caregiver, does he appear weepy, frightened, or anxious?

6. If you suspect a problem in a facility or with a hired caregiver, report the situation to a supervisor and provide as much information as you can.

7. Contact Adult Protective Services to report an abusive situation. These services work with local police departments to investigate allegations of abuse and neglect.

8. Make an appointment with your parent's physician for a complete medical examination. The results of an examination may be helpful to determine if your parent is abused or neglected.

9. Review chapter 18 for more helpful information.

J. MY JOURNAL

Use this page as a safe place to express your feelings and concerns. Putting thoughts and feelings on paper helps you to see them more clearly. What bothers you? How do you feel about the situation? When you read what you have written, you may see a new pathway to help resolve stressful issues. For example:

"My father was always so outgoing, I should have known something was wrong when he became so timid and shy . . ."

"Mom was so bruised. How am I ever going to forgive myself . . . ?"

_____

_____

_____

_____

_____

K. TIP SHEET

- Take immediate action if you suspect that your parent is the victim of elder abuse or neglect. Immediately step away and get help if you are the abuser.
- Observe your parent at different times of the day with and without his caregiver.
- Look for physical signs of abuse, such as black and blue marks, hand grab marks, soiled clothes, poor grooming, excessive weight loss, uneaten food in the refrigerator, dehydration, or bed sores.
- Educate yourself regarding the different types of abuse such as physical, emotional, financial, and familial. Knowledge is paramount in keeping your parent safe and secure.
- Forgive yourself if your parent is the victim of abuse or neglect. You may be as much a victim as your parent. Take the time to begin the healing process.

19

MAKING DECISIONS ABOUT HOUSING: WHEN? WHAT? HOW?

A. EVALUATING THE NEED FOR CHANGE

"My aunt Molly was always independent and very stubborn. She is eighty-six years old and her memory is failing. She has one son who lives very far away and he is not involved in her life. I have been shopping for her and taking her to doctor appointments. Her apartment is small so she is very against having a home health aide. She says, 'Gloria, where am I going to put her?' I suppose she's right. A few days ago I received a telephone call from one of Aunt Molly's neighbors. My aunt decided to make toast, it burned, and she opened the front door of her apartment. As the smoke billowed into the hall, the alarms rang and the fire department was quickly on the scene. I told Aunt Molly, enough is enough. It is time for a change. She was not agreeable until I said that the next time she may hurt someone else. Aunt Molly moved one week later into an assisted living facility."

Gloria, Florida

"Dad confuses me. He confuses the doctors very often. He appears so sharp when we go to the doctor, yet I know how he lives. He lives in a pig sty. No, that's too kind. I don't understand how he smells so good and his house is so dirty and unsafe. I have to do something and soon. I have to help him make some changes, but I just don't know where and how to start."

David, Georgia

Change is often particularly difficult for older adults to accept because they usually find comfort in familiar things, surroundings, and people. Even though your parent may have experienced the loss of family and friends, her home provides her with a sense of stability. Talking about this topic may not be easy, but it is crucial for you to understand your parent's feelings and for her to understand yours. Try to talk to your parent about this subject while she is physically and cognitively able to participate. Express your concern for her future and your hope that she can have the type of life she wants. The information she provides is vital for you to keep in mind as part of your parent's "wish list." When and if the time comes to make a change, hopefully you will honor her wishes to the best of your ability.

You do not have to make this decision alone if your parent cannot participate in the process due to poor health or if you find yourself in an emergency situation. A geriatric care manager can help you and your parent assess and identify your parent's needs, consider what he wants now and in the future, and suggest alternative housing options.

"I know that I went to a lot of trouble, probably more than I should have, to keep my mom at home with me. I built my mom an apartment in my basement. She lives there with a live-in home health aide. I thought if she lived with me I would stop worrying. I worry just as much. My husband and I are fighting all the time and there is no place to run and hide. It's just not working because she is getting worse. If I had really thought about it I would have moved her to an assisted living facility from her apartment. Now I have to uproot her again and I'm sure she is going to get more confused."

Louise, Maryland

"My dad always lived in a big house. He always said little spaces make him crazy. I know what he means, because I don't like small rooms either. His house has fifteen rooms and it is very expensive to maintain. Five years ago he accepted the fact that in order to stay in the house we had to sell some of his land and close off a few of the rooms. We also hired a home health aide to live with him. In the past few months his Parkinson's disease has gotten worse and he is more confused. This man who loved space now lives in one small room in this huge house. He is so confused he doesn't know where he is or who he is with. It is time to move him out. The money we get for the house will pay for his care. I tried to do what he wanted for five years, I can't any more."

Sherry, Massachusetts

Keeping your parent in his home or yours may not be the best decision for him, and it may place undo pressure and stress on you. Try to resolve this dilemma by doing what is best for both of you.

Safety and Quality-of-Life Issues

"I grew up in the house, so everything seemed very natural to me. The area rugs and the staircases leading to the second floor and basement are all part of our home. One afternoon I stopped into see my mother. It's a good thing I did. She was on the floor of the basement and her left leg was twisted like a pretzel. I called for an ambulance, but I knew her hip was broken."

Pat, Maine

"I only see my dad a few times a year. He lives with the same aide who took care of my mother before she died. We found the aide through a friend of mine, but she didn't work for an agency. She agreed to stay and live with my dad. I figured it worked OK for mom, so I thought it would be good for Dad. I guess the aide was afraid to lose her job, so she didn't tell me that Dad stopped eating and taking his medications. But when I visited I knew something wrong. She said that in the past few weeks dad seemed more confused and he thought she was trying to poison him. He wouldn't take anything from her. She didn't tell me because she thought she could handle it herself. If I had allowed this to continue, I don't know how much longer he would have lived."

Sheryl, New Jersey

If your parent is living in an unsafe situation, and her physical and emotional health is suffering, then it is time to act. In order to help you evaluate your parent's willingness to move and her safety and quality of life, complete this phrase with one of more of these statements. *If my parent . . .*

1. *Expresses a desire to move into a supportive environment because she recognizes her limitations (i.e., inability to take care of her home, garden, or day-to-day needs) we should begin to talk about moving.*
2. *Has difficulty walking or requires a wheelchair and he lives in a home that is not handicap accessible, we should consider the possibility of remodeling his house or moving to a more appropriate environment.*
3. *Lives alone in a large house and he uses only one or two rooms because he feels safer in a smaller area of the house, we should consider the possibility that he may feel more comfortable in an apartment, adult home, or assisted living facility.*
4. *Is cognitively impaired and he rejects anyone I hire to help him with his medications, food, clothing, bathing, and other daily activities, he cannot remain in his home because it is not a safe environment.*
5. *Is cognitively impaired and does not recognize that he is in his own home and he becomes easily frightened and anxious, he probably requires a supportive environment and professional supervision.*
6. *Is physically frail and she requires two or more people to care for her at a time, she may require a nursing home to meet her needs.*

7. *Requires extensive skilled nursing care twenty-four hours a day, seven days a week, and her home is too small to accommodate several staff members, or she has limited finances, she may require a nursing home.*

8. *Is depressed, lonely, and anxious, because he is isolated and does not have many opportunities to socialize with his peers or family, he may enjoy a better quality of life in an adult home or assisted living facility.*

9. *Is diagnosed with a degenerative or chronic illness that will require specialized medical geriatric care, she may receive more comprehensive treatment in an appropriate nursing facility.*

10. *Lives far away from me and I could care for her if she was geographically closer to me.*

If you completed the phrase with any one of the ten statements you may want to think about moving your parent. *These statements do not apply if your parent has resources to remain safely in his home and if he is cognitively able to make the decision for himself.* Keep in mind that the most significant thing is for your parent to reside in a safe environment and for her to feel physically and emotionally secure.

Guilt Issues

Anyone who tells you not to feel guilty about your relationship with your parent doesn't understand guilt. No one can make guilty feelings disappear or take guilt away from you as if it were some tangible object. Guilt is often a pervasive feeling that oppresses you from the inside out and may take its toll on your physical and emotional well-being. Guilty feelings probably began a long time ago when you lied about your report card or your parent made you feel guilty over something you thought was unimportant. Will you ever stop feeling guilty? It's hard to say, because everyone is different. But you can try to feel better by trying to do what you can to make the best decision for your parents when they can't make it for themselves. (See section F in chapter 5 for more information about dealing with guilt.)

- Consider all of the options. Review the above ten-point list and rename it your "guilt-free list." The ten criteria give you permission to make a decision about alternative living arrangements based on your parent's wants and needs.

- If, after you consider your options, you still feel uncertain, ask another person. You can ask your parent's doctor, nurse, social worker or geriatric care manager for their opinion.

- Reconsider what you did, how you did it, and if you or the person you consulted have any other ideas. Ask yourself, "Did I consider all of the options? Do I feel like I did my best?" If you answer "yes" to both questions then it's time to *accept your decision.*

- If the time comes and you have new knowledge and want to change your decision, then pursue it. It's OK to change your mind.

- Once you reach acceptance, you can move on to a new challenge, helping to make your mother's new living arrangement comfortable and secure. (In chapter 20, section L you will learn how to create a home away from home.)

If guilty feelings continue to overwhelm you and interfere with your life, it may be time for you to join a support group to meet and talk to others who are in the same situation. Contact your local mental health clinic or your primary care physician for a referral to a therapist to talk about your feelings and concerns.

B. ADAPTING YOUR PARENT'S HOME FOR SAFETY AND SECURITY

The most important fact to consider is your parent's safety and security. It does not matter if she lives in a large two-story house or a small apartment. Instituting a few simple safety measures and maintaining them is one of the most effective, least costly, and easiest ways to avoid many accidents and injuries. For example, falls resulting in broken hips, wrists, and legs due to faulty stairs or objects in the way; poisoning due to expired food and outdated medications; fires because of worn electrical cords, heaters, and old-fashioned stoves; and a host of other disasters. It only takes one of these horrible incidents to physically, financially, and emotionally disrupt your lives.

Deciding to deal with these problems is only the first step. Your parent may feel you're intruding on her life or resent your help. Stay strong, determined, and get creative. Invite another family member or friend to help. Give your parent a gift of a thorough house or yard cleaning.

If you need help to assess your parent's home, you can hire a geriatric care manager or a social worker. In many areas, the police and fire departments will send a community liaison for an in-home safety assessment. There is generally no fee for the service. There are furniture removal companies that specialize in moving and discarding old furniture, clothes, and so on. The fee for this type of service varies. Check in the local yellow pages.

There are many ways to help modify and secure your parent's home. *We recognize that this is a very extensive list of recommendations.* Review the list for suggestions and select those items that you think are most critical for your parent's safety. Do the best you can to rectify each of the most significant problems. Try to tackle one thing at a time. Ask your family or a friend to give you a hand and don't forget to ask your parent to help if she can. Whether you make some small changes or you tackle a remodeling job, give yourself a well-deserved pat on the back for eliminating as many dangers as you can.

Kitchen

1. Try to purchase appliances that turn off automatically, such as irons, electric heaters, and fans. Check for stoves with this feature.
2. Check stove and appliances for grease buildup (exhaust, oven, burners).
3. Check the refrigerator, freezer, and food pantry for spoiled or rancid foods. Discard any outdated or spoiled food. When you purchase new food, clearly mark the packages with an expiration date. If your parent continues to have this problem, talk to her primary care physician. He may recommend a physical and cognitive examination to determine if her forgetfulness is due to dementia.
4. Purchase a microwave oven only if your parent is capable of following the directions and she does not wear a pacemaker to regulate her heart. A microwave oven can interfere with the pacemaker. Even if she is capable of learning how to use the oven, it may take several verbal explanations followed by clear and specific written instructions.

5. Check pots and pans. Be sure that they are not too heavy or too lightweight, and that the handles are securely fastened and do not retain heat.
6. Install revolving shelves in the kitchen for easy access.

Living Areas

1. Paint door frames a different color than the walls, and doors a different color as well. Use contrasting colors for furniture, drapes, and floor coverings. Try to use this concept throughout the house for tablecloths, placemats, dishes, and other items. Sometimes aging eyes have difficulty differentiating between similar colors. Seeing things clearly is critical for safety.
2. Upgrade wattage on bulbs and make sure that lamps and fixtures can handle a higher wattage. Get rid of three-way bulbs. In an effort to save money, your parent may keep the bulb on the lowest wattage. If your parent can't see clearly, it may interfere with pleasurable activities such as knitting, doing word puzzles, reading, or watching television. Due to the dim lighting she may fall and suffer unnecessary injuries. Feelings of depression may result from light deprivation from poor or low lighting, particularly in the winter months.
3. Remove clutter and unnecessary furniture wherever you can. The less clutter, the more room to move around freely and less risk of falls and accidents.
4. Use heavy, firm furniture. Lightweight chairs can tip backward when your parent tries to sit down or stand up.
5. Replace shag carpets with a low-pile carpet that is easier to walk on. Make sure the carpet is secure to the floor with appropriate padding. Remove area and throw rugs to avoid trips and falls.
6. Eliminate sharp edges around tabletops and counters by covering them with rubber corner guards.
7. Check sinks, counter heights, closets, and doorways for clearance and access if your parent uses a wheelchair.
8. Check all electrical outlets and extension cords for safety and wear. Reposition wires that run across the floor so that they are out of the way.

9. Be wary of electrical heaters. Be certain they are in working order and turn off automatically. If you are concerned, take the heater to the nearest fire department for an assessment. When in doubt, toss it out and buy a new one.

10. Install night-lights throughout the house, particularly in the bathroom, hallways, and near staircases. Don't assume your parent will turn on the light in the middle of the night. You may find that you can use an automatic timer to turn on the lights.

Bedroom

1. Check the height of your parent's bed. Your parent's feet should touch the floor while sitting on the bed and he should be able to sit easily without falling backward.

2. Be sure that the room has sufficient lighting and that your parent can reach the light from the bed. A light at the entrance to the bedroom will help to ensure that she sees her way clearly into the room.

3. Purchase a portable toilet or commode for the bedroom for easy access during the night.

4. Rotate the mattress a few times each year.

5. Avoid electric blankets. If the blanket becomes too hot it can burn sensitive skin.

Bathroom

1. Obtain a tub or shower seat and an elevated toilet seat. If your parent has difficulty with stairs he will also probably have difficulty stepping in and out of a tub or shower. He may require assistance with bathing. If you remodel a shower stall for your parent, consider a handicap accessible area. Use nonskid surfaces or mats to avoid falls.

2. Install grab bars for the shower, tub, and toilet area. Grab bars are made of steel and coated with a rustproof exterior. Your parent will feel more secure when she holds onto the bars to help maintain her balance. Grab bars must be installed properly to avoid accidents or injuries. Try to impress upon your parent that a towel rack is not

safe or strong enough to hold his body weight. If she uses a towel rack instead of a grab bar, she is at a high risk for accidents and injuries. Check to see that all towel bars are securely fastened to the wall.

Medications

1. Gather all of your parent's medications. Check medicine cabinets, closets, pantries, shoe and hatboxes etc. for all medications. Write the names on a piece of paper and fax or bring them to your parent's primary care physician.
2. Ask the pharmacist or your parent's doctor for an evaluation of all the medications you find and if your parent is supposed to take any or all of the medications. Once you are clear which medications your parent needs, remove or discard all other medications from the house.
3. Purchase a medication organizer with boxes for each day of the week, morning, mid-day, afternoon, and evening. Make sure your parent understands how to use the pillbox. If your parent is forgetful or confused and she has a home health aide, place the pills in the pillbox and ask the aide to keep it for safe keeping.
4. Purchase a first aid kit for your parent. Learn about the most suitable kits from her physician, professional care manager, or pharmacist.

Outside Safety

1. Make sure that there is sufficient lighting on the outside of the house, near stairs, and walkways. For added protection and if your budget allows, buy sensor lights that turn on automatically when someone walks through the area.
2. Remove large bushes and overhanging branches from walkways.
3. Repair broken and uneven stairs and walkways.
4. Be certain that steps have a back (called a "riser") so that your parent's foot cannot go too far in, causing loss of balance and a possible fall. Mark steps with nonskid tape or different paint colors so that your parent can see them clearly.

5. Wind up and store hoses and other garden tools so that they do not interfere with walkways.
6. Check all electrical wires and equipment.
7. Remove all poisonous plants from the yard and indoors.

Miscellaneous

1. Set hot water heaters so that the maximum temperature does not harm your parent's skin. Older skin may be more sensitive to heat, so he needs a lower temperature than you do.
2. Replace current cabinet knobs, sink controls, and doorknobs with levers in the kitchen and bathroom. Levers are easier to use if your parent suffers from arthritis.
3. Mark any poisonous bottles with the word POISON or a large letter X. Try to use a contrasting color. This is particularly important if your parent has impaired vision. If your parent has dementia or memory loss, remove all poisons such as bug spray, most cleaning solvents, and medications. If your parent lives with a home health aide, you can direct the aide to keep all of the above items out of sight and locked in a secure cabinet.
4. Install loud smoke alarms, particularly if your parent still smokes cigarettes. Place large ashtrays around the house and post clearly written directions in each area of the house where your parent smokes to remind her to extinguish her cigarettes.
5. Check burglar, fire, smoke, and carbon monoxide detectors regularly for batteries and other faults.
6. Check the furnace and air conditioning filters on a regular basis for dirt and soot buildup.
7. Clearly post all emergency telephone numbers by every telephone in the house. Securely tape the phone numbers to the tabletops or walls.
8. For more suggestions you may contact the fire or police department in your parent's community, the Area Agency on Aging, or the Alzheimer's, Heart, Diabetes, or Parkinson's associations. The local library may have more helpful tips.

Assistive Devices and Helpful Equipment

"When my mother reached her eighty-ninth birthday she had some difficulty walking. The doctor recommended several tests, but my mother had her own theory. She said that she felt a little unsteady because she was more nervous walking alone. She agreed to try to use a cane. After a few days with the cane she said that she walked for an hour and really enjoyed it. When I asked her why she thought it made such a difference, she responded, 'Something to hold on to.'"

Grace, Illinois

"My dad is a follower, a good old boy. He often does what his old-time army buddies do, whatever it is. We tried to convince him to use a walker and he refused over and over again. One day my sister decided to invite Dad out for lunch. As they were approaching the restaurant Dad saw two—not just one, but two—of his buddies with walkers. He turned to my sister and said, 'You know I think it's time I got one of those.' The moral to this story is whatever it takes…"

Josh, Pennsylvania

To give your parent an extra sense of security, talk to her about the items that cannot only make her life easier, but also allow her to remain as independent as possible. Insurance programs do not usually cover most of these items. Check with your parent's insurance carrier. You may purchase many of the items in a surgical or homecare supply store. Here is a list of assistive devices to help your parent with his day-to-day activities.

- Handheld shower for more convenient bathing and hair washes. A handheld shower is flexible and convenient to handle.
- Tub or shower bench or seat with or without a back. Ask the surgical supply professional for his opinion regarding which seat is the best for your parent.
- Adjustable toilet with or without safety rails. Seats without rails are

generally more economical. Ask the surgical supply professional to evaluate your parent's needs.

- Extra large nonskid tub mats to ensure a secure, safe surface. Tub surfaces are often slippery due to soap and shampoo.
- Grab bars for the tub and bath area. The bars come in a variety of sizes and configurations. It is very important for all grab bars to be installed properly. You may want to contact a licensed carpenter or plumber or ask the surgical supply professionals for a recommendation.
- Large-button telephones help ensure easy dialing for your parent with visual impairment. Telephones with a lighted button or an extra loud ringer are helpful for the hearing impaired. Contact the local telephone company for more information about specialty telephones.
- Folding walker, or a walker with an attached cart for shopping or for holding your mother's purse. A walker helps your parent with balance and ambulation.
- Lift-out recliner chair eases your parent out of the chair with the press of a button. This type of chair generally is available in several fabrics and colors.
- A long metal gripper helps your parent reach into cabinets without stretching or standing on unsafe chairs or ladders.
- An extra-long shoehorn makes getting shoes on easier and with less physical exertion.
- Zipper hooks help with side and back zippers that are hard to see and grip.
- Kitchen items such as rubber jar openers; specially designed forks, knives, and spoons; and can openers help parents who may have trouble gripping a regular utensil.
- A sense of security and peace of mind may sometimes come from just one piece of equipment, so talk to your parent about some of these ideas. If she rejects the idea of helpful devices, remember they make great gift ideas.

"We put a big red bow on this beautiful new lift-out recliner chair and my dad was thrilled. He kept saying no, but when it was in front of him, he grinned from ear to ear like it was a brand-new car. We did the same thing with a raised toilet seat, and we filled the seat up with his favorite soap, toilet tissue, and a bath brush with an extra long handle. We all had a good laugh."

Jessie, Michigan

C. MOVING YOUR PARENT INTO YOUR HOME

No matter what expectations you or your family have before your parent moves into your home, it is important to consider how this will effect your day-to-day life, your family dynamics, and the actual room space that is available for another person.

These two caregivers approached this situation in very different ways.

"When mother had a stroke I was convinced she was going to die. I promised myself that if she lived I would take care of her. I told my husband—I guess I never even thought about asking him—that I was going to work part-time instead of full-time and hire someone to help Mom when I wasn't home. I didn't give him a choice. Then I told the kids. My son is seventeen and my daughter is fourteen. One of them had to give up his room. I decided that my son's room was more conducive to taking care of Mom, so I basically told him he could sleep on the couch or bunk with his sister. What was I thinking? One week after my mother moved into the apartment, my son ran away from home. Thankfully, he ran to my sister's house in the next town. We decided, given the situation, that he would stay with my sister and her family. I threw my son out to let my mother in. I can't forgive myself."

Marsha, New Hampshire

"My mother and father always told us that in our family children take care of their parents. When I think about it, they started telling us this as soon as we could understand. I guess they knew what they were doing. So when Mom died and Dad was alone I invited him to stay with us. I have a nice house and an extra room on the ground floor. Dad had his own entrance, bathroom, and television. Until six months ago we saw him only at dinnertime and on the weekends. Six months ago he started to get forgetful and confused. The doctor called it early dementia. He walks around the house all night, and scares the kids when they are sleeping. Things are definitely different now. We have someone living with him downstairs, and we don't have the same freedom we had in the past. The kids are upset, my husband is telling me he doesn't want Dad living with us anymore, and I'm stuck right in the middle."

Janet, Nevada

Before you make the decision to move your parent into your home, try to answer the following questions.

- Do I really want to make this commitment?
- What are my motivations?
- Is this the best choice for my parent and my family?
- How will this move impact our daily lives?
- What type of care does my parent need and can my home accommodate that need?
- What are my financial obligations to my parent? Do I charge my parent rent? Who pays for her food, clothing, medications, and so on?
- What if this doesn't work out? Can I move my parent once he is accustomed to my home?
- Can my brothers and sisters help us with doctor's appointments or respite time for my family? Or can they keep Dad company one afternoon a week?

Take the time to think about these questions before you jump into a very complex situation. Try to consider your family, lifestyle, finances, and living situation before you make the decision. If you decide not to move your parent into your home, talk to him about your feelings and explain your reasons. Present him with the best alternatives. This chapter provides you with many of those options. If you decide to move your parent into your home try to work out as many details as possible *before* moving day. The fewer surprises, the better it is for all of you.

Space and Territory

Space is a precious commodity, no matter where you live. It doesn't matter if it is a large house or a small apartment. Everyone wants his own space. For instance, how often have you heard a chair referred to as "Dad's chair," or a seat at the dining room table as "Mom's spot?" Years and years go by and no one dares to sit in the designated chair. Why? Because everyone wants a place to call his own.

If you decide to move your parent into your home, plan to give up some of your space. If your parent is ambulatory, probably no space is off limits.

> "I leave for work at six in the morning and get back about seven at night. I told the aide to make sure my Mom is fed and dressed for bed by the time I get home. She said sometimes my mother doesn't cooperate and she can't have her ready. I get very angry because I want some time for myself. It's just Mom and me. I need a little time alone after a very long day at work. I like her to go into the den or to her room for just an hour, and then we can watch television. That's how I cope with the situation. I need my couch, television, and quiet for just one hour. Is that asking too much?"
>
> *Sonya, Georgia*

Sonya may seem a little tough, but she is simply setting limits and giving herself the time she needs to cope with the realities of her life. You may need to set the limits that fit into your lifestyle, such as "down time" when you get home from work or dinner in a restaurant with your friends without inviting your mother to join you.

Look around at the space in your home and consider the possibility that as time goes on your parent may require more physical space for assistive devices such as walkers and wheelchairs and even a hospital bed.

- Set limits that are clear and reasonable. For instance, if you do not want your mom using the stove because you are afraid she will forget to turn it off, make that clear from the beginning. Leave a clear, written sign on the refrigerator or countertop reminding her that the stove is off limits. Remove the knobs off the stove if you have to. If you need time off after work, as Sonya did, set the routine in motion from the first day and try for consistency.

- Consider the amount of room your parent needs to live comfortably. If you don't have the room, don't consider the option of your parent living with you. If you have the room, but you want to set limits on the use of space, be open and clear. Let your parent know which room(s) is available for her and which are not. Always be clear and periodically reinforce the information.

- Think about how much space you need to care for your parent. If your parent is bedbound and she requires a home health aide or nursing care, be prepared that several people may come in and out of your house daily. You may need space for several assistive devices such as a wheelchair and commode.

- Try to base your decision on what your parent needs and your ability to cope with the situation. Can you give up some of your living space and more of your time without anger and resentment? Are you making this decision based on emotional need or guilt? Be realistic and answer these questions honestly to make the best decision.

Adapting Your Home

Many of the suggestions in the above section Adapting Your Parent's Home Safely and Securely will work well in your own home. In addition, if your parent is physically challenged, you may want to consider:

- Widening two exit doorways for easy access and safety if your parent uses a wheelchair or walker.
- Constructing a ramp to the most convenient door to provide easy access in and out of the house.
- Lowering door locks and latches and handles so that your parent can reach them.
- Removing raised thresholds so that your parent does not trip, or else modify the threshold with a ramp.

- Making sure doormats are securely fastened to the floor to avoid falls or remove them completely.
- If your parent is cognitively impaired and forgetful, you will probably consider having someone stay with her when you are not available. You may also want to think about a few additional safety features:
- Try to cover door locks with a cloth the same color as the door. If the door is painted white use a white cloth, if it is painted blue, use a blue cloth, and so forth. This camouflages the lock, but does not interfere with your ability to open the lock. Because of your parent's cognitive impairment she will hopefully not see the lock and she will not try to leave or wander away from your home.
- Place locks and latches high up on the door so that they are out of your parent's eyesight and reach. Anyone staying with your parent can open them quickly in the event of an emergency.
- Remove or lock up all poisonous materials, medications, homeopathic remedies, over-the-counter medications, cleaning solutions, etc.
- Remove the dials from the stove or oven to avoid any cooking mishaps.
- Try to remove money, checkbooks, and expensive jewelry. Keep them in a safe and secure place. Your parent may find a one-dollar bill or pocketwatch very appealing and put it away for safekeeping. Unfortunately, no one knows where it is and he cannot remember.

When you adapt your house to meet your parent's needs there are some things you may not think about until you are living together. For instance his sleeping and eating schedule may be different than your family's, or he may play his radio or television too loud because of a hearing impairment. Many programs offer the dialogue to be read by the hearing impaired. Talk about the compromises you will all have to make to accommodate your parent. Ask for his consideration on lowering the radio or eating dinner when you do. You will learn that flexibility and a little patience will be your most helpful allies.

D. ADULT HOMES

> "My mom is still in good shape at ninety, but her house is too big. One day it's the plumbing; the next day she tells me the washing machine is not working. I finally told her, enough, it's time to think about moving. We looked together and we found a lovely place where she'll have two rooms and a bathroom. They cook and clean. We both think it's about time."
>
> *Louise, Rhode Island*

If your parent feels like Louise's mom or you feel that she is often alone and isolated, talk to her about an adult home. Sometimes older adults get squeamish about the thought of a "home" or a "facility." They visualize a nursing home and sick, frail, people sitting in wheelchairs. Immediately, set the record straight and emphasize to your mother or father that an adult home is nothing like a nursing home. An adult home is like a senior hotel for active, relatively healthy, independent older adults. Very often it is the ideal environment for your parent if he does not want the responsibility of a house or apartment.

You can probably find an adult home in most urban, suburban, and even some rural communities. An adult home may look like a high-rise apartment in New York City or a large country house in Massachusetts. Some builders had the initiative to renovate apartment houses, motels, and hotels to accommodate the needs of senior citizens. In most instances you walk into a lobby that has seating areas, a television room, and maybe a library. Bedrooms are generally simple and serviceable, and bathrooms are generally handicap accessible. Some homes supply all of the furniture and you bring the accessories. Other homes give you the option to bring your own furniture or use some of theirs and some of your own.

The fees for an adult home vary from community to community. Meals and housekeeping services are included in the basic fee. If your parent requires special meals, be sure to check with the admissions department before you make a final decision. You can expect additional fees for any type of special programs, such as a trip to a museum or to attend a play, cable television, telephone, and beauty parlors.

Generally, your parent can count on planned activities seven days a week. Most adult homes are non-sectarian so they accommodate all religions by providing a variety of religious services and holiday celebrations. Other activities may include movies, card games, lectures, musical performances, and arts and crafts. Your parent does not have to participate in any activity unless she wants to. Many adult homes provide some transportation services to a doctor's office, clinic, or hospital. If you are not sure if your parent is an appropriate candidate for an adult home, a geriatric care manager or social worker may help you assess your parent's eligibility. Here are a few ways to initiate a discussion with your parent.

- Talk to your parent about the idea of moving into an adult home. Be prepared for this conversation with information and a few brochures from adult homes in her community.
- Explain that she will retain her freedom and independence and that an adult home is simply a "new home base."
- If you think she will find it enticing not to have to cook, clean, or grocery shop, use that information to your advantage.
- Talk about how she can decorate her room and make it comfortable.
- Remind her that you will continue to visit her the same way you did in the past.
- Emphasize the social aspect of spending time with peers who enjoy the same television shows, books, and music.
- Invite her to join you for lunch or dinner at the adult home. Contact the social worker and set up a date and time.
- If she rejects the idea, leave the brochure on the table with a little note that says, "Think about it." Wait a few weeks and bring up the topic again.
- Talk to the staff about a possible week's vacation for your mom. Many homes will accommodate your parent with a discounted, introductory offer in order for her to try it out.

E. ASSISTED LIVING FACILITIES

"When I walked into the special unit I knew that this was the right place for my mother. The women and a few men looked like her. Everyone was well dressed and groomed, but they all looked a little lost and bewildered. That's Mom. She has dementia and Parkinson's disease and she has the same look. The staff was so kind to everyone. I was delighted when I heard the piano player start to sing 'You Are My Sunshine.' They don't know how appropriate that song was right at that moment."

Marge, Pennsylvania

"My mother is eighty-three years old. She is so frail and I feel she is unsafe in her own home. She fell on two occasions and she says that the house 'overwhelms' her. She takes several medications and she sometimes feels too weak to dress herself. She also lost many of her friends and she feels lonely. My friend told me about the assisted living facility her mom moved into six months ago. It sounds like a good place. When I told her about it, she was a little skeptical, but she said, 'I always had an open mind, I'm not going to close it now.'"

Annette, Illinois

Here is a list of some of the differences between an adult home and an assisted living facility (ALF).

- Assisted living facilities accommodate the needs of a physically frailer and cognitively impaired population.
- Many facilities have specialized units that cater to the needs of a parent who has Alzheimer's disease or a related dementia. *These units have:*

    1. Staff specially trained to handle your parent's special needs, such as her memory impairment or anxiety. The unit may have a higher staff-to-patient ratio for added safety.
    2. Special programs to meet the needs of a memory-impaired or confused patient.
    3. Secure units to help prevent your parent from leaving the unit alone and unattended.
    4. Special support groups for you and other family members to help cope with your parent's illness.

- Some facilities have a registered nurse on staff twenty-four hours a day, seven days a week. A physician is usually on call at all times.
- Some facilities will accommodate a resident who requires a wheelchair. Ask the facility admissions director if this accommodation is available. Keep in mind if your parent requires a wheelchair, he probably will need additional or even full-time care. Consider this aspect of his needs when you calculate the total monthly costs.
- Medical, psychiatric, and podiatry services are available in the facility on specific days of the week.
- Medication monitoring is done on a continuous basis.
- Different levels of care to accommodate your parent's specific personal care needs. Most ALFs charge extra for the additional time your parent requires for personal attention. Be very sure that you understand the different levels of care and the costs. This type of care may add significantly to the basic monthly fee.

When your parent is ready for an assisted living facility he may or may not be capable of taking part in the decision-making process. If he is capable, then ask him to join you for a visit or a meal at the facility. If he is not capable of participating in the process, you may need help making the best decision. Contact a geriatric care manager, your parent's physician, or talk it out with a friend or family member. Although you may make the choice about which facility you prefer for your parent, the facility will conduct its own evaluation to determine his eligibility and appropriateness.

An assisted living facility can provide your parent with a better quality of life and allow you to feel that you did your best.

F. NURSING HOMES

Chapter 20 provides you with detailed information on making the decision about nursing home placement, finding the best nursing home for your parent, special programs, staffing, and how to make your parent as comfortable as possible.

G. MOVING YOUR PARENT

Moving is a very emotional experience. Moving implies change and change does not always feel good, even if you all agree it is the best thing to do. Your parent may see this move as a loss and a last chapter of her life. You may have mixed emotions. You may feel sad because your parent has lost her independence, but you also may feel relieved because she is receiving the care she needs.

Before you begin the task of moving your parent, it is helpful for you to acknowledge your feelings and let your parent express hers. You may experience the change differently. You may feel the loss when you close the door on your mother's house and many of your childhood memories, or the loss of your parent's ability to enjoy an independent lifestyle. She may feel the loss of things that are safe and familiar as well as her independence. If you abruptly move your parent from a hospital bed into a facility, all of her and your emotions may undergo a shock. Once she is settled in her new home you may begin to experience a void that is hard to explain, but you know it's there. It is important to talk about your feelings and make sure that your parent has the opportunity to express her doubts and concerns to a geriatric professional, such as a registered nurse or social worker. If your parent cannot verbally express herself, it is even more important that the professional staff help her with the transition.

A period of transition takes place between the time you move your parent into a facility and when she settles into her new environment and routine. It is a time when your parent may feel confused, disoriented, and frightened. You can make this transition period less stressful by doing the following:

- If your parent had a home health aide in her home, try to keep the aide with her during the transition period into the facility. Try to reduce the hours gradually while she is adjusting to the new environment. For example, if she had an aide for eight hours a day, seven days a week, ask the aide to spend six hours a day in the facility. After two weeks reduce it to four hours, four days a week. Then four hours for three days and so forth. This provides her with a sense of continuity and familiarity. It also encourages your parent to take part in the assisted living community and enjoy the activities. Check with the facility regarding their home health aide policy.

- Allow about four to six weeks for your parent to adjust to the change in environment. Some people take less time and some take more time.

> "We moved my mother into an adult home three months ago. Every time my sister and I came to visit, we heard the same old story. 'Take me home, I hate you for doing this to me.' My sister cried and I thought it would never end. I don't know exactly what happened, but about a week ago when we decided to visit, she was friendly, kissing, hugging, and telling us what great daughters we are. We jokingly asked the social worker what mom's drinking and she said, 'I knew she would come around; it just takes time.'"
>
> *Joanne, Illinois*

> "My dad is legally blind and he requires someone to be with him all the time. When it became impossible for him to be at home, we moved him into a wonderful assisted living facility. Although we realized that he can't see the beautiful flowers in the garden or the lovely furniture we felt good bringing him there. We hired two women to take care of him, one for the day shift and one at night. It was a big expense, but we felt it was worth it. Dad was miserable. He cried and cried, but he didn't seem to know what was wrong. A very wise social worker said to me that my dad was suffering from a huge loss of touches, smells, and people that were familiar to him. She said that as the room began to smell familiar and he adjusted to his caregivers and he felt more confident walking around his new room, he would begin to calm down. Eight weeks later dad seemed different, content. It actually was simpler than I thought. He needed to give his new world a chance to become as comfortable as the old one was to him. Time works wonders."
>
> *Alicia, Nevada*

- Try to visit a little more often during this period or ask a family member to help you out. It will help your mother if you or someone she enjoys spends a little extra time with her.
- Give the staff an opportunity to know your parent and you by making appointments to speak to the social worker, director, social or recreational director, and the nursing staff. Talk about the things your parent likes to do and the things that she doesn't seem to enjoy.
- Try to do something special if you can. It is essential for her to feel like she is still a vital member of the family. Order a small bouquet of flowers once a week and have the florist deliver them from her grandchildren. Send a drawing or picture from a grandchild or great-grandchild. Ask some family members to send a card or note in the mail once a week.

Who Does What?

Who does what in preparation for a move depends on several factors. Are you an only child? Will your brothers and sisters help you? Can you count on other family members to help? Can your parent help? Do you want to hire someone to take over the job? Try to make the choice based on the size of the job and the time you have to complete it.

- Think about how much you have to do before you can move your parent. Do you have to discard fifty years of clothes, furniture, and bric-a-brac? Sell the house in order to pay for the long-term care? Or do you simply have to pack a suitcase and a few personal items?
- Think about who is going to help you. If no one is available, prioritize everything you have to do. If a family member or friend is going to help, delegate some of the responsibilities. Write a list of everything you have to do, no matter if you do this alone or with someone else. For instance, assign a task with a date of completion, such as in these two examples:

   1. By Friday, December 5—Gather, coordinate, and label all clothes items with a sew-in or iron-on label or write the name in the item with a waterproof laundry marker.

2. By Sunday, December 7—Purchase toiletries and other personal items such as underwear, hosiery, and socks.

Review section L in chapter 20 for guidelines on the amount of clothes your parent needs. If she is moving to an adult home or assisted living facility, you will want to add to the other list approximately seven to ten casual outfits and two or three dinner outfits and appropriate shoes.

- If you decide to hire a geriatric care manager to assist you, make an appointment to discuss what you need her to do and how long she has to do it.

Once you know who is going to help, the next step is to figure out what your parent needs.

Paring Down Your Parent's Belongings

> "My mother saved the first coat she owned, dozens of pocketbooks, fifty or sixty hats and a million and one unnecessary things. I don't know where to begin, but I know since she is moving to a warm climate she doesn't need twelve pair of rubber sole boots and two fur coats. What should I do with the old paintings and huge pieces of furniture? I wish someone would just come and take it all away."
>
> *Nina, California*

The truth is someone *can* come and take it all away. There are companies who specialize in cleaning out houses. Nevertheless, before you decide that the best way to deal with the situation is to call for a clean-up crew, stop and think about what your parent may want.

- Ask your parent what he wants from his house.

> "My dad collected dozens of pens, watches, and small radios. As he got older and more confused he hoarded more and more of the same stuff. Drawers filled to capacity with things that were

outdated or didn't work. When we had to move him into an assisted living community, he really carried on about 'his stuff.' We decided to bring a small extra dresser for 'stuff.' We told him to pack whatever he wanted in the drawers. We weren't worried about anything he put in the drawers because we discarded anything that could possibly be dangerous. Dad got his 'stuff' and we didn't get too aggravated."

Marlene, Minnesota

- Take measurements of his new room(s), or space if he is sharing a room.
- Begin the process of paring down furniture and personal items by figuring out what fits comfortably in the space he has. Don't overcrowd a room with furniture or personal items. Clutter is dangerous and your parent may trip and fall.

  1. If Mom has a dinner service for twelve people and she wants to keep her dishes, pack a service for four.
  2. If Dad has a collection of wooden boats and he only has one dresser to display things on, decide on two or three boats.
  3. If you are moving Mom's bedroom set that consists of two dressers and two nightstands and your space is limited, select one of each.

Continue with this process with any other items in the house. By working with your parent you are helping to ease the stress of moving into a new home.

H. ADVOCATING AFTER THE MOVE

You and your parent deserve and expect professional, appropriate, and caring service. Introduce yourself to the director, social worker, and nurse. Also take the time to meet the men and women who help your mom dress in the morning and feed your dad at lunchtime. Let them get to know you. If you are dissatisfied with your parent's care, it is important to let someone know. You have a voice that needs to be heard. You do not have to be confrontational or disrespectful to any of the staff. What you have to do is organize your thoughts and be clear about what you think and expect. In emotional circumstances, caregivers may react with a "knee-jerk reaction" or simply without thinking. Try the following three steps before you respond.

1. Walk away from the situation before you react inappropriately.
2. Take a few minutes or a day to compose yourself before you talk to the staff about a problem. You may want to ask a family member, friend, or professional healthcare provider or attorney to join you for a meeting, if you perceive the situation as an emergency.
3. Try to listen to all sides of a story. There are often three sides to every story, your side, the other side, and somewhere in the middle is the truth. If you listen to the full story you may find a quick and suitable solution to most problems. You need to establish a balance between showing your respect and appreciation to the staff and letting them know when something needs improvement. Show your appreciation each time you visit by saying hello and thank you if you know someone has done something special for your parent.

"I told the personal care aide that my mom loves chocolate pudding. I always visit unannounced, but whenever I arrive there is a container of chocolate pudding on her nightstand. I thanked her for being so thoughtful."

Terry, Connecticut

- Visit at different times of the day so that you can become acquainted with the staff members who work on various shifts. This is helpful if your parent has a complaint about someone or if she enjoys one of the staff members. It also gives you a better understanding of the care she is receiving during different shifts.
- Be observant but try not to jump to conclusions. If your parent's hair is dirty, ask the staff what happened. You may learn that your

mom refused the hairdresser appointment or the hairdresser is sick with the flu. (In chapter 20, section I you will learn about Who's Who in the Complaint Department.) This chain of command may vary slightly from an adult home to a nursing home, but basically you will talk to the same people if you have a problem.

- Keep written notes regarding any problems you see or hear about. If you do not receive satisfaction from a meeting with the appropriate person (i.e., the floor nurse for medication issues or a nurse's aide for feeding and bathing), put your complaint in writing and add any pertinent documentation such as the names of the people you spoke to, the incident you are reporting, and the date and time. Send the information to the director or administrator of the facility. Request a meeting to review the situation.

If you continue to be the advocate for your parent with little or no results and he is not receiving the care he deserves, find another facility to meet his needs. It may mean another period of adjustment, but once the transition period is over, your parent will be in a better place.

I. VISITING YOUR PARENT

Deciding how often you visit your parent is an individual choice.

> "I visit my mother every week, but my friend visits her mother three times a week. She makes me feel like she is a better daughter than I am."
>
> *Sandy, Washington*

There is absolutely no correlation between how many times a year you visit your parent and whether or not you are a caring child. Time, family obligations, and job responsibilities have a great deal to do with the time you have to visit with your parent. Whatever time you spend, try to make it pleasant for both of you. If you have a strained relationship with your parent or your parent has difficulty communicating because of a loss of language due to a stroke or dementia, these ideas will help to stimulate conversation and bring you closer together even during a brief visit. If you enjoy a loving relationship you will find these suggestions a pleasant way to spend the time.

- Bring pictures, photo albums, and videotapes of the family. Your parent will enjoy the connection to the family and it helps to stimulate old memories. It also gives you and your parent something to talk about.
- Word games, simple puzzles, and books sometimes help keep your mom focused and alert.
- Think about subjects to talk about in advance. For instance if you went on a trip, bring some pictures or souvenirs to talk about.
- Bring a small gift with you. Some of the best gifts include a colorful lap blanket, flowers, a plant, a picture frame, hair brush or comb, some homemade cookies in a pretty tin (if your parent is not on a restricted diet), or a small battery-operated radio.
- If your parent suffers from dementia and is agitated at times, don't stay too long if your parent is not receptive to your visit.

> "My dad fights with me whenever I walk into the ALF. He makes me feel like I shouldn't bother. Someone told me to stay as long as he is pleasant. When he gets abusive I learned to say, 'Dad I can't talk to you when you say things like that. I'll be back another day to visit.'"
>
> *Tara, Maine*

Decide on a visiting schedule that is best for you and your parent. It's not how long you stay or how many times you visit that brings you together. It's your history, love, and family experiences that join you. When your visit is not what you hope for, try Tara's approach, stay for a while and come back another day.

J. WORKSHEET: MAKING THE DECISION TO MOVE YOUR PARENT

Safety and quality-of-life issues are paramount in making the decision for your parent to move to alternative supportive housing. Check off the answers that best describe your parent and his or her situation. The answers to these statements will provide you and your parent with a clearer picture of the reality of the situation.

1. My parent presently lives in ❑ my home ❑ his or her own home ❑ with another family member or friend.

2. My parent is living in an environment that is ❑ safe ❑ unsafe.

3. My parent talks about moving because ❑ he or she recognizes his or her own limitations ❑ he or she feels lonely and depressed.

4. My parent requires a wheelchair and her home is ❑ handicap accessible ❑ not handicap accessible ❑ can be renovated ❑ cannot be renovated.

5. My parent is cognitively impaired and not safe living alone. He or she ❑ accepts the home health aid ❑ rejects anyone I hire ❑ expects me to be with him or her twenty-four hours a day seven days a week.

6. My parent is physically frail and she requires ❑ at least two people to care for her at the same time ❑ extensive skilled nursing care twenty-four hours a day, seven days a week ❑ his or her home is too small to accommodate several staff members at the same time.

7. My parent expresses feelings of ❑ loneliness ❑ isolation ❑ depression ❑ anxiety.

8. My parent lives a long distance from me and it would be easier to care for her if ❑ she lived closer ❑ if she lived in a facility where she could receive appropriate care and support.

9. If you find that many of your responses indicate that it may be time to move your parent, see the worksheet below, Moving Your Parent, for important steps to help you and your parent through the move.

WORKSHEET: MOVING YOUR PARENT

If the time comes to move your parent, you will have many things to do. Read this "to do" list. As you complete a task, check the item off of your list. Staying on top of things will give you a sense of control and accomplishment.

1. ❑ Select a moving date. Discuss the date with anyone who is involved in the move.

2. ❑ If your parent is moving out of an apartment, check with the superintendent or landlord regarding the approved moving hours.

3. ❑ If your parent is moving to an assisted living facility, nursing home, or any other type of housing, check with the staff regarding approved moving hours or if there is a moving coordinator to assist you with the details.

4. ❑ If you need a moving company to help you, try to obtain estimates from two or three companies. Contact the local Chamber of Commerce and the Better Business Bureau to check for complaints against the companies.

5. ❑ Measure your parent's new living space so you know what will fit and what you can bring. Try to arrange your parent's room in a similar fashion to the way it was arranged at home. Try to place his or her clothes in the same drawers and spaces. This helps decrease confusion and ease the transition.

6. ❑ If your parent is capable, ask him or her to tell you what he or she would like to take to the new space. If your parent cannot help you, try to select the things that you think would give your parent a feeling of home, family, and familiarity.

7. ❑ Install a telephone and the cable for television if necessary three to five days before the move. Make sure that heating and air conditioning systems are in working order.

8. ❑ If your parent is cognitively impaired, try to have a friend or hire a home health aide to accompany you and your parent to help keep him or her company and distracted.

9. ❑ Review chapter 19 for more information on moving your parent.

K. MY JOURNAL

Use this page as a safe place to express your feelings and concerns. Putting thoughts and feelings on paper helps you see them more clearly. Am I doing the right thing? Who can help me make this decision? Am I hurting or helping my dad? For example:

"My mother wants to remain in her home but I know that she is not safe. How can I explain this to her without hurting her feelings . . ."

"Dad is so stubborn. I know I'm right, but he makes me feel so guilty . . . ?"

L. TIP SHEET

- Look at your mother's needs and wants to help you determine if she is ready to make a move.
- Talk about the alternative housing options with your parent if he is able to participate as well as with other concerned and involved family members.
- Be aware that everyone needs time to adjust to the new living arrangements.
- Create a home away from home for your parent by bringing some personal items, pictures, and furniture into the new living situation.
- Advocate for your parent when it is necessary to ensure her safety, well-being, and continued quality of life.

20

EVALUATING THE MOVE TO A NURSING HOME

A. MAKING A DIFFICULT DECISION

"I agonized over the fact that my dad needed hands-on care. The doctor said someone had to be with him day and night. I did not want to send him to a nursing home, but I knew in my heart that I couldn't make the commitment to even supervise caregivers. It was too much for me. On the day of the move I asked my best friend to help me. She actually was the one who accompanied Dad and helped him to settle down in his room. I visited later in the day and he was fine, just fine. What a hard choice to make. It all seems so final, but I did what I had to do for him."

Andie, Arizona

A nursing home may not be your first choice, but it may be the best choice you have when it comes to providing your parent with the most appropriate care. The emotional struggle begins the moment you even think there is a possibility that your parent requires a nursing home facility. You may ask yourself: What are my options? Where is the best facility? Who will pay for it? Will my parent think that I am deserting her? Is it the right thing to do?

"I read about this problem all the time, but now it's not someone else's. It's ours. I feel like I'm on an emotional roller coaster."

Elaine, New Jersey

The desire to keep your parent at home is sometimes so strong that adult caregivers describe the feeling as *"oppressive and tormenting."* The death of a grandmother or great-grandmother in a nursing home haunts and clouds the family's ability to think about the situation clearly. They often find fault with someone or something connected to the nursing home. The family tends to forget that their grandmother reached her one hundred and first birthday. True, at times a person's untimely death is due to poor care or neglect. That is why, for your peace of mind, it is so important for you to make the best decision.

To help you understand why you feel the way you do, try to think about finding a nursing home as a process that affects you on two levels. For most people, the first level is the emotional turmoil that makes you question your motives and choices and keeps you up at night. The second level is understanding on a practical and necessary basis that your parent needs to be moved into a nursing home.

Follow the stories of two family caregivers who made the decision to place a parent in a nursing home. One based her decision on her mother's needs and the other struggled with her emotional conflicts until she exhausted herself and every option.

The first family caregiver, Janet, enjoyed a healthy but geographically distant relationship with her mother. When Janet was twenty-two years old she moved to another city, and took a job with a large accounting firm. She spoke to her mother once a week on the telephone and saw her a few times each year. One day Janet received a telephone call from a doctor. He said that her mother had a stroke and she was medically stable but in intensive care. Janet said she would be there as soon as she made some arrangements. When she arrived her mother was alive but in serious condition and her prognosis was poor. Janet remained with her mother for ten days and at the end of that time, the doctor recommended that she place her mother in a nursing home for long-term care. She wanted to do the right thing, so she met with the hospital social worker. The social worker asked her if she would consider moving her mother to a nursing home near her. Janet felt that her mother would not want to leave her hometown because she still had some friends and family in the community. She knew that seeing these people was important to her mother's quality of life. As an accountant she approached most things methodically and with a purpose. With the assistance of the social worker, Janet compiled a list of questions and visited three nursing homes the next day. That night when she returned to her mother's house, she thought a great deal about what her mother would want. The next morning Janet telephoned one of the nursing homes and made the arrangements to transfer her mother.

The second family caregiver, Marie, was a loving daughter, mother, spouse, and friend. She cried if the dog lost her bone or the home baseball team lost a game. She devoted her life to her children, friends, and family, but especially to her seventy-eight-year-old mother. They lived two blocks from each other and they saw each other every day. At times the relationship with her mother created tensions with her husband and children. Marie described the day her mother had a heart attack as "the worst day of my life." During her mother's hospitalization she spent many hours each day taking care of her mother. Marie's devotion was overwhelming to the hospital staff. The coronary episode left her mother weak and very frail, so she required oxygen and nursing care. Marie insisted that with proper care her mother could live at home. She did not listen to her friends, husband, or doctors. She arranged for homecare, nursing visits, and physical therapy. She spent hours and hours at her mother's house at the expense of her own family and her health. After a few months Marie began to feel tired and depressed. She attributed her condition to tension and stress. As her mother's condition declined, the time she spent with her mother increased. Finally, her best friend told her that she looked ill and she encouraged her to see a doctor. A few weeks later Marie learned that she had cancer. She neglected herself for months and unfortunately paid a price with her own health and that of her young family. In order to treat her cancer, Marie placed her mother in a nursing home.

This is not to say that attending to your mother will give you cancer. How you make the decision to place your parent in a nursing home is as individual as your situation. For most of you the decision and the process will not be easy, and you should try not to do it alone. Even if you have supportive siblings and other family members to help you through the difficult times, you may still benefit from a completely objective and independent opinion. A geriatric care manager can provide an objective, independent assessment of your parent's condition, and make the appropriate recommendations to help you through the emotional and practical process. One caregiver described the geriatric care manager as *"her peace of mind."*

B. CHOOSING THE RIGHT NURSING HOME

"My mother cried when we left her at the home, but I didn't cry. I cried a lot before I finally made up my mind. When I realized that they would take good care of her I was OK. I know it sounds silly, but I felt like I did when I left my son at school when he was five years old. He cried too, but I knew it was time to let go and trust someone else to take care of him."

Wanda, Michigan

The right nursing home is the one that can effectively manage your parent's condition with dignity and respect, and provide you with emotional serenity and a sense of security. This is not a fairy tale. It is what you hope for your parent. Unfortunately, you may read or hear about the horrors of nursing homes, poor staffing, dirty conditions, and abusive situations. The truth is that not every home is a horrible nightmare, but nothing in life is perfect. As a caregiver from New Mexico learned, you will always have some problems. *"The nursing home looked beautiful. The rooms were decorated in soft pastels and everyone and everything looked clean and fresh. Mom seemed to receive good care. But one day I arrived at her room to find Mom sitting on her bed naked. Yes, naked. I asked the nurse what happened and she explained to me that Mom said she was hot and took off her clothes. As the nurse was about to dress her there was an emergency down the hall. She simply ran to the emergency and forgot Mom. The moral to this story is: nothing is ever perfect and always ask questions before you jump to conclusions."* Begin your search with the understanding that if you have realistic expectations, you have done the best you can.

Your parent may require a rehabilitation center or skilled nursing facility. Some rehabilitation centers are freestanding buildings that deal solely with short-term care. Short-term rehabilitation refers to a few months of intensive physical and or occupational therapy. Within a long-term care nursing home, the rehabilitation center may be one department or a couple of self-contained floors. For example, if your parent suffered a stroke, required hip or knee surgery, or was hospitalized for a long period of time due to a serious illness, his physician may recommend a rehabilitation center in order for him to regain his strength, independence, and full use of his arms and legs. When he is ready to leave the rehabilitation center, he may be discharged to his home, or a long-term care nursing home, sometimes referred to as a skilled nursing facility.

"My dad had pneumonia and he was very weak. He desperately wanted to go home to 'his bed, his television, and his chair.' As a family we told him that unless he went for rehabilitation to regain his strength he could not go home. After a great deal of persuasion from us and the doctors, he consented to go to a local facility. After two days he told us how much he enjoyed the people and even though they [the therapists] tired him out he enjoyed their company. They called him 'the Mayor' because he was so friendly. Dad spent two weeks at the facility and when he went home he admitted that it was a really good idea."

Jack, Florida

A skilled nursing facility is necessary when your parent's physical or cognitive impairment is unmanageable at home. This type of facility addresses your parent's needs including medical care, grooming, bathing, dressing, feeding, and socialization. Before you make a decision about the type of facility your parent needs, consider these steps.

- Be sure that you understand the type of care your parent requires. If you are not clear, ask her doctor or contact a geriatric care manager for a professional assessment.
- Make an appointment with the admissions director at three to five nursing homes. Ask for a referral from a doctor, social worker, nurse, or family and friends. Sometimes the best recommendation comes from a friend whose parent is in the facility.
- Before spending the time to tour the nursing home, talk to the admissions director about your parent. For instance if your parent suffers from Alzheimer's disease, he may require a specialized unit. If the nursing home cannot accommodate your parent, don't waste your time.
- Discuss your parent's condition honestly with the admissions director. In some states pre-admissions evaluations are necessary before the nursing home will consider your parent for residency.

> "I made every attempt to hide my mother's psychiatric condition. I know she suffered from psychotic episodes, but I described her in the nursing home admission forms as 'confused.' I purposely left out her psychiatric diagnosis and medications. The day she was admitted to the home we walked in the building together. When my mother realized that she was not in her home, she ran through the facility screaming and physically attacking anyone in her way. The admissions director was very upset and he contacted the nursing home psychiatrist. He determined that my mother was not appropriate for the facility. My only option was to have her hospitalized and reevaluated for placement in an appropriate geriatric psychiatric facility."
>
> *Brenda, North Carolina*

- Discuss the financial arrangements and be open and honest about your parent's finances. Nursing homes require a financial disclosure before admission. Let the admissions director know how your parent will pay for the nursing home and discuss any insurance coverage. Medicare pays for a time limited amount of days in a nursing home under very specific guidelines.

- Consider the traveling time you will spend in order to visit your parent. See section C in this chapter on the importance of the location of the nursing home.
- When you tour a nursing home, think about your first reaction, and try to get in touch with your feelings. It is important for you to feel at ease because this is your parent's new home. Ask yourself these questions:

1. How do I feel when I walk into the building?
2. Does it make me uncomfortable or depressed?
3. How do the residents look? Do they look clean, comfortable, and content?
4. What do the rooms look like? Can I make my mother's room comfortable and homey?
5. What kind of quality of life will she have in the facility?

Be honest with yourself and try to understand that you made every effort to make the best decision. Once you have selected a facility, give yourself and your parent a period of four to six weeks to adjust to the new environment. During that time get to know the staff, the doctors and the personal care aides. Continue to ask questions and visit when you can. If you are unable to visit, ask a family member, friend, or a hired caregiver to help you.

C. LOCATION

"The geriatric care manager smiled at me and said,'I wish I could build you a building around the corner from your home, but I can't. I wish I could make every room filled with sunshine, but I can't. I can only offer to help you find the best nursing home for your parent.'"

Emma, Mississippi

The location of the nursing home is very important for several reasons. If your parent is cognitively aware of his environment, he may feel more comfortable in a facility that is close to home. He may realize that he is never going back to his home, but he may find comfort in knowing that the place he lived in for many years is not too far away. Location is important to you and your family because of convenience. Some family members are willing to travel thirty to forty minutes in one direction, while others will not want to travel outside their community. It is essential to remember that this is an individual choice.

- Be honest with yourself and realistic about what you want to do and what you *can* do. If driving or finding transportation to a nursing home is too difficult or time consuming, you and your family will probably not visit often.
- If your father is in a nursing home and your mother still lives at home and she wants to visit your father, consider her transportation needs.

"My mother insisted on visiting my dad every day. She took two buses and walked several blocks to reach the nursing home. After a few weeks I realized that she couldn't make the trip. My sister and I talked to my mom and within a few days we transferred Dad to a nursing home one short bus ride from Mother's house. When she felt tired, she treated herself to a taxicab. Because of the short distance the fare was within her budget."

Patti, Maryland

"We had two choices for my dad. One was to select an older nursing home with a good reputation in our community. The other was a new, and more appealing nursing home with the same reputation but an hour's drive in each direction from our homes. The family consensus was that because of our work and family obligations, traveling a long distance posed a real problem. Fortunately, we recognized our limitations and based our decision on what was best for Dad. We decided on a facility that provided good care and a convenient location over a facility with new upholstery so that all us could see him on a regular basis."

Joanne, Nevada

Location is important but it is only one of many things for you to consider when you are making the best decision for your parent.

D. RELIGIOUS PREFERENCES

> "My mother and father are not religious people, but they enjoy the traditions of our faith. When I looked for an assisted living facility for them I made sure that they could enjoy the foods that they liked and that a clergyman was available if they wanted to talk. My father suffered from mild dementia and he was very docile. It didn't seem so important to him. On the other hand my mom is physically frail, but she has a real dynamic personality. She said to me, 'Honey, you did a good thing. Daddy and I are comfortable here because we are surrounded by people who understand what we need. This is a good place. Thank you.'"
>
> *Honey, Illinois*

Many nursing homes are nonsectarian, which means that they welcome individuals of all faiths. They accommodate the diversity of their residents by providing specific religious services and by celebrating many different holidays. Religious observances and holiday celebrations are never mandatory for residents. For example, a December recreational calendar in a nonsectarian nursing home may include a celebration for Christmas and Chanukah. The communal area of the facility may display a well-decorated Christmas tree and a shiny Chanukah menorah.

Some facilities are under the auspices of a particular faith and tend to decorate the communal areas and rooms with more religious pictures, items, and books. They may encourage visiting clergy or may engage clergy as members of the staff for counseling, prayer, and support.

Selecting a nonsectarian or a religious facility is an individual choice. If your parent is able to participate in the process, explain the options and allow her an opportunity to make a decision. If your parent is too ill to participate in the decision, think about the way she spent her life. Ask yourself these questions:

1. Did she go to church, synagogue, temple, or mosque on a regular basis?
2. Was she active in religious activities?
3. Did she enjoy an active social life through her place of worship?
4. Would she enjoy a more diverse group of friends?
5. The answers should help you select the best-suited nursing home for your parent.

E. DIETARY REQUIREMENTS

If your parent requires a specialized diet, it is critical to discuss his needs with the admissions department before you make your decision about a nursing home. Although most nursing homes accommodate special dietary needs, you cannot make any assumptions. If your parent requires Kosher or vegetarian food, for instance, it is important to inquire what type of meals the nursing home will provide for him. Will the specialized food be fresh or frozen and prepackaged? Other dietary needs may range from a regular diet consisting of three meals a day plus a few snacks to a diet of pureed or soft foods. How will the nursing home accommodate your mother if she has a poor appetite and requires supplemental liquid drinks to boost her caloric intake? Whatever the need, nutrition plays a significant part in your parent's overall well-being. Without proper nutrition and a sufficient intake of fluids, your parent may suffer from such problems as skin ulcers, increased confusion, agitation, and dehydration.

- Become familiar with your parent's needs and dietary restrictions by speaking to his doctors.
- If your parent has a very complicated medical history you may want to meet with the nursing home dietician and alert her to your parent's specific condition.

  "My mother has high blood pressure and kidney problems and she retains fluid. I walked into her room during lunchtime and found her eating a salty ham sandwich and a bag of potato chips. I went wild. My mother's aide said that's what they gave her for lunch. I took the tray and walked down to the kitchen. They were not too happy to see me. The excuse they gave was that they ran out of turkey and they always give chips with a ham sandwich."

Andrea, Maine

If something like this happens, try these few steps to help you avert another food disaster:

- Immediately report the situation to the nurse in charge of your parent's care.
- Insist on a new tray and try to wait with your parent until it arrives. If you do not receive satisfaction, bring the situation to the attention of the supervising dietician or nursing supervisor.
- If you continue to have a problem, ask to speak to the social worker or the patient advocate for assistance. Your parent's diet is vitally important for his health and strength. It can also provide him with a little comfort and pleasure.
- If your parent is still capable of deriving pleasure from eating foods he enjoys, he deserves them. Talk to his doctor and the dietician about bringing a favorite meal or dessert to the nursing home.

"When I walked into the dining area, my father was sitting with two women. He's legally blind. As I walked closer to him, I saw more food on his lap than on the plate. When he heard my voice, he smiled. I asked him if anyone helped him and he said no. I didn't know what to do."

Lillian, Pennsylvania

- Speak to the nurse in charge of your parent's care.
- Ask for someone to assist your parent during mealtime. If your father is cognitively intact but visually impaired, the assistant can provide a verbal picture of where the food is on the plate by referring to the face of a clock. For example, the peas are at twelve o'clock, the fish is at three o'clock, and the potatoes are at six o'clock. If your parent does not have use of a hand or arm, the assistant will help feed your parent. Ask the nursing home admin-

istrator if there is an additional fee for this type of service so that you do not have any surprises.

- If your parent is cognitively impaired the assistant can help feed and orient your parent to the meal, the time of day, and the different foods on the plate.
- Some nursing homes provide "feeding or nutrition stations." Several residents sit at a semicircle shaped table. One assistant supervises and assists the residents. Your parent may enjoy the company of other residents rather then sitting alone. The downside to this arrangement is that in order to accommodate all of the residents, the meal may be rushed.

F. SPECIALIZED CARE

Some nursing homes dedicate a floor or wing to care for residents with specific conditions, such as brain injuries, muscular dystrophy, strokes, dementia, cancer, Alzheimer's, Parkinson's, or pulmonary conditions. In this setting residents receive specialized care. For example, a nursing home that has a special dementia unit may create an atmosphere that allows patients to move around freely and safely, called a secure or locked unit. You may find a security device with a keypad at all of the exits. Because the residents suffer from dementia, it is unlikely that they understand or can interpret the exit code. This keeps the residents safe and secure within the unit. The residents participate in specific and appropriate social activities. (You can read more about dementia specific units in chapter 16.)

In a medical unit you may find a higher ratio of staff to residents to insure that the residents receive specialized attention. And you'll find the latest in high-technology wheelchairs, beds, and bathing equipment.

> "The decorations on Dad's cancer unit were bright and uplifting. If you wanted music they piped soft music into each room. But the best was that every day at four o'clock they served snacks from a rolling dessert cart. The atmosphere brought such humanity to my father's life."
>
> *Caroline, New Mexico*

Finding the most appropriate nursing home with a specialized unit to meet your parent's needs requires you to ask very specific questions.

- Contact the nursing homes that you are interested in for your parent. Ask to speak to the admissions director or a social worker.
- Be very specific when you ask about a specialized medical or dementia unit. For example, "My mom was diagnosed with Alzheimer's disease. Do you accept residents with dementia?" If the answer is yes, you can then ask, "Do you have a dedicated unit?" If the answer is yes, make an appointment to tour the unit.
- Try to see the unit during lunch or dinner and then during the middle of the day in order to observe the recreational activities.
- Try to visit on a Saturday or Sunday to give you a more complete picture. It is possible that during the weekend there is less staff and activities in the nursing home.
- Observe how the residents are dressed and listen to the interactions between residents and staff. Does the staff appear respectful, caring, and supportive? Does the staff take the time to help the residents?
- If you see family visitors, ask them if you can have a few minutes of their time. Ask how they feel about the unit and if it meets their parent's needs and their family's expectations.

Once you gather all the information you need to make an informed decision remember that nothing is written in stone. You can transfer your parent to another facility if you find that the nursing home does not meet your expectations and your parent's special needs. Ideally, once you select a facility, you hope your parent can remain there for as long as necessary. However, it is important for you to understand that you have options and the ability to make changes to meet your parent's specific needs.

G. CLEANLINESS

"I felt like I was going to gag. The lobby of the building had an odor. I saw dead flowers in pots all over the place. Then I saw two men sitting in wheelchairs by the window, just looking outside. There was food all over one man's face and I saw stains on the other man's pants. I ran out of there, but I couldn't forget the smell."

Ellen, New York

When you visit a nursing home in the morning you may smell urine, medicine, and antiseptic cleaners. Odors seem to dissipate after they clean the rooms and residents receive a bath. Realistically some odor is hard to avoid due to the fact that there are probably many incontinent patients. If you visit at different times of the day and the nursing home always has an unpleasant odor, it is probably not the right place for you or your parent.

Old buildings, furniture, and carpets sometimes give the impression that they are not clean, but something that is old is not necessarily dirty. Try to take into account the difference. Even if old furnishings do not appeal to you, your parent may feel more at home than in a modern facility because it reminds her of her own home.

Keep the following list in mind when you are touring a nursing home:

- Be aware of acrid odors that are pervasive throughout the day and appear masked by the smell of strong antiseptic cleansers.
- Look around at the floors, peek under the bed, and walk into a bathroom. You want to see clean floors, bathroom tile free of mold and mildew, and clean bed linens, covered pillows, and blankets.
- Residents should be clean, well groomed, and free of odor.
- Staff should dress appropriately and appear clean and neat. Observe staff members while they are attending to the residents or serving food. Do they use rubber gloves? Do food servers wear hairnets or caps?
- Do not accept excuses like, "We don't have enough staff to clean the floors," or "we don't have enough staff to bathe all of our residents every few days." This is not acceptable or the right place for you or your parent. Floors should be clean and all of the clients should receive a bath or shower every few days.

The cleanliness of the facility often reflects the attitude of the staff as well as the quality of care. You should immediately eliminate any institution from your research that does not provide clean, sanitary conditions for the health and well-being of your parent.

H. ACTIVITIES FOR RESIDENTS

Activities in a nursing home are essential to your parent's quality of life. They give your parent something to focus on, help to pass the time, and provide entertainment as well as physical and mental stimulation. Most nursing homes have a specific staff member, a recreational specialist or therapist, to plan and arrange all of the activities. Sometimes a social worker acts in this capacity. The recreational therapist plans a calendar of events for each day of the month. The family receives a recreation calendar in the mail and one is displayed on the resident's floor or in the common areas. A calendar of events may include, music therapy, chair exercises, movies, bingo, musical entertainers such as a piano or accordion player, holiday parties, and birthday celebrations. Some homes have a relationship with an animal shelter or pet shop that brings puppies and kittens to the nursing home for pet therapy. Holding and cuddling a pet allows your parent to express and receive love and affection. The calendar usually reflects religious services and the availability of hair stylists or barbers.

Not all nursing home patients participate in the activities. Some do not enjoy group activities; others are too sick and frail. In some homes these residents enjoy a one to one session with the recreational therapist.

> "My father was not very sociable; as a matter of fact, he was very snobby. I thought it might change because he was so sick, but it didn't. He would never go to activities and if they wheeled him into a music program or something like that he would scream and disrupt everything. So they stopped bringing him in. What he did enjoy was when the recreational therapist came to his room and sang songs and played her guitar. I think it really soothed him."
>
> *Susanne, California*

It is important to ask about the activities. But even more important, to let the staff know about your parent's hobbies, the type of music she likes, if she enjoys games, and dislikes watching television. Many recreational therapists will ask you to fill out a questionnaire with this information. If your parent's nursing home has a family day or family dinner, try to join in the festivities. It is a great way to spend some quality time with your parent.

I. WHO'S WHO IN THE COMPLAINT PROCESS

When you have a grievance, the way you handle the complaint may make all the difference.

> "I know I have a temper. But my mother is sick and confused and she lives in the dementia unit of a nursing home. One day at noontime I found her still in bed and dressed in a nightshirt. Her face and hair looked dirty to me. I ran over to the nurses' station to complain, but no one was available so I ran into the office of the nursing home director. I screamed at him, 'Isn't my mother important? We pay our bills, you have to do something right now.' The director was stunned because she he didn't have a clue why I was so angry."
>
> *Jack, New York*

> "My father had a serious roommate conflict. For five months he enjoyed the company of a nice, quiet roommate. The man died and my father's new roommate was loud and very nasty. I asked for a room change. The nurse in charge of my father's care said she would make the request, but that was over four weeks ago."
>
> *Sally, Washington*

If you feel that your parent is not receiving the best possible care and attention, or if you believe that your parent needs your help immediately, try these steps:

- If you believe your parent is in danger or there is a medical emergency, find a supervisor or call 911.
- Try to avoid screaming matches or impossible threats. Most people will respond more favorably to a soft but firm voice.

- If it is not an emergency try to follow a chain of command. For example, begin with the aide who handles your parent's personal care. If you do not receive satisfaction, contact the supervisor for the aide. If it is a medical or medication issue speak to the nurse in charge of your parent's care. If you do not feel you received a satisfactory answer, request a meeting with the nursing supervisor and the physician in charge of your parent's care. You may want to meet with the social worker or patient advocate for their input, support, and participation in any meetings you have with other staff members.

- If you still do not feel satisfied with the situation, make an appointment to meet with the nursing home director or administrator. Prepare for the meeting with a list of your complaints, what you have done so far, whom you spoke to and the response. Be very specific regarding compensation for lost clothing by producing receipts. If you want to change a situation, like your parent's room, ask for an approximate day and date the change will take place.

- Everyone has a complaint at one time or another. It's perfectly all right to voice your complaint in an organized and calm manner. People respond better and more quickly to someone who can state a problem and ask for help politely and respectfully. Try to keep in mind that you can and will accomplish what you need to do for your parent with dignity and respect for the people around you.

J. MEDICATION/PAIN MANAGEMENT

"I tried to visit my mother twice a week. A few times I noticed that my mother ate very little of her lunch and supper, and she always seemed tired after each meal. I finally discovered something that was very disturbing. Her aide left the food tray on the nightstand instead of helping her with the meal. Mom needed someone to help her eat. I can't believe that no one knew that. She always received her medications right before supper so that she would have some food with the pills. I figured the reason she was so tired was probably because she was receiving the medication on an empty stomach. Once I realized what was happening I insisted that someone feed her. I knew that if she

received a good meal, her body would probably react better to
the medication. I was right."

Jackie, Illinois

If you think your parent maybe receiving an inappropriate medication, or too much or too little medication, speak to the nurse in charge of
her care. Talk to her about your concerns.

1. If your parent expresses that she is in pain or if you feel she is in
   pain, ask the nurse to have your mother evaluated by the physician. She has the right to be pain-free.
2. Speak to her doctor regarding all of her options for pain control
   and management.
3. Don't bring medication from home and give it to your parent. It is
   unsafe and dangerous.

"I know I was stupid, but she seemed so miserable. I gave her
one or two of my pain pills. I didn't think that my pills and her
pills would have such a bad interaction. When I received a telephone call in the middle of the night that my mother suddenly
became ill, I knew NOW what had happened. I called her
doctor right away and told him. She's OK now, but I'll never
forget that night."

Georgia, Wisconsin

Medication is essential to your parent's health and quality of life.
You have the right to expect your parent to be as comfortable as possible.
Exercise your rights by asking questions and insisting on a doctor who is
willing to work with you and your parent for the best possible outcome.

K. PATIENT ADVOCATE AND BILL OF RIGHTS

As a resident of a nursing home your parent has certain rights. One of
these rights is to representation if she has a problem. The representative
or patient advocate listens to her complaints and acts as an intermediary

between your mother and the nursing home administration. In some states these advocates are volunteers referred to as ombudsmen. Although a nurse or aide may try to help you with certain problems they may not have the time or the expertise to be effective. Ask to speak to the patient advocate when you have a specific problem or a general question regarding the nursing home. The primary role of the patient advocate is to help you and your parent resolve problems swiftly and satisfactorily.

Every nursing home should have a Patient's Bill of Rights. You will probably find the Bill of Rights in the nursing home admission packet, and you will find it displayed in the lobby or common areas. This adaptation of the Nursing Home Bill of Rights from the State of New York will give you an example of what to expect.[1] The Bill of Rights may vary from state to state. Ask for a copy whenever you tour a nursing home. If you are the primary advocate for your parent be aware of these rights and do not hesitate to speak to staff members regarding any issues that concern you or your family members. If you do not receive satisfaction, speak to local authorities if you believe that your parent is being neglected or abused in a facility. (See chapter 18 for more information.)

Every nursing home resident has the right to:

- Dignity, respect, self-determination, and the right to his or her individuality.
- Privacy and confidentiality.
- Approve or refuse personal or clinical records to anyone outside the nursing home.
- Receive or send private written communications and the right to access stationery, postage, and pens and pencils.
- Access to handicap-accessible telephones that are usable by visually or hearing impaired residents.
- Access to the legal right to vote.
- Bring a cause of action for poor care and treatment.
- Request, read, and examine all nursing home records pertaining to his or herself.
- Be free from physical, verbal, or sexual abuse and chemical or physical restraints.
- Fully understand his or her medical condition and ask questions and have them answered.

- Refuse all experimental research.
- Refuse medications and treatments as long as the resident understands the consequences.
- Choose a personal physician from doctors permitted to practice at the nursing home and receive the physician's name, address, phone number, and specialty.
- Participate in and approve his or her care and treatment.
- Participate in the resident's council.
- Choose social activities that he or she likes.
- Receive notice before a roommate or room is changed.

L. MOVING TO A NURSING HOME

The day arrives and your parent is moving into her new home. It is not like the day she moved into her new house fifty years ago filled with anticipation and hope for the future. This is a different kind of move; this is a move of necessity.

> "My mother never wanted to go to a nursing home, but we didn't have a choice. She needed so much care."
>
> *Juliet, New Hampshire*

The truth is that nothing will make moving day easy, but some preparation will help make the transition more organized and alleviate some of the emotional stress.

1. If your parent is cognitively alert and aware but physically incapacitated, talk to her about what will happen the day she moves into the nursing home. Provide her with as much information as you think she can handle. If it is too difficult for you to discuss the move with her, ask another family member, friend, or health-care professional to be with you.
2. Decide whether you want to be a part of the move or if you would rather someone else move your parent. If you think you will find the process too difficult, then don't do it. Ask another

family member, friend, or healthcare professional to assist you. If you hire someone such as a geriatric care manager or home health aide, tell her to contact you as soon as she settles your parent in her room.

3. Talk about the transportation you will use for the move. If she requires an ambulance, you may want to have someone she knows accompany her for the ride, such as a home health aide. If that is not acceptable to the ambulance service, then you and or the home health aide can follow behind in a car or taxi. This is an emotional time for everyone and you will need support.

4. If your parent is cognitively impaired be sure you have one or even two people with you for help and support.

"I always thought of myself as a good Girl Scout, always prepared. But the day I moved my father into the nursing home was a rough day. I hired a geriatric care manager to help me on moving day. I drove the car and the geriatric care manager sat in the backseat with my eighty-year-old father. A block from the facility a large, brightly lit sign said, 'Welcome to _____ Nursing Facility.' Although my father suffered from dementia and a history of psychological problems he still could read. He read the sign out loud and started to scream. I tried to remain focused on driving the car, but it was a miracle we didn't get into a serious car accident. I was so grateful because while I was trying to keep the car on the road, the care manager called ahead on her cell phone to alert the staff."

Bunnie, Pennsylvania

5. If someone other than you escorts your parent to the nursing home, think about when you would like to visit. Some family caregivers prefer to wait a day or two until their parent settles into her new surroundings. This is a personal decision. Try to base it on your ability to cope with the situation. Don't feel like you are deserting your parent if you decide not to visit on the first day. Call the nurses' station and see how she is doing, or ask another family member, friend, or hired caregiver to visit.

6. If your parent has a home health aide, arrange for her to spend time with your mother in the nursing home. Some family caregivers find that if they retain the same aide for approximately four to six weeks (or longer if necessary) for several hours each day, it helps their parent's adjustment to the new environment. Some nursing homes may not permit hired caregivers in the facility. Before your parent moves into the facility speak to the admissions director or a staff social worker about the policy. Sometimes the facility is willing to make arrangements to accommodate special circumstances. If the facility does not permit outside staff then you can arrange a "family schedule" to provide a little extra support in the first few weeks. One family found that between the children and grandchildren they spent three to four hours a day with Grandma. The adults visited in the early evening and some of the teenagers visited after school. After five weeks their grandmother seemed to feel more comfortable, and they decreased their visits.

7. Decorate the room and make it as comfortable as possible before your parent moves. This may help to provide him with a sense of family, home, continuity, and security.

8. Talk to the admissions director or social worker about any special concerns. For instance, if your parent is going to share a room, you may want to know about his roommate(s), how much space he has in the room and the policy regarding televisions and telephones.

9. Give the nursing home staff a chance to do their job. You may try to think of everything, but there are some things that happen that you cannot control. If your mother doesn't get just the right dinner the first night, let the staff know and give them a chance to correct their error. If she is supposed to receive a tub bath every other day and you find out she received showers during the first week, let the staff know you are aware of the error and give them a chance to rectify it.

10. Assure your parent that you and your family will visit and talk to her on the telephone.

"I couldn't believe my mother, she took my hand and said, 'It's OK if you don't visit all the time; just remember, I'm still here.'"

Karen, New York

Making the Room Comfortable

Many times you hear children say, "It smells like Grandma's house," and generally, this is not a bad thing when it reminds you of chocolate chip cookies, a special birthday party, holiday celebration, or a family reunion. But if you think about your parent's house, you will probably remember that it really does have its own distinct aromas. Most of the time they represent an accumulation of cooking smells, colognes, perfumes, dogs and cats, old furniture, and carpets. Hopefully, they are the smells and memories that make you smile.

Making your parent's new home comfortable may take a little time, creativity, and a trip down memory lane.

- Talk to your parent if she is capable of participating and making some choices. Ask her what will make her happy. Make some suggestions about bringing her favorite blanket or pillow, but don't be surprised if she rejects the idea. If your parent was reluctant about the facility she may feel if she agrees to bring things from home, she is agreeing to stay. Sometimes you have to wait until she adjusts to the move, before you bring things from home.

  "My father reluctantly moved into a facility, but asked me to keep all of his belongings in plastic bags next to the door. After a few months he slowly let me unpack his things."

  Janet, Ohio

- Use your best judgment if your parent is cognitively impaired and is not capable of participating in making selections. Bring a pillow, blanket, or comforter and pictures of the family. Try to include old pictures to help stimulate memories and some new pictures to assist with orienting your parent to the present.
- Pare down family pictures by bringing five or six instead of twenty.

A wonderful caregiver from Pennsylvania said, *"There wasn't much wall space in my dad's room so I made a collage of pictures. One collage was filled with the grandchildren's pictures and the other was of his old army buddies. He loved looking at the pictures and the walls looked homey."* Use two throw pillows to decorate her bed instead of four. A small end table instead of a large armoire can help recreate a part of your parent's home in the facility.

> "We found a simple way to enhance our mother's room. First, we selected two blankets, two pillows and one afghan that our mother always enjoyed. We covered one wall in family portraits and snapshots and another wall in the needlepoint pictures she made over the past thirty years. Then we added an old kitchen radio to rest on the dresser drawers. Our mother always liked the smell of pine in the house, so we hung a room deodorizer in the bathroom that smelled like pine trees. The room smelled like home and looked like home. When we asked her how she likes the room, she said, 'It's not home, but it's pretty close.'"
>
> *Cheryl and Cynthia, Connecticut*

Not every nursing home room is bare or sterile. Many facilities have added colorful draperies, wallpaper, plants, and flowers to provide pleasant surroundings. The extra touches from home will provide your parent with continuity, and a warm feeling that she is still a part of the family.

Clothing

The idea that your parent is going to live in a bathrobe or hospital type gown is not necessarily true. When it comes to clothing in a nursing home the optimal words are "comfort" and "accessibility." But if your parent always took the time and interest to dress fashionably, she does not have to completely give up her sense of style. Here are five suggestions that pertain to men and women.

1. Try to purchase washable clothes. If the tag says DRY CLEAN ONLY it is not appropriate.

2. Label every item of clothes from underwear to overcoats. Use preprinted name labels that you can sew or iron into the clothes or a black laundry marker that does not fade in the laundry. Once your parent is a resident, some facilities will provide a labeling service.

3. Do not purchase expensive clothes. Variety, color, and comfort are far more important. Clothes sometimes disappear in the nursing home laundry.

> "My ninety-three-year-old demented aunt never wore slacks. One day when I visited her she was wearing a pair of brown slacks with her favorite blouse. I said, 'Hi Aunt Betts, great slacks.' Without missing a beat she said, 'I must have just bought them.' When I asked the social worker, she said that sometimes the residents' clothes get mixed up."
>
> *Elizabeth, Rhode Island*

4. Both men and women need outerwear. Depending on the geographic location and climate in the area of the nursing facility, your parent may need a woolen coat, hat, and gloves or a lightweight raincoat or jacket. Your parent will need the outerwear if he transfers to a hospital or other nursing facility, participates in a nursing home outing, or a family celebration.

5. Because of laundering schedules most facilities will ask for at least ten days to two weeks of clean clothes, underwear, nightclothes, and socks.

For women only:

1. Cotton underpants. Cotton is usually more comfortable then synthetic fabrics. If your parent is incontinent, you do not need the underpants because she wears adult diapers.

2. Cotton bras or undershirts. Bring three or four bras if your mother prefers a bra or her doctor recommends it. Some women do not feel comfortable in a bra and prefer men's cotton undershirts with a cap sleeve.

3. Nightgowns or pajamas. Every woman has her preference, but in a nursing home setting, convenience, comfort, and easy access take priority over aesthetics. Before purchasing any nightclothes ask the social worker or nurse on your parent's floor what type of night clothes are preferable for your parent's physical condition. If you have a choice, try to bring her own nightclothes or purchase items that are similar. Continuity is important in every aspect of care.

4. Housecoats, sometimes called snap coats or dusters, are very comfortable and presentable. You can purchase them in most department stores and they come in a variety of fabrics, colors, and sizes. Try to purchase the coat a little larger than is actually necessary. It is usually more comfortable and easier for the staff to assist your parent in the bathroom or transferring from the bed to a chair or wheelchair. Some nursing homes prefer housecoats that snap in the back. The reason is that if your parent is cognitively impaired she may try to undo a housecoat with a front closure. This type of housecoat is not as common, but some nursing homes provide a "shopper's day" every few months. At that time vendors provide family and staff the opportunity to purchase clothing specifically designed for a parent with incontinence or dementia. If you are not available on the designated shopping day or you are a long-distance caregiver, you can ask the nursing home social worker to purchase the clothes.

5. Sweaters or sweatshirts with snaps or zippers are comfortable and attractive over a housecoat. If your mother was always style conscious, try to coordinate her sweaters with her housecoat. She'll look good and you will both feel better.

6. Socks and shoes or sneakers should fit comfortably. Cotton socks are usually preferred over synthetic fabric. If your parent is ambulatory and tends to walk around in her socks, then you might want to purchase socks with a skid-free bottom. You can find these socks in department stores and in some shoe stores. Try the socks with her shoes or sneakers. Sometimes even cotton socks are too heavy for certain shoe styles. Even if your parent cannot walk, she will be uncomfortable if her shoes are too tight, or the socks are too big. Some nursing facilities have a connection with a shoe

company. A representative measures your parent's shoe and sock size. The representative takes the orders and delivers the items to the nursing home. Ask your parent's social worker about this service. Many women use knee-high stockings as their socks. Check with your parent's nurse or doctor because sometimes this type of hosiery maybe too constricting around your mother's leg.

7. Sweatpants and sweatshirts are comfortable, affordable, colorful, and washable. They are easy to coordinate and they are warm in the colder climates. Many sweatpants have elastic around the ankle. In order to avoid problems with tightness or discomfort you can remove the elastic and hem the pants. If your parent is incontinent take into account the extra room she'll need for the adult diapers. Many of the sweatpants and shirts are suitable for men and women. Try to purchase sweatshirts without a hood. Hoods are sometimes bulky and uncomfortable when your parent lies in bed for a nap.

8. Jewelry is sometimes a meaningful accessory, but don't bring the family heirlooms to the nursing home, because they may be lost or stolen. Some caregivers have the jeweler make a copy of a favorite necklace or pin, or they bring a few pieces of inexpensive costume jewelry to match an outfit or two.

9. Your mother may still enjoy carrying her purse. Bring a favorite pocketbook, makeup case, or wallet. You may want to put a dollar or two in the wallet to give your mother a sense of familiarity and control. You may add an old handkerchief or small brush, or keep the bag empty. Mirrors, perfume bottles, or makeup may not be appropriate if your mother is cognitively impaired. Ask the nurse in charge of her unit what items are safe and appropriate. If your mother wears lipstick or other makeup, label each item with her name and give it to the aide or nurse for safekeeping.

For men only:

1. Underpants and undershirts should be comfortable. If possible, cotton is always preferred over synthetic fabrics. If your father is incontinent you do not have to worry about underpants, because he wears adult diapers.

2. Bathrobes and pajamas should be comfortable and washable. A cotton or terry robe is preferable over flimsy silk or polyester fabric. Ask the social worker or nurse what type of pajamas are appropriate for your father's needs.

3. Socks, shoes, and sneakers must fit comfortably and securely. (See section six in the "for women only" list above for details about shoes and socks.)

4. Many men enjoy wearing sweatpants and sweatshirts. Other men like to dress in slacks and a button-down shirt or sweater. In most cases your father should be able to enjoy either style. What's important is that all of his clothes are wash-and-wear, and wrinkle resistant. Many family caregivers report that their parent looks "sloppy or messy." Clothes that need ironing do not belong in a nursing home. If possible, avoid pants that require a belt or suspenders, because it makes it more difficult for the staff to assist your father in the bathroom. If he is cognitively impaired and uses the bathroom on his own, he may not remember how to unbuckle a belt or remove the suspenders and he could hurt himself with the buckle. This delay may increase bathroom accidents.

5. Bringing jewelry is usually not an issue for most men, but if it is, do not bring expensive pieces. They may be lost or stolen. If your father wears a watch, purchase an inexpensive watch with a large face and clear numbers. Even if he does not use it, wearing it may make him feel better. If he always wore a neck chain, ask the nurse or doctor if it is safe for him to continue doing so.

6. Many men like to carry a wallet. If your parent is ambulatory but suffers from dementia he may forget where he is and think he needs money to buy food or even gasoline for the car. Put a few pictures of the family in the wallet and a dollar or two to give your father a feeling of being in control.

At some point your parent's condition may decline and she or he will not need to wear anything other than a nursing home robe and nightshirt. If and when that time comes, you can bring a colorful bed jacket or sweater for your mom and a bright, comfortable sweater for your dad to keep him warm and comfortable. It will make all of you feel better.

Valuables and Personal Items

There is a simple rule that applies to all nursing homes. Don't bring valuable jewelry or family heirlooms, such as an antique pillow or afghan. Do provide moderately priced televisions, radios, and CD, cassette, or DVD players for your parent's enjoyment. Many nursing homes are large institutions with hundreds of staff members and residents. Even smaller, private institutions sometimes have difficulty keeping track of clothing, and personal items. In many instances your parent's belongings are well cared for, but sometimes things get lost, stolen, or misplaced.

The truth is, be prepared to lose whatever you bring.

> "I bought a holiday afghan for my mother. Although she has dementia she seemed to respond to the colorful design. I put it on the edge of the bed so she could look at it. When I visited the next week I noticed that the afghan was not on her bed and a torn and discolored afghan was on her lap. I asked the nurse what happened. The explanation was that my mother's afghan was lost in the laundry, but she said, 'maybe it will turn up.' I told the social worker, who apologized and said, 'These things happen.' About two weeks later I was walking down the hall into my mother's room and I noticed an afghan wrapped around the legs of another resident. It was my mother's. I told the nurse and she returned it to Mom with a flimsy apology. I guess we were lucky to get it back. I hear that things get lost all the time."
>
> *Mary, New York*

Personal items help create a sense of warmth and comfort in your parent's room. Even if your parent is confused, disoriented, or in poor physical condition, don't underestimate the power of familiar things, smells, colors, and sounds. If your parent is sharing a room with two or three other residents, there are some limitations. (See the section on Making the Room Comfortable in this chapter for more details on how to create a comfortable room.) The following suggestions apply to a large single room or a small area in a larger room.

Even in the smallest quarters you can bring one pillow, a small radio, and one or two pictures or small paintings, and a blanket cover or coverlet from your parent's home.

- Family pictures add warmth and memories to any space.
- Try to purchase an inexpensive radio and leave it on a low volume. You may want to bring a VCR or DVD player and videos of the family. Place a note by your parent's bedside reminding the nurse or nurse's aide to put the radio volume on low or put a particular tape or disk in the VCR or DVD player. This is particularly meaningful for a parent who is bedbound. Your parent may enjoy popular music from the thirties or forties, classical or ethnic music. Sometimes listening to music in her native language is soothing. For example, if your mom speaks Italian, Spanish, or French she may enjoy music in that language.
- Try to purchase a small television set. Even if your parent is unable to follow or understand a television show, he may enjoy the familiar voice of a talk show host or just the sound of other voices in the room.

Keep the valuables at home and remember that the things your parent treasures the most are not necessarily measured in dollars and cents.

M. WORKSHEET: EVALUATING THE MOVE TO A NURSING HOME

It may be one of the most difficult decisions you have to make for your parents. To ease some of your burden, use this guide to help you make the best decisions.

1. Be sure that you understand your parent's diagnosis and prognosis.
2. Ask your parent's physician what kind of care your parent needs now and in the future.
3. Ask a friend, physician, social worker, nurse, or family member for a referral to several nursing homes. Try to visit three to five facilities. Make an appointment with the admissions director or administrator for a tour of the facility.

4. Be prepared by bringing a list of written questions. Because this is such an emotional issue, try to bring someone you trust with you when you visit the nursing homes.

5. Discuss your parent's condition with the admissions director. Be honest and open about his or her physical and cognitive needs.

6. Discuss the financial arrangements. Be candid about your parent's financial situation and be prepared because you will be asked to provide proof of your parent's ability to pay. If your parent cannot pay and he or she will require public assistance, discuss this with the admissions director.

7. Select a nursing home that not only meets your parent's needs but also is geographically desirable for you. Consider your traveling time and your ability to visit your parent.

8. When you tour the nursing home, ask yourself how you feel in the environment.

9. Look around at the people. Do they look well cared for and comfortable?

10. If your parent requires specialized care, such as that to be found in an Alzheimer's unit, make sure that this type of unit is available.

11. Ask the staff about recreational activities, holiday celebrations, and special events.

12. The answers will indicate to you the quality of life in the nursing home.

13. Review this chapter for a comprehensive look at nursing homes.

N. MY JOURNAL

Use this page as a safe place to express your feelings. Putting thoughts and feelings on paper helps you see them more clearly. What bothers you? What changes do you want to make? When you read what you've written, you may see a new pathway to help resolve stressful issues. For example:

"Placing Mom in a nursing home was the most difficult thing I had to do. I feel like I left her to fade away and die, but I know that I couldn't have done anything else . . ."

"Dad doesn't know me anymore. It hurts when he looks at me and can't remember who I am or my name. I feel so sad and alone . . ."

O. TIP SHEET

- Visit three to five nursing facilities at different times of the day to determine which facility is the best for your parent.
- Do an Internet search for vital information regarding most nursing homes to help you with the decision-making process.
- Take into account location, religious preference, dietary requirements, and any specialized services your parent may need.
- Talk to staff members and observe the interactions between staff and the residents during meals, social activities, or as they pass a resident in the hall.
- Allow yourself all the feelings you have regarding this very difficult time and reach out to family and friends to help you.

21

DATING, SEX, AND REMARRIAGE

A. YOUR PARENT'S NEW RELATIONSHIP

"I wanted my mom to have a life of her own. She spent so much of her time living my life. It was so burdensome feeling as if I have to keep her company. One day she called me and said that her friend Mary introduced her to her brother. They went out for coffee and she said that she had a good time. I was glad and sad at the same time. Happy that she found a companion, and sad it wasn't my dad. Mom's doing great and I'm adjusting to my stepfather."

Jackie, Florida

"My mother is a healthy seventy-year-old. She lives about three thousand miles away from me. That's fine with me because we never had a great relationship. I have my own family, two daughters, twenty and eighteen. One day I screamed at my older daughter about something she did or didn't do. After the shouting match, I looked in the mirror, and I started to cry. I realized at that very moment that I sounded like my mother. It was a startling revelation. A few weeks later, my mother called to tell me about her upcoming marriage. I was pretty shocked, but do you know what I said? 'Does he have any money, and can he buy you a house?' Those were the exact questions my mother asked me twenty-four years ago when I was planning my own wedding."

Mary Beth, Connecticut

"My parents seemed so happy all of the time. I just didn't see the problems or maybe I didn't want to see. Whatever the case, when Dad died Mom just wanted to be alone. I didn't understand why she felt the way she did but I accepted it. Over time she seemed to come out of her shell and socialize with friends. One day she told me that she met a man. I was surprised to say the least and more shocked when I met him. He was disheveled, dirty, and he was actually missing a tooth. I was disgusted and I told my mother. All she said was, 'You just don't understand.' I guess at the time she was right. We haven't spoken to one another in over two years. Maybe I should have just kept my opinion to myself."

Suzanne, Michigan

Jackie, Mary Beth, and Suzanne are responding to their parent's new relationships in very different ways. Each woman brings a different perspective to the situation based on who she is and how she feels. Given a similar situation, which reaction would be yours?

1. I am happy that my mother has a new relationship.
2. I wish my father wouldn't tell me anything about his new girlfriend.
3. I am jealous of the new woman in my father's life.
4. I hate that miserable man.

The tone of all of these statements is filled with strong emotions and feelings, but the statement is not complete. What is missing from each statement is the "because." For example, "I am happy because . . ." Your emotions play an enormous part in how you react to this type of news. Balancing your emotions with common sense and reason may help you to understand why you feel the way you do. When you understand your feelings, you may be better equipped to handle the new events and changes in your parent's life and yours. Think about the statement that may apply to you and substitute your own "because."

1. I am happy that my mother has a new relationship because she is lonely and she will have someone else to spend time with and do the things she likes.
2. I wish my father wouldn't tell me anything about his new girlfriend because I know all about her. She already had two rich husbands and everyone who knows her history says she is looking for a third.
3. I am jealous of the new woman in my dad's life because he and I are very close. I am afraid that she will take over.
4. I hate that man because he is not my father and he wants my mom to move into his house with his things. I know she will sell her house and I am afraid my memories will go with it.

Once you add the reason, your reactions begin to take on a new meaning, and your feelings begin to make more sense. Clearly verbalizing how you feel may give you a new perspective. Now you can begin to look at the situation and your attitude more rationally, and you can begin the process of trying to accept the change in your parent's life by:

- Acknowledging your feelings. Think about, evaluate, and try to discover the reasons you feel the way you do. Talk it out with a friend, a counselor, or a therapist. Sometimes writing how you feel will help you release your thoughts and understand them better. *Use the journal at the end of this chapter to help you express your feelings in a safe and private place.*
- Talk to your parent in private. Do not make this into a family counsel because not everyone may feel the way you do. Prematurely bringing your feelings to the attention of the rest of the family may add to the tension.
- Try to remain open to your parent's feelings. Sometimes we think

we know what someone else is thinking or feeling, but our thoughts and ideas are not even close to the reality of the situation. Acknowledge how he feels, and let him know how you feel.

- If you have any serious concerns regarding financial issues or housing, try to discuss them with your parent. Your parent may not want to talk to you about these issues, and he has the right to his privacy. If he is willing to talk to you, try to keep your emotions tempered and focused on concrete facts and information. Prepare written notes to help you remember specific issues. For example, explain to your father that you know his new wife talked about starting a savings account for her grandchildren like he has for his grandchildren. Ask him to give the relationship time before he makes any financial commitments to her family. Let him know that you want his assurance that the money he saved for his grandchildren is safe. Talk to him about your concern that he may be planning to give his new spouse the country cottage that he promised you and your children. If he says he is not sure what he plans to do, ask him to give his relationship some time before he makes his final decision.

- If your parent is in a relationship and he is very happy, he may want to share his joy and good feelings with you. If you are not ready to accept his relationship, explain to your parent that you simply need time to adjust. Assure him that your reluctance about the relationship doesn't mean you don't love him or you don't want him to enjoy his life. You are just not ready. Ask for his patience and understanding.

A period of getting to know this new person may make all the difference for you and your parent. *Don't be too hard on yourself if you find this new situation awkward or unsettling.* Even if your first impressions were unfavorable, time may change some of your feelings and allay some of your concerns—or the reverse!

B. REMARRIAGE

"My mother said, 'Doreen, what's the problem? I haven't been a virgin for over fifty years. Your father and I loved each other, but we didn't make love for the past twenty years. I feel so wonderful. Can't you be happy for me?' And what did I do? I ran out of the room crying, 'How can you cheat on Daddy's memory?' I feel like a fool. I really wanted to go back and put my arms around her and tell her I was sorry. Of course I want her to be happy. But most of all I wanted her to put her arms around me and tell me that I am still the most important one. How old am I? I'm fifty-two."

Doreen, New Mexico

"My father came to visit and announced that he met a woman. My brother said, 'That's the way to go, Dad.' I just looked at him in total disbelief. He said, 'She lives in my apartment complex, and we see each other very often. I met her children and two of her grandchildren this weekend. You'll love them.' Love them? I wanted to say, I don't even like my own sister. Instead, I just sat there and listened to my father tell me how we are all going to be one big, happy family."

Lois, New York

It may be difficult to admit, but your parent's remarriage is not about you. It is an opportunity for him to start over, and maybe enjoy a better, fuller life. "[Researchers] find that married elderly persons are more likely to eat breakfast, wear seat belts, engage in physical activity, have their blood pressure checked, and not smoke than widowed elderly persons."[1]

That's the good news. The bad new is that everyone is emotional, scared, and unsure about the future. You may say things that you really don't mean, and do things that are out of character. Why? You might feel jealous of the new person in your parent's life, or you may begin to question your parent's loyalty to your deceased parent. If your parents are divorced, you may feel an allegiance to one parent over another, and struggle with feelings of abandonment by the parent who is getting married or spending time with a new partner. You may feel that this stranger sitting in your father's favorite chair or sleeping in your mother's bed is trying to replace your dear mother.

"I walked into my parent's room and saw a new comforter and sheets on the bed. My mother followed me. I turned and said, 'Did you at least turn the mattress?' She started to cry and said, 'How lonely do I have to be to keep you happy?'"

Merry, California

Over the years, your family may have created many special traditions. For instance, they may equally divide all holidays between the two sides of the family: this is an unwritten family law that has withstood the test of time and a few family arguments. Your family may open birthday presents only at the kitchen table after the ice cream cake's been served, or you may spend Thanksgiving in a country house and every other holiday in the city. Along comes someone new, your parent's future husband or wife. His family may not have many traditions, but if they do, they are also entitled to enjoy the ones they have established. The first months of "getting to know you" are filled with changes, conflicts, and emotional highs and lows. You can still try to help your parent during this period of adjustment and discovery. Here are some frequently asked questions.

Q. I'm really struggling with how I feel about my mother's new husband. Mom seems so happy, and I really want to help her. She has a whole new family to deal with, and her stepchildren seem a little cold. How can I help her?

A. When it is possible, try to reach a compromise. Not every situation is going to develop into a crisis, but sometimes the simple day-to-day issues are enough to frazzle your nerves and create havoc in the family. Suppose that every year everyone spends the holidays at your house, and this year your mom says she is going to her stepdaughter's house. You may feel slighted, but your mom may be under pressure from her new husband to spend the holidays with his daughter. Instead of arguing and making it more difficult, tell her you understand, and suggest to her that they join you and your family for dinner the next week. It may not always be easy to compromise, but it can save a great deal of aggravation.

Q. We are so used to doing things the same way year after year— family things that make us feel good. My mom's new family is so different. It seems like nothing is sentimental or important to them. How can we maintain our family traditions without making it harder on Mom?

A. Don't feel like you have to give up your family's traditions. Begin to think about modifying some of them. If your mother's new husband wants her to spend Thanksgiving day with his great-aunt Mary, then maybe you can move your dinner to the weekend. If your dad's new wife has high cholesterol or she cannot eat milk products, don't make your family's traditional ice cream cake for her birthday. Talk to your new relatives about things they enjoy. You may even create some of your own traditions if you are willing to take the time to listen to one another.

Q. I loved them both, but I realized at a very young age that my parents had a very ordinary life. A big night out was a movie and coffee at the local diner. They enjoyed this for many years until my dad died. After a few months, my mother became a "swinging single." She blossomed into this beautiful woman. It was as if she were free from some burden. I guess maybe it was my father. She met a man about her age at the library and they began to date. She was a new woman, and I really was happy for her. She wanted me to accept him and care about him, though I was not ready, willing, or able to cope with a new man in our lives. I stopped calling her, and it's been very stressful for all of us. What can I do to make things better?

A. Coping with this new situation by not talking about it only makes matters worse. Set aside a time when you and your mother can be alone. Tell her you want to understand how she feels, and you want her to listen to how you feel. First, listen carefully for her message. She may want you to know that her future husband makes her feel good and safe. She may want you to know that she needs to have the financial security that he can provide. She may simply tell you that she loves him and would like you to accept her feelings. Let her know how you feel and try to express why you feel the way you do. For instance, do you feel jealous of the time they spend together? Do you feel like she is betraying your father? If you walk away from this first conversation feeling as if you did not accomplish anything, try again. You may want to see a family therapist or a counselor if you feel that you and your mom cannot work this out on your own.

It appears that everyone experiences the news of a remarriage in very different ways. There is no right or wrong way to deal with this new and often emotional situation. What it takes is the willingness of all of you to try and listen to one another, learn what you can about your new parent and his family, and keep an open mind and heart to the journey ahead.

Give your parent a chance to live and learn and love. Give yourself the time to understand that his need for a partner does not mean he does not need you or is sullying the memory of your mother.

Financial/Legal Issues

> "I live on the East Coast, and my future stepfather's family lives on the West Coast. Our parents retired to a senior community in Florida. Mom calls us up and says she and this man are getting married. We were in shock. Our mother is independent and wealthy. According to Mom, his children were also in shock. Their father was a widower for twenty years, swinging, single, and rich. This was not going to be a marriage; it was more like a merger."
>
> *Cindy, Virginia*

Cindy may be right. Sometimes a second or third marriage may seem more like a business deal or financial arrangement than a love match.

> "My mother was married and widowed three times. Her marriages became the family joke. My uncle said the next man she meets better buy himself a pair of sneakers and start running. Mom remarried for money and position in the community. She was lucky because she is attractive, bright, and bakes a great apple pie. My father worked in a factory and left her with bills. Her second husband was an accountant who left her with stocks, and her third husband was a businessman who left her a hefty life insurance policy. When she met number four, Mom was worth a lot of money. We wanted to protect her, but she wouldn't listen to our suggestions and married him anyway. He convinced her to sign over some of her accounts to him, and before we knew it, he took most of her money and left."
>
> *Lily, Connecticut*

When you are young, people talk about marrying for "the right reasons." There is no right or wrong reason, however, because people marry for a wide range of reasons based on love and passion, convenience and companionship, and shelter and security. Whatever the reason is or is not for your parent, it is understandable that you want to try to protect her from unnecessary misunderstanding, harm, or loss.

If your parent is particularly excited about her upcoming marriage, she may not be too receptive to even consider the fact that her future spouse wants her money or house. Your parent may not want to discuss this issue with you. It is important for you to try to understand how she feels and to respect her need for privacy. If she is willing to involve you in this particular matter, how can you help to protect your parent and ensure her future security?

- You may be surprised to learn that your mother and her future husband never spoke about what they intend to do about their finances. If they did discuss their plans, ask her about the specific details. Gently suggest that she speak to her accountant, a financial planner, or an attorney before she makes a final commitment.
- If she has financial assets and property, encourage her to see her accountant, a financial planner, or an elder law attorney to discuss her options. Offer to make the appointment and go with her as soon as possible. If you have siblings who are actively involved with your parent, ask her if they can join you.
- Encourage your dad to learn as much as he can about his future wife's spending habits and debt problems. Does she have several credit cards? Does she use the cards on a regular basis? Does she pay the balance every month or does she allow it to accumulate? It is important for him to know what his financial responsibilities may be in the future.
- Be prepared with all of the financial information including savings bankbooks, checking account statements, stock and bond certificates, deeds, insurance policies, a list of her jewelry, art, and antiques, and so on.

"My mother gathered her bankbooks and checking account information. She even brought the deed to her house. The attorney looked at the information and said, 'Irma, I thought you had other assets.' I said, 'Mom, where are your stock certificates?' She looked at both of us and said, 'I didn't realize they count.'"

Sally, Ohio

- If your mom has antique jewelry or she inherited a silver tea set from her grandmother, talk to her about the sentimental and monetary value. Explain to her that if she wants to protect these family treasures for you and her grandchildren, she should have them appraised, photographed, and insured, and mentioned in her will.
- Explain to her that although you hope her marriage is successful, she might want to consider a prenuptial agreement. "A prenuptial agreement is a contract entered into before two people marry, settling out what each will be entitled to if they later divorce or one dies. Instead of relying on state law to settle property and support issues, the couple sets out their own solution. Often, these agreements focus on property owned by the wealthier of the two spouses. In general, the agreement needs to be in writing, signed by both parties, witnessed by as least two disinterested parties (those not receiving anything in the agreement), and notarized."[2]
- Talk to her about her partner's family. Express your concern that although they appear to be nice people, you don't know much about them, and she should reserve judgment and her money. Discourage her from giving large monetary gifts or loaning money. Suggest that she protect her last will and testament from any interference.

In some situations, your parent may be remarrying not only for companionship, but also for financial security. What guarantee does she have that if her new husband predeceases her, she will have the financial security she needs and wants?

"Mom was sure that her new husband was a 'really good man.' I thought he was, too. We didn't know until he died that he was not too smart. Before he died, he told my mom that she could live in his house for the rest of her life. It was all paid for, and she would have a limited amount of expenses. He never told his son about the arrangement, and Mom never asked for anything in writing. Two weeks after her husband died, his son told her to pack her bags and leave. She begged him to allow her to stay for a few months, but he said no. She moved into my house the next day."

Sylvia, California

Although this is an extremely sensitive subject, try to emphasize that you are only concerned about her best interests. You are simply making suggestions that she can think about in order to protect her own future. By encouraging her in this way, you are supporting her and giving her the power to control her own destiny.

- Talk to her about your concerns, and give her a chance to tell you if she has discussed her future security with her fiancé. Be very specific. If they buy a house together, who will live in it if they separate? Who pays the household bills? Are they going to purchase life insurance, and who is going to pay the premiums?
- If they have worked out an agreement, encourage her to see an attorney for a written contract or a prenuptial agreement. If they have not worked out the details, encourage her to do so before the wedding. Gently but firmly let her know that waiting until after the wedding may complicate matters because it might lessen her negotiating power.
- If your mother's future husband has adult children, encourage her to ask him to talk to his children about the arrangements he made for her. Explain to your parent that it is important for her fiancé to put his intentions in writing for his family and hers so that there will be no misunderstandings in the future. A family meeting prior to the wedding may help to keep everyone informed. This type of communication may also help to avoid an unnecessary family feud.

> "My stepfather was a cheap, arrogant man, but he did one thing right. He told his son and daughter his intentions, and he left written instructions with his attorney that if he died before my mother, she could live in the house for as long as she wanted to. After he died, an estranged son came back into town. He harassed his family and Mom. He tried to get her out of the house. Of course he wasn't successful, but after a few months she decided that it was not the best place for her anymore. It's very different when you can make that decision on your own and not feel as if someone is throwing you out. I never liked my stepfather, but I'll always be grateful for what he did for Mom."
>
> *Yvonne, Georgia*

- If he refuses to put their agreement in writing, she may want to reconsider the marriage. If she is angry with you because you suggested reconsidering the marriage, talk to her about a short delay. Suggest that she try and work things out more carefully.

You may offer very helpful advice and support, and desperately try to safeguard and protect her right to safety, security, and peace of mind. But, no matter how hard you try or what you say, your parent may decide to ignore your warnings. She may marry or decide not to marry and simply live with her new partner. She has a right to self-determination and to expect you to respect her decision. You cannot stop her, but you can be there to support her if and when she needs you.

C. DATING, LOVE, AND INTIMACY

"I watched from a distance as my ninety-three-year-old father and his girlfriend held hands. They live in an assisted living facility. He is in a wheelchair, and she uses a walker. After a while, she stood up and they walked to his room. I followed a few feet behind. She bent down and kissed him on his mouth, and without a second to spare, he patted her gently on her behind. Two days later my father was rushed to the hospital, and he died. I was so glad he had that kiss."

Myra, Texas

The need to feel the touch of another human being begins at birth. It doesn't matter if you are eight days or ninety years old. Your parent's need for human contact and companionship is natural and healthy. Like Myra, many of you will see your parent's desire for this type of friendship and love as something special. You may even encourage him to join social groups and functions to meet people. Senior centers, church and synagogue groups, and widow and widower groups provide opportunities for seniors to meet other seniors with similar backgrounds and interests. These organizations sponsor programs, outings, lunches, and dinners to accommodate older adults in the community. Senior summer camps may provide your parent with a well-rounded experience that may include hiking and swimming as well as stimulating lecture series.

> "My mother joined a summer camp last year. She's seventy-eight years old. I thought I was sending my teenage daughter to camp. We labeled Mom's clothes, picked out two new bathing suits, and helped pack her suitcases. The first postcard arrived about ten days after she left. It said something like this, 'I met a boy. Having a great time. Love, Mom. P.S. He is a retired teacher.' That says it all. What a great sense of humor."
>
> *Emily, Illinois*

Some college campuses cater to a senior population by offering courses in history, art, and music. In some states, retirement communities are built in close proximity to a college campus for just this reason. All of these groups focus on lifelong learning and bringing older adults together to socialize and develop new relationships.

> "I met this woman at a lecture on eldercare. She started to talk about her father, and I started to talk about my mother. Something clicked, and we decided to introduce them to each other. We invited them to join us for lunch. By the end of the meal, they had plans for Saturday night. The woman is now my stepsister. We couldn't be happier for our parents and ourselves."
>
> *Sarah, Virginia*

Even if you recognize that developing close relationships in later years is important for your parent's health and well-being, some of you may still feel embarrassed and uncomfortable that your parents want the companionship of a partner. Because you are having problems with this issue, you may say things to her such as "Grandmas don't do that," or "How can you embarrass me like this?" You may even make her feel guilty, and she may try to justify her actions. This sometimes complicates the situation and may make both of you feel uncomfortable and unhappy.

Calmly explain to her that you would like to understand why she needs this new relationship when she has you, her grandchildren, and sisters. She may tell you that she would like you to understand and accept the fact that she loves and needs all of you, but she also wants and needs a partner.

Try to accept the fact that your parent's desire for love, companionship, and security is a normal part of life, and her life is far from over. Consider how fortunate she is that she can still find joy and fulfillment at eighty or ninety years old. Think about how lucky you are to have a parent with a healthy state of mind.

Sexuality and Sex

"My parents divorced after thirty-eight years of marriage. Dad took off for someplace out West, and Mom continued to live in a small town in the East. She met a very nice man, and they began to travel together. 'Travel together' was her way of saying they were 'sleeping together.' I guess it sounded better to her. When she told me this, all I could think of was this is way too much information. I really don't want to know about my mom's sex life."

Carol Lynn, Massachusetts

"My mother was a very stern, nasty woman. When I grew up and had my own family I was sure she would mellow, but she didn't. Dad died suddenly at the age of eighty years old. I figured Mom would become nastier and meaner. She didn't; instead she met a man and she was never happier. One day she confessed that she never loved my dad and, although it was hard to hear, it explained her misery. She was finally happy and fulfilled. I guess it's never too late to find love."

Nancy, Maine

"Most older people experience some interest in sexual intimacy. Many people are sexually intimate well into their eighties and beyond. We've not all of a sudden become asexual beings; our capacity for sexual intimacy will be with us our entire lives."[3] The thought of your healthy parent in a sexual relationship with her partner shatters the image of old folks rocking on a porch. You may even chuckle and feel uncomfortable, but if your parent is enjoying a sexual relationship, "believe it or not the 'happiness payoff' of having sexual relations is greatest for the old."[4]

Does your parent's sex life affect you? It shouldn't, but it does. Unfortunately, it may make you feel like a child again. Remember when your parents locked their bedroom door and announced that it was time to watch the Saturday night movie? Guess what? It's fifty years later, and the movie is still not over. You may feel embarrassed by this type of relationship. You may still feel like a child, no matter how old you are today, when a discussion of sex and your parent is the topic of conversation. "As we all approach later life, two of the things which brought us the greatest joy—our children and/or our careers—are no longer as prevalent in our every day. This means that our personal relationships take on an increased importance. It is a way of solidifying our relationship with our partner and taking refuge from the sometimes harsh reality of the world. Sex is a way to affirm the love of life. It is an expression of the satisfaction gained from the present. It expresses the closeness of our deepest relationships and is an important measure of the quality of life."[5]

> "I couldn't believe my ears. My mother said that she and her friend were going across the country in a camper. My mother never camped a day in her life, but she was so excited. She invited me over to see the camper. My first thought was that there was only one bed. I said, 'Mom, where is Sam going to sleep?' Without hesitation, she said, 'With me silly, with me.' Silly is not the right word. I felt like a naive fool. I looked at her and said, 'Go for it, Mom.' She's never been happier."
>
> *Roberta, North Carolina*

Can you ever get over feeling awkward or embarrassed in front of your parent or his partner? Some of you may always feel uncomfortable because you still find it hard to believe that your parent likes holding hands, enjoys a kiss, or has sex. Others may try to accept a situation that is considered natural.

If it is very difficult for you to change your attitude and you feel your behavior is hurting your relationship with your parent, try these suggestions:

- Try to talk to your parent about the situation. Explain to him that you are happy for him, but you don't necessarily need to know all the details of his sex life. In the section on safe sex in this chapter, you will learn when it is important for you to know what is going on and how to react when you have the information.
- Be calm and gentle when you talk to your parent. Explain to him that not wanting this information has nothing to do with your love for him or your interest in the rest of his life.
- If your parent and his wife or significant other are overtly affectionate and it makes you uncomfortable, try not to make unkind or rude remarks. Instead, try to talk to them as a couple. If you address them as a couple rather than alone, you are reducing the risk of either of them misunderstanding your intentions.
- If you believe your parent wants to keep his relationship private, try to respect his wishes and let him know that you are available if he wants to talk to you.

Sexual desire and the need for intimacy does not stop just because your mother celebrated her eighty-second birthday, or end the day your dad retired from his job. If you think about your parent as a lively, energetic person who also happens to be your parent, you may begin to accept and understand that his feelings are normal and healthy.

Safe Sex

The plea to practice safe sex is heard and seen in the media, advertised on the sides of buses and billboards, and displayed in your children's and grandchildren's schools. The media developed many strong advertisements that clearly alert the public to the danger of AIDS. You can learn about AIDS (Acquired Immune Deficiency Syndrome) and the elderly population in chapter 15.

If your healthy parent is sexually active and she has unprotected sex, meaning sexual intercourse without the use of a condom, she is also at risk for many sexually transmitted diseases. For your parent's health and your peace of mind, this list of suggestions is adapted from "Safe Sex" tips.[6]

- Encourage your parent to try to remain loyal to a partner who also wants a monogamous relationship. Advise him how important it is to carefully choose a new sex partner. Many older men are enjoying the company of multiple partners strictly because of the availability of older women.
- Your parent should make every effort to limit the number of his sexual partners. One is best, but if he feels he wants more than one sexual partner, he should try to limit the number. Remind him that it is imperative that his partners limit their contacts as well. Caution your parent that he's sleeping with everyone his partners have slept with.

> "Mother was always a very attractive woman. When she and my dad were divorced, she became someone I didn't know or like very much. She started dating one, two, three, four men at a time. Who am I kidding? She wasn't dating; she was having sex with one man after another. I found out about it because my girlfriend's mother lives in the same retirement development. I did confront her, and she thought it was very funny when I said, 'Mom, I understand you have a few male friends. Want to tell me their names in alphabetical order?' It wasn't funny because my mom became involved with one man too many, contracted a sexually transmitted disease, and infected other partners."
>
> *Terry, California*

- Your parent may find some humor in your suggestion, but encourage him to always use a condom for all sexual encounters to protect him against many serious diseases.
- If he has not had a sexual relationship in a very long time, he may want to speak to his doctor or the pharmacist about the latest forms of added protection, such as a spermicidal product.
- Encourage your parent to talk to his partner(s). Talk to him about not drinking alcohol when he first meets someone new. Keeping his mind clear will help him make better and more appropriate decisions about a new person.
- Encourage your parent to inform his doctor that he is sexually

active. Testing for the AIDS virus and other sexually transmitted diseases is not only important for him, but for all of his sexual partners. Impel him to see his doctor immediately if he is concerned about anything.

The message is clear that age has nothing to do with risky sexual practices. What can you do if you know your parent is sexually active and he may not be practicing safe sex? Don't panic. This is a serious problem, but you can help your parent by being open, honest, and understanding. Remember, he may not want to discuss this subject with you, and he has the right to privacy and confidentiality. If he is willing to discuss this personal and intimate subject, these suggestions may help you.

- Before you approach your parent, decide if you think you are the right one to talk to him about this issue. If you think you can talk to him, refer to the information provided for you in this chapter.
- If you feel too embarrassed or you are concerned that your parent will not be responsive to you, contact your parent's physician or therapist about approaching your parent and discussing the health risks. If your parent has a close friend, he may be able to approach this subject with your parent.
- Contact the local AIDS center for literature on AIDS and other sexually transmitted diseases and a possible referral to a trained counselor. First make an appointment for yourself. Learn what you can, and then try to discuss it with your parent or refer him for counseling. Try to provide your parent with current pamphlets and literature that addresses this information.

As difficult as it may be to discuss this topic with your parent, it is crucial to advise him about his risky sexual behavior. Try not to chastise or make your parent feel as if he is your fifteen-year-old son. Talk to your dad the way you hope he would talk to you, calmly, respectfully, and with understanding. Safe sex means health and peace of mind for your parent and you.

D. MY JOURNAL

Use this page as a safe place to express your feelings and concerns. Putting thoughts and feelings on paper helps us see them more clearly. What bothers you? What changes do you want to make? When you read what you've written, you may see a new pathway to help resolve stressful issues. For example:

"*I wish my mom would talk to me about her new boyfriend. I feel left out of her life and very much alone . . .*"

"*If Dad spent as much time with my kids as he did with her grandchildren everything would be better, maybe . . .*"

E. TIP SHEET

- Try to talk to your parent about his new relationship in order to help both of you adjust and support one another.
- Encourage your parent to receive financial and legal advice if he decides to remarry.
- Try to understand your parent's need and desire for love and intimacy at any age.
- Don't hide under the covers if your parent is sexually active. Try to make her aware of safe sex practices and the importance of medical intervention if she has any questions or problems.
- Talk to a close friend or counselor about your feelings or concerns. Use the journal in this chapter to write your feelings in a safe, secure place.

22

DEATH AND DYING

A. FACING YOUR FEELINGS AND FEARS

"No one in my house ever talked about death out loud, they always 'whispered.' I know it sounds ridiculous, but I began to believe that if I never talked about my parents dying, they just wouldn't die! Dad died years ago and I don't think I ever came to terms with that. Now Mom's sick and even though I'm sixty-one, I still can't cope with the thought of being an orphan. If I can't handle it, how am I going to comfort her or make plans with her? How am I going to say good-bye before she dies?"

Paul, Texas

"My dad said, 'Elizabeth, if you don't explain my illness to Nick and Jack and let me talk to them, they may wonder if they did something to cause my death and you'll have a helluva time convincing them they didn't. I'm a doctor; listen to me. It's important that they learn how to handle the deaths of loved ones now, before they create their own damaging scenarios. I'm begging you, Liz. This could affect the rest of their lives.' I must be the world's worst mother. I'm so wound up in my own fear of death that my dying father has to remind me to take care of my kids. Is it possible to react 'well' to death? If so, please tell me how."

Elizabeth, South Carolina

"The nursing home called around 1:00 AM. I don't have any idea what they said exactly, but they called to tell me my father was dead. Isn't that odd? Most people never forget those words, and I can't remember them. I guess I just could never say them so I wiped them from my memory. Even though I knew the call was imminent, I wasn't ready for it. The minute the phone rang, I felt a pain that reached all the way into my soul. That's all I can say about it."

Jennifer, Kentucky

It's not unusual for children to know their parent's wishes for burial or cremation, nor is it unusual for parents to sprinkle conversations with the phrase, "After I'm gone . . ." Both subjects deal with after death, and both are generally accepted as part of a conversation as long as they don't become a mantra and they're not specific about the absolute act of dying. For example, how many times have you heard a friend or coworker say, "We knew it was coming, but now that it's happened, I can't believe it." Your bereaved friend made no identification or specific confirmation of the fact that someone is dying or has died. She just used the word "it." How can something that happens to every single one of us, regardless of sex, religion, or nationality, be so hard to discuss in a normal conversation? There is no easy answer. We may shrink from talking about death because of the pain of losing a parent or the experience of how that parent died. "Our culture often makes the quality of death a lower priority than the quality of life."[1] Some caregivers may feel guilty for not being there at the exact moment of their parent's death. Or your parent's death may remind you that you, too, are mortal, and then the fear of your own death may become the underlying issue.

Many of us were taught as children that polite and sensitive people do not talk about "it." If you accompanied your parents to a funeral when you were a child, you probably wondered why the adults whispered instead of speaking in a normal tone of voice. You may have become frightened because a friend's or a relative's death made your very strong parents cry. You may have thought, if death could make the people I rely on most for safety and stability cry, surely I should be frightened of it. When we grew older and began attending services for our own family members, friends, or colleagues who died, most of us did exactly what we learned to do as children. We wore dark clothing, cried, and spoke in whispers. Through example, we began preparing our children to feel exactly as we do.

> "My mother said, 'Linda, you are going to have to tell the children. They know something is wrong and they are frightened. I want to be able to say good-bye to them. What are you afraid of?' I stared at her, mute, while my eyes filled with tears. I don't know what I was afraid of. The only thing I know is that I couldn't say it out loud."
>
> Linda, New Hampshire

When your parent dies, you may have so many diverse and conflicting thoughts and emotions whirling around in your head that you may feel numb. That is your own body raising its protective shield. It is giving your system the time it needs to absorb the pain and shock of finding out that your parent is dying or has already passed away.[2]

Don't expect every member of your family to react in exactly the same way you do. Be prepared for every sort of emotion. One family member may remain calm, show no visible distress, and begin organizing, leaving you to wonder if she really cares that your mother just died. Another may break down and sob hysterically. Some may begin to deny the issue ("No, she couldn't be dead."); others may become angry and say, "She didn't deserve to die, not her of all people." Still others will be too stunned to cry, talk, or help in any way. Grief and shock do not produce identical feelings in every person they touch. If one of your siblings had a poor relationship with your parent, he may not feel or show any sadness at all or may not display great guilt. This is not a time to change perceptions. As hard as it may be for you, try to accept everyone's feelings.

Fears about death and dying encompass our deepest feelings and emotions and our most dearly held traditions. Mourning, grieving, or learning to live with the loss of your parent is so personal and is so dependent on your individual life experience that there is no right or wrong approach. However, learning from the experiences of other caregivers who have shared similar feelings and fears may help you find a less painful approach to dealing with your grief.

> "My mother-in-law looked my husband straight in the eye and said, 'Frank, why won't you talk to me about this? You have to face the fact that I cannot be treated and I am going to die. You are a grown man with three adult children. Did you honestly believe I would live forever? I've faced it. Why can't you talk about it?'"
>
> *Charlene, Texas*

One of the first steps you can take to help yourself accept and manage your fears is to learn to open your heart and talk about death and dying. This can be one of your most difficult challenges, but it may also be one of your most rewarding and important achievements. Don't automatically assume discussing death is something you "could never" do or could "easily do." If you don't succeed the first time, try again. If you break down and cry, don't worry. It's normal to cry when a beloved parent receives a terminal diagnosis or dies. Tears help protect and heal us by reducing stress and anxiety. Talking about your fears out loud makes them less frightening. Not everyone will be successful at this. That's normal, too.

Why go through the pain of even trying? If your mother is terminally ill, she may want or need to talk to you openly and honestly about her own feelings. If you deny her impending death and she cannot share her thoughts and hopes, or her deepest fears with you, she may feel as if she is facing death alone. Many family members find this beyond their capacity. If you sincerely feel that talking to your parent about her death is something you cannot do alone, try bringing another person into the conversation. Think about another close family member, a very close friend of hers, or a member of the clergy. That way the third person can contribute to the conversation.

"I know a lot about death and dying. I've read the books. But I haven't been in the situation of being with people close to me who were ready to make that leap. I wanted to be with them and I was scared, too. Overcoming my own fears to be present was a time of major growth for me."

Ilya, Missouri

Identifying your own feelings and talking about a subject that disturbs you is a time-honored method of dispelling fear and overcoming panic. If you need help to face the situation and can afford a professional counselor, choose a psychologist, a social worker, or a nurse who has specific training in death and dying issues and in grief counseling. Caregivers who cannot afford professional assistance can still help themselves by talking to family members, clergy, trusted friends or companions, consultants from community organizations, or counselors from the illness-specific organization that relates to their parent's illnesses, or by working through their company's human resources programs. Be realistic in your objectives. Your parent may be seriously ill or may have recently died. If you love your parent, it's unrealistic to expect to totally eliminate your sadness or pain. However, it is within your reach to feel less afraid, and more understanding and accepting of the fact that death is one issue you cannot control. This isn't easy. It takes a great deal of courage to examine your feelings and talk frankly about love, hate, fear, anger, guilt, or even relief. There are no guarantees: you may find peace of mind, or you may find nothing. But it's worth trying. If you succeed, you can make a positive difference as a caregiver and a parent by teaching your children how to handle your death and the deaths of others they love. Consider these options:

- Do you have a true "best friend" or someone you can tell your deepest thoughts to without worrying about what she will think or that she will repeat your thoughts to others? If you do, take a walk or have a cup of coffee with her. Have dinner, clean out a closet together, or just get away from your everyday surroundings and go to a place where you can talk privately and without interruption.

"Sarah and I have been good friends for years. When I got divorced, she talked me through it. When her son died, I stayed at her apartment for two weeks and took care of everyone and everything while she grieved. When Mom got nearer to the end, Sarah was the only one I told my horrible secret to: I wasn't sure how many more times I could visit my mother while she was dying because I couldn't stand to watch her rot away. Then she told me about her father. I knew her parents were dead, but we'd never talked about how or why. Her story was worse than mine. Just getting my feelings out in the open made me feel better. Knowing I wasn't the only one who ever felt that way helped me feel less guilty and ashamed."

Karen, New Mexico

- Many adult children benefit from individual professional counseling or a support group. If you've thought about it but haven't made the call, ask a family member or a friend to help you summon the courage to make an appointment. Remember, the key to getting help is to begin the process and make a decision on whether it is helpful to you after you've tried it, rather than working off assumptions that it won't help. It's also not a good idea to make this decision based on someone else's experience. Your personality and the counselor you choose may provide a totally different experience. Ask for a referral from a source you already trust like your doctor or the specific organization that relates to your parent's illness, such as the Alzheimer's Association, the American Heart Association, or others. If your parent is in a hospital, ask the social services office. You can also call the Area Agency on Aging.
- Does the company you work for have a human resources counselor? If so, take advantage of this benefit. Ask for a referral to a bereavement counselor. Don't be embarrassed and don't worry about letting someone know you need help. Your request is just one of many the human resources counselor hears every day. Logic should prove to you that if you were the only one who needed help, there would be little need for this benefit, and your company probably wouldn't have it.

- Make some time to spend with your brothers and sisters, aunts, uncles, and cousins. You may be surprised to find yourself laughing and smiling warmly about both the good and the bad times you have shared over the years. Often, talking about good memories from the past will help ease your pain. Talking about bad memories is equally important. Everyone in your family may not have had a good relationship with your parent, but each family member's feelings and perceptions are meaningful. If one family member has particularly bad memories and they are too painful for you to hear, don't become angry and aggressive. Just excuse yourself and leave the room.

> "I didn't like her. She was never a 'mother' to me. She was always more interested in herself. But I was her only child. It didn't seem right to desert her—even though that's what she did to me when I was little. So I visited her every day. I brought her foods she liked and paid for a homecare aide so she could die in her own bed. When she died, I walked away and never looked back."
>
> *Cyd, Florida*

- You may be feeling guilty because it has been your habit to feel that way when anything goes wrong. You may feel that you could have done a better job of caregiving, or recognized your parent's illness sooner. You may feel guilty because you are well and your parent is sick enough to die.[3] You may regret than you didn't have a better relationship. Though you may not deserve any of your guilty feelings, it's hard to ignore them or make them go away on your own. Help yourself by finding counseling in a support group or in private sessions. Ask for a referral from your human resources department at work, a hospital, or a group that works with caregivers for your parent's illness: the American Stroke Association, the Parkinson's Association, and so on. The truth is, "For many caregivers, feeling guilty is better than feeling helpless."[4] If you acknowledge that, then you are ready to ask for help.
- Sometimes adults feel that if they talk to their children about a grandparent's death, they will upset their children and cause them

unnecessary pain. Talk to your children. Silence is far more painful than helping them air their fears and feelings. They, too, need the opportunity to say good-bye in some way, or if it's appropriate, to help with caregiving duties. If you don't explain death, you may leave them wondering if they did something to make their grandparent leave them, or if they actually caused their grandparent's death. If you have qualms about this conversation, there are many wonderful children's books written just for this purpose. You can also get help from a counselor or a member of the clergy.

Learning to acknowledge your own feelings and fears can help you be more receptive to your parent's feelings and fears.

B. WHAT ARE YOUR PARENT'S FEELINGS AND FEARS?

"My father discussed the entire procedure with my mother. Notice, I said 'procedure.' I still have a hard time saying 'funeral.' But she didn't. When my father found out he only had about six months to live, he began talking to my mother about his death and her life. He helped her take care of all the details. They decided who they wanted to speak at the service, and she called and asked them. He told her not to tell anyone how much money they had because he didn't want anyone marrying her for her money. Marrying her! He wasn't even dead yet! She cried, but she knew he was just talking about life going on. Could I ever do that with my Fred? Could he? How can they?"

Linda, New Hampshire

"At first, my father wouldn't let my mother discuss her 'problem' with me. About the millionth time he said 'problem,' I lost whatever control I had left. I screamed 'What are you trying to do? Drive me crazy? How can I help you or even talk to you if you keep insisting this is just an ordinary problem? Do I look stupid? I know Mom's dying. Dad, you are going to have to face this sooner or later!' He just looked at me in amazement. 'We want to talk to you. We faced it long ago. We just didn't want to upset you until we had to.' They weren't afraid for themselves, they wanted to protect me. I'm fifty-nine."

Kitty, Massachusetts

Many elderly individuals are not afraid to die. After reaching a certain age, they accept death as a natural sequence in life. Some will tell you they welcome it as a way to escape illness, loneliness, and pain. Others will show shock and disbelief and begin working through the same process we all go through to come to terms with the reality of death. In other words, everyone faces death differently. However, it's a pretty safe assumption that your parent wishes to die without pain and with dignity. Wouldn't you want the same for yourself?

If your parent tells you she has a terminal illness, you can begin to help her by gathering your courage and talking honestly with her about what her diagnosis is and whether or not additional treatment is an option. If you don't feel you can do this, your reluctance is understandable. If you want to try, but not alone, ask your brother or sister, your parent's friend, or a member of the clergy to help you begin. But consider your role carefully because it is demanding and difficult. Some caregivers find themselves emotionally unable to take on this responsibility. If you can make the commitment, a good first step is to tell your parent you love her and that you will be there with her and for her as she faces the end of her life. Then make every effort to keep your promise and stand by her.

- Try to understand that as your mother faces death, she may feel a variety of constantly changing emotions. This is the time for "Active Listening" (see section D of this chapter). Be open to her moods and feelings. Let her show them to you without fear of your response. Accepting her actions and attitudes tells her that you accept the fact that she is dying. Your acceptance of her condition may be one of the keys to her peace.
- Your parent may want to sit quietly and reflect on the past or even the future. Don't assume that you have to "make conversation." Quiet moments do not necessarily mean your mother is depressed.

Her silence isn't an automatic signal for you to begin talking to fill the void. Sometimes just sitting in the same room, quietly reading, watching TV, walking, or holding your parent's hand is the most supportive and appropriate service you can perform.

- Don't try to impose your wishes or your "way" of doing things. What you want or what you think is the best way to do things is no longer important. If you haven't faced a terminal illness, you cannot know how your parent feels. What difference can it possibly make in the long run if she's a little late for dinner? How will it affect her life or your life if she changes her hair to a style you don't like or wears clothes you consider inappropriate? This is no longer about you.

- Give your mother the time she needs to work through her grief. There are five stages of grief: denial, anger, bargaining, depression, and acceptance.[5] Understanding them and their purpose will help you both through this painful time. At first, your mother may deny she is dying. Be gentle. Denial is usually a temporary defense and buffer after unexpected shocking news. It gives your mother time to collect herself and begin to mobilize other, less radical defenses to help her adjust. Next, she will probably become angry, maybe with her doctors, maybe at God—and blame them for letting this "happen to her" unfairly. Once her anger subsides, she may decide to "bargain" for her life by giving to a charitable cause or promising to become more "religious" or to never smoke or curse again. As she becomes weaker and her physical appearance declines, she will not be able to avoid seeing that she is becoming sicker, and the fourth stage of grief, depression, may set in. Allow her to express her sorrow. Don't tell her to "not be sad." If your mother cannot work through her depression into the fifth stage, acceptance, it's a good idea to bring in a professional counselor. "Acceptance is not a resigned and hopeless giving up or sense of 'what's the use.' Nor is it a happy stage. It is almost devoid of feelings. Your parent may be tired and weak, and sleep more often. Many dying persons in this stage have found some peace; they wish to be left alone and not stirred by news and problems from the outside world."[6] You can help most by letting your parent know that everything is taken care of and she can rest peacefully.

When she seems ready, talk to your parent. She may enjoy reminiscing with you or talking about the future. Both of you may cry at the thought that she will not see her grandchildren graduate from school or be at their weddings. If she wants to talk, even if you're both crying, don't stop her from venting. Your parent may want to talk to your children, but is concerned about her ability to do so without breaking down or their noticing her sickly appearance. You can accommodate her by helping her make a video or audiotape recording about the family's history or her feelings for them. It can serve as a legacy for them and for their children. As difficult as this may sound, caregivers have told us that quiet conversations like these often create a special time toward the end of a parent's life. Some say they experienced a closeness that enriched their lives and lasted forever as a warm, loving memory.

"My sister and I sat with my mother for several days until the end. We talked about almost everything in our lives. We asked each other questions we'd never dared to ask before. I think we each answered honestly. I know we were surprised at the answers. Some of the revelations were amazing. It was one of the most meaningful times I remember in my entire life."

Marilyn, South Carolina

"My whole life changed when I found out my mother was dying. My brother and I always argued about whether or not she was a bitch. I'd hated her for so long that it seemed like a fraud to go see her before she died and pretend that I cared. My brother finally convinced me to go. He said, 'Look Bon, if you go and you still hate her, well then you can just forget about her. But if you don't go, you might miss your last chance to get some peace.' When I got there, she asked me 'why' I disliked her so. I was furious. I expected her to cry and apologize, not talk to me rationally about my feelings. Something in me told me to answer exactly the way she asked: calmly and quietly. Later I realized that I heard my brother's voice telling me not to blow my last chance to make my peace. Not hers, mine. I ended up staying for hours. I went back every day. I cried when we buried her. It felt good to care again."

Bonnie, California

It would not be unusual for your mother to become more spiritual as she faces death. Her prior beliefs do not matter. She may begin to talk about and question the meaning of life or death. She may question accepted definitions of good and evil, or the value of her faith and yours. Support her in her quest for meaning. These are difficult questions, and she doesn't expect you to have the answers or to agree. Whether you have a strong faith or don't believe in God at all, your honest response will support her in her quest for a deeper understanding of her own feelings and need for peace of mind.

C. COPING WITH THE DEATH OF A CHILD

"When Dad died, Mom handled his death normally. She cried, but she also laughed with friends when they remembered their experiences together. She always enjoyed looking at pictures of dad. Last year, my forty-year-old sister was attacked and shot. We expected the same reaction Mom had to Dad's death, but when Mom heard Fran had been killed, she collapsed. When she could stand, she went into her bedroom and stayed there with the door closed, refusing all help. She cried quietly, moaned loudly, screamed, and scared us out of our wits. We called the doctor, but she wouldn't talk to him or take the medicine he prescribed. Her best friend, Joan, probably saved her life because Mom let Joan feed her and give her medicine. We all grieved and we're still angry, but eventually we went back to our lives— except Mom. She still isn't back to her normal self."

Serena, California

"When Mom heard about my daughter's cancer diagnosis, she was almost unreachable. She retreated into another place and lost all her zest for life. She always enjoyed a full social life, but refused to go out in case she missed our call. Or I guess I should say, 'the call,' telling her that Rebecca died. I tried to tell her this cancer wasn't anywhere near fatal and explain how lucky we were to catch it early and have a great doctor, but nothing got through to her. She answered every telephone call with a quiet, fearful 'yes?' She lost twenty pounds. Her skin lost all color. She looked like she was going to end up in the hospital. Rebecca's been out of treatment for almost a year and Mom's just getting some of her sparkle back. I don't what we'll do if Rebecca gets sick again. It's hard enough dealing with cancer without dealing with Mom's reaction to it."

Lilly, Texas

As children many of us may have asked, *"Mommy, where did Grandpa go? Why did he leave us? Is he coming back?"* As heart wrenching as the answers may have been for your parent, they were also comparatively simple because we've all been taught by events and the explanations we're given for death that our parents will die before we do. The reason is clear: our parents will grow into old age before we do and eventually old age leads to death. It's always been that way, not only for you, but the for the world, so it makes sense and although we grieve and mourn, we accept a parent's death because it is an integral part of the order of life as we know it.

There is nothing as physically and emotionally painful for a parent as the loss of a child. The grief is boundless, the concept literally unbelievable. The code of life and death that your mom has lived by for sixty-five, seventy-five, or eighty-five years no longer applies. The unexpected and unfair loss of this limb of her family tree signifies the death of part of her family's future. This can turn her belief system and her world upside down, leaving her emotionally adrift because in her current state of shock, the answers she has relied on all her life no longer apply.

It's not unusual to hear a parent talk about a child or grandchild using phrases like, "He is a gift" or, "She's the best thing that ever happened to me" or, "I would die for him." Losing a child or a grandchild suddenly or to a prolonged illness is a blow to a parent's or grandparent's strongest and most protective human feelings. Mom may withdraw from family and friends, leaving you to grieve alone. This doesn't mean she loves you less. When a child dies, a part of the parent and grandparent dies as well. She may become overprotective and fearful for her other children. You may hear a series of *ifs* or *could haves* or *should haves*: *"If* I had been there to protect her, I *could have* insisted the doctor keep trying to save her. I *should have* more understanding." Guilt sometimes makes us feel that we had control over uncontrollable events. Feeling guilty may seem far more acceptable than feeling lost and without control.

Your love and the love of other family members or friends is extremely important when your child is very ill or has died. As much as you want to "be there" for Mom, it is important to acknowledge and care for your own needs. Try verbalizing or writing your feelings down. If your parent is too stricken to comfort you, you may feel alone. Take the time to talk to a best friend or family member. Coping with and healing from the death of loved one begins with expressing your feelings and talking about the pain, anger, sadness, or even relief you feel in your heart.

> "We made a huge mistake in telling Mom that my brother died. She can't remember what day it is and half the time she can't remember who I am, but somehow she manages to remember that someone died. The problem is she forgets that it was Ben who died. Sometimes she thinks I died, sometimes other relatives, sometimes friends. This has been going on for months with no end in sight. She calls us eight or ten times a day from her assisted living community to tell us she just heard uncle Henry died or that I'm dead. Then she cries over our deaths. I don't know how to describe the feelings I have trying to console my mother, who's crying because I just died. God, I hate this disease."
>
> *Delia, Colorado*

No matter how well intended, trying to bring a person with dementia into your reality generally results in problems. Because we can't enter their worlds, we are never totally certain how people with dementia will process what we say. Neither we nor they have any control over their interpretation of our words or whether they will single out and become obsessed with one thought or phrase. They will sometimes take it totally out of context, and at other times, change it to what we consider a falsehood. They may mangle your conversation beyond recognition and be terrorized by their version of the event.

You may find differing opinions on the subject of "when and how much" to tell, but following one of the basic rules of communicating with a person with dementia should help you make a better decision:

Do not try to bring your disoriented parent with dementia into your reality. She cannot accommodate or understand your wish. It is usually better to enter her reality. Loose translation: if Mom is demented and someone close to her dies, try not to tell her. If she asks about the person, tell her, "Ben sends you his love, Mom." Then change the topic of conversation to distract her. If the concept of compassionate deceit is hurtful to you, consider the amount of pain Mom may feel if her reality becomes clear for even one second and she understands her son or grandson died— or the pain she may feel with an ongoing distorted memory of the deaths of many friends and family members. You can rest easy in the knowledge that your kindness saved her (and you) a great deal of unnecessary sorrow.

D. ACTIVE LISTENING

> "I learned how important it is to take care of yourself emotionally. You have to acknowledge your emotions and do whatever you need to do, whether that's writing or crying or praying— whatever makes sense for you to fortify yourself so that when you're with the person who's dying you can focus on that person and get yourself out of the way."
>
> *Lucy, Florida*

Active Listening is an art. Active listeners use all their senses during a conversation. They can often hear a person's *feelings* in a tone of voice rather than accepting the perfunctory "I'm fine, thank you" answer we all give.

The art of Active Listening begins with the listener's ability to focus on the speaker. Evaluate your current listening expertise: How well do you listen? Do you think about other issues or ideas when you're involved in a lengthy conversation or do you "actively" focus on the speaker's words and sensitively respond to his needs? Do you mentally wander during a colleague's or boss's long explanation? Are you easily distracted by noises or other people around you?

When spending time talking or just sitting quietly with a dying or grieving parent, it's important to practice active listening. These suggestions will help you understand what active listening entails, but they are general and should be tailored and individualized to meet your needs and those of your parent.

- Take a few minutes before your visit and quietly prepare yourself by thinking about your parent.
- Look your parent in the eye while he speaks. Focus 100 percent of your energies and thoughts on what he says and try to "feel" the content of his words.
- Your father may or may not want to discuss his approaching death or the death of your mother. Let it remain his choice and follow his lead.
- Try not to think about your response while your parent talks. You'll lose part of the conversation. It's okay to take quiet periods to think before you answer.
- Don't state your views or interrupt your parent's thoughts until you have listened to his full comments on the subject.
- You don't have to agree with your parent's thinking. Listen, respond, and comfort nonjudgmentally.
- Turn your cell phone off and don't constantly check it for messages. This is the time to focus on your parent.
- Don't say, "I know how you feel," and give an example. You can't know and it's unlikely your example matches the magnitude of your dying parent's emotions.
- Allow your parent to talk at his own speed with rests and quiet periods. Don't worry about talking through the quiet moments. Your presence is enough.

The death of a parent is a trying time that often includes unrealistic expectations forced on us by family or by ourselves. Don't ignore your own limitations. Give what you can give, but if you cannot emotionally or physically cope with spending long periods of time with your dying parent or making funeral arrangements, seek help by bringing someone else into the mix to help you. Anyone who has ever experienced the death of a loved one will understand your feelings. Take care of yourself by talking to a friend, family, or clergy, and asking them to help you manage during this difficult experience.

E. HONORING YOUR PARENT'S WISHES

The best way to ensure your father's wishes for his end-of-life treatment are carried out is to discuss them with him. Although this may be a difficult conversation to have, it's your best option. Explain to your father that unless he tells you what his wishes are, he may have no voice in his own care. He may also be placing an unnecessary burden on you and other family members. Without a clear direction, your family may have opposing views on how and how much to treat your father if he is at or near death. He may have decided that under certain circumstances he doesn't want excessive life-support options or continued resuscitation, only palliative care. "Palliative care" means that he will be treated only for pain and discomfort with no attempt to prolong his life. Unless he tells you about his wishes, and formalizes them in a legal document, called an advance directive, neither you nor he may have any control over what treatment he receives. Helping your parent formalize his wishes can help avoid additional stress during a very emotional and difficult time.

Advance directives are legal documents that are used only when a person is unable to make his wishes known. If your parent was seriously injured in an automobile accident or suffered a massive coronary and couldn't speak for himself, his advance directives would direct both the family and the physicians to help them follow his wishes. The same would be true if your parent was legally declared incompetent to make decisions on his own behalf. The laws regarding advance directives may vary by state, so it's important to prepare a document that is valid where your father lives. You may be able to obtain state-specific copies of these documents from a hospital or the Area Agency on Aging in your father's state. You can also retain the services of an attorney in the same state where your parent lives. Any competent individual over age eighteen may prepare an advance directive.[7]

- A living will (also known as a healthcare directive or a healthcare declaration) spells out the types of medical treatments and life-sustaining measures your parent does and does not want, such as mechanical respiration and tube feeding.[8]
- A durable power of attorney (DPOA) for healthcare designates someone your parent has appointed to make medical decisions on his behalf (a healthcare agent), but only in the event he is unable to do so for himself. This document is different from the power of attorney that can authorize someone to make financial transactions on his behalf.[9]
- Be certain the designated healthcare agent, your parent's physician, and you all have a copy of your parent's documents so that one of you can present them to a hospital when necessary.

> "My mother took me aside and gave me a piece of paper. She said, 'Lucy, I've taken care of everything. You just have to do what this paper says.' When I read what she'd written on the paper, my mouth dropped open. My mother and I had never discussed her death or her will. She was eighty-two and had been widowed for forty years. She didn't drive. Yet, without any help from my sister or me, she had investigated and chosen the nursing home she wanted to go to if she needed long-term care. She had planned her funeral down to and including a very short mourning period, after which she expressly asked that we go back to our lives and live them fully. When I caught my breath, I thanked her for sparing me the burden of making all those decisions on her behalf later. Isn't she wonderful? You can't imagine how proud I am to be her daughter."
>
> *Lucy, New Mexico*

If your parent's wishes for his end-of-life medical treatment are different from what you would want for him or for yourself, try to understand that it's his wishes that count. Although you may not be able to imagine stopping treatment, if your parent is cognitively intact it is his choice, not yours. If you are aware of your parent's wishes, consider taking the time to visit the hospice organization near you for a better understanding of how palliative care works. Hospice is the premiere organization and place for end-of-life palliative care. The hospice staff concerns themselves with quality of life and quality of death. They are dedicated to helping patients die without pain and with dignity, and to helping families cope with death and dying. Their overall goal is peace of mind for the patient and the patient's family. If this type of care is your parent's wish, try to keep an open mind until you learn all you can about how the process works. Ask your parent's physician or the hospital or nursing home social worker for a referral to the hospice organization where your parent lives.

F. FUNERAL ARRANGEMENTS

One of the worst moments after a parent's death arises when a family member has to make hurried and complex choices for the funeral. If you know your parent is dying, you can save yourself a considerable amount of extra stress by planning the funeral in advance. You can also save a considerable amount of money. Very often, the overwhelming sorrow we feel at the death of a parent is joined by feelings of guilt that hamper our ability to make logical, cost-effective choices. We fear that other people may judge our love for our parent by the amount of money we spend for the funeral, and that other people may judge our families by the number of people who attend the funeral. Even though we know our parent's successes in life are not measurable in these types of numbers, these feelings inhibit our ability to make logical, cost-effective choices, and before we know it, the cost for the funeral becomes a significant financial burden.

In their 2004 survey, the National Funeral Directors Association found the average cost of a funeral to be $6,500.[10] However, funerals can easily cost as much as $30,000 if arrangements are made at the time of death.[11] You may consider funerals the aftermath of a tragedy, but make no mistake about the sales representatives of the funeral homes. They may acknowledge your grief and sympathize or empathize with your loss, but in the end, they have a business to run, and you are a customer who represents the potential for a very large sale.

The most significant factor in exorbitantly expensive funerals is the vulnerability of the bereaved person who makes arrangements at the time of death without benefit of comparison pricing.[12] In a survey of several thousand funeral directors, in response to the question *"Why would you say funerals cost so much?"* more than 85 percent replied, *"Emotional overspending by the family."*[13] Unscrupulous funeral directors may thus take advantage of people who are at their most vulnerable during this trying time.

With or without guilt or worrying about the perceptions of family members and friends, you are still very likely to have to make quick decisions on issues you know nothing about. How many funerals have you planned? Regardless of the size of the funeral you are planning, you will have to balance complex financial and religious realities with the needs of your family and your parent's friends to say good-bye, and to remember and celebrate your parent's life.[14] Perhaps you and your family have spent weeks of sleepless nights at the bedside of your parent. Or you may be in shock from your parent's sudden and unexpected death. You or a grief-stricken, emotionally exhausted family member will have to immediately interact with the funeral industry on a range of emotional and expensive decisions. First, the hospital will want to know which funeral home will pick up the remains.[15]

> "I've been in healthcare for thirty years and done a lot of death care. My mother had been hospitalized and dying over a period of five months. On the day she died, the staff asked me which funeral home to call. I was totally unprepared for that question. I marveled that I hadn't thought ahead given the extended hospitalization. I used the yellow pages. It wasn't a good time to be thumbing through the yellow pages."
>
> *Dana, Oregon*

Enlist a friend who can remain objective or the services of a professional funeral consultant. Professional funeral consultants provide you with the options and the information you need to make informed decisions, and then take care of the details for you. There are two types of professional funeral consultants: consumer's consultants and consultants who offer their services to funeral homes rather than directly to families.[16] Look for a consultant who is a member of the North American

Association of Certified Funeral Consultants (NAACFC). The group is family-oriented, and its members undergo training in all facets of the business. Funeral consultants charge a fee, but your savings can easily make their fee worthwhile.

Whether you organize your parent's funeral alone or with assistance, some knowledge of what you are entitled to will help you remain in control. Don't hesitate to be assertive about what you want. These explanations may help:[17]

1. Funeral home business practices are regulated under the 1984 Funeral Rule, which is enforced by the Federal Trade Commission and governs disclosure of information to the consumer by the funeral home. The rule's purpose is to make it easier for you to choose only the goods and services you want and to pay only for those things you have selected.

2. The rule requires that the funeral home disclose the specific prices for all goods and services on a general price list. They must provide this information by phone, if requested, or in a written general price list given to those who visit in person. They must present you with an itemized statement of funeral goods and services selected following the discussion about funeral arrangements and allow you the time to consider the choices you've made and make changes if desired.

3. Prices for the goods and services selected should be itemized like they are on the funeral home's general price list rather than represented in categories such as "services" or "facilities." The statement should include specific cash-advance items such as obituary notices, clergy honoraria, pallbearers, musicians, and so forth, with a good-faith estimate of the cost of these cash-advance items.

4. You should not be charged for anything you have not selected.

5. Funeral homes that offer cremation must offer alternative containers that can be used in place of a casket. (Alternative containers that enclose the body and allow dignified handling may be made of fiberboard, composition materials, or heavy cardboard.)

6. Any cemetery, crematorium, or local laws that require the use of any specific item or service you did not ask for must disclose the charge for that item or service in writing on the statement.

7. You must be advised that embalming is not required by law except in selected special situations. Further, the statement must advise you that embalming will be done only with your approval and is not required when you select an option such as cremation or immediate burial.

8. The funeral home must advise you when it charges you for, or receives a commission, rebate, or discount for, cash-advance items it arranges on your behalf.

An amendment to the original Funeral Rule allows each funeral home to establish a non-declinable basic services fee that is added to the cost of other selected goods and services to pay for the services of the funeral director and staff. The funeral home is required to disclose this fee on the general price list and advise you that it will be added to the cost of other arrangements. The same fee applies to the simplest or the most elaborate funeral. It is another place where comparative shopping can save as much as $1,000.

The modern funeral industry recognizes that it is a service business, and offers many alternatives.[18]

In-Ground Burial

Your cemetery may require a burial vault or grave liner to prevent the ground from sinking in as the casket deteriorates over time. These are boxes placed into the ground to receive the casket. They are made of concrete or reinforced, layered materials and range in cost from $600 to $10,000.

Caskets are typically the most expensive item in a funeral and range in cost from $600 to $9,000 and up. A casket and embalming are not required for direct burial (burials that occur immediately after death). For these, a simple cremation container may be used. A heavyweight cardboard box is sufficient to ensure dignified handling of the body. There are a variety of online sites that will ship caskets within forty-eight hours and offer prices that are 40 to 50 percent less than funeral home pricing. By law, funeral homes cannot refuse to use products purchased from outside sources. The Federal Trade Commission recommends that caskets not be purchased too far in advance because of problems that occur when companies go out of business or styles/lines are discontinued. If your parent wishes to prefund his funeral and the price includes a casket, read the contract carefully and preferably include a picture of the selected model. For online resources, refer to chapter 24.

Veteran's Burial

Veterans have the option of burial at sea or in a national cemetery, on a space-available basis. The veteran's wife and dependent children are also eligible for this benefit even if they predecease the veteran. The veteran's benefit includes the space, a grave liner, a headstone or marker, opening and closing fees, and perpetual maintenance. Benefits change periodically. For the most current information and more details, call the Veteran's Administration at 800-827-1000 or go online at www.va.gov or www.cem.va.gov.

Mausoleum/Above-Ground Burial

The mausoleum offers a variety of structures for above-ground burial. They may be quite ornate and famous like the Taj Mahal or a simple wall beside a scenic lake. Urns rest in spaces called niches or columaria. The location of these spaces is one determinant of the cost. Most people consider these to be very expensive spaces, and they can be. However, when compared to the full price of in-ground burial, mausoleums may offer a cost-effective option. For online resources, refer to chapter 24.

Cremation

Cremation is an increasingly popular option, though it is still not an accepted practice in some ethnic and religious groups. Cremation does not require a casket, though you may use one if you wish. To ensure dignified handling of the body, you may choose a heavyweight cardboard box. You may have both cremation and a traditional funeral service by renting a casket (ask the funeral home for information on this option) to hold the cremation container during the funeral service. Cremation urns are substantially less expensive than caskets and are readily available online at significantly discounted prices.

If you are planning to ship your parent's remains from where he died to another location, it is far less costly to do so with ashes than with a body. In this situation, you can have the cremation in one location and a memorial service somewhere else.

Seniors facing a Medicaid spend-down should check with an elder law attorney regarding setting aside funds to pay for funeral arrangements.[19]

Another option for a wide range of assistance and education regarding funeral issues is a memorial society. In many communities these groups have negotiated contracts with local funeral homes, cemeteries, and crematoriums to allow members substantial discounts on services and products. For more information, visit the Funeral Consumers Alliance Web site at www.funerals.org.[20]

While funerals are emotional experiences to mourners, they are profit-producing services to others. Unfortunately, not all service providers are ethical. If you feel you were treated unfairly, you may have grounds to file a complaint with the Funeral Consumers Alliance Ombudsman. E-mail the details of your story to ombudsman@funerals.org.

G. GRIEF AND MOURNING

"My father was inconsolable. He tried to throw himself into the grave. He and Mom had been together for over fifty years, and he always expected to die first. He just couldn't imagine life without her. After the funeral, he kept on talking to her, right out loud, as though she was still here. He always finished his conversations with 'I'll see you soon, sweetheart.' He died peacefully in his sleep six months later. It reminded me of the stories I told my kids when they were little. You know, the ones that went 'wish it hard enough and it will happen.' It's the first time I've ever considered 'wishing to die' as a good thing. It was very hard losing him so soon after Mom died, but I knew he wanted to go. I like to think they're together again. This may sound like a strange thing to say about the recent death of a father I loved very much, but I'm happy for him."

Sandra, Maine

"Even my husband didn't understand. I just went back to work as if nothing had happened. They couldn't understand that as far as I was concerned, when my mother died, it meant nothing to me. I hadn't felt anything at all for her when she was alive. Nothing changed when she died."

Joanne, New York

"My mother was diagnosed with Alzheimer's twelve years before she died. Fortunately, for her, she finally got pneumonia and escaped from her demented life. I arranged the funeral my family expected, sat dry-eyed through the service, and wandered through my house in a daze when people came to call. I finally drove over to a seawall on the bay and sat by the water by myself. I didn't think or cry; I just sat peacefully. I felt guilty as hell, but the truth was, the woman I knew as my mother died years ago as Alzheimer's ate her soul away. I cried then. Oceans of tears. I felt bad, and I was glad my father wasn't here to see the state she was in when she died, but tears? I cried myself out years ago."

Patrice, Maine

When a parent has had a long-term serious illness with a poor prognosis, grief and mourning often begin before she dies. You may continue to fight the illness until the very last moment of your parent's life. But as your parent becomes progressively sicker, you begin to process the conscious thought that she might die. When she does, your reaction at the time of death may be very different because you have had time to mentally and emotionally adjust to the concept of her death. You may feel sad, you may cry, but the shock you experience may be significantly less than if her death had been sudden or accidental. It would be perfectly normal for you to also feel relieved because you realize that your parent is no longer suffering or because the strain of caring for a dying parent is over.

"I savor my freedom now. I have great empathy for those with multiple living parents."

Dana, Colorado

If your parent dies suddenly, your emotions may suffer a huge traumatic blow. In this situation, there is often so much to think about and so many added responsibilities between the time your parent dies and the funeral that it's not unusual to begin your actual mourning after the funeral or memorial service. Reality begins to take over when everyone has gone home and you're left in the quiet alone or with your newly widowed parent. What can you do to help your parent and yourself adapt to your new situation?

- Allow yourselves to grieve. Allow your surviving parent and yourself to be emotional. Death is a shock, and it takes more than a funeral or memorial service to feel "normal" again. Your parents may have been together for forty or fifty years. Your mother may feel empty; either of you may accidentally call your deceased father's name. You may feel the need to walk or sit in a park, or you may have a desire to hear music and dance or sing. All of those feelings are acceptable. If you work, don't feel the need to prove how strong you are by returning to work immediately.
- Talk about your deceased parent.

> "My father died four years ago. As far as I know, my sister does not talk about him. Ever. I know she loved him, so I asked her why she refused to discuss old times with us. She explained that if she did, she would have to talk about him in the 'past tense'—like he was dead—and she just couldn't bring herself to do that. I didn't know what to say."
>
> *Jane, Georgia*

Not talking about your deceased father will not bring him back to life. Look at old pictures and talk, tell funny stories, and remember the times you enjoyed together. You and your mother may remember your father differently, as he was twenty years ago or last week. That is your choice. Talking is a cathartic experience. It sometimes cleanses the mind and the soul.

- Remember to take care of yourself and your mother physically as well as emotionally. Because you and your mother have suffered a traumatic shock, you may lose some of your focus or concentration. You may lose your appetite or feel listless and fatigued. Try to eat nourishing foods and get enough rest.

- Allow your friends and neighbors to be kind to you. They may bring flowers or meals to your house. Some may want to just come and sit with you so that you don't feel so alone. Let them. But don't feel obligated to entertain them, talk to them, or serve them snacks or refreshments. They are there to help you.

If you truly aren't ready to have friends visit, tell them so. Thank your friends and neighbors, and ask them to return in a few days. Tell them you feel the need for some time alone. Taking this time to contemplate your loss may help you over the initial void. You can devote this time to feeling deeply and to grieving freely.

Saying Good-Bye

If a parent is so ill and frail that you both know her time is short, saying good-bye can be heartbreaking. Speaking from your heart can help alleviate some of your pain. If you love your parent but have been uncomfortable expressing your love, do it now. Just say, *"I love you, Mom."* If your parent can no longer speak, you can help yourself and relieve and comfort her by speaking for her, *"Don't worry, Mom. I know you love me."* If your children need to say good-bye, let them express their love. Respond to them and be the voice of your parent if she cannot answer.

If both of you or either of you have something to forgive, this is a good time to voice your forgiveness. Again, if your parent is unable to talk, help her leave peacefully and yourself live peacefully by gently saying, *"It's okay, Mom. I know you forgive me and we both know how much we love each other."* Family members often expect their parents to pass away immediately upon saying their good-byes, but your parent may linger for one or several days more. You may repeat your loving statements again and again. Love is the feeling that is impossible to show too often.

> "I don't know how long it actually took me to get over my parents' deaths. My husband said, 'Jan, it's been months. Snap out of it! You're a grown woman.' It's just that I'm an only child, and

when my last parent died, there was no one left to talk to me about when I was young. No one was left who knew my history as a person. It's as if a whole part of my identity disappeared. How long does it take to get over that kind of loss?"

Jan, Vermont

There comes a time when you must say good-bye to your grief and return to your normal life activities. This doesn't mean that you should try to "forget" your parent. It doesn't mean to never feel sad about his death. It simply means that it's time to remember that all those who are born must die. It is a natural end to life. You can continue to honor the memory of your parent by living every moment of your life to its utmost advantage. Everyone feels the death of another person differently, and each of us separates from this feeling differently. If you or another family member had a truly negative relationship with your parent and you feel no grief, it is no one's business but your own. You are entitled to any and all of the feelings you have. However, if you find you cannot leave your tears and sorrowful feelings behind after several weeks or months, it's probably time to ask for help.

"My father's been dead for over thirty years, and I still cry when I think about him. It still hurts me. I loved him so much. I still miss him, but it's more than that. Maybe it's the way he died. He had been such a proud man. Always totally self-sufficient, helping out others in our family who didn't do as well in life. At the end, he was a shell of his former self. He couldn't even scratch his own nose—he had to ask someone to do it for him. That's worth crying about, don't you think? Maybe I'm crying for the way things could have been. Or should have been. Maybe I feel guilty because I didn't do more. Maybe I'm afraid I'll die like that. Maybe it's all of those reasons jumbled into one. I don't know. I'll probably never make my peace with it."

Janet, Alabama

"We were stunned when my brother-in-law died of a heart attack at thirty-eight. When my father-in-law died of a massive heart attack, I began to be afraid. I could hardly breathe at the wake. Would my husband be next? I never stop worrying, but it's really bad when someone dies. Then I can actually taste the fear in my mouth."

Sally, Alabama

A grief counselor won't ask you to forget memories and feelings that you cherish. She may help ease your pain by helping you understand and learn to cope with the feelings that trouble you. You may learn how to use your memories to make you stronger and enjoy a warmer relationship with your family and friends. You have the option of group counseling or individual counseling. You may find a bereavement group you can join at your local hospital or the local organization that represents the disease your parent died from, or ask your physician for a referral to a private counselor. Making yourself feel whole again is the best way to remember your parent.

H. WHAT IS POST-TRAUMATIC CAREGIVER SYNDROME?

Dear Readers: You won't find PTCS in the medical books because, although the condition has existed for decades, the authors created the name specifically for this edition of *Eldercare 911*. It is our sincere hope that society's eldercare focus will soon broaden to include much needed care and assistance for family caregivers.

"I'm doing a lousy job at work. I may have a few good days and then I think that I'm okay again, but it doesn't last long. I go right back to remembering Dad's last few months and his suffering. Mostly what I remember is how helpless I felt. Then I start yelling at someone or something and I feel like I'm out of control. I've got to stop this or I'll lose my wife and my job."

Bernie, Indiana

"This is the first time in the last eight years I haven't been a caregiver. It's hard to describe if you haven't been there, but picture the CEO of a large company that's going down the tubes. To keep my company, aka 'Mom' running, I dealt with insurance, day care, homecare, doctors, physical therapists, medications, nutrition, moving Mom to a nursing home, making sure they paid attention to her, sorting through her stuff and deciding what to give to whom. Can you understand the physical and mental chaos I went through? Then she died and bingo, the past eight years of constant response to her needs abruptly ended. In the blink of an eye chaos dissolved into nothingness."

Beverly, New Jersey

If you spent several years caring for your parent, chances are your life changed dramatically during that time. Prior to becoming a caregiver you may have spent many hours of enjoyable time with family or close friends, on volunteer work or hobbies, traveling, working at your career —staying involved in work or pastimes that brought pleasure. As your parent's condition worsened and his needs increased, it is likely you had fewer and fewer hours left for personal enjoyment. Eventually, caring for him may have devoured most or all of your free physical time and created a great deal of emotional stress. Post-traumatic Caregiver Syndrome (PTCS) is a way of describing the aftermath of the years you spent carrying the heavy burden of caregiver responsibility.

If your parent has passed away, you may find yourself in an emotional or physical void. You can also expect those feelings if your parent depended on you and you are suddenly freed from multiple responsibilities. Or, you may finally be able to give in to the exhaustion that built up during your years of carrying the caregiving burden. If you've spent months with the understanding that death is imminent, anticipatory grief may take over your emotions. Later, when your parent dies, you may be astonished to find that your most dominant feeling is relief. These emotions are an expected aftermath of a significant loss. Grief is our natural way of coping with the trauma of losing someone we love. We all grieve differently, but most of us find healthy ways to let our sorrow and pain out, and we learn to cope with our loss without professional help.

Post-traumatic Caregiver Syndrome (PTCS) is a serious form of burnout that prevents us from appropriately discharging and disengaging from our sorrow and pain. We continue to feel strong negative emotions without relief.

Instead of helping us find coping mechanisms so that we can return to enjoyable activities, this syndrome may feed on itself and intensify, increasing our distress. Perhaps you lack the energy or desire to leave your home or get out of bed. You may begin projects and abandon them. You may be unable to focus, suffer headaches or stomach upsets, cry frequently, sleep too many or two few hours, drink too much, or feel an overall strong and persistent sadness or loss or grief. When this happens your immune system may not function up to par and you may find yourself visiting doctors for any number of ailments you don't remember having prior to your parent passing away or entering a nursing home. You are suffering trauma that "post-dates" your caregiving tenure.

> "Go back to what life? For ten years, all I've been or done involved caregiving—if I'm not a caregiver anymore, who am I? Where should I go? And when I get there, what am I supposed to do? The only place I want to go is back to bed or to the kitchen for a glass of bourbon."
>
> *Bernice, Kentucky*

Caregivers suffering from PTCS may no longer be able to martial the pre-caregiving physical and emotional resources we all depend on for mental health. They find it difficult, sometimes impossible, to fend off negative thoughts such as guilt and failure.

> "It's been four years since my father died. I tried my best to keep him alive, but I couldn't. Not only that, I borrowed money on the house to get him the care he needs, so I'm broke, too. I failed on every level."
>
> *Pam, Arkansas*

If your after-loss trauma persists over a long period of time, it's critical to seek treatment. Left unidentified and unresolved, PTCS may increase your pain and sadness and cause you physical and psychological damage for years.

> "I spent seven years as Mom's full-time caregiver. I did everything for her. I even cradled her in my arms and sang to her when she couldn't sleep. I haven't slept more than three or four hours a night since the night I lost her. I can't maintain focus or make a decision. I have a hard time holding on to my job. Even the little decisions are huge almost impassable obstacles for me, like whether to leave at 10 AM or 10:15 AM. I'll never have a husband or kids. I never want to care for anyone again and it would be too painful if one of them died. I don't even want the responsibility of feeding a dog."
>
> *Angie, Tennessee*

Many caregivers tell us they had to try more than one therapist before finding the "right fit." That's time consuming and emotionally upsetting under the best of circumstances, but Post-traumatic Care Syndrome multiplies the degree of difficulty. As hard as it may be for you to begin again, don't give up. Open, honest, communication with your therapist is one of the most important keys to wellness. Unless she knows what you're thinking or feeling, she can't reach you emotionally to provide the support and guidance that will help you. If you aren't connecting with her, if you're uncomfortable with the relationship, it's unlikely you'll be completely open or honest about your feelings and thoughts.

If you're too tired or have given up, try to take one more step and ask your physician or a friend for assistance finding the help you need. Jared's story shares the benefits of forcing yourself to take that next step and keep trying:

> "I was in the fourth grade when Pop was diagnosed with multiple sclerosis and eighth grade when Mom was diagnosed with Alzheimer's. Kids don't understand 'illness'; they're just afraid their parents might leave them forever and they'll be left alone with no one to love them and no way to survive. I can't remember too many days over the age of nine without a caregiving task, and each one was a graphic reminder that I should be scared as hell. And I was. There was no close aunt or uncle, no one at all who said 'don't worry, sweetheart, we'll all be fine' or reassured me in any

way. So I survived by burying it all somewhere in my head and then burying my head in books. Social relationships were too scary. At sixty-five, I had three failed therapist relationships behind me and no intention of wasting my money on a fourth one. Thank God a friend convinced me to try her therapist, Joan. Thank God. She's the first person who truly understood and respected my feelings of love, resentment, and failure while I cared for my parents, but also why my life's been in turmoil for the decades since they died. She helps me understand how my past impacts my actions today. You can't ever 'forget it,' you have to learn how to acknowledge your pain and finally deal with your emotions. Then you can get well and have the life you want."

Start by explaining your feelings to your physician and asking for a referral to a qualified therapist or grief counselor. A professional will help you examine your emotions and provide you with the emotional coping skills you need to make the adjustment from caregiver back to mom, dad, boyfriend, girlfriend, career-building professional, or someone's friend.

Now that you can take the time to care for yourself, give yourself the opportunity to heal and regain your strength. It's one of the most life-giving, worthwhile journeys you can make.

I. A NEW BEGINNING

"When my mother died, my entire family had to regroup and start from scratch. She always kept us in touch with each other on a weekly basis. She actually called us all and carried the news from one to the other. We all gathered at her and Dad's house for major holidays. She was in charge of most family traditions. I always had a sneaking suspicion that those traditions really weren't very 'old' at all. I think she started most of them. It was her way of keeping us all close together. I took over most of the traditions and dinners. I never dreamed how much work she put into it. But I want to keep them going for my children. Like I told my dad and brothers, we're still a family."

Sandy, Nebraska

"My mother is eighty-eight. She's in relatively good health and could probably enjoy a reasonably good life. As far as I can see, she has no joy in her life at all. My father died decades ago. She has been married two more times, and she's survived both of those men. My brother died of a heart attack when he was sixty-six. I think the death of my brother finally broke her spirit. She flatly refuses anything I suggest to help her heal. She just keeps repeating all the things she 'shoulda' done, 'woulda' done, or 'coulda' done for all the people she's lost. Like their deaths are her punishments for not 'being' enough or 'doing' enough for them. It hurts me terribly to hear her keep reliving the past. She's missed so many years of what could have been a good life."

Julie, New York

"If you could've seen my eighty-two-year-old father learning to use a washing machine and a vacuum cleaner for the first time, you wouldn't have known whether to laugh or cry. I did both. I nearly split my sides. Then I got all teary-eyed. What a champ he is. Definitely my hero."

Ricki, New Jersey

"It took my father two years to go out with anyone but the family. It took him one year to start playing cards again. Beginning his new life was hard for him. His friends never waited that long after their spouses died, but he missed my mother so much. I don't know what happened. I guess time and reality finally took care of it. Maybe he just was too lonely to continue. He's a survivor. It took him a long time to begin his new life, but he did it. He still talks about Mother, but I think he's almost happy again."

Margaret, Ohio

There are many "new beginnings" when a parent dies. You may become the oldest person in the family or the only person in your family. You may take over family traditions, or you may start new ones. Whatever it takes, you and your parent have probably already proven many times in your life that you can stand up to great challenges. New beginnings can be difficult. If your new responsibilities hurt for a while, let them. If they bring tears to your eyes when you remember why you have them, cry. Suffering the loss of a beloved parent is a good reason to cry. When you feel good about something, enjoy it to the utmost. Take the time to celebrate. If you are still a caregiver for a parent, and he needs you, try to help. If you can, make it your goal to help him help himself to be more independent.

J. REMEMBERING TO CARE FOR YOURSELF

Personal needs are often forgotten when traumatic events enter a caregiver's already often chaotic life. When we've spent so much time and energy caring for others, we often get into the habit of ignoring our own needs. As difficult as it may seem, tending to your mind and body's health is actually one of the most important coping strategies you can use to help you manage during the first week and for emotional and physical healing for the months that follow.

This list will give you ideas for basic physical and mental coping techniques.

1. Some future thoughts and planning are necessary and natural. Initially, try to focus on one day at a time until your thoughts include a future with some joy in it.
2. Make a list of what "must" be done and stick to that list. If you can't accomplish what "must" be done, ask a family member, clergy, friend, or neighbor for help.
3. Surround yourself with comforting people you can talk to or be silent with. Avoid toxic people; ask a friend, relative, or clergy to manage them.
4. Avoid too much alcohol or junk food. Eat nutritious foods that can keep your body fueled and up to the tasks you face.
5. Drink water. It's essential to stay hydrated during periods of extreme stress.
6. Do not take medications that mask pain or stress without a physician's supervision.

7. Keep as much normalcy in your life as possible. Try taking your kids to school, playing golf, whatever it is that nurtures you.
8. If you regularly work out, continue your routine to stay physically and emotionally strong.
9. If you don't regularly exercise, try taking walks. Exercise helps improve our emotional outlook, which leads to better coping skills and other positive actions.
10. Talk to friends or join a group of peers who have experienced the loss of a parent. Sharing your feelings in a supportive environment can help lessen your pain.

Most of all, try to have as high a regard for your own courage or for your parent's courage as you do for others who surmount difficult obstacles. Look around. Look back. Look to your future. You have earned your own respect. Give it freely and accept it with a knowing smile. You understand "new beginnings," and you are in control.

K. WORKSHEET: HONORING MY PARENT'S WISHES

Use this worksheet to help you determine what your parent's wishes are for end-of-life treatment. Obtaining this information now may help ease your burden later.

1. My parent ❑ has a living will ❑ needs a living will.

Date of will: _____ Location of will: _____

People with copies: _____

To do: _____

2. My parent ❑ has a durable power of attorney (DPOA) ❑ needs a durable power of attorney.

Healthcare agent's name: _____

Address: _____

Telephone number: _____

Date of DPOA: _____ Location of DPOA: _____

People with copies: _____

To do: _____

3. My parent wants:

❑ palliative care only, under the circumstances as described in his living will.

❑ curative medical treatment regardless of circumstances.

4. My parent wants:

❑ an in-ground burial in a cemetery he/she has chosen.

❑ his/her ashes to be placed in a pre-selected above-ground mausoleum.

❑ cremation with ashes scattered at _____.

5. My parent ❑ has (❑ has not) purchased a burial plot.

6. My parent ❑ has (❑ has not) purchased a ❑ casket and/or ❑ cremation urn.

Cemetery name: _____

Address: _____

Plot location and I.D. number: _____

Location of contracts/purchase agreements: _____

To do: _____

7. Review this chapter for additional information on honoring your parent's wishes.

L. MY JOURNAL

Expressing our thoughts on paper often helps us see our feelings more clearly and that makes it easier to arrive at solutions to our problems. What bothers you? What changes do you want to make? What or who are you grateful for? When you read what you've written, you may see a new pathway to help resolve stressful issues. Use this page as a safe place to express your feelings. For example:

"Dad's been driving me nuts since Mom died. It's gotten so bad I can hardly stand to be around him and that makes me feel so guilty. Something's gotta' give before I say something I won't be able to take back. I always think I can handle anything. I never thought about it until I wrote this, but I guess this is outside my capabilities. I'll call hospice to ask about counseling tomorrow. Maybe we both need help?"

"My house is full of people 'celebrating' my mother's life. I haven't gotten to that point yet. I'm still crying because of her death. I'm glad so many people cared for her, but I need to be alone right now and remember her in my life, not in theirs. I'll ask my cousin to explain. Then I think I'll start writing down my memories so they'll stay fresh with details for my kids when they're older."

_____

_____

_____

_____

_____

_____

_____

_____

_____

_____
_____
_____
_____
_____
_____
_____
_____
_____
_____
_____
_____
_____
_____
_____
_____
_____
_____

M. TIP SHEET

- Each person grieves differently. Don't expect other family members to grieve the same way you do.
- Don't say, "I know how you feel." You can't know how the person feels unless you have actually experienced the same loss.
- Help yourself manage your feelings and fears by talking with a friend, relative, or counselor.
- Practice Active Listening with your parent to help you understand his feelings and fears.
- Use the "Honoring My Parent's Wishes" worksheet to compile funeral wishes and documents before your parent becomes ill.
- Ask a friend or family member for help with funeral or other arrangements.
- Use the "My Journal" worksheet to help manage grief and other feelings.

23

CAREGIVER VOICES

*B*elieve in yourself. You already have the strength and courage you
need.

You are not alone.

Caregivers face unique emotional and physical challenges that can
often escalate to life-altering levels. To add to their burdens, society and
circumstances frequently relegate caregivers to facing their problems
alone.

Where do caregivers find the inner resources to help them conquer
their fears? Can we learn to manage the resentment we sometimes feel
due to adjustments and frustrations that caregiving has imposed on our
lives?

How do we open our hearts to friends or family for emotional support
or practical help? Where can we go to find the confidence to be successful
in caregiving and in life in general?

Renew your strength and draw peace from these caregiver voices. Let
their experiences help lighten your heart as you face the day. Use their
wisdom to calm your fears during a difficult night.

No one knows more about creating pathways for the caregiver

journey than those who have found peace of mind as they traveled this arduous road.

A. ABOUT COMFORT

You brought hope when your family forgot how to hope. You found moments of joy for them when they could not find their own. Now, other caregivers offer their voices to comfort you.

"Living with someone who has Alzheimer's can really wipe the smile from your face. Somehow, reminding myself that before I became a caregiver for my mother, there used to be joy and wonder in most of my days helped me recognize that if I tried really hard, I might still find them. When I did, I was so happy to find a personal moment of inner joy that I kept it to myself. Then one day I began to share: 'Listen, Mom, a bird is singing to you' or, 'Look how cute that kitten is, Mom.' The happiness in her eyes intensified my pleasure and our shared experiences of 'joy and wonder' became a daily event. Don't get me wrong; we had plenty of bad days. After all, she still had Alzheimer's. But every night when I remembered that day's joy and wonder, I felt comforted and felt the peace it brought me during the day wash over me all over again. Mom's been gone for over a year, but I've made it a habit to continue looking for joy and wonder in the day. Not only do I enjoy my day more, but it helps me remember her differently than I might have if we hadn't shared those experiences."

Natalie, California

"I've been caring for my mother for years and always felt inadequate as a caregiver. Mostly I felt guilty because I thought I should spend more time with her, but with two young kids and my job, there was just no way to do that on a regular basis. Recently the nurse in mom's doctor's office touched my arm and said, 'She's so lucky to have you.' I was stunned, 'Me?' She kept her hand on my arm and smiled. 'You have no idea what a difference you've made. Without you advocating for her, she would never have the quality of life she has now. Give yourself some credit.' She was the first person who ever said anything like that to me. I know this sounds silly, but her acknowledgment made a huge difference—she changed how I see myself as a caregiver and a son. That took some of the emotional burden off my back. We really ought to have a 'tell a caregiver he's terrific' day."

Larry, Florida

How important it is to listen to your inner voice when it reminds you that comforting the person you care for is only one part of the caregiving process. You too need reassurance and support. Very often the comfort we need is available if we seek it out and open ourselves to accepting it. Be open with those around you and allow them to help.

B. ABOUT STRENGTH

Eldercare 911 salutes the power of *your* power. Your personal force and creativity is evident in everything you do. Your willingness to continually dedicate your strength to those who need you has forever changed your life and the lives of those you love.

"I found my strength in the same type of water wings that helped me stay afloat when I was a child. When I didn't think I could take another minute of arguing with doctors or insurance companies, or watching mom fade from a diagnosis called 'failure to thrive,' I went to the store and bought two pair of water wings in the largest sizes I could find. I put mom's arm through one side and told her to stay afloat. I struggled into the other pair and we ate dinner wearing those water wings night after night, laughing at ourselves. Until those water wings, we had pretty much stopped laughing. A few weeks later, mom started feeling stronger. Since the doctors never knew what was wrong with her, it was no surprise that they had no idea why she recovered. Mom and I know. For us, 'failure to thrive' means reaching a point when you can't stay afloat any longer without someone and something to hold you up."

Suzanne, Indiana

"When I was tired, exhausted, emotionally drained, I tried to remember to take a deep breath and suck it up, because you know what? No matter how bad it got for me, and sometimes my situation felt pretty bleak, I had to remind myself that it was a bazillion times worse for Mom. I am so glad I made myself continue, because now, years later, I realize I got a lot out of caring for Mom. It was hard to see it that way then, but looking back, I see how close we were. It was definitely a two-way service we provided for each other. Recognizing that doesn't erase all the trauma, but it does helps me manage my feelings about giving up a relationship and the loss of opportunities for advancement in my career during all those years."

Mike, Wyoming

We may find the strength we need within our thoughts or in an unusual form from an outside source. The hardest yet most basic part of the search for the resources that we require is to acknowledge their presence when we find them. Keep your heart and your mind open. Think about your capacity to provide care, then seek out the help you need to feel strong.

C. ABOUT COURAGE

You exhibit courage unparalleled in its abiding ability to change the lives of those you care for. Wherever you go, whatever you do, you will have the spirit and determination to follow your life's path.

"It took sixty-three years, but I finally got it: I've always thought that success in life meant being happy all the time. Not only was that naive, it may also have been the ultimate denial. Being a caregiver for both my mother and my father taught me that we can plan and shape our lives to some degree, but it will always be more like a series of small journeys and no two journeys can ever be exactly the same. Some are wonderful, others not. Caregiving is like that. You never know what the day will bring—happiness, anger, fear, love. Yet we just keep going and that's the beauty of the journey. The part I finally got is this: for me, the sweetest journey of all is knowing that I have the inner strength to dig deep and find the courage I need to keep trying."

Joan, Colorado

"People who are successful will tell you they are successful in part because they feel successful. For me, feeling successful is a good part of what it takes to *stay* a caregiver for years and years. We all need the 'outside support' of people we trust telling us we're doing a good job, but to feel successful I think we also need our own 'inner support' system. Your head has to get in the game. 'Inner support' is something you have to feel or do for yourself by creating an inner dialogue. I think the dialogue needs to say, 'You're good, you've done well; now take the time you need to appreciate and care for yourself.' Or even something stronger: Whatever the mantra is that works for you. Everyone is different and this is very individual, but the result is the same: the dialogue you need is the one that makes you feel like you're doing a good job. When I'm finished listening to my inner dialogue, I feel more confident and I'm more productive, like the successful people I mentioned at the beginning."

Ellen, New York

It takes a special kind of courage to wear a caregiver's shoes, but once you've worn them, you need never again doubt your ability to take on a challenge and succeed. Never fear a test of your commitment or strength. Take time every day to acknowledge and appreciate your accomplishments. You've done well.

D. ABOUT FRIENDSHIP

Sharing our feelings with friends who open their hearts can change the nature of our caregiving experience. We are happier and healthier when we reveal and celebrate our joy and sorrow with those we care about.

"There are four of us, all women who have been friends for decades. We've always gone to dinner, yakked on the phone for hours, taken care of each other without reservations. It's the kind of friendship where you can always tell the truth or just sit and not talk (like that ever happened!). We never worried about judgments or embarrassment or anyone telling our secrets. One day Sheila showed up at my house wheeling in a luggage carrier with a cardboard box. She was furious, really burning mad. She said, 'Here, take this, we cooked enough food for a week. Unfortunately, we also drank wine while we cooked so we're not sure what this stuff tastes like. None of us knew what else to do at this point.' She got louder and louder until she was literally yelling at me. 'You know, you don't *HAVE* to do this *ALONE*. You think you're superhuman, but the truth is you look like hell, you have no sense of humor left, have no time for us, and you still won't talk to us or let us help. When did you become a moron? When did we become untrustworthy? *WHAT IS YOUR DAMN PROBLEM?!*' By that time I was crying. Then Mom yelled, 'The TV is too loud! I can hear them yelling all the way in here!' and we both started laughing. All I could do was hug her and say, 'I love you.'"

Lynne, Ohio

"My father was in a nursing home and I had sole responsibility for him. I lived more than thirty miles from the home and worked ten-hour days. He was physically failing, but still had all his mental capacity. He looked forward to the evenings that I visited so I tried to go on the same nights during the week and not skip a visit. One night the combined stresses of caregiving and career finally got to me and I had an emotional meltdown. I just couldn't visit him and I was wracked with guilt. My brother and sister lived in other parts of the country so I was his only visitor. My best friend offered, 'I'll go see him for you.' She had never even met him but that didn't concern her. She saw that we both needed help and she stepped in. She went that time and once again when I had the flu. My father enjoyed having a new visitor and I experienced another dimension to what friendship means. His last years were a very difficult time for him and for me, but my friend's capacity for kindness made me feel less alone. Ultimately, I shared my feelings with other friends. That was a turning point for me. I'm still a very private person, but whenever I don't want to be bothered getting involved in someone's problems, I remember how much her being there meant to me and my father, and I reconsider offering help."

Kathy, Georgia

When you're caught up in caring for a parent, it's easy to feel that you're too busy to continue social relationships. No matter how full your day is you do not have to live your caregiving life in solitude. In fact, the most effective caregivers share their joys and sorrows with others. The healthcare and insurance systems are too multifaceted to tackle them alone. The emotional and physical needs of other family members are so time-consuming and the demands of our jobs so enormous that in most cases the only way caregivers can maintain their quality of life is to be open about their situation and accept help. Try it. Choose a friend or family member and talk about your caregiving life. Keep trying until you find the right person. You'll know her/him because the right person's compassion and ability to listen will help lift your spirits and allow you to once again enjoy other facets of your life.

E. ABOUT HOPE

You continue to dig into your heart and soul to bring forth the promise of tomorrow, even during the most painful times. You help others understand that life and hope are inextricably intertwined.

"I think all caregivers feel hopeless from time to time, but losing hope was the worst trial I faced when I was caring for my dad. I can't believe I'm saying this to you but feeling hopeless may have been more painful than Dad dying. Can you imagine how awful it feels to lose your ability to smile? At the time I thought it very unfair that no matter how disheartened I felt, my career and caregiving responsibilities remained the same. But now I know that hope is connected to the broader world. When I lost my connection to others—friends and strangers—I was so insulated that my problems seemed larger and more insurmountable. Interacting with people gave my mind a break. I call it respite for my mind and I use it all the time. Whether I talk to someone about what's bothering me or just take a mental break from the hassle and forget about it for a few hours, I always feel better. Life is tough for caregivers, but it's important to not let the problems break your spirit. For me, that meant learning to accept that when my problems couldn't be resolved the way I hoped, I had to face the bad news and transfer my hope to other things in my life that I can look forward to."

Francine, New Mexico

"When I was a kid, my father used to tell me to stop hoping for things that I couldn't have. He'd say, stop wishing for 'what isn't' and pay attention to what is.' I always answered, 'yes, sir,' but I never stopped because I always thought he was wrong. I'm seventy-eight and I've been a caregiver for many years, first for my parents and now for my husband. You learn a lot about your life when you care for your loved ones. The most important lesson I learned is that there is more to being a caregiver than dealing with practical matters. You have to tend to your dreams, no matter how far off they seem. Otherwise you take the chance of losing your capacity to hope. How can you live a good life if you have no hope for your future?"

Donna, Illinois

What *is* is this: we can't live a good life unless we acknowledge and respect our practical needs and the reality that surrounds us. *Hope* is a crucial component of our reality and our practical needs. It is vitally important for our physical and mental health to understand that *hope* is essential to life. How often have you hoped for sunny weather? For a hole in one? To find just the right outfit for a special evening? Hoped for a friend's recovery? Whether your wish is simple or complex, your hopeful thoughts acknowledge that you expect to have a future and you believe in the potential for a better tomorrow.

F. ABOUT FEAR

Despite your fears and sadness, your understanding and acceptance of the needs of those you love helps them to face their own uncertainties and challenges with dignity.

> "It's really challenging to tell the truth. I went about my life thinking, 'eighty-six is not that old.' Well, the truth is, it's old. There's a part of me that just wanted to think that my parents would be okay, but I've learned enough about aging to know they're going to have more and more needs. It's extremely difficult to bite into that reality sandwich and say, 'This is the last part of my parents' life and I want to be supportive and I want them to have the best quality of life that they can have. But at this point, they make the decisions. If their poor choices lead them to a place where they can't make good decisions, then I'll help but it's time to understand that there's a point at which you can't do any more.' I never knew how frightening and stressful it could be to just sit back and wait for problems rather than work to prevent them, but I've finally come to terms with reality. I sometimes wonder if they're as afraid as I am, but if they have the strength to go on trying to remain independent, the least I can do is look my own fears in the face and reflect some of their courage. One of the truths I had to acknowledge is that I will probably do exactly the same thing when I'm eighty-six."
>
> *Sandy, Colorado*

"Can you tell professionals that we're smart enough to recognize false hope and platitudes? When medical science runs of out options, we still have human methods that can help. My fears won't stop me from doing whatever I have to do, but there are times when this burden becomes so heavy that I would give anything just to borrow someone else's strength for few minutes. All it would take would be a few moments of conversation about my fears or the warmth of a hand or a steadying touch on my arm that I can carry with me and use to feel less frightened at night when I lie awake and wonder 'what's next?'"

Judy, Kentucky

"A month ago I was a vice president of my company, thoroughly enjoying my life and my climb up the corporate ladder. Then Mom had a stroke and I became a caregiver. In four short weeks I've become an 'expert' on strokes, rehab, specialists, physical therapy, the medical system, Medicare, Medicaid, long-term care, nursing homes, and her current and future financial needs. For God's sake, I'm a furniture designer! How do I know where she should live or what kind of care she should have? My nature is to accept the fear and slog through it—just put one foot in front of the other. I'm a tough city girl, but I have to tell you, I don't feel so tough now. I won't let her down. I mean, she needs me and I'll be there for her, but I'm terrified."

Pat, New York

No one goes through this experience without fear or sadness. When you become a caregiver, you enter unfamiliar territory and face an unknown future. You may be expected to manage medical care or know when and how much to intervene for your parent's safety. You may wonder how to divide your time or worry about your career. Your fear of the unknown is rational, as are your concerns about your career, managing your time, and overseeing your parent's healthcare and financial matters. If it seems impossible for you to handle all these issues, well, you're right. You can be a more effective caregiver by getting help from your spouse, a trusted relative, your children, a geriatric care manager, or other professionals. Adding more competent people to the caregiving mix can help lower your anxiety and increase the quality of life for your parent and for you. Make the call now.

G. ABOUT LOVE

If you are lucky enough to be a caregiver because of love instead of circumstance, take the time to nourish your relationship and cherish the special warmth you share with your parent.

> "People ask me, 'where did you get your enthusiasm, your zest for life?' The answer is always 'my father.' While he was teaching me how to fish and throw a ball, he also taught me to enjoy whatever I was doing. I didn't realize it, but my wife says he also made sure I knew how to use my heart. She calls it 'soft macho.' Mom died years ago, which left him alone. So when he became sick and started withering away, it was time for me to use my 'soft macho' and give him back some of the joy he gave me throughout my life. I took a leave of absence and moved in with him so I could be close to him. My brother and sister thought I was crazy, but I'm so much like him and I knew having family around him would ease his pain at least a little. His body became useless, but his mind was still sound, which meant he suffered even more, so the fact that I had come home to him made me glad. I didn't do much. I just read the paper to him and we watched TV together. One morning, we were watching television and laughing at a politician's remark. I looked at him and in that instant he closed his eyes and rested for good in the best way possible. I will always be grateful that I could help my father die the way he wanted to: with dignity, a smile on his lips, and someone who loved him at his side."
>
> *Antonio, Kansas*

> "It's such an odd experience being human—we're taught from childhood that we should be goody two-shoes and that's what

ends up hurting us. I was angry with Mom a few times and those moments haunted me even while I continued to care for her and for a long time after she died. I finally learned what she knew all along. Being human means experiencing all kinds of feelings, not just the pleasant ones. I know now that the thousand times I loved Mom far outweighed the few episodes of anger or impatience I showed her. I also know I was the only one who remembered those angry moments. They meant nothing to her. She never doubted my love."

Mike, Wyoming

This is your personal truth: Your gifts to others are bountiful: love, kindness, sympathy, and encouragement are only a few of the wonderful contributions you make on a daily basis. We applaud your courage and strength.

H. MY JOURNAL

Who gives you comfort? Strength? Courage? What are your hopes? Fears? What would you like to say to your friends? Who brings love into your life?

_____

_____

_____

_____

_____

_____

_____

_____

_____

_____

_____

24

CAREGIVER ORGANIZATIONS AND RESOURCES

T his resource section is divided alphabetically into ten specific categories: Caregiver and Senior Organizations; Elder Abuse; End of Life; Government Agencies; Healthcare; Housing; Medical and Disease-Related Organizations; Professional Organizations; Relaxation for Your Body and Mind; and Travel.

Most of these resources are relevant for professionals as well as caregivers. Look for your particular category of interest. If you don't find what you need under the first category, please check under another heading.

A. CAREGIVER AND SENIOR ORGANIZATIONS

The following Web sites provide caregivers and seniors with comprehensive up-to-date information, education, advocacy, and support.

AARP (American Association of Retired Persons)

www.aarp.org
888-687-2277 (888-OUR-AARP)
601 East Street, NW, A1-200
Washington, DC 20049

Alzheimer's Association

www.alz.org
800-272-3900
225 North Michigan Avenue, 17th Fl.
Chicago, IL 60601

Alzheimer's Society of Canada

Web site in English and French
www.alzheimer.ca
800-616-8816 (valid only in Canada)
416-488-8772
20 Eglinton Avenue West, Ste. 1200
Toronto, ON M4R 1K8

American Federation for Aging Research (AFAR)

www.infoaging.org
212-703-9977
55 West 39th Street, 16th Fl.
New York, NY 10018

American Health Assistance Foundation (AHAF)

www.ahaf.com
800-437-2423
301-948-3244
22512 Gateway Center Drive
Clarksburg, MD 20871

American Health Care Association (AHCA)

www.ahca.org
202-842-4444
1201 L Street, NW
Washington, DC 20005

Benefits Checkup

www.benefitscheckup.org
This National Council on the Aging Web site has a database of federal and
state assistance programs for the elderly. This site can help identify
benefits your parent is entitled to but may not have applied for.

Canadian Association of Retired Persons

www.fifty-plus.net
416-363-7063
Fifty-Plus Net International, Inc.
27 Queen Street. East, Ste. 300
Toronto, ON M5C 2M6

Children of Aging Parents (CAPS)

www.caps4caregivers.org
800-227-7294
P.O. Box 167
Richboro, PA 18954

Eldercarelink

www.eldercarelink.com
190 Front Street, Ste. 201
Ashland, MA 01721

Elderweb

www.elderweb.com
309-451-3319
1305 Chadwick Drive
Normal, IL 61761

Family Caregiver Alliance

www.caregiver.org
800-445-8106
415-434-3388
180 Montgomery Street, Ste. 1100
San Francisco, CA 94104

National Adult Day Services Association

www.nadsa.org
877-745-1440
85 South Washington, Ste. 316
Seattle, WA 98104

National Family Caregivers Association (NFCA)

www.NFCAcares.org
800-896-3650
301-942-6430
10400 Connecticut Avenue, Ste. 500
Kensington, MD 20895-3944

National Hipanic Council on Aging

Web site in English and Spanish
www.nhcoa.org
202-347-9733
734 15th Street, NW, Ste. 1050
Washington, DC 20005

National Hospice and Palliative Care Organization

www.hospicenet.org
800-658-8898
1700 Diagonal Road, Ste. 625
Alexandria, VA 22314

National Respite Network

www.respitelocator.org
919-490-5577
800 Eastowne Drive, Ste. 105
Chapel Hill, NC 27514

Partnership for Caring/National Hospice and Palliative Care Organization (NHPCO)

www.caringinfo.org
800-658-8898
1620 Eye Street, NW, Ste. 202
Washington, DC 20006

Rosalynn Carter Institute for Caregiving

www.rci.gsw.edu
229-928-1234
Georgia Southwestern State University
800 GSW Drive
Americus, GA 31709-4379

Senior Resource

www.seniorresource.com
4521 Campus Drive, #131
Irvine, CA 92612

Solutions for Better Aging (Eldercare Network)

www.agenet.com
866-414-4143
5976 Executive Drive
Madison, WI 53719
This Web site contains products, clothes, gifts and much more.

Well Spouse Foundation

www.wellspouse.org
800-838-0879
63 West Main Street, Ste. H
Freehold, NJ 07728

B. ELDER ABUSE

The National Center on Elder Abuse (NCEA)

www.ncea.aoa.gov
800-677-1116 Help hotline
302-831-3525
University of Delaware
297 Graham Hall
Newark, DE 19716
The National Center on Elder Abuse is an excellent resource for information about elder abuse, reporting options, the latest research, and resources.

C. END OF LIFE

Funeral Help Program

www.funeral-help.com
877-427-0220
1236 Ginger Crescent
Virginia Beach, VA 23453
The Funeral Help Program advises consumers of their options and rights. The Web site provides a wide range of resources for education, including books for download, articles, and information on professional funeral consultants.

Growth House, Inc.

www.growthhouse.org
415-863-3045
Growth House, Inc., offers resources for life-threatening illness and end-of-life care. The organization is dedicated to improving the quality of compassionate care for people who are dying. The site offers links to many helpful healthcare Web sites.

D. GOVERNMENT AGENCIES

Administration On Aging (AOA)

www.aoa.dhhs.gov
800-677-1116
202-619-0724
One Massachusetts Avenue, Stes. 4100 & 5100
Washington, DC 20201
The AOA is part of the US Department of Health and Human Services that provides a wide range of services and resources for the elderly and their family caregivers. In addition to their services, the AOA can direct you to the nearest Area Agency on Aging as well as many other

sources of state and local assistance. This Web site is available in several languages.

Administration for Children and Families

www.acf.dhhs.gov
370 L'Enfant Promenade, SW
Washington, DC 20201
The contact page on this Web site provides specific nationwide telephone numbers as well as regional offices throughout the United States.

Center for Medicare Advocacy

www.medicareadvocacy.org
860-456-7790
P.O. Box 350
Willimantic, CT 06226

Centers for Disease Control and Prevention (CDC)

www.cdc.gov
800-311-3435
404-498-1515
1600 Clifton Road
Atlanta, GA 30333

Centers for Medicare and Medicaid Services (CMS)

www.cms.hhs.gov
877-267-2323
7500 Security Boulevard
Baltimore, MD 21244
The Centers for Medicare and Medicaid Services is a comprehensive, user friendly Web site for consumers as well as professionals, providing up-to-date information on Medicare, Medicaid, and related programs.

Department of Veteran Affairs (VA)

www.va.gov
800-827-1000
800-273-8255 Talk Hotline
The Department of Veteran Affairs Web site provides information and programs for veterans who qualify. Benefits and services include, healthcare, pension, and burial. The national office can answer questions about qualifying for VA benefits and refer you to the VA nearest you.

Eldercare Locator (Administration on Aging/ US Department of Health and Human Services)

www.eldercare.gov
800-677-1116
The Eldercare Locator helps older adults and their caregivers find local services for seniors. The Web site provides an extensive glossary, caregiver resources, and referrals.

Healthfinder

Web site in English and Spanish
www.healthfinder.gov
P.O. Box 1133
Washington, DC 20013-1133
The Healthfinder is a federal Web site that includes a health library, containing healthcare information organized specifically by age for men, women, and children. The site provides information for caregivers and healthcare professionals on long-term care issues, insurance, and related topics.

Joint Commission

www.jcaho.org
630-792-5000
One Renaissance Boulevard
Oakbrook Terrace, IL 60181

The Joint Commission evaluates healthcare organizations throughout the United States in order to maintain quality care.

National Association of Area Agencies on Aging

www.n4a.org
202-872-0888
1730 Rhode Island Avenue, NW, Ste. 1200
Washington, DC 20036
The National Association of Area Agencies on Aging is the umbrella organization for all the local Area Agencies on Aging. The site provides important information on services for the elderly and advocacy, and supports the dignity of maintaining the elderly at home.

National Institute on Aging (NIA)

www.nih.gov/nia
301-496-1752
Building 31, Room 5C27
31 Center Drive, MSC 2292
Bethesda, MD 20892
The NIA is a federal government agency that funds and promotes research on life expectancy, age-related diseases, special problems, and needs of the aged, as well as other topics related to the well-being of older Americans.

National Institutes of Health (NIH)

Web site in English and Spanish
www.nih.gov
301-496-4000
9000 Rockville Pike
Bethesda, MD 20892
The NIH Web site offers consumers health information, a health database, free fact sheets, brochures, articles, and handbooks with timely information on health maintenance and illness prevention.

National Institutes of Health Senior Health

www.nihseniorhealth.gov
The Web site offers specific information on the cause, prevention, treatment, and research on a variety of illnesses that affect the elderly.

Social Security Online

Web site in English, Spanish, and other languages
www.ssa.gov
800-772-1213
Social Security Administration
Office of Public Inquiries
Windsor Park Building
6401 Security Boulevard
Baltimore, MD 21235
The Social Security Administration's Web site answers questions and provides full information on all aspects of benefits, including statement requests and applications for retirement, disability, and survivors benefits.

E. HEALTHCARE

American Health Assistance Foundation

www.ahaf.org
800-437-2423
22512 Gateway Center Drive
Clarksburg, MD 20871
The Web site provides timely information as well as the symptoms, treatments, causes, and cures pertaining to diseases and illnesses of the elderly.

The Arc of the US

www.thearc.org
800-433-5255
301-565-3842
1010 Wayne Avenue, Ste. 650
Silver Spring, MD 20910
The Web site contains information and resources for individuals with
   mental retardation and related disabilities.

Barton Medical Equipment

www.bartonmedical.com
877-8 BARTON
512-476-7199
5727 Highway 290 West, Ste. 103
Austin, TX 78735
Barton Medical Equipment specializes in innovative medical equipment
   to allow one person to securely and safely transfer patients. The site
   provides pictures of equipment and specific product details.

Center Watch Clinical Trials Listing Service

www.centerwatch.com
617-856-5900
22 Thomson Place, 47F1.
Boston, MA 02210-1212
Center Watch Clinical Trials Listing Service offers a wide range of information related to clinical trials and new drug therapies recently
   approved by the Federal Drug Administration. This information is
   offered for patients interested in participating in clinical trials.

Dr. Koop

www.drkoop.com
Dr. C. Everett Koop's Web site provides a wide range of information on
   physical and mental health, and fitness. The site also gives informa-

tion on complementary and alternative medicines and their potential interactions with traditional medications.

Enable Mart

www.enablemart.com
888-640-1999
360-695-4155 (Outside the US)
5353 South 960 East, Ste. 200
Salt Lake City, UT 84117
EnableMart provides assistive devices for hearing and vision impairments as well as mobility equipment and much more.

Familydoctor/American Academy of Family Physicians (AAFP)

Web site in English and Spanish
www.familydoctor.org
Familydoctor.org provides comprehensive healthcare information for all ages on many illnesses and conditions, including cancer, heart disease, asthma, allergies, stomach problems, and mental problems.

Link to Life

www.link-to-life.com
888-337-5433
297 North Street
Pittsfield, MA 01201
Link to Life's Web site provides Personal Emergency Response Services (PERS) to the sick and elderly. A PERS system provides emergency advice and help at home when needed. These services are available nationwide.

The Low Vision Center

www.thelowvisioncenter.com
800-658-3500 Extension 3303

2800 Third Street
Rapid City, SD 57701
The Web site provides a multitude of products for the visually impaired,
including watches, talking clocks, games, and magnifiers.

Mayo Clinic

www.mayohealth.org
The clinic's Web site includes a Healthy Aging Center that provides information on medical conditions, diet, exercise, stress reduction, risk
avoidance, and physical, mental, and emotional health. The site also
provides Mayo Clinic specialists to answer some of your specific
health inquiries at no charge. A free e-newsletter is available.

Maxi AIDS.com

www.maxiaids.com
800-522-6294
42 Executive Boulevard
Farmingdale, NY 11735
The Web site contains products for the hearing and vision impaired as
well as assistive devices for mobility, activities of daily living, technology, and more.

Medline Plus/A Service of the US National Library of Medicine and the National Institute of Health

Web site in English and Spanish
www.medlineplus.gov
8600 Rockville Pike
Bethesda, MD 20894
The Web site covers 740 topics on illness and wellness. The site includes
a medical encyclopedia and dictionary as well as many other important and timely resources.

Pharmaceutical Research and Manufacturers of America (PHRMA)

Web site in English and Spanish
www.helpingpatients.org
888-477-2669
Helping Patients.org is a free confidential Web site of PHRMA. The site assists patients in finding appropriate programs to acquire their specific medications.

WebMD

www.webmd.com
212-624-3700
111 Eighth Avenue, 7th Fl.
New York, NY 10011
The WebMD Web site is a comprehensive health resource for consumers, physicians, nurses, and educators. The site offers free newsletters, up-to-date news and information, chat forums, and special health quizzes.

F. HOUSING

American Association of Homes and Services for the Aging (AAHSA)

www.aahsa.org
202-783-2242
2519 Connecticut Avenue, NW
Washington, DC 20008-1520
The American Association of Homes and Services for the Aging promotes excellence in services to the aging. The association represents thousands of alternative housing communities and serves approximately one million older persons throughout the United States.

Care Pathways

www.carepathways.com

877-521-9987

Care Pathways provides information and resources about assisted living facilities, nursing homes, and long-term care. Facilities are listed by state. The site includes important links for elder abuse information and a medical and prescription drug dictionary.

Medicare

www.medicare.gov

7500 Security Boulevard

Baltimore, MD 21244-1850

The Medicare.gov Web site provides extensive information about Medicare and Medicaid nursing homes throughout the United States. Find specific facilities by name, geographical location, or the proximity to your home.

National Center for Assisted Living (NCAL)

www.ncal.org

202-842-4444

1201 L Street, NW

Washington, DC 20005

NCAL Web site includes in depth information about assisted living facilities, finding the appropriate facility, and making the move to a facility. The site also includes a variety of resources for the consumer.

G. MEDICAL AND DISEASE-RELATED ORGANIZATIONS

The following Web sites provide up-to-date disease specific information, resources, services, support, research, prevention, and advocacy for professionals and consumers.

About GERD (International Foundation for Functional Gastrointestinal Disorders)

www.aboutgerd.org
888-964-2001
414-964-1799
P.O. Box 170864
Milwaukee, WI 53217-8076
GERD is an acronym for Gastroesophageal Reflux Disease or "reflux." The GERD Web site provides information and education about the disease.

All About Vision

www.allaboutvision.com
Access Media Group LLC
7590 Fay Avenue, Ste. 302
La Jolla, CA 92037
This Web site provides comprehensive information about eyeglasses and contact lenses, as well as diseases of the eye such as glaucoma and cataracts.

Alzheimer's Association

www.alz.org
800-272-3900
225 North Michigan Avenue, 17th Fl.
Chicago, IL 60601

Alzheimer's Disease Education and Referral Center (ADEAR)/ National Institute on Aging

www.alzheimers.org
800-438-4380
P.O. Box 8250
Silver Spring, MD 20907

Alzheimer's Foundation of America (AFA)

Web site in English and Spanish
www.alzfdn.org
866-232-8484
322 Eighth Avenue, 7th Fl.
New York, NY 10001

Alzheimer's Society of Canada

Web site in English and French
www.alzheimer.ca
800-616-8816 (valid only in Canada)
416-488-8772
20 Eglinton Avenue West, Ste. 1200
Toronto, ON M4R 1K8

Alzheimer's Store

www.alzstore.com
800-752-3238
678-947-4001
3197 Trout Place Road
Cumming, GA 30041

American Academy of Allergy and Asthma Immunology (AAAAI)

Web site in English and Spanish
www.aaaai.org
414-272-6071
555 East Wells Street, Ste. 1100
Milwaukee, WI 53202-3823

American Academy of Dermatology (AAD)

www.aad.org
866-503-7546
202-842-3555
1350 I Street, NW, Ste. 870
Washington, DC 20005-4355

American Cancer Society

Web site in English and Spanish
www.cancer.org
800-227-2345

American Diabetes Association

www.diabetes.org
800-342-2383
1701 North Beauregard Street
Alexandria, VA 22311

American Gastroenterological Association (AGA)

www.gastro.org
301-654-2055
4930 Del Ray Avenue
Bethesda, MD 20814

American Heart Association

www.americanheart.org
800-242-8721
7272 Greenville Avenue
Dallas, TX 75231

American Lung Association

Web site in English and Spanish
www.lungusa.org
800-548-8252
212-315-8700
61 Broadway, 6th Fl.
New York, NY 10006

American Parkinson's Disease Association (APDA)

www.apdaparkinson.org
800-223-2732
718-981-8001
135 Parkinson Avenue
Staten Island, NY 10305

American Stroke Association

www.strokeassociation.org
888-478-7653
7272 Greenville Avenue
Dallas, TX 75231

Arthritis Foundation

Web site in English and Spanish
www.arthritis.org
800-283-7800
P.O. Box 7669
Atlanta, GA 30357

Asthma and Allergy Foundation of America (AAFA)

www.aafa.org
800-727-8462

1233 20th Street, Ste. 402
Washington, DC 20036

Brain Injury Association of America

Web site in English and Spanish
www.biausa.org
800-444-6443
703-761-0750
1608 Spring Hill Road, Ste. 110
Vienna, VA 22181

Cancer Care

Web site in English and Spanish
www.cancercare.org
800-813-HOPE (800-813-4673)
212-712-8400
275 Seventh Avenue
New York, NY 10001

Fisher Center for Alzheimer's Research Foundation

www.alzinfo.org
800-alzinfo (259-4636)
One Intrepid Square
West 46th Street and 12th Avenue
New York, NY 10036

Harvard Brain Tissue Resource Center

www.brainbank.mclean.org
800-272-4622
McLean Hospital
115 Mill Street
Belmont, MA 02478

Hospice Foundation of America

www.hospicefoundation.org
800-854-3402

Macular Degeneration Information Center

websites.afar.org/site/PageServer?pagename=IA_d_macu_home
212-703-9977
American Federation for Aging Research
55 West 39th Street, 16th Fl.
New York, NY 10018

The Merck Manual of Geriatrics

www.merck.com/mkgr/mmg/home.jsp
908-423-1000
One Merck Drive
P.O. Box 100
Whitehouse Station, NJ 08889-0100
The Merck Manual of Geriatrics Web site provides the reader with free
   comprehensive information about geriatric illnesses, specific condi-
   tions, and problems.

National Alliance for the Mentally Ill (NAMI)

www.nami.org
800-950-6264
703-524-7600
Colonial Place Three
2107 Wilson Boulevard, Ste. 300
Arlington, VA 22201-3042

Cancer Information Service/National Cancer Institute

http://cis.nci.nih.gov
800-422-6237

National Eye Institute (NEI)/National Institutes of Health

www.nei.nih.gov
301-496-5248
31 Center Drive, MSC 2510
Bethesda, MD 20892-2510

National Institute of Diabetes and Digestive and Kidney Diseases (NIDDK) (National Institutes of Health)

www.niddk.nih.gov
301-496-3583
Building 31, Room 9AO6
31 Center Drive, MSC 2560
Bethesda, MD 20892-2560

National Multiple Sclerosis Society (NMSS)

Web site in English and Spanish
www.nmss.org
800-344-4867
733 Third Avenue, 3rd Fl.
New York, NY 10017

National Osteoporosis Foundation (NOF)

www.nof.org
800-231-4222
202-223-2226
1232 22nd Street, NW
Washington, DC 20037-1202

The Susan G. Komen Breast Cancer Foundation

www.komen.org
877-465-6636

5005 LBJ Freeway, Ste. 250
Dallas, TX 75244

H. PROFESSIONAL ORGANIZATIONS

American Board of Medical Specialties (ABMS)

www.abms.org
847-491-9091
1007 Church Street, Ste. 404
Evanston, IL 60201-5913

The ABMS coordinates and publishes information for twenty-four approved medical specialty boards in the United States. It has a list of all board-certified diplomates and provides information to the public on certification status and standards.

American Geriatrics Society/
AGS Foundation for Healthy Aging

www.healthinaging.org
800-563-4916
212-755-6810
The Empire State Building
350 Fifth Avenue, Ste. 801
New York, NY 10118

The Web site contains pertinent up-to-date information, education, and resources for professionals in the field of geriatrics. Visitors to the Web site can share their healthcare experiences and learn about upcoming AGS events.

American Medical Association (AMA)

www.ama-assn.org
800-621-8335
515 North State Street
Chicago, IL 60610

The AMA Web site provides comprehensive information for the medical community through medical education, advocacy, and policy issues. The consumer finds helpful information on health issues and a clear and simple way to locate specific physicians through Doctor Finder.

American Nurses Association (ANA)

www.nursingworld.org
800-274-4262
301-628-5000
8515 Georgia Avenue, Ste. 400
Silver Spring, MD 20910-3492
The ANA Web site provides nurses with information, education, career opportunities and more.

American Society on Aging (ASA)

www.asaging.org
800-537-9728
415-974-9600
833 Market Street, Ste. 511
San Francisco, CA 94103
The ASA provides information, educational programs, training, and other resources to practitioners, educators, administrators, policymakers, business people, and other professionals concerned with the physical, emotional, social, economic, and spiritual aspects of aging.

Council of Social Work Education (CSWE)

www.cswe.org
703-683-8080
1725 Duke Street, Ste. 500
Alexandria, VA 22314-3457
CSWE Web site provides up-to-date resources, education, and information for social workers. Visitors to the site will find career opportunities and timely articles and publications.

National Academy of Certified Care Managers (NACCM)

www.naccm.net
800-962-2260
P.O. Box 669
244 Upton Road
Colchester, CT 06415-0669

The National Academy of Certified Care Managers is an organization designed to ensure the professional skills of care managers through a standardized examination and to provide quality care management to all. The Web site provides several important professional links.

National Academy of Elder Law Attorneys (NAELA)

www.naela.com
520-881-4005
1604 North Country Club Road
Tucson, AZ 85716

The NAELA Web site provides addresses for elder law attorneys throughout the United States who work with older clients and their families on issues such as public benefits, probate and estate planning, guardianship, and healthcare and long-term care planning.

National Association of Professional Geriatric Care Managers (GCM)

www.caremanager.org
520-881-8008
1604 North Country Club Road
Tucson, AZ 85716-3102

The GCM provides addresses for geriatric care managers throughout the United States to help older clients and their families access counseling, treatment, and the delivery of concrete services and dignified care by qualified certified providers.

National Council on Aging (NCOA)

www.ncoa.org
202-479-1200
1901 L Street, NW, 4th Fl.
Washington, DC 20036
The NCOA provides resources, information, and advocacy to consumers
and organizations on issues such as Alzheimer's disease, arthritis,
heart attacks, personal relationships, and safety. The site also offers a
Benefits Checkup, which helps locate programs for seniors that may
pay for some of the costs of their prescription drugs, healthcare, util-
ities, and other essential items or services.

Nursing Education of America

www.nursingeducationofamerica.org
Nursing Education of America offers nurses continuing education
through a large selection of courses, including geriatrics, mental
health, and palliative nursing care. There are several course levels to
meet specific individual and professional needs and requirements.

Society of Certified Senior Advisors (SCSA)

www.society-csa.com
800-653-1785
1325 South Colorado Boulevard, Ste. B-300
Denver, CO 80222
The CSA educates insurance, accounting, law, clergy, health, real estate,
and other professionals to better understand the needs of seniors in
twenty-three key areas, including housing, Social Security, Medicare,
Medicaid, and financial and estate planning. The Web site helps
locate a CSA near you.

I. RELAXATION FOR YOUR BODY AND MIND

American Yoga Association

www.americanyogaassociation.org
941-927-4977
P.O. Box 19986
Sarasota, FL 34276
The American Yoga Association Web site provides information, education, and instruction to individuals interested in yoga. Check the online store for videos, CDs, and books.

Ellis Island Records

www.ellisislandrecords.com
212-561-4588
The Statue of Liberty-Ellis Island Foundation, Inc
Attn: History Center
17 Battery Place, Ste. 210
New York, NY 10004-3507
The Ellis Island Records Web site provides the ability to search for individual family members, purchase Statue of Liberty and Ellis Island mementos, and as a foundation member create a family scrapbook.

iVillage

www.ivillage.com
The iVillage Web site brings women extensive, timely, information on diet, fitness, health, parenting, home, and garden, and much more. Their free newsletter, Women.com, features articles on entertainment, beauty, dating, and other diverting topics.

Men's Health

www.menshealth.com
800-666-2303

733 Third Avenue, 15th Fl.

New York, NY 10017

The Men's Health Web site includes timely information and articles on men's fitness, nutrition, and health.

National Women's Health Information Center
(US Department of Health and Human Services)

www.4woman.gov

800-994-9662

The National Women's Health Information Center Web site provides a wide range of free health information for women.

Women's Health America

www.womenshealth.com

800-558-7046

1289 Deming Way

Madison, WI 53717

The Women's Health America Web site provides education, advice, and options for women on a variety of healthcare issues such as menopause, bone health, antiaging, diet, and exercise. The Web site includes a health library, mini courses, and an e-newsletter.

J. TRAVEL

Society for Accessible Travel and Hospitality (SATH)

www.sath.org

212-447-7284

347 Fifth Avenue, Ste. 605

New York, NY 10016

The SATH Web site helps alert the public to the needs of all travelers with disabilities. The Web site names hotels and helps to provide opportunities for travelers with disabilities all over the world.

Vacations to Go

www.vacationstogo.com
800-338-4962
5851 San Felipe, Ste. 500
Houston, TX 77057

The Web site has a new addition: Travelers with Special Needs. The visitor is provided with easy, accessible information to help assist individuals with disabilities such as hearing and vision impairment or poor mobility to plan a vacation on land or sea.

NOTES

PREFACE

1. Kenneth Dychtwald, *Age Wave* (New York: Bantam Books, 1990), p. 241.

2. KNOWING WHEN YOUR PARENTS NEED HELP

1. Jennifer Southerland, "Changes in the Aging Eye," *Jupiter Medical Center Health Update* 15 (Fall 2001).

12. MANAGING MEDICAL ISSUES

1. Adapted from *Merriam-Webster's Medical Dictionary* (online), network edition, 1997.

2. Ibid.

3. Adapted from "Patient Education," *MU Health*, http://muhealth.org/~patient/rights.shtml, University of Missouri Health Care, 2001.

4. Ibid.

15. DEALING WITH SERIOUS ILLNESS

1. William B. Abrams et al., *The Merck Manual of Geriatrics*, 2nd ed. (Whitehouse Station, NJ: Merck Research Laboratories, 1995).

2. Jeffrey Lauer, "The Aging Faces of AIDS," *Jacksonville Medicine* 50, no. 8 (1999).

16. COPING WITH ALZHEIMER'S DISEASE

1. "What Is Alzheimer's Disease?" Alzheimer's Association, www.alz.org (accessed February 2002).

2. Ken Gies and Raymond D. Tremblay, adapted from "Farmer Fred," *Geriatric Nursing* 12, no. 5 (September/October 1991): 242.

17. WHEN HOSPITALIZATION IS NECESSARY

1. Susan Beerman and Judith Rappaport-Musson, *The Eldercare 911 Question and Answer Book* (Amherst, NY: Prometheus Books, 2002), pp. 185–89.

18. DETECTING AND DEALING WITH ABUSE

1. *Black's Law Dictionary*, 7th ed. (St. Paul, MN: West Publishing, 1999).

2. Ibid.

20. EVALUATING THE MOVE TO A NURSING HOME

1. Jean Murphy, Jennifer Weiss, and Lora Meyers, eds., *Eldercare in New York: The Consumer's Guide to Long-Term Health Care*, 7th ed. (New York: FRIA, 1999).

21. DATING, SEX, AND REMARRIAGE

1. Agency for Health Care Policy and Research, "Marriage Encourages Healthy Behaviors among the Elderly, Especially Men," press release, October 26, 1998, Rockville, MD, http://www.ahcpr.gov/news/press/marriage.htm.

2. "Prenuptial Agreement," http://www.mycounsel.com/content/familylaw/marriage/prenuptial.html (accessed February 7, 2002).

3. "Sex and Aging," Sexual Health Info Center, http://www.sexhealth.org/sexaging/index.shtml (accessed February 3, 2002).

4. "Sexuality in Old Age," Trinity University, http://www.trinity.edu/mkearl/gerosex.html (accessed February 3, 2002).

5. "Sex and Aging," http://www.sexhealth.org/sexaging/index.shtml (accessed February 3, 2002).

6. "Safe Sex," http://seniorliving.about.com/library/weekly/aa031901d.htm (accessed February 7, 2002).

22. DEATH AND DYING

1. Mark Matousek, "The Last Taboo," AARP, *Modern Maturity* (September/October 2001), http://www.aarp.org/mmaturity/sept_oct00/lasttaboo.html.

2. Adapted from Norm Bouchard, "Grief and Loss," Society of Certified Senior Advisors, Certification Class Presentation, February 8, 2002.

3. Adapted from Rev. Howard R. Gorle, "Knowledge of the Grief Process," Hospice Net, http://www.hospicenet.org/html/knowledge.html (accessed February 8, 2002); adapted from American College of Physicians, "What You Can Do to Be a Supportive Caregiver," Hospice Net, http://www.hospicenet.org/html/supportive_how.html (accessed February 8, 2002).

4. Harold Kushner, *How Good Do We Have to Be? A New Understanding of Guilt and Forgiveness* (Boston: Little, Brown, 1996).

5. Adapted from Elisabeth Kübler-Ross, *On Death and Dying* (New York: Simon & Schuster, 1996), pp. 51–146.

6. Adapted from Norm Bouchard, "Grief and Loss," Society of Certified Senior Advisors, Certification Class, February 8, 2002.

7. "Advance Directives, Making Your Wishes Known," Mayo Clinic, www.mayoclinic.com (accessed February 12, 2002).

8. Ibid.

9. Ibid.

10. Donna Sylvester, "Funeral Planning," Society of Certified Senior Advi-

sors, Certification Class and Manual, February 8, 2002; National Funeral Directors Association, www.nfda.org.

11. Sylvester, "Funeral Planning."

12. Ibid.

13. R. E. Markin, *The Affordable Funeral: Going in Style, Not Debt*, Funeral Help Program, www.funeral-help.com.

14. Adapted from "Funeral and Memorial Planning," Growth House, Inc., http://www.growthhouse.org/funeral.html.

15. Sylvester, "Funeral Planning."

16. Ibid.

17. Ibid.

18. Ibid.

19. Ibid.

20. Funeral Consumers Alliance, www.funerals.org (accessed February 2002).

GLOSSARY OF ELDERCARE TERMS

AAA (Area Agency for Aging): An organization with offices throughout the United States that provides direct services, information, and referrals to individuals who are sixty-five years of age and older.

Activities of daily living (ADLs): Refers to the ability to perform such tasks as personal grooming, shopping, cooking, eating, using the toilet, dressing and undressing, and doing laundry.

Acute care: Refers to specific treatment due to a medical illness or accident. This type of short-term care is usually provided in a hospital.

Admitting doctor: The physician who provides access to a hospital for a patient who requires medical treatment.

Adult day center: A structured environment that offers socialization, custodial and respite care, nutrition, exercise, therapeutic services, and support for frail and/or physically or cognitively impaired individuals one day to several days per week.

Advance directives: Legal documents that express the wishes of an individual if he becomes incapacitated and unable to make medical, legal, or personal decisions for himself.

Adverse drug reaction: A result occurring when two or more drugs react with each other to create an unexpected side effect that may sometimes be dangerous or even deadly.

Ageism: A misconception that old age in and of itself limits an individual's abilities.

Aging in place: The ability of an individual to remain in his own home because of the availability of supplemental supportive services such as homecare.

Agitation: A behavior that may result from a physical or cognitive impairment, or from too much or too little mental stimulation. It may take the form of yelling, hitting, or restlessness.

Alcohol abuse: The overconsumption of alcohol by an individual that interferes with his daily life and ability to function.

Alzheimer's disease: An irreversible, degenerative brain disorder that causes loss of memory and cognitive function.

Assessment: A comprehensive evaluation of an individual's physical, psychological, emotional, social, and environmental needs. A registered nurse or a social worker usually conducts this type of assessment.

Assisted living facility (ALF): An alternative living option that provides a room, meals, personal care, medication management, socialization, and recreational activities in a supervised, safe, and secure environment.

Assistive devices: Any type of equipment that aids an individual and provides increased independence or support, such as a wheelchair, a walker, tub rails, or a cane.

Bereavement counselor: A trained professional or volunteer who provides counseling and support services to individuals who are grieving the death of a family member or a friend. This type of counselor is also helpful for people who witness a tragedy such as an airplane crash or an automobile accident.

Board-certified physician: A medical doctor who completed all medical school requirements and passed a medical qualifying examination.

Burnout: Emotional and physical exhaustion resulting from long-term burdens of overwhelming stress and responsibilities.

Caregiver: Any individual who provides personal, emotional, financial, or supportive care for another person.

Care management: A fee-for-service business that evaluates every aspect of an individual's life, and provides ongoing planning, supervision, and management of services to meet medical, psychosocial, emotional, and quality-of-life needs.

Care manager: An independent, privately hired and paid for registered nurse or licensed social worker who assesses, plans, coordinates, implements, monitors, and supervises all aspects of a client's daily life.

Case management: A service that is often paid for by government programs or some form of insurance. Contact, interventions, and degree of involvement with clients is often time-limited due to benefit limitations.

Case manager: A registered nurse or a social worker who works for a social service agency or in connection with a hospital or an insurance company and provides a clinical assessment of an individual's needs. Often the same entity determines needs and provides services.

Certified nurse's aide (CNA): An individual who earns a state license or certification by completing specific homecare and patient training. A hospital, a nursing home, an assisted living facility, or a private patient may employ an individual with these credentials.

Cognitive impairment: A decline in an individual's ability to perform tasks, make decisions, or think clearly.

Combativeness: Acting out through verbal or physical behaviors, such as yelling, hitting, or physical aggressiveness.

Community-based services: Services provided by the community to help the elderly reside in their own homes, such as senior centers, adult day care programs, and home delivered meals.

Companion: A nonprofessional trained individual or a volunteer who provides company and support for another individual.

Compliant: The ability to respond appropriately to another person's directions, such as accepting medication from someone in a timely manner or complying with physicians' orders.

Continuing care retirement communities: Housing communities that provide an individual with levels of care: independent housing, assisted living, and skilled nursing care. An individual will move from one level of care to another based on physical and cognitive need.

Continuity of services: Services provided to an individual without any lapse in time by the service provider.

Custodial care: Nonmedical care provided by a home health aide or a certified nurse's aide at home or in a short- or long-term care facility.

Dementia: A neurological condition that results in memory loss, changes in personality, difficulty in learning or retaining new information, language problems, and mood swings.

Depression: A mental illness marked by symptoms that are severe and last over an extended period of time, such as loss of appetite or weight, loss of interest in pleasurable activities, crying, feeling helpless and hopeless, and suicidal ideation, thoughts, and plans.

Diagnosis: A definitive identification of an illness or condition.

Disorientation: A state of confusion resulting in an inability to identify or relate to a person, place, or time.

Do Not Resuscitate (DNR): A document that allows a legal representative to make the decision to not allow resuscitation if an individual stops breathing.

Drug abuse: The accidental or intentional misuse of prescription medications, over-the-counter medicines, homeopathic products, or any other drugs.

Durable power of attorney: A legal document that allows a competent individual to appoint another individual to make decisions for him when he can no longer make his own decisions. This document remains effective in the event the individual becomes incapacitated.

Durable power of attorney for healthcare: A legal document that allows a competent individual to appoint another individual to make healthcare decisions for him when he can no longer make his own decisions. This document remains effective in the event the individual becomes incapacitated.

Eldercare professionals: Individuals who specialize in the care and needs of the population age sixty-five and older.

Elder law: A specialty in the field of law that deals with financial, legal, and personal needs of individuals age sixty-five and older.

Environmental assessment: A comprehensive study of an individual's home to identify and correct safety hazards.

Estate planning: Provisions for the disposition of an individual's wealth for the benefit of her family.

Flextime: An individualized work schedule that allows an employee to work convenient and flexible hours.

Geriatric care manager: An independent, privately hired and paid for registered nurse or licensed social worker who assesses, plans, coordinates, implements, monitors, and supervises all aspects of an elderly client's life.

Geriatric nurse practitioner: A licensed registered nurse who has advanced training and specializes in the care and treatment of the population age sixty-five and older, after receiving extensive training, education, and clinical experience.

Geriatric physician: A medical doctor who receives extensive training, education, and specialized clinical experience in the care and treatment of individuals age sixty-five and older.

Guardian: A court-appointed individual who makes financial and/or personal-care decisions for another individual who can no longer make decisions for himself.

Healthcare proxy: A legal document that allows a competent individual to appoint another individual to make healthcare decisions for her when she cannot make her own decisions.

Homecare: A service business that provides personal care and assistance with activities of daily living in the home environment.

Home health aide: An employee trained to provide personal care and other associated services in the home, such as cooking, light housekeeping, and laundry.

Home modifications: Adapting a home to accommodate the needs of a physically ill, frail, or mentally challenged individual. The change may be as simple as removing scatter rugs to help prevent falls, or the total reconstruction of a kitchen and bathroom to provide the individual with a safe and comfortable environment.

Hospice care: Specialized, compassionate care at home or in a facility for an individual suffering from a terminal illness.

Human resource counselor: A trained professional who works for a small business or a large corporation and provides counseling and support services for employees.

Incapacity: A legal term that describes the inability of an individual to make decisions for herself.

Incontinence: The inability to control bladder and/or bowel functions.

Independent living: An alternative living option for an individual who is physically and cognitively capable of residing in an independent environment.

Intervention: Involvement in an individual's life in order to help maintain, rescue, or assist that person.

Living will: A legal document that allows a person to identify in advance the type of medical care he wants under specific circumstances, usually relating to serious illness or impending death.

Long-distance caregiver: Any individual who is geographically distant but involved in the care of another person.

Long-term care facility: An institution that provides medical and/or custodial care for more than a few weeks or months.

Long-term care insurance: A private insurance policy that covers some of the costs of extended healthcare needs at home or in a nursing home.

Long-term memory: The ability to remember past experiences, people, places, and things.

Medicaid: A federally funded program managed by individual states to cover the cost of certain medical care at home, in nursing homes, and in some assisted living facilities. The purpose and design of the program is to meet the needs of individuals who have a limited income.

Medicare: A multi-part federal insurance program that provides health-care benefits for individuals age sixty-five and older.

Medigap: A private insurance plan designed to cover some of the costs not covered by Medicare.

Memorial service: A special tribute to remember the life of a deceased individual. This type of service may take place in a funeral home, a church, a synagogue, a cemetery, a private home, a park, or in any place that brings family and friends together.

Memorial society: A nonprofit group that negotiates contracts with funeral homes, crematoriums, and cemeteries. The benefit of this type of group is that members receive discounts on specific products and services.

Memory impairment: The inability of an individual to remember recent and/or long-term events.

Mobility: The ability of an individual to walk independently without the assistance of another person or an assistive device such as a cane or a walker.

Multi-infarct dementia: A non-Alzheimer's type dementia, sometimes known as vascular dementia.

Neurologist: A medical doctor who specializes in diseases and illnesses of the nervous system.

Non-durable power of attorney: A legal document that allows a competent individual to appoint another individual to make decisions for her. This document is generally used for a limited purpose such as providing an attorney the legal power to represent you at a house closing or other business transactions. This document is no longer effective if the individual becomes incapacitated.

Nonverbal communication: An individual's ability to communicate without the use of language skills, such as with the use of eye contact, signing, or body language.

Nursing home: A facility that cares for the specific needs of physically ill and/or cognitively impaired individuals.

Opthalmologist: A medical doctor who specializes in the care and treatment of the eyes.

Paranoia: A mental disorder in which the individual suffers from delusions or disturbances in thinking.

Patient advocate: A social worker or a trained volunteer who acts as an intermediary between the patient and the staff in hospitals or other institutions.

Personal emergency response system (PERS): A call button or voice-activated system that connects an individual to emergency assistance. The individual wears an alarm button around his neck or may carry a small device the size of a beeper.

Preventive intervention: A method of identifying risks and creating a plan to help an individual before a problem actually arises.

Primary caregiver: An individual who is foremost in the daily care and needs of another person.

Primary care physician: The first doctor that an individual sees for all medical needs and who helps coordinate the individual's medical care.

Private-duty nurse: A registered nurse who is paid for privately and assigned to care for one patient in such places as a hospital, a nursing home, an assisted living facility, or the patient's home.

Professional funeral consultant: An individual who provides families with options and information that allows them to make informed decisions regarding funerals and takes care of all aspects of it.

Prognosis: The possible outcome of a particular medical condition.

Registered nurse: An individual who successfully completed nursing school and passed all of the appropriate licensing examinations.

Respite service: Care provided on a temporary basis in a facility or in an individual's home to relieve a caregiver of caregiving duties and associated stresses.

Self-neglect: An individual's failure to care for her personal needs.

Senior center: A building or place for people over the age of sixty-five to join in socialization, education, and nutritional programs.

Sexually inappropriate behavior: Unsuitable or aggressive sexual behavior toward another individual.

Short-term memory: Recall of recent events.

Skilled nursing facility (SNF): A long-term care facility that cares for the specific needs of a physically ill, frail, or cognitively impaired individual.

Sliding scale fee: A fee that is determined by an individual's income level and ability to pay.

Social worker: An individual who completed an accredited school of social work.

Specialist: An individual who has expertise in a particular field, such as a geriatrician who specializes in the care of the elderly.

Telephone tree: A support system whereby several individuals contact one another on a daily basis. If someone does not answer the telephone within a certain time limit and had not notified the group that he would be out of town, an emergency protocol takes effect.

Toileting: Helping an individual to use the bathroom facilities.

Transferring: Moving from one position to another with or without assistance, such as moving from a wheelchair to a bed.

Urinary tract infection (UTI): An infection of the bladder or the urinary tract.

INDEX

ABOUT THE AUTHORS

Susan Beerman, MS, MSW, is president and founder of Barrister Advisory Services, Inc., a consulting firm specializing in geriatrics and individuals with special needs in Queens, New York. She is a member of the National Association of Social Workers, the National Council on the Aging, and the American Society on Aging, as well as various caregiver organizations. Sue brings twenty-five years of experience to her well-received public speeches especially designed for the specific needs of caregivers who require up-to-date information and support. Through her seminars and as an educator, Sue reaches out to healthcare and legal professionals through her lectures, radio show appearances, and writing.

Judith Rappaport-Musson, CSA, is a partner and cofounder of Preferred Client Services, Inc., a geriatric care management and health insurance claims advocacy firm in West Palm Beach, Florida, and an affiliate member of the National Association of Professional Geriatric Care Managers. She uses her seventeen-plus years of experience in the elder-caregiving field to answer readers' questions in her successful weekly column, "Eldercare 911," which appears in six Florida Scripps Treasure Coast newspapers. She is a sought after motivational speaker who energizes audiences using equal parts of laughter, comfort, and practical information to help caregivers become more effective advocates and maintain their own quality of life.

Susan Beerman and Judith Rappaport are the coauthors of *The Eldercare 911 Question and Answer Book.*